The Me262 Combat Diary

The Story of the
World's First Jet Fighter in Battle

by
John Foreman
and
S.E.Harvey

Air Research Publications

ESSEX COUNTY
COUNCIL LIBRARY

First published 1990 by.
Air Research Publications
PO Box 223, Walton–on–Thames,
Surrey, KT12 3YQ
England

Revised edition published 1995

Reprinted 2008

© John Foreman and S E Harvey 1995

All Rights Reserved.
No part of this publication
may be reproduced, stored
in any form of retrieval
system, or transmitted
in any form or by any
means without prior
permission in writing
from the publishers.

Printed and bound by
CPI Antony Rowe, Eastbourne

ISBN 978-1-871187-51-9

CONTENTS

Foreword		5
Introduction		12
Acknowledgements		14
Chapter One:	'It was if the angels were pushing'	21
Chapter Two:	Into Service:	37
Chapter Three:	Tactical Operations and Kommando Nowotny	55
Chapter Four:	Bleak Winter	103
Chapter Five:	Jets at Night	131
Chapter Six:	Into the Jet Age	139
Chapter Seven:	Jet Crescendo	163
Chapter Eight:	Bloody Twilight	217
Chapter Nine:	Too Little and Too Late	263
Chapter Ten:	The Phœnix Rises	279
Chapter Eleven:	Post Mortem and Remembrances	297

Appendices

Appendix I:	Known Me262 Pilots	313
Appendix II:	Known Losses of Me262 Aircraft	325
Appendix III:	Prisoner Interrogation Report: Generalleutnant Adolf Galland	349
Appendix IV:	USAAF Air Combat Claims against Me262 Aircraft	355
Appendix V:	RAF Air Combat Claims against Me262 Aircraft	365
Appendix VI:	Known Claims by Jet Pilots	369
Appendix VII:	Royal Air Force Crash Report on Me262	379
Index:		381

Foreword

Oberst Hermann Buchner
Luftwaffe

I was very pleased to comply with the request of the authors of this book, who asked me to write a foreword. The authors have compiled the details for this *Combat Diary* after careful research and by contacting and interviewing many English, American and German airmen also historians from various countries, preserving the records for posterity. For this they merit our thanks.

The war in Europe was already three years old by 1942 and the air forces of all participating nations had survived many combats and had acquired much knowledge and experience. With the entry of the United States into the theatre of war the balance of power between the air forces changed enormously. New and only partly attainable impositions were placed upon the German Air Force fighter units. In the summer of 1942 the US units carried out the first incursions into occupied France using four-engined bombers in groups of thirty machines; the strength and tactics of the German air defences were to be tested. At the beginning of this phase, the German fighter defence was still in the position of being able to hinder incoming formations from fulfilling their objectives. For years the fighter units on the Channel Front, in spite of almost impossible demands having been made upon them, had, by skilful flying, been fighting a debilitating war against the RAF, while the remaining fighter units were deployed in the East and the

South. Thus in Germany itself there were no units available apart from *JG 11* and night fighter units.

After the Allied invasion phase, the Allied commanders agreed on how the future air war against Germany would be prosecuted. Targets in occupied zones and in Germany itself would be attacked by RAF squadrons by night and US squadrons by day. The combined attacks by Allied bomber squadrons on Hamburg during July 1943 called forth strident demands for strengthened home defences. Squadrons from the East were recalled to Germany. The Armament Authority (RLM) issued an 'urgency notice' for the Me262, which was still being tested, while Galland, as General of Fighter Command, tried to build up a fighter reserve.

For a short time the additional fighter units were able to make things difficult for the invaders. The fighter defence produced results and the US bomber commanders demanded better fighter cover for their bombers flying over Germany. With the introduction of the long-range Mustang and Thunderbolt fighters the situation changed and the advantage passed to the Allied air forces. The defence requirement problems for the Me109 and FW190 pilots were, from 1944, almost insoluble in the face of the overwhelming air superiority of the enemy fighter escorts. The pilots fought on with the courage of despair, sometimes achieving spectacular successes, but they also had to take account of their own heavy losses.

Too late: in the third quarter of 1944 the legendary Me262 went into operation. Pilots were withdrawn from various *Luftwaffe* squadrons and sent for training. The bomber groups (KG) were allocated Me262s for use as *Blitz* bombers; it was a momentous decision. The Me262s were withdrawn from the fighters. After an all too brief training period and without practice we Germans faced the enemy, who were surprised, some even shocked. Trial sorties with Me262s of *Kommando Nowotny* were flown from Achmer/Rheine in October and November, but there were too few aircraft and too few experienced pilots available and the sortie results were zero.

Too late: came the possibility of fighting the bombers with greater numbers. The high speed of the Me262 made it possible to break through the US escorts and successfully attack the bombers direct with the cannon. In spite of the massed defence put up by the valiant gunners, the Me262 pilots were able to score some notable successes. The escort fighters tried again and again from ever higher positions to foil the Me262 attacks. Both the USAAF and the RAF and we Germans were looking for useable tactics; the Germans tried to turn speed and surprise into success and the Allies tried to engage the attacking jets successfully. However the Me262 was about 200 km per hour faster than the escorting fighters and it was fitted with 4 MK108 (3 cm) guns and, from February 1945, it also carried R4M rockets.

Too late: only 380 of the production of 1,294 Me262s reached the fighter units; the majority went the bomber (KG) units or were damaged on the ground in air raids. Even the free-ranging deployment of the jet pilots could no longer impede Allied air superiority. As the loss of territory increased and Allied ground troops advanced, the depth of operations became less and less, the supplies for our own units grew ever more difficult as the struggle moved relentlessly to its conclusion. The Allied fighter escorts had shorter flights and could, therefore, wipe out the Me262s on their bases in Germany. The landing places still available were blanketed by Mustangs or Thunderbolts, but in spite of this the jet units of the German Luftwaffe fought on, using all their flying skills and ready to sacrifice themselves. They remained fair until the last day of operations and respected their opponents in the air and on the ground, despite the ferocity of the air battles.

Too late and too little: the Me262 was certainly an aircraft that could have given the German pilots the ability to win back mastery of the air, but sadly it came too late and in too small a number for deployment as a fighter weapon. The Me262 was an aircraft that marked a turning point in both civil and military aviation and in the achieving of air superiority, even if it could not bring about mastery of the air.

The pages of this book show in a straightforward way extracts from combat reports by participating pilots in the period during which the jet aircraft was introduced, combat reports of air battles that will go down in the history of military aviation.

Hermann Buchner,
Hörsching Austria
December 1989

Formerly with the Austrian Air Force, Hermann Buchner transferred to the *Luftwaffe*, becoming a fighter and close-support instructor. He joined the *4th Staffel* of *Schlachtgeschwader 1* in Russia in the spring of 1942 and flew with this unit (later renamed *6./SG 2*) until June 1944, when he became Staffel Leader of *4./SG 2* for a short time. After another period as an instructor he was selected as one of the first pilots to join the Me262 *Erprobungstelle* at Lechfeld in November 1944. One month later he joined the cadre of *III./Jagdgeschwader 7*. While flying as a fighter-bomber pilot on FW190s he achieved 46 combat successes, including one against the Western Allies, and claimed a further twelve victories whilst flying the Me262 jet fighter, nine of them four-engined bombers. During his service he was awarded the *Ehrenpokal, Deutsches Kreuz, Eisernes Kreuz* 1st and 2nd Class, and the *Ritterkreuz*. He joined the new Austrian Air Force after the war and was trained to fly Vampires at De Havilland's in England, flying one of the first Austrian Vampires back to Hörsching airfield He later served on control duties until his retirement with the rank of Oberst (Colonel). He now lives peacefully in Austria.

Major Urban L Drew
U.S. 8th Air Force

John Foreman and Sid Harvey have done a masterful job of handling a difficult subject. Since those days when the Me262 first appeared in European skies, very little factual writing has properly been done on the subject. And never before have the combat actions been so well documented. What Foreman and Harvey have done is to write a book about the people who flew and fought in the Me262 and the pilots and aircrew who fought against them in aerial combat. This of course is what it was all about.

Aircraft themselves are products of designers, engineers and manufacturers who construct them; of themselves, they are inanimate objects. While over the years, in all air wars, historians are wont to dwell on specific aircraft, their colour schemes, their serials etc., none of that information is really germaine to the subject at hand. What really matters is the men who flew these machines, who mastered their traits, men who mounted these steeds of war and so became legends in the doing.

The many great *Luftwaffe* aces who flew this Messerschmitt 262, already famous in their own rights, became legends while operating and fighting in the Me262. Men such as *Major* Georg-Peter Eder, would make the Me262 serve him as had the FW190 and Me109 before it. The Allied fighter pilots who fought this great jet aircraft, realising its vast superiority over their own mounts, developed tactics to combat it and, with raw courage, fought the Me262 over its own turf.

The authors have presented a serious historical document, but have written it in such a manner that it reads like a novel, truly a great accomplishment. I could not put the manuscript down, once I started reading it.

Not only should this book prove to be an invaluable reference work for the serious historical students, but it has done much to correct the record in stating the actual role the Me262 played over the skies of Europe during World War II.

My own engagements with the Me262, while flying the Mustang, were most vividly brought to mind as I perused the manuscript, even though the actions described took place over 45 years ago.

I take this opportunity to congratulate John Foreman and Sid Harvey on an exceptional work.

Urban L Drew,
Pretoria, South Africa.
December 1989

'Ben' Drew arrived in Britain in May 1944 after serving as a fighter instructor aqt Bartow, Florida. He flew operationally with the 375th Fighter Squadron, 361st Fighter Group, flying P-51D Mustangs from Bottisham, Cambridgeshire and later from Little Waldon, Essex. During his 75 combat missions he was credited with the destruction of six enemy aircraft in aerial combat and another on the ground. On October 7th 1944 he became the first fighter pilot in history to destroy two Me262s in combat, and the first of only two men to shoot down two in a single mission. He later served in the Pacific theatre, flying P-47 Thunderbolts from Iwo Jima, and was awarded the Air Force Cross, two Distinguished Flying Crosses and fourteen Air Medals. He retired from the USAAF with the rank of Major, and now resides in South Africa, as a successful businessman, still involved with aviation.

Group Captain J.B.Wray, CBE, DFC,
Order of Orange Nassau,
2nd Tactical Air Force, Royal Air Force

Fortunately for the Allies the Me262 did not appear in the air battles of Europe until the last year of the War. Even flying their latest and fastest fighters Allied pilots found themselves in combat against an aircraft the performance of which far exceeded their own.

John Foreman and S.E.Harvey have amassed a formidable and intriguing array of evidence and information on these combats and associated events and have presented it in such a way that the skill, dedication and, at times, the desperation of the combatants is vividly portrayed.

The Germans in their Me262s were fighting their last battle, but despite this they fought with a ferocity as if it was their first. The Allies with their domination in the air were almost brought up short by this new and devastating attack, but they fought back with skill and determination. The result, as is shown so clearly in this book, was a series of great air battles which will go down in the annals of air warfare.

John Wray
Guildford, England
December 1989

John Wray joined the RAF in 1935, serving first with Army Co-operation Command. He flew Blenheims with 53 Squadron during the 'Phoney War' and, after a period instructing, went to 25 Squadron, nightfighting with Beaufighters, where he rose to become a Flight Commander in 1941. He took command of 137 Squadron in 1942, flying Whirlwinds and later Hurricanes. Following a period at No. 13 Group Headquarters, he joined 150 Tempest Wing as supernumary Wing Command, then successively led the Manston Wing, 125 Wing - with Tempests and Spitfire XIVs - and in October joined 122 Wing as Wing Leader. In two separate engagements with Me262s he became the only RAF fighter pilot to destroy two. In January 1945 he became Chief Instructor at 56 Operational Training Unit, and remained in the RAF after the war, holding many Staff appointments both in Britain and abroad before retiring 1n 1967 with the rank of Group Captain.

Introduction

This book is an account of an aircraft born in war; the Messerschmitt 262 fighter and fighter-bomber, which with a single step placed the *Luftwaffe* at least five years ahead of their opponents in the field of aviation technology and fighter performance.

First flown in 1942, it could have been in service as an interceptor fighter perhaps as early as 1943, but for two delaying factors; the insistence of the *Luftwaffe* High Command that the tailwheel configuration be replaced by a tricycle undercarriage, and the interference of Adolf Hitler, who ordered that it be produced primarily as a bomber - a role for which it was manifestly unsuitable. When it did appear, the western Allies received possibly one of their greatest shocks of the war. Their best fighter aircraft had, at a stroke, become obsolete, for the jet aircraft enjoyed a speed superiority of more than 100 mph over the fastest Allied escort fighter, the North American P-51D Mustang, and could enter combat or disengage at will. It also carried the heaviest armament in the world, four 30mm cannon, which with a single round could destroy an Allied fighter and required an average of only three strikes to bring down a heavy bomber. When this armament was supplement by a battery of air-to-air rocket missiles, the result was, as one B-17 gunner was to say 'A nightmare fighter'.

Less than 1,500 of the jets were built, and many were destroyed before reaching their assigned units, or were bombed on the ground, but those that did become operational were flown into combat against overwhelming odds over the German homeland during the great air battles in the spring of 1945; sometimes as few as twelve of the jet fighters would take on more than 1,500 Allied aircraft, yet the jet fighter pilots gave a creditable account of themselves, and wrote a page into history that should not be forgotten. Modern accounts seldom mention the part played by this aircraft, and the popular view that it was of little significance, total victories claimed by it's pilots numbering no more than one hundred, is a sheer propaganda myth.

This is the story of that aircraft, the men who flew it, and those that fought against it, often told in their own words It includes all known air engagements between Allied aircraft and the Messerschmitt 262 units. Many records are of course lost, destroyed by the Germans in those days of the crumbling Reich, but it is hoped that from those documents that remain, and the memories of people who were there, the authors have assembled an accurate record of the events that took place.

John Foreman *S.E.Harvey*
Radlett, *Wrentham,*
Hertfordshire *Suffolk*

June 1995

Notes, Sources and Acknowledgments

Five years ago, the original Me262 Combat Diary was published and the authors were quite surprised at its reception. Our account of the meteoric rise and fall of the world's first jet fighter resulted in a great deal of correspondence with readers, many of whom had met the fighter in combat and indeed some who had flown it. They were willing to share their experiences and knowledge with us, which resulted in so many corrections and additions that, when added to the continuing demand for the book that is now long out of print, that the publisher asked us to update the book and have it reprinted. We hope that this new version is as well received as the original.

1.) Claims and Losses.

Claims submitted by fighter pilots are always a matter of some contention. Overclaiming always happened in large engagements; the larger and more involved the air combat, the greater the overclaim rate became. With opposing aircraft of similar performance, the 'normal' overclaim rate, averaged throughout the war, tended to be three claimed victories to two actual losses. It should be appreciated that air combat was, and still is, a fast and fleeting business. The pilots were young, charged with adrenalin and, with little time to observe the results of an attack, were very likely to misinterpret the effects of their actions. In the case of the Me262, the sheer speed differential added to the problems; a pilot had just a few seconds to select his target, position his aircraft, and deliver his attack. It is hardly surprising that overclaiming occurred; indeed it is more surprising that the claims were as accurate as they were. In addition to claiming aircraft destroyed, the German pilots regarded the 'cutting out' of an enemy bomber from its formation as an achievement worthy of note. It was fairly easy for a fighter pilot to attack a lone straggling bomber, but to hurtle into the midst of a huge 'combat box' of 72 American heavy bombers, each mounting ten or more .50 inch calibre machine guns, took a rare degree of courage and tenacity. Thus the 'cutting out' or *Herausschuss* was considered as important as a confirmed combat success, and these are included both in the text and in the known individual claims in Appendix I. It should also be remembered that the losses of Allied aircraft are total losses, and that conventional fighters (mainly Bf109s and FW190s) were nearly always involved in the large air combats.

The losses of Me262 aircraft are difficult to determine; while it would have been nice to include every jet loss, this has not proved possible. The *Luftwaffe* Quartermaster General Returns for 1944 have been lost, perhaps forever, and the situation during 1945 was such that records are missing, destroyed, or in many cases, not even maintained. Those that have survived are included in Appendix II. Thus where an Allied fighter pilot claimed the destruction of an Me262, and no such loss appears in the listing, it does not necessarily mean that the claim was inaccurate. Such losses frequently did occur, and many claims could be supported by the combat film exposed during the action. As will be seen, many jets were lost and pilots killed, of which no record remains of their passing. A great pity, for courageous men, of whatever nationality, deserve at least to be remembered. Thus it is to the aircrew who flew the aircraft, those who flew against them, and particularly those German pilots, the true jet pioneers, who lost their lives during the huge battles over the Reich with no record of their demise that this book is respectfully dedicated.

2.) Ranks

In general, the *Luftwaffe* ranks equalled those of the Allies, but often carried far greater responsibility. Often the the command of a *Staffel* (8-12 aircraft) was entrusted to an *Oberleutnant* or even a *Leutnant*, while a *Gruppe* was often led by a *Hauptmann* or, on occasion, an *Oberleutnant*. In both the RAF and the USAAF, such positions would be held by officers of much higher rank. The Operational flying ranks are listed below, with Allied equivalents where appropriate.

Luftwaffe	USAAF	RAF
Flieger	Airman	Aircraftsman
Gefreiter	Lance-Corporal	Leading Aircraftsman
Obergefreiter	---	---
Unteroffizier	Corporal	Corporal
Feldwebel	Sergeant	Sergeant
Oberfeldwebel	Technical Sergeant	Flight Sergeant
Stabsfeldwebel	Staff Sergeant	Warrant Officer
Fahnenjunker-Feldwebel	---	---
Fahnrich	---	---
Oberfahnrich	---	---
Leutnant	2nd Lieutenant	Pilot Officer
Oberleutnant	1st Lieutenant	Flying Officer
Hauptmann	Captain	Flight Lieutenant
Major	Major	Squadron Leader
Oberstleutnant	Lieutenant Colonel	Wing Commander
Oberst	Colonel	Group Captain

Note: *Flieger* (Airman) was not an Allied aircrew rank, and the ranks of *Obergefreiter* (Senior Lance-Corporal), *Fahnenjunker-Feldwebel* (Colour-Sergeant), *Fähnrich* (Officer Cadet) and *Oberfähnrich* (Senior Officer Cadet) have no direct Allied comparison.

3.) Abbreviations

American Bombardment Groups are shortened to 'Bomb Group', Photographic Reconnaissance Groups to 'Photo Recon Group', and *Luftwaffe fighter* and bomber Geschwadern to 'JG' and 'KG' respectively, thus *JG 7, KG(J)54* etc. The '(J)' in the latter abbreviation, meaning *Jäger* (fighter) was incorporated into bomber unit designations when conventional bomber units converted to the Me262, indicating that the units were to be employed on fighter-bomber duties. As far as Allied Tactical Air Forces were concerned, the abbreviations for the American 1st Tactical Air Force (Provisional) of USAAF and the British 2nd Tactical Air Force will be found as 1 TAF (Prov) and 2 TAF respectively.

Finally, the combat reports submitted by Allied aircrew contain many sometimes confusing abbreviations. While no words have been changed, the authors have decided to expand such abbreviations for ease of reading and comprehension, particularly for those readers who are unfamiliar with aviation 'jargon'.

While we accept that weights, performance etc. of a German aircraft should be expressed in metric units, it is felt that such matters will prove confusing to many readers; few English-speaking people can readily appreciate or visualise the terms '750 kph', '600 kg thrust' or '6,000 m'. Imperial measures have therefore been used throughout, with equivalent metric units bracketed where it is thought appropriate.

4.) Acknowledgements and Sources

Germany and Austria:

Oberst a.D. Hermann Buchner, Georg-Peter Eder, Rudolf Sinner, Rolf Ole Lehmann, Georg Lang, W.Honig, Hans-Joachim Ebert, Otto Pritzl, Erich Liebe, Hans-Dieter Weihs, Herbert Scholl and Günter Wiesinger.

USA:

General Harry M Chapman, General Edward B Giller, General Stanley F H Newman, Urban L Drew, (South Africa), Frank Belasco, Harold E and Esther Oyster, A A Raidy, Charles M Bachman, Frank M Mead, Ira J Purdy, J W Nielson, Howard P Husband, Ronald Cole, Dale E Karger, John A Kirk III, Lawrence B Bird, Gordon A Denson, Paul C Roberts, Jack Ilfrey, Duane Sears, Paul F Sink, Leo Freedman and the Editor 'Air Force Magazine'.

Netherlands:

Peter Monasso and Gerrie G Zwanenberg MBE

South Africa:

Colonel P M J McGregor and Captain D Becker of the South African Air Force.

Canada

Squadron Leader R I A Smith DFC, Group Captain E.G.Ireland, J J Boyle DFC, Squadron Leader James E Collier, Colonel J W Garland, A Hugh Fraser, Leonard N Watt, Robert Bracken, Ron Lowry, Gus Platts and Frank McLeod.

Australia:

Russell Guest and the War Memorial, Canberra.

United Kingdom:
Group Captain J B Wray CBE DFC, Mr and Mrs H J S Pietrzak, J S Baker, L.C.Betts, A.Hill, Dennis Richardson, Hubert Hammett, George M.Hirst, Bruce Lander, Brian Cull, Frank Marshall, Stephen Burns, Simon Parry, Clive Gosling, Harry Hawker, Robert Collis, Fred Read, Malcolm R Holmes, Martin Bowman and Sharon Tansey.

Particular thanks are due to Mr D W Goode, Chief Librarian of the Royal Aircraft Establishment, Farnborough and to Mr F Flowers, Senior Assistant at the Royal Air Force Museum, Hendon. Especial thanks go to Hermann Buchner, Urban Drew and John Wray not only for their individual contributions to the foreword, which thus gave a balanced view by representatives of the three major air forces, but also to their accounts of air combat. Also to Rudolf Sinner and Hans-Dieter Weihs, who gave us much of their time to offer welcome constructive criticism of our original book and provided further details of their own experiences; to Günter Wiesinger, who provided us with numerous 'shoot-down reports', identifying Allied aircraft that fell victim to jet fighters; to Rod Smith and Hugh Fraser in Canada, who gave so freely of their time. Last but by no means least, to Chris Shores, who did a masterly job of editing the original manuscript. Our thanks to you all.

Sources:

Public Record Office:
   Squadron Operation Record Books (Air27 series)
   Group Operation Record Books (Air26 series)
   Fighter Command documents (Air 16 series)
   Bomber Command documents (Air14 series)
   Intelligence documents (Air 40 series)

Published Works:

Manfred Boehme:	Jagdgeschwader 7
Alfred Price:	Instruments of Darkness
Roger A Freeman:	The Mighty Eighth
	The Mighty Eighth War Diary
Jeff Ethell:	Escort To Berlin
Kenn C Rust:	The 9th Air Force
Frank Olynyk:	American Fighter Claims of World War Two

Acknowledgements, Sources and Notes

Wolfgang Dierich:	Kampfgeschwader 51 "Edelweiss"
Merle C Olmsted:	The Yoxford Boys
	The 357th Over Europe
Kenn C Rust and William N Hess:	Slybird Group
Gemeinschaft der Jadgflieger e V:	Jagerblatt (various)
Pierre H Clostermann:	The Big Show
David Irving:	Rise and Fall of the Luftwaffe
Blake Publishing, USA: (various)	Fighter Pilots in Aerial Combat
Christopher F Shores:	Second TAF
	History of 80 Squadron
Chris Thomas and Christopher F Shores:	The Typhoon And Tempest Story
Werner Girbig:	Start Im Morgengrauen
Johannes Steinhoff:	Im Letzter Stunde
Adolf Galland:	The First and the Last
USAF	Study 85
Luftwaffe Quartermastergeneral	Returns of Aircraft Losses

Jagdgeschwader 7
by
Manfred Boehme

The authors feel that a fuller acknowledgement should be accorded to Herr Manfred Boehme for his work on *Jagdgeschwader 7*, now in English translation. Although the vast majority of fighter claims submitted by pilots from that *Geschwader* and quoted in this book came to us largely from other sources, they were almost entirely culled from his book and appear only due his painstaking research. Without that vital information, this book would not have been possible and we fully acknowledge that fact with our gratitude. It is indeed a remarkable work of original research and we believe it should be read by all students of aviation history

- J.F and S.E.H.

Chapter One
'It was as if the angels were pushing'
- Generalleutnant Adolf Galland

The spring sunlight glittered upon the grey waters of the North Sea far below as Major John C Meyer, commander of the 487th Fighter Squadron of the 352nd Fighter Group, led his P-51D Mustang fighters towards their rendezvous with a formation of American heavy bombers en route for Germany. They were nearing the Friesian Islands when a flight of three twin-engined aircraft were sighted some way below. Meyer decided to investigate and, taking two sections of Mustangs, eased into a dive. Then it happened; the three aircraft suddenly picked up speed and pulled steadily away from the pursuing Mustangs. As the American pilots opened their throttles wide the unidentified aircraft lifted and climbed with unbelievable speed until they were lost to view in the blinding eye of the sun. The Mustang pilots were left doubting the evidence of their own eyes. Meyer and his pilots climbed to rejoin their formation in a state of shock and self-doubt. Until that moment they firmly believed that they were flying the most formidable fighter aircraft ever built, the P-51. The Mustang had, in that early Spring of 1944, proved more than a match for the Messerschmitt Bf109G and Focke-Wulf FW190 fighters then equipping the German units opposing them. They had become the scourge of the *Luftwaffe*, escorting the Fortress and Liberator forma-

Maj John C Meyer of the 352nd Fighter Group was one of the first Allied pilots to be impressed by the Me262's performance.
(Via Roger A Freeman)

tions, ranging far and wide across the Reich and pitilessly ambushing the Germans wherever they could be found. But the sight they had seen that day was to prove an ominous portent for the future.

The bomber escort mission was accomplished and the 352nd Fighter Group returned to their base at Bodney, Essex, where the eight fighter pilots submitted sighting reports to their Group Commanding Officer, Colonel Joseph L Mason. All agreed that they had never seen anything like it before; three very fast aircraft climbing away from their Mustangs and vanishing as if they had never existed. Had not all eight witnessed the fact, then they would have thought that their eyes had played them false. The reports were submitted to 8th Air Force Fighter Command, but no light was thrown upon what these aircraft could have been. It was to be only a short time before the facts emerged. They had undoubtedly been among the first Allied aircrew to witness the startling performance of Professor Willy Messerschmitt's new jet fighter - the Me262.

Development of Willy Messerschmitt's jet aircraft began in 1938, when the *Reichsluftfährtministerium* (Technical Department of the German Air Ministry - normally abbreviated to *RLM*) gave the Messerschmitt Company a design contract for an airframe to house two axial-flow turbo-jet engines. The engines, BMW P-3303 power plants, then in the design stage at the BMW factory at Berlin-Schönefeld, were expected to produce a nominal thrust of 1,320 lb. It was planned that the first of the new units would be available for installation by December 1939.

The design study had specified no combat capability, but from the very beginning the Messerschmitt design team had recognised the potential of the new aircraft as a short-range interceptor fighter. When on June 7th, 1939 the design - known as *Projekt 1065* - was presented to the *RLM*, this option was heavily emphasised.

Projekt 1065 was specified as an all-metal, low wing cantilever monoplane, with the two turbo-jets buried in the wing roots. A full-size mock-up of the aircraft was built and was inspected and approved by *RLM* officials in January 1940. Maximum

'It was as if the angels were pushing'

Master aircraft designer Professor Willy Messerschmitt chats to his Chief Test Pilot, Flugkapitän Fritz Wendel. (via ARP)

speed in level flight was estimated to be 560 mph. On the basis of the design a contract was issued to the Messerschmitt Company in March, 1940, for four airframes. Three of these were for flight testing and one for static trials. The designation of this new aircraft then became 'Me262'. During this period, Ernst Heinkel had also been studying the possibilities of jet-powered flight and had also produced a design study for an aircraft of similar capabilities. An element of rivalry was introduced since a contract was also issued to the Heinkel factory for prototypes of the He280.

Meanwhile, the development of the jet engines was running into difficulties. BMW had not only been over-optimistic in their estimate of delivery date, but the physical size of the engine, now designated BMW 003, was substantially larger than had originally been planned. This made it impossible to mount the power plants in the wing roots of the Me262. A major redesign was called for and the new proposals were presented in May, 1940. The resulting design was far different from that originally envisaged. The aircraft that emerged had a smoothly streamlined fuselage of triangular section, with the wings mounted flush with the flat underside, the huge engine nacelles underslung at approximately quarter-span, and the tapered outer wing sections slightly swept. At a stroke, the Me262 had introduced a completely new concept in design and had leapt into a new age.

Work on the prototypes began at Augsburg in July, 1940. These initial machines featured a retractable undercarriage with a fully retractable tailwheel, but it soon became apparent that although work on the airframes was proceeding satisfactorily, the engines were presenting further unforeseen problems. The initial bench runs of the BMW 003 produced a thrust of only 570 lb, instead of the promised 1,320 lb. The Junkers factory, which had also received a jet power plant contract, was faring no better. Only time would tell.

The first prototype (Me262V-1) was completed by the end of 1940, but the engines were far from ready. It was therefore decided that, in order to allow some measure of flight testing, a conventional piston engine should be mounted in the nose and the jet nacelles not fitted. Consequently on April 18th 1941, the Me262V-1 coded PC+UA and powered by a Junkers Jumo 210G piston engine, was rolled out for its first flight. The combination of a fully loaded weight of 5,864 lb, high speed wing profile and the relatively poor acceleration offered by the Jumo engine gave the Messerschmitt Chief Test Pilot *Flugkapitän* Fritz Wendel a serious take-off problem. The machine, as it stood, was grossly underpowered; the whole of the grass airstrip was utilised as Wendel eased the aircraft from the ground, just clearing the boundary hedge but, as he raised the undercarriage, the speed increased to 260 mph. Wendel then experienced for the first time the delightful handling qualities. Wendel ventured shallow dives, but at full throttle and at speeds in excess of 335 mph, severe elevator buffeting was experienced. This was a minor problem, however, and following subsequent test flights by Wendel and Karl Baur, modifications were made that eradicated the problem. Success now only waited upon the engines.

The first two BMW 003 turbo-jets were delivered to Augsburg in November 1941, tested to a thrust of 1,015 lb each, and work commenced to fit them to the Me262V-1. However, as a safety precaution, it was decided to retain the nose-mounted Jumo as a temporary measure. A number of ground trials were carried out before the machine was pronounced fit to fly, but once more the take-off posed problems. Wendel again only just cleared the boundary. He had reached just 165 feet and was about to raise the undercarriage when the port engine suffered a flame-out, followed at once by the starboard. With consummate flying skill Wendel coaxed the overburdened aircraft around the airfield circuit on the piston engine alone and landed safely. It was then discovered that both engines had sustained turbine blade failures. The BMW 003 could not do the job.

Meanwhile the Junkers factory had overcome their problems with the Jumo 004 turbo-jet and the first engines soon arrived at Augsburg. It was found that they were rather larger than those supplied by BMW. The Me262V-3 was chosen to house the new units, the nacelles being increased in size to accommodate them and the fin area was enlarged to compensate for this. The whole Me262 flight testing programme was then moved to Leipheim which, while no larger than Augsburg, had the advantage of a tarmac runway, which would improve the take-off performance considerably.

At this time, British Intelligence was speculating about the German jet aircraft development programme. It was known that the Heinkel factory had a viable jet engine, but information on Messerschmitt projects was sparse. Various odd designations were being mooted, such as 'Me209', 'Me215' etc., but no definite data had yet been gathered.

By mid-July 1942, the aircraft, coded PC+UC, was ready for its first flight with the Jumo 004A-0 pre-production engines. Fritz Wendel commenced high speed taxiing trials and it was discovered that the elevators were proving ineffective at the calculated 'unstick' speed of 112 mph; he could not raise the rear fuselage. During hurried discussions with the design team, it was postulated that a brief touch on the brakes, applied at 112 mph, might well raise the tail. At 08.40 hours on 18th July, Wendel again ventured into the unknown. With the turbo-jets at full power, the Me262V-3 accelerated down the Leipheim runway. The speed rose quickly. At 112 mph Wendel touched the brakes. Instantly the tail rose, the elevators bit into the airflow and the Me262 - now unofficially known as the *Schwalbe* (Swallow) - lifted smoothly into the air. The engines ran sweetly and Wendel was overjoyed with the performance and handling of the aircraft. After a 15 minute demonstration before the delighted Messerschmitt team, he brought the aircraft down to a smooth landing. '....it was a sheer pleasure to fly this machine.', he said. 'Indeed, seldom have I been so enthusiastic during my first flight with a new aircraft as I was with the Me262.' The jet age had begun.

Wendel flew the aircraft again at 12.05 hours, testing the banking characteristics; the small problems encountered on this and several subsequent flights were quickly rectified by minor modifications. Within a matter of weeks, Wendel had the *Schwalbe* up to 435 mph -considerably faster than any Allied aircraft then flying - and it was decided to allow a test pilot from the *Erprobungsstelle Rechlin* to test-fly the V-3. Dipl.Ing. Beauvais arrived at Leipheim on 17th August and Wendel carefully explained the flying techniques - particularly the 'tail-raising manoeuvre' - but on take-off, Beauvais misjudged the moment. He held the tail down for too long, clipped the corn in an adjacent field, and the wingtip struck an unfortunately placed manure heap, ground-looping the aircraft to an ignominious halt. Beauvais was relatively unhurt, but the aircraft was badly damaged, resulting in a serious setback to the flight development programme.

In the meantime, Wendel and Baur had continued test-flying the V-1, still fitted with the Jumo piston engine in the nose. On

'It was as if the angels were pushing'

The Me262V-3, with the larger Junker Jumo engines, ready for its first flight. The tailwheel undercarriage gave it a somewhat ungainly look but when a tricycle system was fitted it transformed the appearance remarkably. (via ARP)
On 18th July, 1942, Fritz Wendel lifted the graceful Schwalbe from the runway at Leipheim. From the very beginning he was impressed by its speed and handling characteristics.

1st October, 1942 the first flight was made with new Jumo 004 engines fitted to the V-2 (PC+UB) and the jet programme was again underway, now to be based at the *Erprobungsstelle* (experimental station) at Lechfeld.

The German Aviation Minister, Ernst Udet, had displayed little interest in the new aircraft. Erhard Milch, who filled this post after Udet committed suicide in November 1941, maintained this attitude for a while. However the undoubted success of the initial V-3 flight tests allowed him to order a further two prototypes and fifteen pre-production aircraft. These latter aircraft were to be equipped with the Jumo 004B, producing the same power for less weight.

Early in 1943, the rebuilt V-3 arrived at Lechfeld from where, a few weeks later, the first *Luftwaffe* fighter pilot - Hauptmann Wolfgang Späte - flew it. He was highly impressed, but on his second flight both engines 'flamed out' during a steep turn. Späte descended rapidly, succeeded in relighting both jets, and landed safely. It was then discovered that a sideslip in the turn had caused the airflow to stop the turbine blades, resulting in complete engine failure. The aircraft, fully overhauled, was subsequently flown by Wendel's assistant, Ostertag, on its next flight. Shortly after take-off the aircraft nosed into a steep dive from 1,600 feet, crashed into the ground at Swabmünchen and killed the pilot. At first, apart from eyewitness accounts that an engine had failed, the cause was not determined. It was only after several other Me262s had been lost in similar circumstances that it was discovered that the manually-adjusted exhaust cones became detached in flight, effectively 'sealing off' the jet orifice and causing a skid, which blanked off the tailplane and made the aircraft uncontrollable.

The development programme was further advanced by the arrival of the V-4 prototype in April 1943. Späte had already reported to *Generalleutnant* Adolf Galland (Inspector of Day Fighters) on the performance of the aircraft in glowing terms and, on 22nd May, Galland visited Lechfeld to try the machine out personally. From the very outset he was impressed and recalled, 'What an aircraft! It was as though the Angels were pushing!' Three days later he reported to Goering: 'This aircraft is a tremendous stroke of luck for us; if the enemy continues to utilise piston-engined aircraft, this puts us way out in front'. The tried and tested Messerschmitt Bf109 was by now in its G-series and was becoming outclassed by the latest Allied fighters. Galland therefore suggested to Goering that production of piston-engined fighters be restricted to the superb FW190, leaving the Messerschmitt factories to concentrate exclusively

On 22nd May, 1943, Generalleutnant Adolf Galland visited Lechfeld to fly the jet. (l to r) Flugkapitän Fritz Wendel, Hauptmann Horst Geyer and Galland. (via ARP)

on the new jet aircraft, Meanwhile *Luftwaffe* representatives, in a meeting with Willy Messerschmitt, had put forward a proposition to convert the aircraft to use a tricycle undercarriage, thus eliminating the take-off problems. Messerschmitt protested that such a change would seriously delay production, adding that '...we can work on the nose-wheel as we go along'. He pointed out that most pilots who had test-flown it had experienced little trouble with take-offs. 'With experienced pilots you could have a squadron in months'. His arguments were of no avail; shortly thereafter a Ministry of Supply meeting released the Me262 for series production, but only if a tricycle undercarriage was fitted for service use.

During mid-August 1943, a meeting was called by Erhard Milch, Minister of Aircraft Production. Milch set out his requirements for fighter production, stating that 4,000 fighters per month were needed. *Generalleutnant* Adolf Galland, still enthused by his exhilarating experience with the jet, at once requested that one quarter of this total be Me262 fighters, but Milch disagreed. He could not be expected to curtail conventional fighter production lines in favour of the jet aircraft and added that, 'The Führer feels that there is no need for the jet at this time', thus showing how truly staggering the gap had become between the *Luftwaffe* High Command and the frontline Commanders. Galland of course knew full well the operational situation; the American 8th Air Force fighter units were becoming stronger daily and, with the advent of the P-51 Mustang, his home defence fighter pilots would became hard-pressed. The FW190 was now the mainstay of the *Reichsverteidigung* (Home Defence) units and could still hold its own with anything - except the Mustang - while the Bf109G was now obsolescent. Arguably the finest fighter aircraft of the early war years, Willi Messerschmitt's creation had now been modified out of all recognition. Gone were the clean lines of the 'E' and 'F' versions, bumps and bulges sprouted from it as larger engines, heavier armour, extra fuel tanks and underslung guns and rocket tubes were fitted, reducing performance to a frightening degree. Its pilots now referred to it as the *Beule* (bulge) and apart from a few old hands, would have much preferred to fly the Focke Wulf.

Galland's arguments were overruled. Milch's contention was that the 'round the clock' bombing had seriously affected the capacity of the German aircraft industry. The *Luftwaffe* fighters had not stopped the raids and therefore more fighters were needed; quantity rather than quality.

Galland was not satisfied. He realised full well that the planned monthly production figure of sixty Me262s would not be met. He also knew that the fighter would be needed in quantity by the spring of 1944. He decided to take more direct action. Shortly after the meeting, he visited *Reichsmarschall* Hermann Goering, taking with him Professor Messerschmitt. Goering, an ex-fighter pilot, was impressed with the arguments put forward and took the matter to Hitler. This resulted in some progress being made.

On November 2nd 1943, a special commission was established under Oberst Petersen, to guide the further development of the Me262 and, on the same day, Goering arrived at Augsburg, having been sent by Hitler to discuss acceleration of the Me262 programme with the Messerschmitt management staff. Others

Even the production Jumo engine was still giving problems. Here PC+UC touches down at Lechfeld amidst clouds of dense white smoke.

present at this meeting included Professor Messerschmitt, *Generalleutnant* Galland, *Generalmajor* Vorwald of the *RLM* and *Generalfeldmarschall* Milch. Goering put to Messerschmitt a direct question from the Führer, 'Can the Me262 carry bombs?' He was told that it would be possible to install two bomb racks beneath the nose. Then he asked how long this would take. Messerschmitt, who had never intended the aircraft to be used as anything other than a fighter, replied casually, 'Oh, two or three weeks after production has commenced'. Goering seemed satisfied and Messerschmitt dropped the subject, hoping and believing that any question of using the aircraft as a bomber would be forgotten. Events were to prove him wrong.

Ten days later Milch, who had received a demand for increased labour from the Messerschmitt company, asked Vorwald whether the Me262 airframe and engine development was advanced enough for full production to commence in early 1944. He was assured that all was well. Meanwhile the Messerschmitt management were making every effort to accelerate the Me262 development programme, but were encountering problems with the tricycle undercarriage system. The Me262V-5 prototype had first flown with a fixed nosewheel on 26th June 1943, but, when this was replaced with a fully retractable unit, initial tests proved disappointing. The take-off distance remained the same as with the tailwheel and, to overcome this, a pair of 1,100 lb thrust Borsig rockets were fitted beneath the rear fuselage. These were ignited electrically when the aircraft reached 100 mph and burned for six seconds. The initial tests were conducted by Karl Baur and, after determining the optimum position and angle for the units, the take-off run was reduced by some 300 yards. Later, when a pair of 2,205 lb thrust rockets were tested, the take-off run was reduced to 400 yards.

By mid-November 1943, a further two Me262s equipped with tricycle undercarriages had joined the flight testing programme; the V-6 prototype was powered by the new Jumo 004B-1, which had a thrust of 1,980 lb and was 200 lb lighter in weight. This aircraft was fitted with gun ports, but carried no armament. The Me262V-7 was essentially similar to the V-6, but was fitted with a clear-vision blown canopy and pressurised cockpit for operations up to 40,000 feet. The initial testing of this aircraft was to be carried out by Gerd Lindner. At this time the veteran *Flugkapitän* Fritz Wendel retired on ill health grounds, leaving the test flying entirely in the experienced hands of Baur and Lindner.

Lindner and Baur took two Me262s to Insterburg on 26th November, where a demonstration was given to Hitler and Goering. The Me262V-4 flown by Baur suffered a flame-out on take-off, but Lindner, in the Me262V-6 gave a masterly exhibition. It is widely believed that during this demonstration Hitler shouted, '*Blitz* Bomber! For years I have requested a high speed bomber and in this aircraft, which you present to me as a fighter, I see my *Blitz* Bomber! It was here all the time and you fools could not see it!' The story continues that he ordered that the aircraft be produced as a bomber only and henceforth forbade any mention of the aircraft as a fighter. This does not appear to fit with the facts, for on 5th December, he despatched a telegram to Goering indicating that he wanted the aircraft to be used as a fighter-bomber. Even so, Galland's dream of an aircraft to sweep the Allies from the skies of the Reich was fading fast.

Production of the Me262 fighter-bomber was given top priority during the middle of December 1943, but the problems

'It was as if the angels were pushing'

A rare shot of a white-painted Me262 rolling down the Lechfeld runway. It is believed that this photograph was taken by a Todt Organisation labourer with a hidden camera. The markings on the jet are clear 'V1+A1', showing that it was the Me262S-4 that was destroyed in a crash during May 1943. (via H Scholl)

continued. Skilled personnel were being conscripted to replace losses on the Russian front, while the Junkers factory staff were still attempting to resolve technical problems with the engines.

Two further prototypes reached the flight testing centre in late 1943. These were the Me262V-8, which mounted four 30mm Rheinmetall-Borsig cannon and the V-10, which would be used to evaluate methods of reducing control forces at high speeds. The V-9 prototype was completed in January 1944, to be used for testing radio and auxiliary equipment. This was closely followed by the V-11 and V-12, to be used for high speed and general dynamic testing. By February 1944, twenty-three Me262A-0 airframes had been completed, but were still awaiting arrival of the turbines; these would not arrive for another six weeks.

At the beginning of December 1943, British Intelligence received the first real confirmation of the Messerschmitt jet programme when a report was smuggled out of Germany, emanating from a French draughtsman employed at the Messerschmitt plant at Augsburg:

> "A month ago two jet propelled aircraft were tested. The first, with the typical airframe of the Me210, had the two jet units in the wings. The second was a tailless aircraft...."

Meanwhile an important step had been taken when permission was granted to form an experimental fighter unit at Lechfeld. On 15th December 1943 *Hauptmann* Werner Thierfelder was appointed to command *Erprobungskommando 262*, which would form at Lechfeld when pilots and aircraft became available. This however would not take place for nearly five months, by which time the British had received further intelligence. Another Frenchman, Lucien Pericaud, had also been working at Augsburg and managed to pass on information concerning the Me262 shortly after he had absconded from there. The data included details of weights, performance and a rough but surprisingly accurate three-view drawing of the aircraft. (Pericaud was later arrested and placed in a concentration camp). This information, when added to other snippets that were slowly being compiled, caused the photo interpreters of the Photographic Interpretation Units to look even more closely at reconnaissance photographs of German airfields. This scrutiny was rewarded very quickly, for on 24th February, five jets were noted at Lechfeld shortly after an 8th Air Force air raid; at least one of the aircraft appeared to have been damaged.

In April 1944, sixteen jets were at last delivered to the *Luftwaffe*, soon followed by another seven. These went mainly to *Erprobungskommando 262*, but during April, Hitler, at a conference with Goering and Milch, discovered that not one of the Me262s already delivered had been equipped to carry bombs. To be fair, Messerschmitt's team were already investigating means of adapting the aircraft as a fighter-bomber, but Hitler flew into one of his well-known rages. 'None of my orders have been obeyed!', he roared. To which Milch weakly replied, 'My Führer, the Me262 was designed as fighter in the first instance'. The furious Hitler would not be placated. It was then

'It was as if the angels were pushing'

An Allied reconnaissance photo of an Me262 on the ground at Lechfeld in the spring of 1944. Much intelligence had already been gained and the time was fast approaching for the Allied bomber forces to attack the Me262s on the ground.

that he ordered that all future Me262s were to be equipped as fighter-bombers and absolutely forbade any mention of it as a fighter. Its fate was sealed - for the present. *Ekdo 262* kept its fighters, however, and these were supplemented by a few more despite Hitler's order.

While it is true that that the Führer's orders had somewhat delayed entry of the Me262 into unit service, much greater contributing factors had been his subordinates' refusal to accept that his word was law and to act accordingly and - most important of all - the non-availability of the turbine engines. Whatever the reason, the fact remained that no full fighter production would take place in the foreseeable future and, due to intentional delays with the fighter-bomber, no such aircraft were to be available to face the Allied invasion.

Meanwhile, on 9th April, three Me262s had been identified at Lechfeld and, nine days later, eight more were photographed at Leipheim. British Intelligence was now receiving frequent reports of the progress of the jet development programme and during May received the information that:

"The Me262 had reached 880 kph (560 mph) and could immediately be put into serial production."

The moment had arrived for the 'Schwalbe's' baptism of fire.

Chapter Two
Into Service: May - August 1944

Early in May, 1944, many pilots from the Bf110-equipped *Stab* and *III Gruppe* of *Zerstörergeschwader 26* were ordered to join *Erprobungskommando 262* at Lechfeld for conversion to the jet and to develop suitable combat tactics. The majority of these aircrew were taken from *III Gruppe* and, since they were experienced in both multi-engined fighters and instrument flying, they had little trouble in converting to the new type once the throttle handling problem had been mastered; if opened too quickly, the engines could catch fire and, if closed too quickly the turbines would 'flame out' and the aircraft could stall. At that stage of the war, the later generation of single-engined fighter pilots had little training on instruments. The basic differences between single and multi-engined handling, which required not only a completely different flying technique, but also a heavy reliance on their instruments - would later prove disastrous for the young Bf109 and FW190-trained pilots. These men would often forget their instruments in the heat of battle and run out of fuel, becoming easy prey for the swarms of Allied fighters. One former *Zerstörer* pilot who flew the Me262 was *Oberleutnant* Günther Wegmann, who stated that after the temperamental throttle handling was overcome, the jet proved an easy aircraft to fly. Wegmann, who was later to fly with *Jagdgeschwader 7*, survived the war with eight confirmed jet victories. Fourteen pilots formed the first group to arrive, but of these, only ten were retained; Wegmann, *Oberleutnant* Hans-Günther Müller (*Staffelkapitän 8./ZG 26*), *Oberleutnant* Paul Bley (*Staffelkapitän 9./ZG 26*) *Leutnants* Joachim Weber, Alfred Schreiber, *Oberfeldwebels* Göbel, Reckers, Strathmann, *Feldwebel* Herlitzius and Unteroffizier Flachs.

Ekdo 262 had few of the new aircraft on strength and flying time was carefully rationed due to the short life of the often unreliable turbines. Only ten hours operating time was permitted before the units were removed and completely overhauled. Later versions of the engine had an improved life-span of twenty-five hours, but were still far from perfect. It is possible that a few of the jets were for a time based at the experimental base at Peenemünde, on the Baltic coast, which would explain the early sighting by Major Meyer's Mustangs (related in Chapter One).

Ekdo 262 sustained its first recorded loss on 19th May, when 'V1+AB' crashed at Lechfeld on a training flight. *Unteroffizier* Kurt Flachs was killed.

While *Ekdo 262* was working up during May 1944, Hitler's directive that the new aircraft be employed as a high speed bomber was also being put into effect. On 29th May, Goering convened a meeting to discuss the Me262 question. Present were *Generals* Galland, Bodenschanz and Korten, together with *Oberst* Petersen. The outcome of the meeting was that development of the aircraft was now to be entrusted to Galland, with the directive that,

> "Some of these aircraft are to be allowed for tests in the (fighter) rôle, as long as this does not affect the development of bomber models turned out. I also suggest that this aircraft be called a 'super speed bomber', not a 'fighter' in the Führer's presence in future. He is well aware of the fighter potential, but wants the Me262 to go into action first in the bomber rôle".

For the benefit of Adolf Galland he added that Hitler was well aware of its potential as a fighter, but wanted the bomber version to proceed until further notice. Next day the 'Führer Befehl' was promulgated, this order stating that initial production would continue as a bomber, but fighter testing would be allowed.

> "Under no circumstances is bomber production to be delayed while awaiting results of such tests.... Not until these tests have been concluded will fighter production be permitted to start. Once this point has been reached there is no reason why production capacity cannot be divided between the two."

Five days later, on 3rd June, the *III Gruppe* of *Oberst* Wolf-Dietrich Meister's *Kampfgeschwader 51 'Edelweiss'* was ordered to relinquish its Ju88 bombers and to proceed to Lechfeld to commence conversion to the new type.[1] As jet production increased, the other *Gruppen* were to follow suit. *III Gruppe* would commence operations in August and were soon joined by *I Gruppe*. *IV Gruppe* would commence jet training in

Into Service: May - August 1944

Line-up of some of the first Me262s delivered to Ekdo 262 at Lechfeld.

August from Munich/Riem, while *II Gruppe*, converting in October, would become operational at Rheine/Hopsten with *I./KG 51*. The unit designation was also changed. It would now be known as *KG(J)51*, the 'J' denoting *Jäger*, or fighter.

In order to utilise the aircraft which, in this bomber configuration would come to be known as the *Sturmvögel* (Stormy Petrel), many modifications were necessary. These modifications made the normally docile machine a difficult and often dangerous aircraft to fly. Extra fuel tanks were fitted, one of 55 gallons beneath the pilot's seat and another of 130 gallons fitted behind the rear tank. This latter, far aft of the centre of gravity, would make the aircraft tail-heavy and impossible to fly if not counter-balanced. This was achieved by the addition of two 550 lb bombs beneath the nose and the removal of two of the 30mm cannon. It was vital that the rear tank be selected and emptied first to balance the aircraft in flight (the reason for the removal of the two cannon). However, if an aircraft was attacked just after take-off, the pilot would have little chance of survival, for to jettison the two bombs would cause the tail-heavy fighter to rear up sharply and only a pilot of considerable experience and strength would be able to maintain control and avoid a stall. Another problem lay, strangely enough, in the cockpit layout; not all Me262 aircraft had been built to the same specification and the position of switches etc., varied between otherwise identical models. This would prove to be a vital factor in combat.

Meanwhile, on 6th June 1944, the long-expected Allied landings took place in Normandy and, by the evening of the following day, the hold on the beachheads had been established. In a discussion with Hitler, Otto Saur, a Nazi Party leader, was told 'The Me262 aircraft are to be bombers, to push the Allies back into the sea'. But it was already too late, for *KG(J)51* could not begin operations for several weeks.

During the spring of 1944 yet another unit was formed. This was *Einsatzkommando Braunegg*, a photo-reconnaissance unit equipped with Bf109Gs and Me262s. The jets, known as the Me262A-1a/U3s, were basically fighter models modified by the removal of armament and the installation of either two RB 20/30 cameras or one RB 20/30 and an RB 75/30. A glass window had been fitted in the cockpit flooring and the cameras were mounted on each side of the nosewheel well. The bomb pylons were retained and used to carry drop-tanks for extended missions. As suggested by the name, The unit was led by *Hauptmann* Herward Braunegg, an Austrian from Graz. He had been awarded the *Ritterkreuz* on 26th March for his reconnaissance work with *Nahaufklärungsgruppe 9* and had taken command of the new unit on 19th May.[2] It is now believed that his unit flew sorties over southern England during the last few weeks of the invasion build-up and that he personally flew three such sorties in the Me262. This has never been reported or even admitted from British records but the fact remains that any such mission could not have been prevented; the only fighter capable of matching the German jet in any respect was the Gloster Meteor, which did not arrive on 616 Squadron until 12th July - too late.

Meanwhile *Ekdo 262* had begun operational testing in June, scrambling aircraft to intercept Allied photo-reconnaissance aircraft in their area.

On 6th July, the Me262 V-12 prototype, minus armament and with a specially-modified flattened cockpit hood, was given a speed trial over Leipheim airfield. Flown by test pilot Gert Lindner this aircraft, Werke Nummer 130008, coded VI+AG, was clocked at the phenomenal speed of 624 mph, well over 150

Into Service: May - August 1944

Above: Me262A-1a/U3 of Einsatzkommando Braunegg. Note the camera blisters on the nose just forward of the 'White 2'. (via ARP)
Right: Hauptmann Werner Thierfelder, first commander of Ekdo 262, was en experienced Zerstörer pilot, having fought in the west since 1939 against France and Britain, then flew in the Balkans and against Crete. He died on 18th July 1944, possibly in combat against 15th Air Force bombers.

mph faster than any Allied fighter in service.

On 18th July *Ekdo 262* suffered a blow when its commanding officer, *Hauptmann* Werner Thierfelder, failed to return from a scramble. His body was found in the wreckage of his Me262 near Landsberg. German reports, state that he was shot down in combat and it would seem that he had become involved in a 15th Air Force raid striking northward from Italy. There were no claims for anything but Bf109s and FW190s made by the American pilots of the 1st, 31st, 52nd and 332nd Fighter Groups, who engaged many *Luftwaffe* fighters in the

Memmingen and Oberstorf areas. Therefore it seems likely that Thierfelder, chasing a reconnaissance machine, had unwitting blundered into the raid, was either hit by gunfire from the bombers and crashed while attempting to return to base, or merely lost control.

Several pilots were lost in July due to technical failures. All had dived into the ground without obvious cause. It was not until one pilot, *Leutnant* Schnörrer, survived such an incident, that matters became clearer. Karl Schnörrer had intercepted an Allied recce aircraft that power-dived to escape and, when the jet pilot followed, the Messerschmitt went out of control. Cutting the engines and operating the elevators had no effect. Realising that a bale-out at such speed would probably prove fatal, Schnörrer jettisoned his cockpit hood - and the Me262 recovered from the dive. It appeared that the jettisoning of the hood had acted as an 'air brake', which had righted the machine. Schnörrer re-lit his turbines and landed safely back at Lechfeld, where the machine was examined. It was found to have sustained severe structural damage, and pronounced a 'write-off'. With the death of Thierfelder, *Hauptmann* Horst Geyer, formerly with *JG 51*, took command of the jet unit.

Next day Fortresses from the 1st Bomb Division mounted a concerted assault on the jet fighters by attacking the Messerschmitt factory at Leipheim, destroying seven Me262s and damaging three more. They also raided Lechfeld airfield and the Messerschmitt works at Augsburg. These raids cut production of jet fighters from fifty-nine in July to only twenty in August; a severe blow to the embryo jet force, although not fully appreciated by the Allies at the time.

On 26th July the first official report of an engagement with an Me262 (Intelligence Report No.2256) was submitted by a Royal Air Force crew. A 544 Squadron Mosquito flown by Flight Lieutenant A E Wall with Pilot Officer A S Lobban as his navigator, had left its base at Benson, Oxfordshire, on a sortie to Munich. At 29,000 feet in the target area a twin-engined aircraft was sighted by Lobban; the aircraft was closing fast and Wall opened up his throttles to escape. At that altitude the Mosquito was capable of out-running any known German type, but the Royal Air Force crew were horrified to find the German

Into Service: May - August 1944

Fortresses unload their bombs on Lechfeld, 19th July 1944.
(USAF, via Roger Freeman)

interceptor overtaking them with ease, but without opening fire. Possibly the German pilot was confirming identification, for he turned again and closed in on them from astern. Now realising that their adversary was jet-powered, Wall broke hard to starboard, but the less-manoeuvreable jet used its superior speed and was quickly behind the Mosquito again, opening fire at 800 yards. Once more Wall broke hard, forcing the German to break away and position himself for another attack. This performance was repeated five times before the Messerschmitt pilot changed tactics and delivered a climbing attack from below. Wall broke again, hearing a loud bang from the underside of his machine, and dived hard for the clouds below, leaving the Messerschmitt behind. Safe in the woolly protection, Lobban removed the inner hatch to ascertain the damage, to find that the outer door had gone. Not knowing what further damage, if any, had been suffered. Wall decided to head for the nearest friendly territory and finally landed at Fermo airfield, Italy. Reports conflict concerning the state of the Mosquito; one states that the aircraft was crash-landed, while another reports a normal landing. When the aircraft was inspected it was discovered that the outer door had been torn off by the violence of the evasive action, striking the port tailplane as it went. Allied Intelligence assumed that this encounter involved the new Messerschmitt Me262, but it was not believed yet to be operational. Wall's opponent had been *Leutnant* Alfred Schreiber, who claimed the Mosquito destroyed in combat over the Alps as the first success for *Ekdo 262*.

Next day, (27th July) the nine Me262s comprising the third *Staffel* of *KG(J)51* were sent out to Chateaudun under command of *Hauptmann* Wolfgang Schenk to commence operations against the Allied beachheads. The unit, operating independently, would be known as *Kommando Schenk* until it joined *I Gruppe* at the Rheine airfield complex on 5th September. These attacks were not particularly successful, since the pilots had strict orders not to operate below 13,000 feet in order to keep from the Allied High Command the fact that the Me262 bomber was operational. No bomb-sight was fitted and the attacks were carried out by releasing the bombs as soon as the target disappeared from view beneath the engine nacelles, but from that altitude the chances of hitting any specific target were negligible. Despite this, the Germans preserved secrecy, for there was no mention of the Me262 in any Allied report during the battle for France. As the Allies broke out of the beachhead on 12th August, *I./KG(J)51* moved back to the airfield of Etampes, near Chartres. Due to the speed of the Allied advance they remained there only four days before moving on to Creil, north of Paris. From here a few sorties were flown before they moved yet again, this time to Juvincourt, arriving on 27th August. Next day they vacated French soil and transferred to Chievres in Belgium and, on the same day, they attacked ground targets along the banks of the Seine, northwest of Paris and in the Melun area.

Although it is clear that British Intelligence was now well aware of the jet threat, is it also plain that the information was both slow in coming and by no means entirely accurate -

Into Service: May - August 1944

Wolfgang Schenk was a highly experienced twin-engined fighter-bomber pilot, having served with ZG 1, E.Gr.210 (later SKG 210), SG 2, finally becoming Kommodore of KG(J)51 in July 1944. He would end the war as Inspector in the Special Staff unit for jet aircraft.

confirmation that the early tactics of *Kommando Schenk* had succeeded in maintaining Allied ignorance of its true status:

> "The Me262 is about to become operational. Apparently three Staffeln based in Holland have nearly finished conversion training. I./JG 3, under *Major* Dahl are believed to be converting to Me262s, but this is not confirmed."

The piece of information was both surprisingly accurate and obtained at a very early date (29th July), for part of *JG 3* was indeed under orders to convert to jet operations - although this would not commence for some time.

Meanwhile, operations continued into August and, on the 2nd, *Leutnant* Schreiber claimed his second success, a reconnaissance Spitfire. On August 8th, *Leutnant* Joachim Weber shot down a 540 Squadron reconnaissance Mosquito near Ohlstadt at 15.38 hours. Both Flight Lieutenant Desmond Matthewman and Flight Sergeant William Stopford were killed. Final confirmation of the jets' status was received on 15th August. Following the loss of several reconnaissance aircraft from operations over southern Germany, a Mosquito of 60 (South African Air Force) Squadron was despatched from San Severo in Italy to photograph Leipheim airfield. This machine, crewed by Captain Saloman Pienaar and Lieutenant Archie Lockhart-Ross, allowed the *Luftwaffe* to demonstrate the operational capability of the Me262 in spectacular fashion.[3]

Their course took them up the Adriatic coast towards Prague in a long feint to confuse the German fighter controllers; they then back-tracked to a point north-northeast of Munich from where they turned and headed straight for Leipheim. As they crossed Memmingen airfield, Pienaar felt that something was wrong; no *Flak* and no fighters had been seen - just clear blue sky. Lieutenant Lockhart-Ross crouched down in the nose as they made the run-up to Leipheim at 30,000 feet, peering through the bomb-sight used to target the cameras, and sighted the well camouflaged base. 'I can see it', he called. 'An aircraft's just taken off. Look at it go!'

Pienaar held the Mosquito steady in the thin air as Lockhart-Ross kept the cameras rolling. Then, in the rear-view mirror he saw a speck in the distance. Fighter! Pienaar realised at once that this was no normal aircraft, for it was gaining on them far too rapidly. Perhaps this was the new secret jet fighter that they had heard rumours of? Quickly he jettisoned his drop-tank and grabbed the throttles, looking again in his mirror to find the fighter - indeed a twin-engined jet -almost upon them. As he broke hard to starboard, the Messerschmitt pilot opened fire, catching the port wing with 30mm cannon-fire that blew the aileron away. The normal evasive technique of Mosquito pilots - and indeed of fighter pilots generally - was a hard break to port; had Pienaar done so on this occasion it is likely that the British aircraft would have caught that burst amidships, which would have undoubtedly destroyed the Mosquito. It was estimated that three 30mm cannon hits were sufficient to destroy a four-engined bomber and in ground tests, one single round blew the rear fuselage of a captured Spitfire completely in half.

The German pilot was good, following the Mosquito around and getting more strikes on the wing root and port fuselage - again without inflicting mortal damage. Pienaar felt the cannon strikes and saw pieces flying off his aircraft before the Mosquito suddenly flicked to port and went into a spiral dive with both engines screaming on full power and the flying and throttle controls not functioning. His observer was prone in the nose, the G-forces pinning him helplessly to the floor as the aircraft plunged downwards. His oxygen mask had come adrift and he was only half conscious, but his pilot could do nothing to help him. Then the engine supercharger blowers cut out as the aircraft descended through 20,000 feet. Pienaar then saw the

Into Service: May - August 1944

Summer at Lechfeld, 1944. (l to r) Leutnant Alfred 'Bubi' Schreiber, who claimed the world's first jet 'kill' and would become the world's first jet ace; Hauptmann Riedel; Hauptmann Horst Geyer, Thierfelder's successor as Kommandeur. (via ARP)

pitch levers hard forward. He eased them back and the aircraft eased out of the dive. He found the controls operating after a fashion and discovered that the machine could be flown using just the rudder and full starboard aileron, as the port engine was still roaring at full power and could not be adjusted. Lockhart-Ross managed to clamber back into the cockpit. As he strapped himself back into the seat he saw the '262 coming at them again and shouted a warning to his pilot. Pienaar simply let the controls go, the Mosquito flicked hard to port and the jet hurtled past, the pilot clearly visible, looking back over his shoulder at them as he gained height for another pass. Ten times the action was repeated, with Pienaar breaking into the attacks and leaving the German no opportunity for a clear shot. Meanwhile he had asked his navigator for a direct course for Switzerland; a bale-out in the Munich area could be dangerous, for it was believed that Allied aircrew had been lynched by civilians angered by the heavy bombing in the area.

They were now down to 5,000 feet and, as the jet turned wide to attack again, Pienaar turned the Mosquito head-on, saying

'I'm going to try to ram the bugger. If we have to go we may as well take him with us.' The jet shot over the top of them, almost close enough to touch, and Pienaar dived hard for some thick cloud at 500 feet. The Me262 followed them down, for as they broke out of the grey protection he came at them one last time before breaking away - obviously short of fuel, since Pienaar estimated that the combat had lasted for nearly 30 minutes - and left them alone in the sky.

Setting course for home, they limped back towards Italy at less then 500 feet. They crossed the notorious 'hot spot' of Udine airfield at zero feet to avoid the *Flak* and out again over the blue waters of the Adriatic where Pienaar climbed to 150 feet. He mused on how surprised the Germans must have been at Udine, normally avoided by Allied aircraft. What had they made of a lone aircraft, streaking over them with one engine roaring and the other throttled back? Nearing Ancona, Lockhart-Ross tapped his pilot on the shoulder, pointing at four single-engined fighters coming down on them and they breathed sighs of relief when these were identified as Spitfires. Pienaar carried on towards San Severo, where he set the crippled aircraft down on its belly in a cloud of dust. The crew, dazed but unhurt, scrambled from the wreckage, for wrecked it surely was. Apart from the damage already mentioned, the port engine nacelle was just a series of bare ribs and a 30mm 'solid shot' round was found buried in the wooden mainspar. The jet pilot had unknowingly made his kill. Although the aircraft would never fly again, the sortie had achieved a conspicuous success; throughout the engagement the cameras had been running and when the film was developed there was a clear shot of the Me262 in silhouette, turning below and ahead of the Mosquito. Thus the existence of the machine operating in fighter rôle was firmly established and the obvious performance gave the Allied High Command food for thought. Pienaar and Lockhart-Ross had brought their crippled aircraft over 400 miles across enemy-occupied territory; had they chosen the easier option - Switzerland and internment - the vital film would never have reached Allied hands. For this exploit, Pienaar and Lockhart-Ross were each awarded the Distinguished Flying Cross.

Into Service: May - August 1944

Above: The de Havilland Mosquito had long enjoyed relative immunity from conventional German fighters, losses being light. The arrival of the Me262 was a considerable shock and made the RAF crews far more wary during sorties to the Munich area.
(C Ellis)
Right Feldwebel Helmut Lennartz claimed the first American 'heavy' on 15th August. He had a great deal of experience against the 8th Air Force, having previously flown Bf109Gs with the 5th Staffel of JG 11 in the Home Defence. (via ARP)

The tale has an interesting sequel, for many years later, Pienaar met Wolfgang Schenk, who had also been airborne in an Me262 that summer day. He had been in radio contact with the fighter pilot involved in the action and who reported how the Mosquito had turned to starboard instead of port. Schenck could not remember the pilot's name, but recalled that he had been killed flying the jet on the Russian Front much later in the war.

On this same day *Feldwebel* Helmut Lennartz had been scrambled from Lechfeld at 12.54 hours and, in company with *Oberfeldwebel* Kreutzberg, encountered a lone B-17 of the 303rd Bomb Group near Gerlingen. This was attacked by Lennartz, who blew the port wing off with his 30mm cannons. On the day following (the 16th) the Americans lost an F-5C Lightning of the 5th Photo Recon Group, which was engaged and shot down by an unidentified Me262 pilot near Raumühle. 2nd Lieutenant R A Kiefer was killed.

Two days later, on 18th August, a small detachment of Me262s was sent from Lechfeld to Lärz to operate independently. On this date a 544 Squadron Mosquito, flown by Flight Lieutenant F.L.Dodd DSO AFC, was intercepted at 30,000 feet over Giebelstadt by one of the jets (possibly flown by *Leutnant* Schnörrer - see Chapter One), but escaped undamaged by diving 10,000 feet into cloud.

There were then no engagements involving the jets for nearly a fortnight - although one Me262 was briefly sighted on 20th August. Three days later, on the 23rd, Flight Lieutenant H.C.V.Hawker flying a 683 Squadron photo-recce Spitfire from Italy, had an unnerving experience when he was intercepted by two of the new jets. His encounter report reads:[4.]

"When I first saw the Me262, I was on an approximately due east course about twenty miles east of Munich at 27,000 feet. I had been having trouble with my wing tanks not feeding; they had cut out several times.

"After having a good weave and look out under my tail, I remember trying to make out the concentration camp at Dachau, which was on my starboard quarter. (The RDF was particularly strong and making a curious moaning sound), when the engine cut and I put my head inside [the cockpit] and cured it by momentarily turning on my main tanks. I looked out to port just in time to see an aircraft, which I subsequently identified as an Me262. He had fairly obviously approached from dead astern. He passed my port wing about 100 feet distant. His aircraft tilted slightly towards me and then he rolled rapidly to port, turning steeply. I selected main tanks, opened up fully, set oxygen to emergency and started turning to port, climbing slightly. I was actually following him through part of his turn, and it was then that I

Into Service: May - August 1944

The clean lines of the Spitfire XI, as flown by Harry Hawker of 683 Squadron. He counted himself fortunate to have survived attacks by two jets on 23rd August 1944.
(C Ellis)

saw another jet aircraft, which was still flying on a westerly course and was probably flying number 2 to the the first aircraft. While I was passing astern of this aircraft, he turned to port and, a short while after, appeared 2,000 yards astern, slightly to port. The first aircraft had kept on turning and had dived away northwards, not to be seen again.

"The remaining aircraft moved up behind me until he was approximately 2,000 yards on my port quarter. I was now getting an indicated height of 30,000 feet and an IAS of 260+ mph. The jet aircraft started to pull over towards me and the range closed, but at about 1,000 yards he would break away to port. He repeated this about three times, always pulling away to port before coming in range. I estimated that 600 yards would be his most effective range and the time to turn into him. I watched him closely, having to weave slightly as the mirror is on the starboard side of the cockpit; it is pretty useless as everything is too small and it vibrates. The rear part of the cockpit cover was not awfully clear, and he was slightly below.

"In his last attack he broke to port again and flew about 2,000 yards away parallel to me on my port side. He remained there for about two minutes. I hoped for a moment he had lost me, but I soon realised that he was watching me, and probably pacing me, as he was just keeping abreast and must have throttled back. He then pulled over behind and slightly below me and proceeded to overtake me fast. I kept a straight course until he was 600 yards astern, then I did the steepest climbing turn that I could make. He followed me for the first quarter of it, and except for the very beginning of the turn he was outside me. I myself was shuddering at the stall, but did not let my speed drop below 240 mph IAS. I had a good view of his plan view, the colour being brown camouflage. I thought the wings looked eliptical, but I did not notice the tail unit, though the cockpit cover was faired into the fuselage and not of the bubble variety of the other aircraft.

The aircraft must have turned through 180 degrees, though I only saw him in about the first 90 degrees and as I straightened up on a southerly course, having completed 360 degrees, I saw him a great distance away, turning to port. I put my nose down slightly, hoping my aircraft would be less conspicuous against the background of the Alps. I was then nearly over Innsbrück. I did not see the enemy aircraft again.

"Some points that impressed me about the jet aircraft are listed below:-

1. In his first pass at me, his speed was 100-150 mph greater than mine.

2. That the jet aircraft was fast enough to attack from below and accelerated rapidly even in a slight climb.

3. His aileron control was remarkably good; he snapped easily into any turn that he made.

4. The actual radius of turn was great, though he might have been able to turn tighter than he did if he had slowed up a bit.

5. The pilot of the second aircraft was very experienced and certainly gave me a feeling of 'mouse and cat'."

"Throughout the engagement I tended to treat the jet aircraft as I would have done a normal single engined fighter attack; this is, if I could not pull away or was jumped, to turn inside the attacking aircraft, though I had heard that the jet aircraft's performance improved with altitude. However, when I realised I could turn inside him, I felt that I had a better chance staying at altitude and moving in the direction of friendly territory than I would have losing height in an aileron turn or dive over the Munich area, where there might have been single engined fighters working in conjunction with the jet aircraft. Also, at lower levels my petrol consumption would be increased.

F/Lt H C V Hawker (119864) 683 Squadron, RAF CMF"

During the latter attacks, he remembered seeing the nose of the German fighter lit up with cannon flashes 'like a gas ring'. He was a lucky man, for next day, the 24th, another such engagement proved fatal. *Oberfeldwebel* Helmut Baudach, a fifteen-victory *Experte* from *JG 2 'Richthofen'*, claimed a Spitfire destroyed, having intercepted another 683 Squadron photo-recce aircraft flown by Flight Lieutenant F N Crane. He shot it down west-southwest of Walchensee and this pilot did not survive.

On the 26th two victories were claimed by *Ekdo 262* pilots; *Leutnant* Schreiber reported a Spitfire destroyed, while *Oberfeldwebel* Reckers claimed to have shot down a Mosquito. The date for Schreiber's victory may be in error, and was possibly a

15th Air Force F-5 reported missing a day earlier. Reckers' opponent was certainly a 60 (SAAF) aircraft, crewed by Lieutenants C.Mouton and D.Krynauw, who were both killed when their Mosquito crashed near Ingolstadt at 12.00 hours.

Meanwhile, *Kommando Schenk* had received reinforcements on 23rd August, but of the nine jets, only five arrived safely in France; two crashed on take-off from Lechfeld, another crashed on take-off from Schwabisch-Hall (the intermediate stop) and a fourth force-landed.

As has already been related, *Major* Kurt Unrau's *I./KG(J)51* had left France on 28th August and on this date the first engagements between jets and Allied fighters occurred. *Oberfeldwebel* Hieronymus 'Ronny' Lauer was returning to base when at 19.15 hours he fell foul of a flight of P-47s from the 78th Fighter Group, operating from Duxford as cover to fighter-bombers. Major Joe Myers reported:

> "We were flying at 11,000 feet in the vicinity of Termonde, Brussels, Belgium, when we spotted a strange aircraft flying low to the ground extremely fast. Leaving four of my flight to give top cover, I led the other three of my aircraft down to investigate in a 45 degree dive. My P-47 was indicating 450 mph when I overhauled the enemy aircraft, which was a twin-jet. The pilot must have seen us closing in on him because at the last moment he took evasive action in the way of flat turns. I was about to open fire when the jet's wing hit the ground and he crash-landed, skidding to a halt after some distance..."

Ronny Lauer had actually crash-landed in order to avoid the 'Spitfires' on his tail. He scrambled from the cockpit and ran for cover in nearby trees, watching as Joe Myers' pilots came down to strafe the wrecked Messerschmitt. Myers No 4 man, Lieutenant M.D.Croy, (who shared credit for this first Me262 victory with Myers) fired on Lauer and claimed to have hit him as he was running from the wreck. The German pilot was not injured and subsequently undertook many more jet sorties and survived the war.

Two days later *I./KG(J)51* (which had now been joined by *III Gruppe*) moved to Volkel and Eindhoven airfields in Holland, from where they commenced flying sorties against Allied positions around Antwerp and Louvain, on the Albert Canal line. *IV.(Erg)/KG(J)51* became established in late August at Munich/Riem, to give *KG(J)51* pilots operational training.

However little is known of their activities; some aircraft are known to have been lost to Allied fighters and the unit eventually moved to Neuburg/Donau airfield in Bavaria, during April 1945, where fifty wrecked Me262s were found by advancing American troops

Notes

1. *Kampfgeschwader 51 Edelwiess*, by Wolfgang Dierich.
2. *Die Österreichischen Ritterkreuzträger in der Luftwaffe 1939-45* by Günter Weisinger and Walter Schroeder.
3. Captain Saloman Pienaar DFC. Interview with *Wings* magazine, 1976.
4. Supplied by Mr H C V Hawker

Chapter Three
Tactical Operations And Kommando Nowotny
September - November 1944

3rd September, 1944
The Royal Air Force paid their respects to *KG(J)51* by attacking the unit's new home at Volkel in strength with a daylight assault by Lancasters and Halifaxes. Many of the ground personnel were injured, including the unit Medical Officer *Doktor* Denkhaus, as well as a few of the aircrew.[5.] How many of the scarce jets were destroyed is not known, but they flew no more operations from Holland, withdrawing instead to Rheine, Hoerstel and Hopsten, where they would remain until March 1945. Ar234 bombers remained however, using the taxiways as makeshift runways.

Carefully towed by a ground vehicle, an aircraft of KG(J)51 displays the classic lines of the Me262. The nosewheel was very delicate and was the cause of many landing and towing accidents.

5th - 6th September, 1944

Ekdo 262 was continuing its operations from Lechfeld and Lärz and *Leutnant* Schreiber claimed the destruction of a Spitfire at 14.40 hours. Lieutenant Robert Hillborn of the 7th Photo Recon Group had taken off from Mount Farm on a sortie to southern Germany on what was to prove his last flight of the war. He was over Stuttgart when the attack occurred. His first knowledge of an enemy aircraft in the vicinity came when his Spitfire XI PL182 was hit by cannon fire from below and behind, following which Schreiber's Me262 rocketed over the top of his aircraft. Moments later, the Merlin engine seized solid and Hillborn took to his parachute, landing safely to become a prisoner of war. Schreiber's combat film showed that his four 30mm cannon had absolutely 'shredded' the Spitfire. Next day *Oberfeldwebel* Göbel intercepted a Mosquito, which he claimed to have destroyed. This was very probably a 540 Squadron aircraft flown by Squadron Leader Fleming, which was reported missing.

8th - 10th September, 1944

I./KG(J)51 sustained its second loss in action when *Leutnant* Rolf Weidemann was shot down by AA fire near Diest. He was killed. Although most of the aircraft was wrecked, the two jet units were recovered and sent to England for examination. Next day (9th September) a 1 PRU Mosquito (NS643) was engaged by a lone Me262 of *Ekdo 262* over Aschaffenburg, but evaded without damage.

I./KG(J)51 sustained another casualty on 10th September *Oberleutnant* Werner Gärtner met the same fate as Weidemann when his '9K+LL' fell to AA gunners at Liege.

Casualties to the Allied photo-reconnaissance squadrons continued at a relatively high rate, the Americans losing at least nine aircraft: five F-5s, three Spitfires and a Mosquito. The Royal Air Force lost four Mosquitos and a Spitfire, plus two more fighter-bomber Mosquitos, one of which landed at Dübendorf airfield, Switzerland. At this time also, the recce, tactical reconnaissance (TacR) and fighter units began to experience heavier losses over Dutch airspace than had hitherto been the case. Since it is known that *KG(J)51* jet pilots claimed victories at this time (although no details are known) it is possible that some of these Allied casualties were the result of jet fighter attacks.

In mid-September, 66 Squadron, Royal Air Force, flew a patrol near Venlo, Holland. The Spitfires were at 15,000 feet when Flight Lieutenant Jim Rosser sighted an aircraft a few thousand feet below, heading west. Rosser broke formation to investigate and as he dived he saw the expanding silhouette resolve into an Me262. No Royal Air Force pilot had yet managed to shoot one down, so he gave the Spitfire IXE full throttle. As he began to narrow the gap, the German pilot saw him coming and opened up the turbines. Plumes of smoke emerged and the jet left the Spitfire standing; in a minute or so it was a mere speck in the distance.

The Messerschmitt was from *KG(J)51* and Rosser, who was shot down over Arnhem on September 26th, never had the opportunity to see another in the air again. He remained in the Royal Air Force after the war and, many years later, was among a group of British officers visiting an airfield occupied by the reformed Federal German *Luftwaffe*. The conversation turned to German jet operations and Rosser related his experience. By an amazing coincidence one of the German officers remembered the event, for it was he who had been flying the Messerschmitt. He had seen the lone Spitfire coming down and said:

> "I opened up my engines flat out 'till I lost it. But if you had kept after me, you would have got me for sure, because I had to shut down my speed after a minute or so, as my fuel tanks were all but dry!."

11th September, 1944

The first engagement between American heavy bombers and jet fighters took place, when a US 8th Air Force formation was engaged near Leipzig. The B-17 Fortresses of the 100th Bomb Group - nicknamed 'The Bloody Hundredth' due to earlier high losses - were taking the brunt of the attack by many conventional fighters, when a few Me262s were sighted. The P-51 Mustang escorts joined the fight, American pilots claiming fifteen German piston-engined fighters destroyed. They lost a total 24 of their own number reported missing, one of which, a Mustang from the 339th Fighter Group flown by Lieutenant Willam A Jones, was seen to fall victim to an Me262 flown by *Oberfeldwebel* Helmut Baudach of *Ekdo 262* and crashed near

Eberbach. Jones baled out to become a prisoner. During the next few weeks, on almost every occasion that the *Luftwaffe* challenged American heavy bomber forces, there were a handful of the new jet fighters amongst the interceptors - a matter of concern to the 8th and 15th Air Force Commands, since it was not yet apparent how many of these fast new fighters the Germans could muster.

12th September, 1944
I./KG(J)51 lost another Me262 when *Unteroffizier* Herbert Schauder was fired on by German *Flak* gunners. He lost his life when '9K+AL' took a direct hit and crashed near Arnhem.

The 8th Air Force Bomber Command sent nearly 900 bombers out to attack various targets including oil refineries and storage facilities. Between 100 and 150 German fighters rose to engage the attackers. Despite the heavy escort, they managed to bring down many of the 35 bombers - 31 B-17s and 4 B-24s - lost that day. Among the claimants was *Hauptmann* Georg-Peter Eder of *Ekdo 262*, who was credited with two Fortresses and a B-17 'probable'.

Bombers of the American 15th Air Force operating from Italy attacked the Messerschmitt factory at Wasserburg, near Ulm, where many vital jigs for Me262 airframe construction were destroyed.

13th - 14th September, 1944
The 8th Air Force made its second claim against jets when on the 13th Mustangs of the 364th Fighter Group patrolled near Stralsund. Lieutenant John A Walker sighted an Me262 to the south, which he attacked and claimed to have damaged. *Leutnant* Weber scored his second jet victory next day by claiming a Mosquito, possibly Flight Sergeant Moylan's 540 Squadron machine that failed to return.

18th September, 1944
Leutnant Joachim Weber claimed another Mosquito and again it would appear that his adversary was a Royal Air Force machine; the 544 Squadron machine flown by Flying Officer Hunter DFC failed to return.

24th September, 1944
Hauptmann Georg-Peter Eder of *Ekdo 262* reportedly claimed a

September - November 1944

With his cap at a rakish angle, Helmut Baudach poses in front of his fighter. In late 1944, he was becoming a consistent scorer against the Americans and British. (H Buchner)

pair of B-17s destroyed plus another 'probable' on this date,[6] but it could not be so. No heavy bomber operations were flown by 8th Air Force due to bad weather, nor did the 15th operate over Germany or Austria. Certainly, no B-17s were lost. It is more likely that this date is in error and actually occurred on the 27th, when heavy raids were carried out, the Americans losing 28 heavies.

26th September, 1944
On 17th September, the Allies had put Operation *Market Garden* into effect by landing nearly three divisions of troops by air around the Grave, Nijmegen and Arnhem bridges. On 26th September - the day that Jim Rosser of 66 Squadron was shot down - a flight of Spitfires from 602 Squadron Royal Air Force patrolled the Arnhem area. One of the pilots, Raymond Baxter (better known today as a commentator with the British Broadcasting Corporation) remembered:

"We were flying in very bad weather at the time, when we were bounced from behind by an unfamiliar black shape that went through the middle of us as we all broke. No fire was exchanged and what we all later realised was an Me262 just kept going down into broken cloud, far too quickly for us to pursue." [7].

The jet was almost certainly one of *KG(J)51*'s fighter-bombers, which were being used in attempts to destroy the Nijmegen bridge. One man who was on the 'receiving end' at Nijmegen was Gunner L C Betts of the Royal Artillery, serving with C Troop, 405 Battery, 123rd Light AA Regiment:

"We first saw an Me262 a few days before we reached Nijmegen, when we were parked on Zeist aerodrome in Belgium. What we now know to be an Me262 flew over. We didn't fire as we were in the travelling position, but some guns further away had a go. He took a sharp turn, lost control and hit the deck. It was too far away from us to be seen, but we did not think that the pilot had any chance of getting out.

"Following the drop by our paratroopers on Sunday, 17th September, and after a few adventures and hold-ups, my battery reached Nijmegen the next Saturday night and were deployed to protect the now-famous bridge there. Early on Sunday morning a formation of Messerschmitt 109s came over our position and we opened fire on them; we were not to see any more in force again in this area. The Me262s now came on the scene, normally only one at any time. They would approach the bridge at between 5,000 and 10,000 feet, coasting, so you heard the whine, and the plane would be a quarter-mile ahead of it. As soon as we opened fire, they would open up and whoosh away. We had 400 mph clock sights and we had to be outside the sight to get anywhere near them. I think they were mostly on reconnaissance, but they did carry a canister of anti-personnel bombs, which they dropped in our lines, and these could be very nasty. We never hit one, but used to scare them off. One day a Spitfire got one by diving onto it from above, but they had no chance to catch them on the level. The RAF brought some Hawker Tempest fighters into the area, but I don't think they had any more success. Anyhow, our main job was to stop Jerry from hitting the bridge." [8].

The 8th Air Force directed a heavy raid against Hamm. Lieutenant Urban Drew of the 361st Fighter Group, was among the Mustang escorts at 20,000 feet, astern of the B-24s nearing the target area when he sighted a strange twin-engined aircraft some 10,000 feet below and obtained permission to investigate. He and his flight peeled off from their squadron and dived their Mustangs steeply, but as they descended, the German aircraft began to pull away from them. The Americans dropped their wing-tanks to gain speed. With the Mustangs shuddering at 500 mph, Drew radioed that they were still not gaining on the German aircraft, now clearly identified as a jet from the amount

September - November 1944

A '262 prepares for take-off. The 'S' on the nosewheel door indicates that this is probably a KG(J)51 fighter-bomber.

of smoke pouring from the engines. The '262 began a shallow turn to port:

> "I immediately started a sharper turn to cut him off. As I was cutting him off he started tightening his turn. When we finally passed each other all I could get was about a 90 degree deflection shot, which didn't do me any good at all. I racked my ship around and started after him again, thinking that his speed would have been cut down some in his turn. As we straightened out I could see that he wasn't pulling away from me but I couldn't gain on him either. I had everything wide open and was indicating about 410 mph straight and level on the deck. I chased him for about 30 seconds when I observed this airfield straight ahead of me..."

It was clear that the jet pilot intended to 'drag' the pursuing Mustangs right across his airfield (Achmer) and expose them to the terrific *Flak* defences, so Drew called his flight to get right down to ground level. He started a right turn to skirt the edge of the field, but his wingman, Lieutenant Daniel F Knupp, either failed to anticipate the *Flak* or took incorrect evasive action. He caught a burst of fire, pulled up to 200 feet and baled out, landing on the airfield. Meanwhile Drew continued the pursuit:

> "I had been firing on the ship in his turns every time I thought I was anywhere near being in range, so I had used up quite a bit of my

ammunition. Just then another jet-propelled aircraft dropped out of the lower cloud layer, which was about 4,000 feet, and headed for my flight. My wingman started a sharp turn into him but the jet pilot kept right on going and made no attempt to stay around and mix it up. The first jet-job started another shallow turn and I started firing from about 1,000 yards. I was too far out of range and couldn't get any hits on him at all. The jet propelled aircraft then headed back for the airfield. I saw other single-engined aircraft taking off. I had fired all my ammunition except a couple of hundred rounds and my wingman had become separated when he turned into the other jet aircraft, so I decided it was just about time I left..." [9.]

It would not be long however before Urban L Drew would make his mark against the jets in a more deadly fashion.

On this same day a 540 Sqn Mosquito crew had an unnerving experience, Flight Sergeant Hill's NS639 being intercepted by two of the jets. Eight passes were made before Hill escaped by diving into cloud at 6,000 feet.

28th September, 1944

Heavy bombers from the 8th Air Force struck at oil targets at Magdeburg, Kassel and Merseburg and sustained heavy losses in determined fighter attacks. The Merseburg raid cost ten of the 34 losses suffered by the 8th Bomber Command. *Hauptmann* Georg-Peter Eder of *Ekdo 262* claimed one B-17 as a 'probable'.

Spitfires from 416 (RCAF) Squadron patrolled over the Nijmegen area during the morning. At 10.10 hours a lone Me262 was sighted at 13,000 feet some ten miles southeast of Nijmegen. The jet went into a dive and was pursued flat-out by Flight Lieutenant J B McColl, who attacked from 600 down to 200 yards. Strikes were seen, but the Messerschmitt pilot took no evasive action, merely opening his throttles and climbing away.

30th September, 1944

Six 441 (RCAF) Squadron Spitfires took off at 09.30 hours to patrol Nijmegen and encountered two fighter-bombers of *KG(J)51*. The jets were at 9,000 feet and were gliding down in a shallow dive, presumably to carry out a surprise attack on Allied positions. One was seen to be carrying a large yellow-painted bomb of about 1,000 lb, slung off-centre beneath the fuselage. One of the '262s disappeared into cloud, but Flight Lieutenant R G Lake engaged the second, closing to between 200 and 100 yards and opening fire. A piece resembling a panel

September - November 1944

The great Georg-Peter Eder, one of the most successful jet fighter pilots of all time. He fought on both European fronts before joining Ekdo 262, finally leading the 9./JG 7.

(J Foreman)

was seen to fall away and the German pilot opened up his turbines and made off at an estimated speed of 450 mph without taking evasive action or jettisoning his bomb-load.

It was on this same date that the RAF opened its account against the jets when a 132 Squadron Spitfires engaged an Me262 in the Arnhem area, Warrant Officer F Campbell claiming it 'damaged'.

An important development in *Luftwaffe* jet fighter operations had taken place on 26th September, when *Major* Walter Nowotny, popular former *Kommandeur* of I./JG 54 *'Grünherz'*, but since February 1944 commander of a training unit, JG 101 at Pau, was chosen to lead the first fighter 'Test *Kommando*', which was formed from part of *Ekdo 262*, plus the remaining pilots from III./ZG 26. Nowotny was at that time one of the leading fighter *Experten*, with 255 victories claimed on the Eastern Front; he had been awarded the Knight's Cross with Oak Leaves, Swords and Diamonds. Next day the new unit, officially known as *Kommando Nowotny* was established at Achmer, near Osnabrück. The unit was planned to be expanded into a full fighter *Gruppe* at an early date, with sixteen aircraft per *Staffel* plus four more in the *Stabschwarm* i.e. a complement of 52 jet fighters. The scene would therefore be set for a battle of epic proportions. In order to counteract the vulnerability of the Me262 whilst taking off and landing, the 'long-nose' Focke Wulf 190D-9s of *Hauptmann* Robert 'Bazi' Weiss' *III./JG 54* were also transferred to Achmer and a *'Flak* corridor' several miles long was set up along the line of the main runway. The four FW190D *Staffeln*, commanded by *Hauptmann* Böttlander, *Oberleutnants* Willi Heilmann, Peter Crump and Hans Dortenmann were to fly fighter cover over the airfield until the jets reached the protection of the *Flak* corridor. It was hoped that these precautions would prevent Allied fighters from engaging the jets while in their vulnerable 'undercarriage down' configuration. Using the previous experience of *Ekdo 262* pilots, the essential 'working up' was completed quickly and, although the unit was far below operational strength, it would be declared combat-ready on 3rd October. The Allies were quickly aware of the new dispositions however, for reconnaissance photographs were now very carefully scrutinized for the tell-tale scorch marks on runways, a sure sign that a particular base was being used for jet operations

1st October, 1944

By late September, most of the Allied tactical fighter-bomber units had moved from their hastily-built landing strips along the French coast and were operating from airstrips in northern France, Belgium and Holland. Fighter-bombers from *KG(J)51* attacked the airfield at Grave, which was situated near Nijmegen and was the most forward of the tactical airfields. On this day the Tempests of 125 Wing arrived to join Wing Commander J E Johnson's Canadian 127 Wing. The Wing Leader, Wing Commander J B Wray, remembered the attack vividly:

> "When we arrived by air, Scotty (Group Captain David Scott-Malden O C 125 Wing) was standing outside the group of vehicles that constituted his office, the Ops rooms and the Air Traffic Control. We taxied in, got out and gathered around these vehicles in small groups chatting. I was with Scotty and the two Squadron Commanders, Johnny Heap and Bob Spurdle, telling him that there had been no problems on the flight from Antwerp. Looking around at the flat featureless area I was also saying to him 'I think the first thing we must do is dig slit trenches'.
>
> "At that moment all Hell seemed to be let loose on the other side of the airfield in 127 Wing. There were explosions and Spitfires caught fire. Funnily enough we did not take all that much notice, thinking perhaps that

September - November 1944

An interesting camouflage variation is displayed by this Me262A-2a 'Sturmvögel' fighter-bomber. Although identified as a KG(J)51 aircraft, it may well be from the new KG(J)54, which frequently adopted such paint schemes on its aircraft.

a bowser might have caught fire during refuelling.

"After the fireworks over at 127 Wing, some ten minutes later their Adjutant arrived in a Jeep with the hood up. He drew up alongside Scotty and myself and said, 'Did you see that? They destroyed five Spitfires and killed or wounded a number of our men'. (I can't remember the number).

"I said, 'What was it?' (Tiger tanks had been seen in the vicinity, because the Germans were fairly close by in the west). He said, 'It was one of those '262s. They come over at altitude so you can't hear them and they drop these bombs from quite a height'.

"It was a clear sunny day with white puffy clouds and as he spoke I heard a dull explosion up above us. I looked up casually and saw a big cloud of white smoke at about 2-3000 feet. I said, 'I wonder what that is?' The Canadian leaned out from under the hood of the Jeep and looked up. He shouted, 'Look out, that's one of them!' and threw himself on the ground. We all followed suit, very conscious of the fact that there was no cover whatsoever, therefore we had plenty of time to review our past lives as we heard this whistling noise from hundreds of little AP bombs coming closer and closer. These AP (anti-personnel) bombs were contained in a large canister, which was designed to explode above ground and spread a carpet of AP across an area. Each bomb on impact made an indentation about the size of a plate and had a wide-spread area for its shrapnel. They could do a lot of damage to personnel and soft targets like aircraft. Although we (125 Wing) had been subjected to AP attack from ground fired weapons we had not yet experienced attacks with these weapons from the air. Moreover, although we knew the Germans had jets, we thought they probably had only a few, which were still very much in the experimental stage and would therefore not constitute too much of a threat. Having been at Manston when 616 Squadron was formed with their Meteors, and knowing something of their problems and limitations, we thought the Germans were in rather same position.

"We lay there, convinced, I am sure, that 'the end was nigh'. Suddenly they arrived in a wild staccato of explosions which, after the first few, appeared to be going away from us. When we realised we were still in one piece we jumped to our feet to discover that in fact the first bombs had landed about 50 yards away and the carpet had run away from us, right across the tented area - and it was lunch time. None of our our aircrew was hit, or any of the ops vehicles. The Wing did suffer quite a substantial number of casualties over in the tented area, where the bulk of the bombs fell.

"An amusing sequel to this attack was that just after we had picked ourselves up from the ground I saw a bulldozer driving along the top of the dyke. (Grave was a strip constructed in an open field below dyke level, which subsequently flooded and had to be abandoned. The landing area was either 'Sommerfeld tracking' (wire mesh) or PSP. Accommodation for us was in tentage, although Scotty lived in a caravan and I was in the kitchen of a local farmhouse). I sent one of the airmen up to the driver to tell him to come and see me. When he arrived he turned out to be an Army Sergeant. I said to him, 'Please dig us a slit trench by these Ops. vehicles'. We then went to see the damage in the tented area.

"When we came back about an hour later the bulldozer was gone. There was the slit trench, about fifteen feet long, five feet wide and twelve feet deep with about two feet of water in the bottom. If we had jumped into it we would have had great difficulty in getting out again!" [10].

The dispersal area of 80 Squadron had been hit by a number of anti-personnel bombs. One of those wounded was Squadron Leader R.A.Ackworth DFC, a notable pilot of the Greek campaign of 1940/41, who had just rejoined the unit as a supernumary.

2nd October, 1944

The 9th Air Force claimed its first jet kill. Thunderbolts of the 386th Fighter Squadron, 365th Fighter Group, were covering other P-47s of the Group engaged upon strafing railyards in the area of Düsseldorf when the low elements spotted four Me262s. Captain Valmore J Beaudrault, leading the top cover at 9,000 feet heard one of his pilots shout, 'My God, what was that?'. He looked around in time to see something streaking into the clouds. It was *Oberfeldwebel* 'Ronny' Lauer of *I./KG(J)51* in

'9K+NL', who had attempted an unsuccessful 'bounce' on the Thunderbolts. Beaudrault took his flight up in pursuit, emerging from the clouds to find only his wingman, Lieutenant 'Pete' Peters, still with him, but the jet was still in view. Instead of losing his pursuers, Lauer made a sweeping turn and came at them with cannon blazing, repeating the attack several more times with the P-47s evading each pass. The aircraft rapidly descended until they were less than 500 feet above the ground. The German fighter shot past them once more, suddenly puffs of white smoke spurted from the turbines and the '262 began to slow down. The American pilots then realised the cause; he had run out of fuel. As the Thunderbolts became the attackers Lauer, too low to bale out, began to weave desperately and, as Beaudrault came in for the kill, one of the Messerschmitt's wings hit the ground. The stricken aircraft cartwheeled and, as it came to halt, exploded; Lauer survived, although suffering serious injuries. Curiously, Beaudrault's victory was credited as 'unconfirmed destroyed'. [11.]

During the morning and afternoon, Me262s of *KG(J)51* attacked the airfield of Grave, where apart from the two Tempest units (80 and 274 Squadrons), two squadrons of the new Griffon-engined Spitfire XIVE fighter (130 and 402 Squadrons) were now based, together with the three RCAF Spitfire IXB squadrons of 127 Wing. The jets came over in singly or in pairs and the bombing caused many casualties to both RAF personnel and to Dutch civilians when bombs fell wide of the airfield. No successes were claimed by the defences during these attacks, which injured three pilots and seven other personnel. Other Tempest pilots of 3 Squadron from Grimbergen sighted Me262s near Nijmegen, possibly those that had attacked the airfield, but could not engage. Spitfire pilots of 442 (RCAF) Squadron were more fortunate, meeting a pair of Me262s near Nijmegen in the late afternoon. Flying Officer F B Young made a diving head-on attack from 500 feet above, claiming strikes on the wing of one of the jets before they disappeared.

4th October, 1944
No American heavy bomber raids were despatched from England due to bad weather, but the 15th Air Force struck north from Italy, losing two B-17s and seven B-24s over

Germany. *Hauptmann* Eder of *Kommando Nowotny* claimed two Fortresses on this date and, if this is accurate, he accounted for one B-17G from the 97th Bomb Group (44-8586) and one from the 2nd (44-8043).

Kommando Nowotny lost the Kapitän of *2 Staffel* when *Hauptmann* Alfred Teumer was killed following an engine failure whilst on final approach to Achmer. His place was taken by *Oberleutnant* Franz Schall, a tough veteran of *I./JG 52* in Russia, where he had claimed 117 victories. Schall himself suffered an accident on the 4th, when he crashed on landing at Waggum, fortunately without injury.

5th October, 1944

An important event - for the Royal Air Force in general and 401 (RCAF) Squadron in particular - took place, when the first Me262 fell to Spitfire pilots. Squadron Leader R.I.A.Smith DFC was leading the unit:

"In the afternoon 401 Squadron, which had moved to a small grass field near the village of Rips in southeast Holland two days before, was sent to do a patrol above the Nijmegen road bridge. Two things were unusual about this patrol. One was that it was set unusually high for the Tactical Air Force - 13,000 feet - and the other was that the sky had become almost clear after two or three weeks of quite low ceilings.

"All was quiet until Kenway called me up and said there was an aircraft to the northeast coming towards us at 13,000 feet. The squadron was in open battle formation over Nijmegen at that moment, so I turned it north-northeastwards, took it up another 500 feet and levelled it off three or four miles northeast of the town. Almost immediately I spotted an aircraft dead ahead of us about 500 feet below. It was travelling southwest towards Nijmegen, head-on to us, very fast. I quickly reported it to the squadron, then swung out some distance to the right to give myself enough room to swing sharply back to the left, all the way round to the southwest, so that I would be able to pull in close behind the aircraft at a small enough angle to its path to be able to aim ahead of it, if it should be obliging enough to keep on coming. Two or three other pilots did the same thing.

"I quickly recognised it as an Me262. It kept on coming and had obviously failed to spot us - probably because we were more or less between it and the sun - and it would therefore have to pass right through us. I felt a peculiar thrill. At long last here was a jet plane that had made a mistake and was going to leave itself open to a burst of fire, if only a short one because of the speed with which it would be able to draw away.

"I then began my final swing back to the left and around to the southwest. Just before it began to pass through us it climbed to the left

September - November 1944

Squadron Leader R I A 'Rod' Smith, DFC. He proved himself a deadly shot over Malta, disposed of six Bf109s in three days over Nijmegen then, on 5th October, led 401 Squadron to bring down the first Me262 to fall to Spitfires. (R I A Smith)

slightly and my feeling of thrill intensified. I was fast pulling into position behind the '262 for a perfect shot and I was already aiming along its path ahead of it.

"But that perfect shot was not to be. Another Spitfire, in a tight left turn like mine, suddenly appeared quite close in front of me, almost in line between the '262 and me. If I fired I would risk the hitting the other Spitfire, but for an instant I was tempted to fire a short burst anyway. I resisted the temptation however. Having to pass up that shot was hard to swallow and on top of that I was afraid that the '262 would simply keep on going and get clean away without a shot being fired at it.

"However a second or two after he passed through us the '262 pilot rolled into a fairly steep dive, then half-rolled the other way to get himself upright and began banking and swerving from side to side, all the while keeping in the dive and crossing Nijmegen in a generally southwest direction. All of us dived down after him. I am as certain as I can be that he must have closed his throttles quite a bit as he entered his dive, natural enough in ordinary circumstances but in his position another mistake. The Spitfire that had come between it and me (which I later found to have been that flown by John MacKay) managed to get within range fairly early in the dive. For several seconds, though, that Spitfire seemed to be withholding fire for some reason. In a burst of impatience, not knowing who was flying it, I called out 'For God's sake shoot - that Spitfire!' I'm sure my call was quite unnecessary, of course, and that its pilot was doing his very best contending with the diving and swerving of the '262."

Flight Lieutenant Hedley Everard was apparently out of Rod Smith's view and ahead of Flying Officer MacKay:

> "It started a slow spiral going straight down. I opened fire from 900 yards and followed it, closing in all the time. At 5,000 feet he began to level out, heading south. Throttling back, not to over shoot, I opened fire with machine-guns only from 150 yards. A streamer of white smoke came from it and it accelerated rapidly, drawing away."

As he broke away, he called John MacKay (his wingman) in to attack:

> "I got onto the tail of the aircraft, saw strikes on the after part of the fuselage and port or starboard wing root. The aircraft was extremely manoeuvreable. The pilot was hot and put the aircraft through everything in the book. We were about 2,000 to 3,000 feet when Squadron Leader Smith came in to attack."

Rod Smith had seen MacKay open fire and immediately two or three cannon strikes appeared on the trailing edge of the wing, next to one of the jet nacelles. Strange-looking smoke began to trail from the place struck by MacKay's shells and for a moment he thought that the engine might catch fire, but this did not happen. Meanwhile other Spitfires had closed in. Flying Officer A.L.Sinclair, leading Blue Section, reported:

> "Red Section fired first, bringing the Me262 across in front of Blue Section. I turned in behind firing a four or five second burst, saw strikes, but was crowded out by two other aircraft coming in from above."

Rod Smith failed to see this attack; he had other things to contend with during those few seconds:

> "Tex Davenport and I had to pull out at about 7,000 feet because we were about to collide with each other, so I lost sight of the action for quite a few seconds. When I was able to look again I saw it had pulled out of its dive and was about 3,000 feet over the southwest edge of Nijmegen, still heading southwest. It was no longer trailing smoke and was increasing its lead over several Spitfires, which were still chasing it but were then out of range.
>
> "I thought the action was over and that the '262 had got away but, quite suddenly, it zoomed up into the most sustained vertical climb I had ever seen, leaving far behind it the Spitfires which had followed it all the way down. To my great surprise and elation its climb brought it up to where Tex and I were. As it soared up to us, still climbing almost vertically, the sweep-back of its wings became very noticeable. Its speed, though still very considerable, was beginning to fall off and, with full power on, I was able to pull up in an almost vertical position to within about 350 yards behind it, the maximum range. I aimed at one of its engine nacelles and fired a burst lasting about eight seconds, shifting my aim to the other nacelle part way

September - November 1944

through. I saw strikes around both engine nacelles and within two or three seconds a plume of fire began to stream from alongside one of them. The '262 was then slowing down more than I was and I was able to close the range to about 200 yards. I did not know that Tex Davenport was behind me and was also firing!"

Flight Lieutenant R.M.Davenport was indeed in the thick of it. After first firing on the jet and hitting it in the fuselage from 400 yards:

"I finally closed into 300 yards line astern and emptied the remainder of my guns, approximately 10 or 12 seconds, into the kite, observing strikes all in engines and fuselage. The aircraft was burning all this time. The pilot seemed to be unhurt and put up a good fight all during this."

The end came quickly as both the '262 and Rod Smith's Spitfire reached the limit of their zoom-climbs. Slowly both aircraft stall-turned to right in formation. Rod Smith continues:

"Halfway through our stall turns, when our noses had come down level with the horizon but our wings were almost vertical, I felt as if I were in slow motion line abreast formation on the '262 to its right, directly below it. As the '262 was only about 100 yards above me I had a remarkable and unhurried look at it, side on. To my surprise I couldn't see the pilot's head, although the canopy was still fully closed. He must have had his head down for some reason.

"It then began to dawn on me that when we had completed our stall turns we would both be facing almost vertically downwards with our positions reversed. The '262 would be close on my tail and I would be helpless. My nose went down and to the right and I had no control for quite a few seconds. Because of the Spitfire's lack of rear vision the '262 was out of sight behind me, which was probably just as well in the circumstances. Tex said later that it fired at me but no-one else reported that. In any event, after what seemed an age, during which I wondered if cannon shells would come smashing into me from behind, the '262 appeared a few yards away on my right. It was diving almost vertically downwards, as I was, but it was picking up speed more quickly and the plume of fire it was streaming had grown much bigger. It plunged on down and crashed within our lines just southwest of Nijmegen, sending up a billowing column of smoke."

Everard then went down to see the result, reporting that the largest piece of visible wreckage was not more than eight feet across.

Their opponent, who had earned the Canadians' admiration for his flying skill, had been *Hauptmann* Hans-Christof Büttmann of *I./KG(J)51*. Although he had fought with skill and courage, he lost his life due to tactical errors and lack of fighter training. His body was found a short distance away from the wreckage, parachute unopened. having baled out at around a hundred feet. 12.

Flying Officer Frank McLeod of 56 Squadron was also on patrol in the area:

> "56 Squadron also engaged in this patrol, and I pursued two of these aircraft, but lacked the power to close on either of them". 13.

I./KG(J)51 lost a second aircraft when *Unteroffizier* Gerhard Franke crashed near Nordhorn and was killed. *Oberfeldwebel* Helmut Baudach, from *2./Kommando Nowotny*, force-landed on an autobahn when his fuel ran out.

6th October, 1944

Encounters with jets were now becoming more frequent; Lieutenant C W Mueller of the 353rd Fighter Group patrolled the approaches to Rheine, hoping to take a jet pilot unawares. It had become clear very quickly that Allied fighters had little chance of engaging Me262s in 'normal' air combat and thus standing patrols - known as 'Rat-catching' - were set up by both the Royal Air Force and the Americans in order to intercept the jets at their most vulnerable moments. When a '262 was reported by radar - a fairly easy identification since the 'blip' moved considerably faster than anything else - a section of fighters would be scrambled and directed to Achmer or Hopsten to await its return. Thus it was that Mueller sighted two jet aircraft in the landing pattern, identified them as an Me262 and an He280 and nosed the P-47 into a dive. The Me262 already had its wheels down and the pilot made no attempt to accelerate as the Thunderbolt closed; he merely started shallow evasive turns. Mueller opened fire and saw the .50 calibre bullets knocking chunks of metal from the wings and fuselage. He reported that two parachutes immediately appeared - which seemed odd for an aircraft believed to be a single-seat fighter. The 'He280' then turned towards him and, as the Messerschmitt crashed short of the Rheine runway, Mueller applied full power and climbed into the clouds. The Messerschmitt had not burned, indicating that fuel was short and also explaining the failure of the pilot to use his superior acceleration to escape. It is possible that Mueller's opponent was *Feldwebel* Joachim Fingerloos of *I/KG(J)51* who was shot down near Rheine and severely wounded. This loss is noted as having occurred on October 5th,

September - November 1944

British officers and men investigate the pathetic remains of *Hauptmann* Hans-Christof Büttmann's *I./KG(J)51* Me262 near Nijmegen.
(R I A Smith)

but it is possible that an error in date has occurred. The description of the two parachutes remains unexplained however; possibly Mueller had seen both the drogue and main parachutes.[14]

On this same date the 7th Photo Recon Group despatched eight F-5 Lightnings and four Spitfires on photo-recce duties over Germany, where one of the Lightnings was intercepted and destroyed by an Me262. It is possible that the jet pilot was *Hauptmann* Georg-Peter Eder of *Kommando Nowotny*, who is known to have claimed a Lightning early in the month. However, another source suggests that it may be a rare 'kill' by *I./KG(J)51*. The American pilot, Lieutenant Claude Murray, baled out over the Zuider Zee, landing on or near a small island. He searched around for any sign of habitation, only to discover that he was quite alone. He was then forced to use his dinghy to paddle to the mainland in order to find an available German to surrender to. After thirteen hours in his dinghy he came ashore, to be found by a member of the Dutch resistance and was hidden away in Muiden to await the advancing British forces.

Elsewhere, an Auster crew of 662 Squadron had a narrow escape when attacked at low level while spotting for artillery units. The jet pilot turned away at the last moment however and, according to the Auster crew, it was at once attacked and shot down by an Allied fighter. If their report was accurate, this may have been *Feldwebel* Fingerloos, but the only Allied fighter claim on this date appears to have been that submitted by Mueller.

7th October, 1944
Some 25 sightings were reported by American aircrew as jets from *Kommando Nowotny* intercepted B-24s attacking Magdeberg/Rothensee. *Major* Nowotny suffered an engine failure on take-off and did not leave the ground, but *Oberleutnant* Schall, *Feldwebel* Lennartz and *Oberfähnrich* Russel each claimed a Liberator destroyed, four such aircraft actually failing to return. One of these was Lieutenant S Greenberg's 489 Squadron aircraft, which fell to a '262 near Osnabrück at 14.30 hours. P-47s of the 479th Fighter Group were acting as escorts on this mission. Colonel H Zemke and Lieutenant N Benoit saw three fighters make their firing pass and as the Liberators went down they fired on one, claiming a Bf109 destroyed, but when their combat films were processed it was discovered that their opponent was actually a '262. In fact they had succeeded in hitting either *Oberleutnant* Bley or *Heinz* Russel's aircraft. Both baled out safely.

Meanwhile, Lieutenant Urban L Drew of the 361st Fighter Group was having his own private war. On this mission he was leading the 375th Fighter Squadron on escort to B-17s attacking targets in Czechoslovakia. On the return flight, he kept a careful watch for jets as they neared Osnabrück and was rewarded as they passed close to the jet base at Achmer. Two aircraft were taxiing out. He called his Deputy Squadron Leader, Captain Bruce Rowlett, to take over. Urban Drew remembers:

> "Waited until both airborne, then rolled over from 15,000 feet with my flight following and caught up with second Me262 when he was 1,000 feet off ground. I was indicating 450 mph. Me262 couldn't have been going over 200 mph. I started firing from approximately 400 yards, 30 degrees deflection and, as I closed, I saw hits all over the wings and fuselage. Just as I passed him I saw a sheet of flame come out from near the right wing root and as I glanced back I saw a gigantic explosion and a sheet of red flame over area of 1,000 feet. The other Me262 was 500 yards ahead and had started a fast climbing turn to the left. I was still indicating 440 mph and had to haul

September - November 1944

Urban Drew of the 361st Fighter Group made history on 7th October, when he single-handedly bounced a pair of Me262s as they took off from Achmer, destroying both. (Urban L Drew)

back to stay with him. I started shooting from about 60 degrees deflection, and just hitting his tail section. I kept horsing back and hits crept up his fuselage to his cockpit. Just after that I saw his canopy fly off in two sections, his plane roll over and go into a flat spin. He then hit the ground on his back at 60 degrees angle and exploded violently. I did not see the pilot bail out. Two huge columns of smoke came up from both Me262s burning on the ground." [15.]

Leutnant Gerhard Kobert was killed when his Messerschmitt blew up and, although it has always been believed that Drew's second opponent had been *Oberleutnant* Paul Bley, (a former Bf110 *Experte* with eight victories to his credit), recent research indicates that this may not be the case, and suggests instead that a *Hauptmann* Arnold was flying the second '262. Urban Drew insists that the pilot could not have survived and records show that Bley baled out. This version is supported by Georg-Peter Eder who had led the flight out onto the runway but was forced to abort the mission due to a flame-out and thus witnessed the engagement from the ground. Bley is more likely to have been shot down in the engagement earlier in the day.

> "Immediately after shooting down the two Me262s, the German anti-aircraft opened up and it was a terrific barrage. I called to McCandliss and ordered him to join up with me and take evasive action at tree-top level. He admitted quite candidly in his report to me many years later, that since it was his sixteenth mission, and to that date, he had never had the opportunity to fire at the enemy, he disregarded my instructions and flew off to attack some anti-aircraft batteries, destroying them. Unfortunately he was not aware of the other batteries ringing Achmer and they picked him off. The last time I saw his aircraft it was blazing from nose to tail and from wingtip to wingtip and I was calling over the RT 'Roll and bail out, Mac, roll and bail!'. I did not see him bail out." [16]

Lieutenant Robert McCandliss, who had witnessed Drew's spectacular combat with the jets, managed to bale out at low level, denying him a witness and, when he returned to base he was disappointed to discover that his gun-camera had not functioned, denying him recognition of his two claims. This confirmation was to be established in a remarkable way, for many years later Drew was introduced to Hans Ring, the German fighter historian. Ring contacted Georg-Peter Eder, who had witnessed the battle from the ground and, from the evidence so provided, the German authorities contacted the American Archives. Drew was astounded to receive a telephone call, informing him that a grateful nation wished to decorate him - albeit thirty-nine years late. He was flown to Washington by the USAF to be belatedly awarded America's second-highest decoration (the Air Force Cross) in 1983. Meanwhile he had met Eder in Germany and the two former adversaries became firm friends; when Eder died of cancer, Urban Drew flew out to Wiesbaden and remained with him, sleeping in the hospital, for the last week of his life.

A fourth Me262 victory was reported by an American pilot when Major R E Connor of the 78th Fighter Group intercepted and destroyed a machine from *I./KG(J)51* on final approach to one of the airfields near Osnabrück, at 12.20 hours. This German pilot baled out unhurt. Earlier, Thunderbolts of the 50th Fighter Group, operating near Karlsruhe, had a fleeting contact with jets, Captain Solon Mamalis claiming one damaged at 10.40 hours.

September - November 1944

Thirty-nine years after his battle over Achmer, Urban L 'Ben' Drew receives the Air Force Cross, bestowed for his heroism by a grateful nation. It was worth the wait; not only did Ben receive recognition, but he also cemented a firm friendship with Georg-Peter Eder, the man most responsible for his belated award. (Urban L Drew)

F-5 Lightnings of the 10th Photo Recon Group were operating over Germany and Captain Robert Holbury reported:

"I was intercepted by jet aircraft (Me262) southeast of Heilbronn. The interception was at 33,000 feet from 6,000 feet below. I estimate the jet was indicating 350 miles an hour in a 45 degree climb, coming into position within 15 seconds after I sighted him. I pulled my plane into a 270 turn to the left as the jet closed in and turned inside of him as the jet mushed on by. I then went into a 450 mph dive with the jet following me. I went into the turning manoeuvre three more times and escaped by continually turning inside of him. After losing him I dove to the deck and came on home". [17].

10th - 12th October, 1944

Kommando Nowotny was in action again when *Oberleutnant* Paul Bley claimed a Mustang (possibly a 341 Squadron Spitfire lost over Holland) and, two days later, on 12th October,

Oberfeldwebel Helmut Lennartz claimed another Mustang. One loss has been traced on that latter date, a British Mustang III of 129 Squadron flown by Warrant Officer Foster, which was reported missing. However the 355th Fighter Group, escorting Liberators to Varrelbusch airfield, reported an abortive pass by two Me262s on the way in. Blue Flight of the 354th Fighter Squadron was the target, but no Mustangs were hit. Three more '262s were sighted near Enschede, but were too fast to be engaged.

Two jet pilots from *Kommando Nowotny* were obliged to make forced landings due to fuel shortage during these operations. *Feldwebel* Helmut Lennartz came down near Bramsche and *Oberleutnant* Plaul Bley near Steenwijk, both without injury.

Grave airfield was also raided again, when at 15.38 hours a lone Me262 appeared out of cloud at 8,000 feet and dropped two bombs, one of which exploded in the middle of the 416 (RCAF) Squadron dispersal, killing five airmen and injuring ten more. One of the Spitfires was destroyed, nine damaged and ammunition and petrol were set ablaze, but prompt action by the Fire Section quickly got the fires under control. During the confusion Flight Lieutenants J B McColl and and D W A Harling risked exploding ammunition to taxi two of the unit's Spitfires away from the danger zone.

Meanwhile, on October 10th, a staff meeting had been held, during which American pilots were called upon to give their conclusions on the initial encounters. They were unanimous that the German aircraft could out-climb both the P-47 and P-51, although the manoeuvreability was not great. The fighter-bomber versions were easier to engage, since the bomb-load reduced their speed by at least 100 mph (When engaged however, the bombs were usually jettisoned and the jets escaped) It was concluded that thus far, Me262s had been brought down by:

a) Diving from above
b) Fatal tactical errors on the part of the German pilots
c) When taking off or landing
d) Running out of fuel or engine trouble.

13th October, 1944
The first success for an RAF Tempests pilot took place when

September - November 1944

Oberfeldwebel Hermann Buchner (rt) chats to a dog-lover on the flight line at Achmer, late 1944. (H Buchner)

Pilot Officer Bob Cole of 3 Squadron sighted a '262 of *I./KG(J)51* near Volkel. The jet pilot, *Unteroffizier* Edmund Delatowski, saw the Tempest coming down on him and accelerated away in a shallow dive. Cole was clocking 480 mph and the jet was still pulling away, but after a chase of some forty miles, the Messerschmitt began to slow down - probably due to fuel shortage - and Bob Cole saw his chance. The big Tempest closed in, Cole opened fire with the four 20mm cannon and Delatowski baled out slightly wounded as the jet exploded over Deventer.

The Americans also reported one combat, when Me262s of *Kommando Nowotny* attempted to engage Liberators over Western Germany. Four of the B-24s lost formation and this group of stragglers was attacked by four jets. P-47 escorts from the 356th Fighter Group intervened however, forcing the attacking German fighters away. No claims were made and none of the Liberators were hit. However, *Obergefreiter* Leuthner crashed on return at Achmer and was severely injured, while *Oberfähnrich* Heinz Russel crashed landing at Hesepe, escaping unhurt.

Another success was credited to the growing Me262 force when a 60 (SAAF) Squadron Mosquito was intercepted near Graz. The unidentified German pilot - almost certainly from *Ekdo Lechfeld* - made no mistake, shooting the reconnaissance aircraft at Passail, killing Lieutenant D.Sheldon and Flying Officer P.Snell.

15th October, 1944

The 8th Air Force gained another success when fighters of the 78th Fighter Group surprised an Me262 of *I./KG(J)51* near Rheine at 10.45 hours. *Fähnenjunker-Feldwebel* Edgar Junghans was shot down by Lieutenant H H Lamb and so severely injured that he died in hospital on the 21st; Lieutenant H O Foster claimed a second fighter-bomber damaged near Böhmte, another from *I./KG(J)51* that crash-landed due to battle damage. Flight Lieutenant Wilson of 400 (RCAF) Squadron had an unnerving experience when he flew a TacR sortie over Nijmegen and was bounced by a 'solid mass' of twenty-four Me262s at 28,000 feet. The startled Spitfire pilot made a sharp turn and hurtled into the clouds.

21st - 28th October, 1944

A sighting of three jets was reported by Mustang pilots of the 355th Fighter Group during a *Ramrod* to Kassel on 18th October, but no engagement resulted. It was not until 21st October that any combat resulted, when Tempest pilots of 3 Squadron claimed two 'damaged' near Rheine, one by Flight Lieutenant A E Umbers and the other by Flight Lieutenant G R Duff and Flying Officer R Dryland jointly. On 26th October this unit strafed Rheine airfield where Umbers, now promoted to command the Squadron, claimed an Me262 damaged on the ground, Dryland sharing another 'damaged' with Pilot Officer Bob Cole. Also on the 26th the Americans had an encounter when the 355th Fighter Group escorted Liberators to Minden. Near the target three jets hurtled out of cloud cover from five o'clock and made a 'roller coaster' pass through a box of bombers, damaging one. A flight of Mustangs dropped tanks to engage, but the jets dived away and could not be caught. Two

September - November 1944

'Checkernosed' Republic P-47D Thunderbolt of the 78th Fighter Group. The big 'Jug', as it was known, was a tough aircraft, but generally lacked the speed to catch the jets. When it did, its firepower of eight .50 machine-guns was usually sufficient. (C Ellis)

days later, on the 28th, Tempests of 486 Squadron patrolled the approaches to Volkel, where a lone jet was sighted. Flying Officer R J Danzey caught it in a dive and scored hits before it accelerated away.

For most of October, *Luftwaffe* opposition to the 8th Air Force had been relatively light, thus it was not until the 28th that any further contact was made with aircraft from *Kommando Nowotny*. Heavy bombers of the 8th Air Force raided Hamm, where a '262 was sighted by Captain Jack Ilfrey of the 20th Fighter Group. The fighter kept its distance however and no engagement resulted. *Kommando Nowotny* claimed two successes on this date, *Oberleutnant* Franz Schall and *Leutnant* Alfred Schreiber reporting the destruction of a Mustang and a Lightning respectively, the latter bringing his score to five and becoming the first jet fighter 'ace'. *Kommando Nowotny* lost one experienced pilot when *Oberleutnant* Paul Bley was killed at Achmer after hitting a flock of birds when taking-off on this sortie. *Oberleutnant* Franz Schall experienced one of the landing accidents for which the Me262 was becoming renowned when the nosewheel of his aircraft collapsed on landing at Hesepe.

29th October, 1944

Fighters from *Kommando Nowotny* were again scrambled after reconnaissance aircraft. *Leutnant* Alfred Schreiber claimed a Lightning, obviously a 7th Photo Recon Group F-5 reported missing on this date, but a subsequent interception by this pilot resulted in his colliding with a Spitfire. His adversary is on this occasion is believed to have been a TacR Spitfire flown by Flight Lieutenant Wilkins of 4 Squadron, who failed to return. Schreiber baled out unhurt. Another RAF pilot, Flight Lieutenant A Lambros of 438 (RCAF) Squadron was attacked by Me262s whilst dive-bombing a railway near Rheine, but the Typhoon escaped without damage. Meanwhile jets from *Kommando Nowotny* engaged Thunderbolts, *Feldwebel* Büttner and *Oberfeldwebel* Göbel each claiming one destroyed.

Another unit had begun converting to jets in September when *KG 54* was redesignated *KG(J)54*. The *Geschwaderstab* and *I Gruppe* established themselves at Giebelstadt, while *II./KG(J)54* went to Neuburg, these units receiving their first Me262s in early November. Conversion commenced, but the programme was badly hindered by lack of both spares and J2 jet fuel. This *Geschwader* would not become operational until early in 1945 as a result. In addition, a training unit - *III./EJG2* - was formed at Lechfeld on 27th September from elements of *Ekdo Lechfeld*. The purpose of this unit would be to supply trained jet fighter pilots for the operational *Staffeln*; command was given to *Hauptmann* Horst Geyer, but would, in early 1945, pass to the redoubtable *Oberstleutnant* Heinz Bar, holder of the Knight's Cross with Oak Leaves and Swords. Bär had already claimed 204 victories and had flown in every theatre of war; during the Phoney War of 1939 and throughout the *Blitzkrieg* in France and Battle of Britain and in Russia with *I./JG 51*, the Middle East commanding *I./JG 77*; to *JG 1* and finally leading *JG 3* on home defence. Jet training was in all respects rudimentary, for many of the pilots were experienced combat veterans. Due to restrictions on fuel, pilots undertaking conversion were given one hour of circuits, two hours of aerobatics, one hour of cross-country flying, one hour of

September - November 1944

Tactical reconnaissance (Tac/R) Spitfires such as this 414 Squadron aircraft were very vulnerable to jet attack. The pilots, concentrating upon the ground situation, could so easily be bounced and a single hit from a 30mm shell could rip the entire tail unit off. (E B Morgan)

high altitude flying and two hours of formation practice. The experienced pilots found little difficulty in conversion and many pronounced the jet aircraft far easier to fly than the Bf109G they were used to. For the novice however, who received no more instruction than the old hand, it was a different story when sent into combat against the battle-hardened veterans of the 8th Air Force who, in addition to skill, enjoyed a 25 to 1 numerical superiority. Accidents at Lechfeld were frequent but, surprisingly, most were due to technical failure rather than pilot error. Another jet unit, *III./EKG1,* is also believed to have been formed at this time for the purpose of training aircrew for Ar234 units. Little is known concerning its activities apart from the fact that it had several Me262s assigned and was based at Alt Lonnewitz. The introduction of the Ar234 jet bomber had improved the situation regarding Me262s in the fighter rôle, for Hitler had ordered that for every Ar234 brought into service, one Me262 would be released for fighter duties.

British Intelligence, using the *Ultra* code-breaking system, were now very well informed of the jet developments, having intimate knowledge of both *I./KG(J)51* and *Kommando Nowotny* dispositions, their operations and daily availability. For example the crew strength of *I./KG(J)51* was known to be thirteen on 13th October, rising to twenty-one on the 31st. The next day an *Ultra* de-crypt revealed that twelve pilots and 315 ground staff were on the strength of *Kommando Nowotny*, followed on 2nd November, by a report that a new auto-pilot - *Robot 11* - was being installed in the fighter aircraft. [18]

During the last three weeks of October, *Hauptmann* Eder claimed a Mustang and Fortress destroyed and another Mustang and Lightning probably so.[19] Regrettably, no exact dates are available. These combats are likely to have taken place on the 13th and 28th, when losses were sustained over southern Germany.

November 1st 1944
Mustangs of the 20th and 352nd Fighter Groups escorted bombers to Gelsenkirchen when four Me262s of *Kommando Nowotny* attacked at 32,000 feet over Holland. *Oberfeldwebel* Willi Banzhaff jumped Yellow Flight of the 77th Fighter Squadron (20th Fighter Group), shooting down Lieutenant Dennis J Alison. who was killed. Banzhaff continued his dive, passing over the bombers with Mustangs of the 20th and 352nd in hot pursuit, while Thunderbolt pilots of the 56th Fighter Group, on escort to Liberators nearby, had seen the action and also entered the fray. Banzhaff continued his dive, leaving the pursuers behind, but then made a mistake; instead of taking cover in the clouds, he effected a climbing turn, allowing the American fighters to close. The 20th Fighter Group Report related:

> "At about 14.23 hours, Lieutenant Raymond R.Flowers, pulling over 72 inches at 3,000 r.p.m., closed on the jet in a broad turn and opened fire. He observed many strikes and a moment later the Me262 pulled up and the pilot baled out."

Flowers' claim was disallowed however. Captain Jack Ilfrey of the 75th Fighter Squadron reported:

> "I saw one P-51 go down, having been hit by one of the jets' fire. I saw one jet shot down by a P-51 of the 77th Squadron, I chased one but he went into a cloud bank, then they were gone, as quick as they had come." [20]

Lieutenant W L Groce of the 56th Fighter Group called, 'Spread it out and we'll get him if he turns!', and a second later Banzhaff made a climbing turn to port. Groce opened fire together with Lieutenant W T Gerbe of the 352nd, gunfire raking the jet from nose to tail. One engine burst into flames and as the '262 fell into a spin, Banzhaff baled out and was shot at whilst descending, but was not hit. Groce and Gerbe were jointly awarded credit for this victory.

2nd November, 1944
An important advance in the operational use of technology occurred when aircraft of *Kommando Nowotny* employed air-to-air rockets for the first time. Five forces of bombers had been despatched to various targets. While the main attacking force of 683 B-17s were being engaged in a huge air battle near Merseberg a formation of B-24 Liberators, flying near Minden with an escort of Thunderbolts, was attacked by a flight of six Me262s. These came in 'en masse' firing their rocket missiles into the formation and damaging a 56th Fighter Group Thunderbolt by cannon fire before making off, pursued by the P-47s. Lieutenants A J Bux and Victor E Bast both opened fire at extreme range, but claimed no hits. The rocket weapons were almost certainly 210mm rockets, fitted in twin tubes beneath the nose, and were a fore-runner of the deadly R4M missiles. One aircraft from the 489th Bomb Group, *'Manistee'*, flown by Lieutenant Horace C Rutledge, dropped out of formation over Holland with engine trouble. Then enemy aircraft were spotted, high overhead, flying a 'figure-of-eight' course. The German

Some 392nd Bomb Group Liberator crews fitted rearward-firing bazookas beneath the wings to discourage rocket attacks by Me262s. The idea did not seem to have proved successful. (C Ellis

fighters dropped into a steep diving rocket attack. They were Me262s. One passed less than 200 feet from the nose of *'Manistee'*. Lieutenant Rutledge reported that they recovered from their dives at 10,000 to 15,000 feet below the bomber stream, 'One then came up under us from 12 to 6 o'clock, going like hell.' Another attacked the bombers head-on with cannon fire, breaking away before getting within range of defensive fire. In all, forty heavy bombers went down that day.

Crews from the 392nd Bomb Group, having been fired on by these weapons, decided to retaliate in kind by fitting rearward-facing anti-tank bazookas to several of their B-24s. These were believed to have been mounted beneath the wings, fused to 450 yards and fired electrically by the rear gunners when jets closed upon the rear of the formation. The weapons were used at least once in combat and were totally ineffective, but were at least a morale-booster for the crews. The fitting of these weapons was unauthorised and it is unlikely that 8th Air Force Bomber Command Headquarters ever knew of it. On this date three victories were reportedly claimed by jet pilots of *Kommando Nowotny*, *Feldwebel* Büttner claiming a Mustang and a Thunderbolt, whilst a second Thunderbolt was reported destroyed by *Oberfeldwebel* Baudach. It is likely that one or more of these claims actually occurred on November 5th. *Hauptmann* Eder of *Kommando Nowotny* was credited with a Fortress destroyed on 3rd November,[21] which is clearly an error of date since no sorties were flown by the 8th and air forces operating over Italy suffered no heavy bomber casualties at all. It is probable that his action took place against the 1st and 3rd Bomb Divisions, which lost 38 Fortresses while raiding Merseburg on the 2nd.

An Me262 was lost by *KG(J)51* on November 2nd when *Hauptmann* Eberhard Winkel, *Kapitän* of *5 Staffel*, was shot down by AA fire at Grave. He was badly wounded, but survived.[22] *Kommando Nowotny* lost another when *Unteroffizier* Alloys Zollner crashed taking off from Achmer and was badly hurt.

3rd November, 1944
Another success for the Tempest units took place when Wing Commander J.B.Wray of 122 Wing again engaged an Me262; he

September - November 1944

Mechanics prepare 'White 10' and 'White 11' of Kommando Nowotny for take-off, Achmer, November 1944. On the far left a group of pilots discuss the forthcoming mission. (H Buchner)

recalls:

"I was airborne in Tempest JBW carrying out an air test, and also doing operational trials on a pair of anti-glare spectacles that had been sent to me for that purpose.

"I was flying at about 18,000 feet when I sighted two Me262s flying in a south-westerly direction and camouflaged blue/grey. They saw me and turned in a wide arc to port, then set off in an easterly direction. I had already launched an attack, opening to full throttle and diving. My speed was in the region of 500 mph.

"I closed to about three hundred yards on the starboard aircraft and opened fire, firing about a four-second burst and hitting the tailplane. The Me262 continued on course and started to pull away, but before he got out of range I fired again. Suddenly a large piece flew off the aircraft and he flicked over onto his back and disappeared downwards into cloud in an inverted position. I followed, but the thickness of the cloud made it impossible for me to maintain contact." [23]

The Messerschmitt was claimed probably destroyed, but was actually shot down; *Oberfeldwebel* Willi Banzhaff of *Kommando Nowotny*, fell near Hittfeld and was killed.

4th November, 1944

Oberfeldwebel Göbel claimed a Thunderbolt destroyed and a B-17 was claimed destroyed by *Hauptmann* Eder. One claim for an Me262 damaged was submitted by the 356th Fighter Group,

Captain R A Rann engaging a jet between Lingen and Enschede in the early afternoon. Flight Officer Willard W Royer was attacked by an Me262 over the Dummer Lake - presumably Göbel - and was shot down and killed. *Oberfeldwebel* Zander of *2./Kommando Nowotny* force-landed, probably due to this encounter. Göbel force-landed at Böhmte due to fuel shortage. Meanwhile Mustangs of the 355th Fighter Group sighted several Me262s about to attack an unidentified P-51 formation between Hildesheim and Lingen. Their attack, though unsuccessful, forced the jets to abandon their original targets and make off at speed. One claim was submitted by the RAF when a Tempest pilot, Pilot Officer H F Ross of 80 Squadron, reported the destruction of an Me262 on the runway at Rheine.

5th November, 1944
Another American formation was attacked by jets. On this occasion the Me262s engaged American escort fighters; one Thunderbolt from the 56th Fighter Group and a 354th Fighter Group Mustang failed to return, both believed shot down by jets. It seems very likely that their victors were *Oberfeldwebel* Baudach (see claim noted on November 2nd) and *Hauptmann* Eder, the latter claiming a Mustang 'probable' between the 5th and the 8th, this probably occurring on this date. A further three Thunderbolts and one Mustang were also lost. The Messerschmitt jets were now engaging the escort fighters during their outward journey, with the object of forcing the fighter pilots to jettison the long-range tanks, thus reducing their range and allowing subsequent attacks upon the bombers by conventionally powered *Luftwaffe* fighters to proceed unhindered.

6th November, 1944
The 357th and 361st Fighter Groups flew escort to B-24s attacking targets near Minden, Germany. When the Mustangs had accompanied the bombers back into friendly airspace, the two Fighter Groups split into sections to fly independent patrols. Near Osnabrück a flight of five Me262s from *Kommando Nowotny* flying in two sections of two and three aircraft was seen by Mustangs of the 357th Fighter Group. The section of two attempted to bounce two of the P-51s, but Major Robert Foy's section chased them away. Captain Charles E Yeager and

Preparations for take-off.

his wingman engaged the formation of three, Yeager getting strikes on one before they pulled away into the haze. A few minutes later these jets were again found, Yeager obtaining strikes on the leader before they disengaged. Then 'Chuck' Yeager, who had become separated, found a himself near a large airfield with black tarmac runways in the vicinity of Assen:

"I spotted a lone '262 approaching the field from the south at 500 feet. He was going very slow (about 200 mph). I split-Sed on it and was going around 500 mph at 500 feet. Flak started coming up very thick and accurate. I fired a single short burst from around 400 yards and got hits on the wings. I had to break straight up and, looking back, saw the jet enemy aircraft crash-land about 400 yards short of the field.... a wing flew off outside the right jet unit. The plane did not burn." [24].

Meanwhile Bob Foy, who had chased one jet before losing it, saw two below. He followed them and watched them land on an airfield near Bremen. The severity of the *Flak* frustrated an attempt to strafe and an attempt upon an airfield at Mahndorf had a similar result. However as he was passing over an autobahn near Meppen he made an important discovery; two Me262s were on the highway in take-off position, with another parked just to the east. Thus came the first indication that the Allied fighter activity over the fixed bases was forcing the *Luftwaffe* to adopt more unconventional means of operation.

At the same time (11.00 hours) another jet was claimed destroyed over Rehburg by Lieutenant J R Voss of the 361st Fighter Group and, thirty minutes later, Mustang pilots of the

4th Fighter Group engaged four jets near Bassum, west of Wildershausen. Lieutenant W J Quinn reported:

> "One suddenly turned into me and I opened fire. I saw my bullets hitting his canopy and he immediately peeled off and went into the ground."

None of *Kommando Nowotny*'s jets were totally destroyed however; *Oberfeldwebel* Freutzer's aircraft was damaged by fighters near Ahlhorn and he force-landed safely, *Leutnant* Spangenberg force-landed near Lahnwerder out of fuel and *Oberfeldwebel* Helmut Lennartz force-landed after sustaining combat damage near Bremen. One victory was reported by the jet unit, *Oberleutnant* Franz Schall claiming a Thunderbolt. Franz Schall was one jet pilot who continued the tradition of *Luftwaffe* heraldry by having his *Ritterkreuz* emblem painted on the rudder of his personal aircraft. He was awarded the decoration following this victory and his subsequent 'kills' would appear below the emblem as victory bars. Another pilot to follow this practice was Hermann Buchner, who not only had his *Ritterkreuz* emblem on the fin, but had *'Strolch'*, his pet name for his wife Käthe, painted in large white letters on the nose of his fighter. 25.

8th November, 1944

Generalleutnant Adolf Galland arrived at Achmer during the morning, meeting Walter Nowotny to discuss any problems with the unit's operations, but very quickly the air raid sirens sounded and the jet pilots dashed to their aircraft, *Oberleutnant* Franz Schall and *Feldwebel* Büttner at Hesepe and *Major* Nowotny and *Oberleutnant* Wegmann at Achmer. Nowotny's aircraft suffered engine failure before take-off and *Feldwebel* Büttner's machine was damaged whilst taxiing, thus only Wegmann and Schall actually took off. These two engaged American fighters, Both pilots claiming a Thunderbolt destroyed. The two jet pilots then returned to their bases but, soon after, another alert was sounded and on this occasion it was Schall, Nowotny and *Oberfeldwebel* Baudach who took off. As the fighters left the ground the first of the enemy formations was visible from the airfield, targetted to attack Merseberg and Rheine. The 'long-nose' FW190D-9s of *III./JG 54* had been scrambled first and were soon engaged by American fighters, but they succeeded in holding the Americans at bay as the jets scrambled. The bombers were just turning away from the target when Nowotny and Schall attacked. Schall claimed two more Mustangs in quick succession but his identification seems to have been at fault. A flight of P-47s from the 359th Fighter Group were bounced by a lone '262, which shot-up Lieutenant Charles C McKelvy's fighter. Lieutenant Edward G Rudd fired a burst as it sped past, but claimed no hits. Then the jet returned, again blasting McKelvy's Thunderbolt and also that flown by Lieutenant William L Hoffert, who baled out. McKelvy, his aircraft severely damaged, headed west, but eventually belly-landed after being further attacked by a FW190D-9 of *III./JG 54* flown by *Oberleutnant* Hans Dortenmann. There is little doubt that this was the work of Franz Schall, who then approached an unescorted box of B-17s near Quakenbrück. A short time earlier, Lieutenant Warren Corwin Jr of the 357th Fighter Group had reported a rough engine while over Merseberg and broke formation accompanied by Lieutenant James W Kenny. They sighted the bomber formation near Quakenbrück and Kenny later recalled:

"We saw a single contrail approaching them from 10 O'clock high. We didn't know what it was at the time, but it seemed to be going pretty fast.

"I asked Corwin if his engine was good enough to escort the bombers home and he replied in the affirmative, so we headed for them. Before we reached them, the approaching airplane went over or through them and went behind and below us heading east. I knew it was something different, but I'm not sure if I knew it was a '262.

"The bogey started a wide turn to come back and we turned into it and started down. The German, which I now identified as a '262, pulled away from the bombers and towards me. I fired and apparently got a lucky shot. I couldn't see any strikes because I was so far away. He turned toward the east and I started after him, attempting to overhaul him, which I did quite abruptly. In fact, I had to drop flaps to keep from over-running him. During the rest of the flight he did not take much evasive action and I made several passes and saw several strikes, but he kept flying.

"There was a solid undercast below and we were descending, when the next thing I knew the pilot ejected and his 'chute opened. I flipped off my gun switch and buzzed his 'chute with the camera going.

"I then called Corwin several times, but got no answer. I could not see the B-17s anymore, so I figured there was no sense in trying to find them and I assumed Corwin was still with them, probably on another channel, so I headed home."

Top left: The Me262 vacated by Franz Schall and photographed by Kenny. (USAF)
Top right: Oberleutnant Franz Schall, who claimed several kills during the 8th November battle. (H Buchner)
Left: Lieutenant Ernest Fiebelkorn of the 20th Fighter Group, credited with a 'half-share' in an Me262 victory on 8th November, is believed to have chased Schall's pilotless aircraft. (via R Freeman)

In fact Corwin, whom Kenny had lost sight of during the first pass with Schall, was probably dead. He had split-S'd out of Kenny's sight and almost certainly ended up in front of Franz Schall, who fired on him. Two other pilots, Lieutenants John Sublett and John England heard him say, 'A son-of-a-bitchin' jet job got me.' They asked about his condition, were told that his aircraft had lost part of his port wing and that he had been wounded in the side, then contact was lost. Although he was at first reported to have crash-landed near St Trond, Belgium, the report was erroneous. No trace was ever found of Corwin or his aircraft.

Meanwhile another 357th Fighter Group pilot, Lieutenant Edward R Haydon, also pursued a jet but, as he dived, several 20th Fighter Group P-51s passed him. Before any of the pilots had a chance to open fire the Messerschmitt rolled onto its back and spun into the ground, denying either Haydon or Lieutenant Ernest C Fiebelkorn of the 20th an actual victory (although they were jointly credited with a 'kill'). It seems probable that this was actually Franz Schall's pilotless machine, falling to destruction.

In the meantime, a box of B-17s had been unsuccessfully attacked by two jets over the Dummer Lake, while *Major* Nowotny had radioed that he had shot down a Liberator and had probably destroyed a Mustang, but then reported the failure of one turbine: 'Am returning to base if I can make it' His final transmission was blurred, either, 'It is burning' or, 'I am burning'. Meanwhile Galland had left the fighter control headquarters and walked out onto the field, accompanied by *Hauptmann* Georg-Peter Eder and other officers. The cloud base was low and the waiting officers heard the sound of gunfire before an Me262 came vertically out of the clouds and exploded on a meadow a kilometre away. *Major* Walter Nowotny, brilliant leader and one of only nine fighter pilots to be honoured with the Knight's Cross with Oakleaves, Swords and Diamonds, was dead. There appears to be little doubt that he had been attacked by Lieutenant R W Stevens of the 364th Fighter Group, who engaged the jet near the Dummer Lake at 12.45 hours and shot it down at Epe. While it has often been postulated that a Royal Air Force Tempest pilot shot Nowotny down, no claims were made, although Eder remembered seeing such fighters in the area at the time. Galland at once promoted Georg-Peter Eder to take command of Nowotny's unit.[26]

A large cairn, with a commemorative plaque and topped with fragments from the wreck was later placed at the site of the crash. It is believed that the wreckage of the '262 still lies beneath it.

A fourth Mustang pilot, Lieutenant Anthony Maurice of the 361st Fighter Group, also claimed success on this date, but far away from the area in which Schall and Nowotny had fallen:

"I was leading the second element of Decoy Blue Flight on 8th November 44. When east of Meppel at 12.30 hours, I observed a contrail diving down in front of us at a 45 degree angle about 90 degrees to our westerly course. I called it in to my Flight Leader, who turned toward it and started to follow it down, along with the rest of the Flight, at a 45 degree dive from 18,000 feet. The jet plane began to pull away although we were doing 475 mph at the time. After about three minutes I observed another aircraft, which appeared to be flying formation with the one we were pursuing. From here on, we began to close on them and, when one pulled off to the left, my Flight Leader called for me to go get him, while he took care of the other one. My E/A chandelled to the left and I saw clearly that he was an Me262. As I was still above him, I made a diving pass to the left and, holding lead on him for 3 or 4 seconds, got in a good burst from 400 yards and observed hits on the fuselage. I then mushed past and had to suck on the stick to get into firing position again. At this point he had slowed down to around 350 mph and I closed fast, but just as I was about to open fire the pilot baled out at 5,000 feet. The E/A dove into the deck, where it exploded in a great flash of brown-red flame." [27].

The 'other aircraft' seen by this Flight Leader proved to be a Mustang and it is evident that the jet pilot had slowed down in order to be sure of a 'kill', but was instead surprised by the Mustangs coming down from above. The identity this Me262 pilot is uncertain, but seems likely to have been Helmut Baudach, who baled out safely.

The Americans reported the loss of two Fortresses, nine Thunderbolts one Lightning and six Mustangs during the days operations, thus Nowotny's reported radio claim for a Liberator must be in error, relating either to a B-17 or a fighter. *Hauptmann* Eder, airborne later in the day, claimed three P-51s shot down and a P-38 as a 'probable', the latter possibly from the 474th Fighter Group (42-104272) reported missing from a sortie over Germany during the day.

9th - 11th November, 1944

Hauptmann Eder claimed a further two Mustangs on the 9th and two days later a lone Me262 bounced four P-51s on Radio-Relaying duties over Holland. None of the American fighters were hit and, after just one pass, the jet made off; this was certainly a *KG(J)51* machine, returning after a bombing sortie. In the meantime, elements of *Kommando Nowotny* were renamed *III./EJG 2* and were then withdrawn from operations, moving to Lechfeld airfield on November 14th, to reform and rest. During the few weeks of jet operations, the *Kommando*'s

September - November 1944

Right: 'Nowi', Major Walter Nowotny, popular Kommodore of Kommando Nowotny and holder of the Knight's Cross with Oakleaves, Swords and Diamonds. He died in action on 8th November 1944 after claiming his 258th victory, 'for people and Fatherland' as his memorial says. The Luftwaffe could ill afford to lose leaders of Nowotny's calibre.
Below: Nowotny's memorial, near Achmer.
(via S E Harvey)

pilots had claimed the destruction of twenty-two Allied aircraft, mostly four-engined bombers. Twenty-six jets had been lost to various causes, including two which crashed on landing due to engine failure, three crashed on take-off, five force-landed after combat, two due to undercarriage failure and one to mid-air collision. Most of the unit survivors were to form the nucleus of *III./JG 7*, which was to become the first regular jet fighter unit of the *Luftwaffe* and was commanded by *Major* Erich Hohagen. Originally formed to be equipped with conventional fighters, this first jet *Jagdgeschwader*, would henceforth carry the honour title 'Nowotny' in memory of the highly respected leader of the test *Kommando* that had preceded it. The early indications of this re-organisation, shown in the British Intelligence note in July, were now confirmed.

12th November 1944
The 15th Air Force operated over southern Germany. Two flights of P-38s from the 82nd Fighter Group escorted a photo-reconnaissance Lightning to Munich and these were engaged by a single Me262. The jet sliced out of a cloud-bank from three o'clock at their level, clearly seeking to attack the camera aircraft, just ahead of its escorts. The '262 turned in front of the fighters, which at once engaged, Lieutenant Bob Berry opening fire at 500 yards and seeing many strikes on the rear fuselage. The jet fighter split-S'd away and the Lightnings returned without further incident. Bob Berry was awarded credit for a 'damaged'.

14th November, 1944
I Gruppe of *KG(J)51* sustained heavy casualties when Rheine airfield was bombed. Many airmen and officers were killed, including at least two pilots, *Oberleutnant* Merlau and *Oberfeldwebel* Hoffmann. A third pilot, *Oberfeldwebel* Köhler, was injured.

18th November, 1944
By mid-November, the Allies were taking the threat posed by the Me262 very seriously indeed. On this date 402 American fighters flew out to Leipheim airfield, the 4th and 353rd Fighter Groups claimed the destruction of fourteen Me262s by strafing. One Me262 was seen in the air by Captain J C Fitch and Lieutenant J M Creamer, which they claimed to have shot down just south of the airfield at 12.45 hours. Five minutes later Lieutenant G E Markham of the 353rd found another south of Augsburg and claimed damage. The 4th lost one Mustang during this attack. *III./EJG 2* jets now began to fly occasional interception sorties from Lechfeld.

19th November, 1944

RAF Tempests were again successful, Flight Lieutenant K B Taylor-Cannon and and Pilot Officer O D Eagleston of 486 Squadron catching a '262 on the Rheine runway and claiming a shared 'probable' (later down-graded to 'damaged'). Not so fortunate was Mosquito MM303 of 544 Squadron, which was intercepted by an Me262 between Mannheim and Karlsruhe and was badly shot-up. Flight Lieutenant Stuart S McKay managed to bring the badly damaged aircraft back to base.

21st - 25th November, 1944

On the 21st *Hauptmann* Eder, since 19th November *Kapitän* of 9 *Staffel*, JG 7, reported intercepting a Fortress formation, claiming one destroyed [28]. One of the 303rd Bomb Group, *'Helles Angels'* (42-102484) flown by 1st Lieutenant A F Chance, had taken a *Flak* hit that wrecked one engine and forced it out of formation. Then a twin-engined fighter - identified as a Bf110, but almost certainly Eder's '262 - stormed in and blew it out of the sky. Two days later (23rd) *Leutnant* Weber claimed a Mustang, while next day claims were submitted for a Mustang by *Leutnant* Göbel, a P-38 by *Feldwebel* Büttner and another by *Oberfeldwebel* Baudach. Two Lightnings are known to have been lost. One was an F-5 of the 7th Photo Recon Group and the other a P-38L of the 14th Fighter Group operating from Italy, in which 2nd Lieutenant Ergott was killed when his aircraft fell to Baudach near Fährenhausen. Next morning (25th) a loss was sustained by *1./KG(J)51* when *Hauptmann* Roesch was shot down and killed by AA fire while attacking Allied positions west of Helmond. Meanwhile over Germany a formation of B-24s sighted three jets over the Dummer Lake, which 'shadowed' them for a while, but did not attack. Hauptmann Eder of *III./JG 7* was airborne, claiming one of the six P-51s lost that day escorting 'heavies' to Misburg and Hamm. He also claimed a B-17 'probable', thirteen actually being lost.

26th November, 1944

Major Sinner, *Leutnant* Müller and *Oberfeldwebel* Buchner took off to intercept reconnaissance aircraft and all three had successful engagements. Hermann Buchner had actually been sent up on an air test, but a few minutes after take-off had been instructed by the Stuttgart fighter controller to investigate a plot nearing Augsburg. At 24,000 feet he sighted a speck ahead and below, travelling very fast. Opening up the turbines, he overhauled it rapidly. It was an F-5 Lightning of the 7th Photo Recon Group, flown by Lieutenant Irvin J.Rickey, heading for Stuttgart. The American pilot was taken completely by surprise; suddenly his aircraft was on fire and he hurriedly baled out, believing that he had been hit by *Flak*. His F-5 (43-28619 *'Ruth'*) crashed near Spesshardt, some twenty kilometres south of Pforzheim, at 12.15 hours, where Rickey was taken prisoner. Meanwhile Rudolf 'Rudi' Sinner had found his target near Munich. The American pilots, from the 1st Fighter Group, were now very wary of jet interceptions and Lieutenant Renne had spotted the jet rapidly closing in on him. At once he dropped his wing tanks and broke hard into the attack, causing Sinner to overshoot. Unknown to Sinner, three P-38J Lightnings were covering the F-5 and, as the German pilot turned for a second pass, the three fighters bounced him. Sinner broke downwards, dived too steeply and lost control; it was only by skilful use of the elevator trimmer that he regained normal flight. The P-38s had been outdistanced and climbed back to continue their escort. Sinner spotted the four aircraft high above and opened his throttles wide to re-engage, attacking from below and shooting down the escort P-38 flown by Lieutenant Julius Thomas, who baled out over Kitzbühl and was taken prisoner. Sinner, low on fuel, returned to Lechfeld without further combat. *Leutnant* Fritz R G Müller, formerly a sixteen victory *Experte* with *III./JG 53*, was able to intercept a Mosquito of 60 (South African Air Force) Squadron operating from Italy, which he claimed to have shot down. Lieutenant P J Stoffberg and Flying Officer Andrews had been on a sortie west of Salzburg when attacked and the port engine of their aircraft was badly hit, pouring smoke. Stoffberg at once turned away and lost height into cloud, the Messerschmitt circling overhead for two or three minutes, Müller obviously convinced that the damage was fatal. In fact Stoffberg was able to get back to Italy on one engine and force-landed at Fano.

The Second Tactical Air Force was operating Tempest patrols during the 26th and aircraft of 3 Squadron strafed Rheine, Squadron Leader Sweetman damaging one Me262 and Flying

September - November 1944

Top left: Like a grey ghost, Rudi Sinner's Me262 flashes past the Lightnings. (USAF)

Top Right: Rudi Sinner, like Nowotny, Schall and Buchner, an Austrian, would rise to command III./JG 7.

Above: The Lockheed P-38 Lightning was an efficient combat aircraft in the Pacific, but sustained terrible losses in northwest Europe. It was no match for a competently handled Me262. (USAF)

Right: Hermann Buchner, the only close-support pilot to join Kommando Nowotny, was originally a fighter instructor.
(H Buchner)

Officer R Dryland and Flight Sergeant Cole another. Other Tempests of 80 Squadron strafed Helmond airfield, Flight Lieutenant Price and Flying Officer Findlay claiming an Me262 damaged. The 50th Fighter Group, US 9th Air Force, was also engaged, Lieutenant L E Willis claiming a 'probable' 40 miles east of Durlach at 11.00 hours. These actions may possibly have resulted in the loss of one or more Me262s; *Oberleutnant* Heinz Lehmann of *I./KG(J)51* died when his aircraft crashed near Kirchwistedt while *JG 7* lost one of its successful pilots when *Leutnant* Alfred 'Bubi' Schreiber, the world's first jet 'ace', died in a crash near Lechfeld. A second *JG 7* pilot, *Oberfeldwebel* Rudolf Alt of *9 Staffel*, was killed while on a test flight near Buchenau. Finally, an aircraft of *I./KG(J)54* was engaged and damaged over Giebelstadt by Allied fighters.

27th - 30th November, 1944
Another Allied reconnaissance aircraft was lost on the 27th, when *Oberfeldwebel* Lennartz intercepted a Spitfire of 683 Squadron near Stuttgart; Pilot Officer L Courtney baled out and was taken prisoner.

Next day a *I./KG(J)51* jet was shot down by Allied AA fire while on a low-level bombing sortie west of Helmond. *Hauptmann* Rudolf Resch was killed, as was *Unteroffizier* Horst Sanio of the same unit, who was also shot down by AA near Helmond two days later.

Meanwhile, *Staffeln* of *II./KG(J)51* had arrived at Hopsten airfield from Schwabisch-Hall. Since October this unit had been 'working-up' in the fighter-bomber rôle and now joined forces with *I Gruppe*, to attack ground targets in the area of Euskirchen, Düren and Jülich. Allied 'Rat-Catching' patrols had become a major problem and thus the main base at Hopsten was supplemented by smaller airstrips at Hoerstel, Drierwalde and Esch. From here the Me262 crews lived a nomadic existence; the Allies would never know at which airfield a particular unit was currently based, nor to which airfield the jet fighter-bombers would return after a sortie. Often Allied fighter pilots, seeing a jet take off from a particular base and being aware of the short endurance of the German aircraft, would wait for its return; this now ceased to be profitable for them. For the Allied ground troops, slowly pushing forward, victory now seemed to be merely a matter of time as the exhausted *Wehrmacht* gave ground. Few at that time had any inkling of the shock awaiting them within a few short weeks; von Runstedt's Ardennes offensive - the 'Battle of the Bulge', would threaten to turn the tables.

Notes

5. *Kampfgeschwader 51 Edelweis*, by Wolfgang Dierich.
6. Letter from R.Sinner quoting correspondence with Eder.
7. Correspondence Raymond Baxter - S E Harvey.
8. Correspondence L C Betts - S E Harvey.
9. Correspondence Urban Drew - John Foreman.
10. Correspondence J.B.Wray - John Foreman.
11. *The 9th Air Force*, by Kenn C Rust.
12. Correspondence R.I.A.Smith - John Foreman, plus 401 Combat Report.
13. Correspondence Frank McLeod - John Foreman.
14. *The Mighty Eighth*, by Roger A Freeman.
15. Personal Encounter Report, supplied by Urban Drew.
16. Correspondence U.L.Drew - John Foreman.
17. The Me262 File, Public Record Office.
18. The Me262 File, Public Record Office.
19. Correspondence Rudolf Sinner - John Foreman.
20. *Happy Jack's Go-Buggy*, by Jack Ilfrey.
21. Letter from R.Sinner quoting correspondence with Eder.
22. *Kampfgeschwader 51 Edelweis*, by Wolfgang Dierich
23. Correspondence J.B.Wray - John Foreman.
24. Personal Encounter Report, held in The Me262 File, Public Record Office.
25. Conversation with Hermann Buchner
26. Correspondence Georg-Peter Eder - S E Harvey.
27. Personal Encounter Reports from the Me262 File, Public Record Office.
28. Correspondence with Rudolf Sinner gave the date as 20th November, but no heavy bomber losses were sustained over Germany and the authors believe that the correct date was the 21st.

Chapter Four
Bleak Winter: December 1944 - January 1945

As far as weather was concerned, December proved to be one of the worst months on record and the Allied tactical air forces were grounded for long periods as the German assault on the Ardennes began. Within five days the *Panzers* had driven the Allies some fifty miles back, and had surrounded the American forces at Bastogne. Me262s had played a vital part in the preparation for this attack, for *Hauptmann* Herward Braunegg's photographic reconnaissance unit, *Einsatzkommando Braunegg*, was operating over the area. These aircraft, virtually immune from interception, ranged across the Allied lines during the early part of December, returning with vital intelligence regarding the Allied positions. Thus when the Germans emulated their May 1940 surprise advance through the Ardennes forest, the *Panzers* went almost unopposed. On December 22nd however, the weather - hitherto the Germans' best ally - improved. The Allied fighter-bombers rose in strength and a combination of air power, dogged ground resistance and lengthening supply lines forced the *Wehrmacht* first to a halt and then to a pell-mell retreat. The *Tiger* tanks, mainstay of the advance, were left abandoned on the battlefield when their fuel and logistic support ran out.

Meanwhile, the Allied High Command had become increasingly concerned over the losses of high-flying reconnaissance aircraft to jet interceptors. By late December all such flights were provided with a small escort of fighters. Following this development, losses of such aircraft were dramatically reduced.

There were few sightings of Me262s during December. The weather conditions allowed only single flights by the reconnaissance and bomber units and targets for the jet fighter pilots were sparse.

2nd December, 1944

First successes were gained by the 15th Air Force, when Lieutenant Walter R Hinton of the 325th Fighter Group claimed strikes on an Me262 north of Munich, during the early afternoon, but *Leutnant* Weber of *III./JG 7* claimed his fifth confirmed success by claiming a P-38, actually an F-5 of the 5th Photo Recon Group. This crashed at 14.10 hours near Steinhöring and 1st Lieutenant K.Skeetz was killed.

3rd - 5th December, 1944

Tempests of 80 Squadron 2 TAF, flew an armed reconnaissance to Quakenbrück in the early morning. Flight Lieutenant J W Garland recalls:

> "My No 2 and I dived and shot up a locomotive south-east of Rheine. As I pulled up I saw an Me262 flying at right angles to us parallel to the railway line at our altitude (about 200 feet). I immediately applied full throttle and turned to follow. On completing my turn I closed on him fairly quickly (my estimate at the time was four miles). As I approached firing range - 300-400 yards - he started a turn to port and I saw his canopy come off. He increased his turn and suddenly flick-rolled into the ground. We were probably at 50-100 feet at this time. I am still not certain whether I fired my cannons and do not recall seeing any strikes." [29]

Garland was rightly credited with this victory. His opponent had been *Oberleutnant* Joachim Valet of *I./KG(J)51*, who was killed when his fighter-bomber exploded. Fighters of *III./JG 7* were scrambled to intercept bombers of the 15th Air Force on this date, *Oberfeldwebel* Lübking claiming the destruction of a Fortress, one of which was indeed reported missing.

Two days later, on the 5th, the 56th Fighter Group had been ordered to act as withdrawal support to heavies. Having come down to fairly low level while chasing a bogey, the 'Wolfpack' pilots saw a large number of aircraft on Neuburg airfield, of which around thirty were Me262s. They strafed the airfield and claimed eleven aircraft destroyed including four of the jets. Captain Michael J Jackson and Lieutenant Norman D Gould got one each and Lieutenant Claude A Chinn got two.

Over Germany, Flight Lieutenant R B Cole and Flying Officer G N Mann of 274 Tempest Squadron claimed damage to another Me262 on December 5th, while an 8th Force Mustang pilot, Lieutenant B Grabovski of the 352nd Fighter Group submitted a similar claim near Osnabrück, when he found a '262 at low

John Garland of 80 Squadron, chasing Joachim Valet's I./KG(J)51 fighter-bomber near Rheine on 3rd December. (Ron Lowry)

level over an airfield and reported hits to the starboard turbine.

8th - 11th December, 1944

Spitfires of 41 Squadron had an inconclusive brush with Me262s on December 8th, while two photo-recce Spitfires were briefly pursued by jets. Next day (December 9th) Lieutenant Harry L Edwards, of the US 358th Fighter Group, attacked '9K+IM' of *4./KG(J)51* north of Schwabisch-Hall, and shot it down, *Stabsfeldwebel* Hans Zander being killed. On December 10th a patrol of 56 Squadron Tempests took off at 14.30 hours. They were near Bevergen when Flight Sergeant L Jackson sighted two jets approaching from 5 o'clock. The leader tried to bounce Green 2, but broke away as Jackson turned into the attack, half-rolled to starboard and chased the '262 in a 420 mph dive, holding the range at 550 yards. The jet weaved, straightened out at 14,000 feet and Jackson opened fire at 600 yards, hitting the starboard side of the fuselage. Black smoke poured out as the jet zoom-climbed into the clouds. He noted that the machine carried a bomb slung between the fuselage and the port jet nacelle, and claimed it destroyed. His opponent was another *KG(J)51* aircraft flown by *Leutnant* Walter Roth, who was wounded, but managed to force-land his '9K+FL' safely. *I./KG(J)51* lost a second Me262 during this day when *Feldwebel* Herbert Lenke was shot down and killed by AA gunners near Aachen while flying '9K+WL'..

On 11th December, Group Captain P B Ogilvie DSO DFC commanding No. 34 (PR) Wing, set out on a weather recce in a 16 Squadron Spitfire. He failed to return, and is believed to have fallen to an Me262, possibly that flown by *Leutnant* Benno Weiss of *I./KG(J)54*, who was himself killed when his jet crashed at Fahrenbach/Baden.

12th December, 1944

I./KG(J)54 sent jets to strafe Allied ground positions and one, flown by *Hauptmann* Kornagel, was hit by anti-aircraft fire. He force-landed safely near Obertraubling. From the south, the 15th Air Force had been sending regular photo-reconnaissance missions into southern Germany and, from 3rd December, pilots had reporting sighting Me262s. Apart from the initial clash on 12th November, none had been engaged. On the 12th, however, four P-38s from the 82nd Fighter Group escorted a camera-Lightning to Munich when they were attacked by two Me262s. The escorts broke into the attack as the jets made repeated attempts to get the F-5 in their sights. They then broke away, without a shot being fired. They were then unsuccessfully engaged head-on by an Me410, which passed them, turned and tracked them, but the American pilots did not engage as the two jets reappeared above them. One came in fast from nine o'clock and Colonel Dickman, with Lieutenant Carper as his wingman, broke into the attack and opened fire head-on, the jet hurtling past them and vanishing rapidly behind. The formation turned for home and, a few minutes later, they were attacked again by a lone Me262. Walt Carper turned inside it, opening fire at 600 yards with a 20 degree deflection. He reported:

> "This pilot made a mistake when he tried to turn to position his aircraft, because evidently the jet lost speed in the turn and his rate of acceleration could not compare favourably with that of a P-38. Although I could not appreciably close the range, the Me262 could not pull away and when I broke away I was at the same range as when I started firing."

He concluded:

> "The P-38 has a definite advantage over the Me262 when the '262 attempts to make a tight turn because he must sacrifice the primary advantage of a jet - speed." [30].

It is clear that the jet pilots were still learning their craft in the new aircraft because the Mission Report commented:

> "Pilots report that jet aircraft would race around formation in a level circle out of range and select a point of attack. Attempts seemed to be experimental on different methods of attack rather than an aggressive attempt to shoot down one of our aircraft." [31].

In the west, a jet was lost when *Oberfeldwebel* Hans Kohler of *I./KG(J)51* was killed by AA fire near Aachen.

15th December, 1944

Lightnings of the 82nd Fighter Group, 15th Air Force, flew another photo-reconnaissance mission to Munich. As they headed south they overflew Lechfeld, and it was at this point that four Me262s engaged them, attacking in pairs. Lieutenant Pete Kennedy, flying close escort to the F-5, faced off two beam attacks, then one of the jets came at him head-on from out of the sun:[32]

> "Both of us fired down as far as possible. The Me262 went over my head by not more than 50 feet. As it went over, I thought I could observe the '262's right wing stream white smoke."

Lieutenant Bill Armstrong. leading the second element, fought off three attacks, then a pair of jets came in from three o'clock high:

> "The first jet made his pass at the photo plane and escort, and the second at me. As before, he broke off early enough for me to make a beam high side attack, firing several bursts at different angles, following around to astern, where the jet started a turn to the left, then whipped over 90 degrees to the right into a 60 degree dive, where I broke off. I observed a burst of white smoke off the bottom of the fuselage, which settled at a heavy broken white stream. The last I saw of him he was in a 45 degree dive towards the Alps."

Kennedy and Armstrong were each credited with an Me262 damaged.

17th December, 1944

The Wing Leader of 122 Wing, Wg Cdr J B Wray, was again successful:

> "On this day the Germans unwisely attempted a fighter sweep through our forward area, something that they had not done for some time. Unfortunately for them, my five Tempest squadrons, Dal Russell's Canadian Spitfire Wing and 125 Spitfire XIV Wing had all just got airborne to carry out various missions. An air battle immediately ensued, in which 122 Wing destroyed eleven, while the other Wings had their share too.
>
> "I had taken off and was scarcely airborne when our Ops Centre, Kenway, called me to say that there were two jets in the area of Weert. I set off, and immediately saw two Me262s travelling west to east about 500 feet below me at about 2,000 feet. I latched onto the leader and told my No 2 to go for the other aircraft.
>
> "The one I was chasing went into a gentle dive, and as we approached the River Maas the German AA opened up. I was going flat out at about 450 mph, but losing speed. He was about 200 yards ahead, but drawing away. The visibility was not too good at the time, and I realised that I might lose

him. I opened fire, and fired about a four-second burst, but with no apparent result. I had hoped at least to get him weaving.

"Because I thought that I had lost him, I was about to give up the chase. Then he started to turn slowly, so I set off again. By this time he was right on the deck, and I was slightly above him, and found that I was catching him up. I opened fire again, and there appeared to be strikes on the wings. He started to weave violently, which was not too clever at that altitude, but this allowed me to close to about three hundred yards. I was about to fire again when his port wing hit a building on the edge of the Rhine, and he pitched straight into the river. Heavy AA fire opened up, and so I withdrew quickly." 33.

John Wray's opponent on this occasion was a fighter-bomber from *II./KG(J)51*, and *Leutnant* Wolfgang Lübke perished. On the same day Typhoons of 430 (RCAF) Squadron flew a patrol during which three Me262s were sighted and attacked without effect.

22nd December, 1944
Mustangs of the 31st Fighter Group, 15th Air Force, flew cover to an F-5 Lightning that had been briefed to photograph objectives in the areas of Munich and Ulm. During this operation a jet was claimed destroyed fifteen miles northwest of Passau by Lieutenants Eugene P McGlaufin and Roy L Scales.

23rd December, 1944
A section of Mustangs from the 353rd Fighter Group escorted two 7th Photo Recon Group F-5s on a reconnaissance sortie and were bounced by Me262s of *III./JG 7* near Magdeburg. One of the Lightnings was at once shot down by *Oberfeldwebel* Büttner, but the jets were then chased down to low level, Captain H D Stump and Lieutenant S E Stevenson each claiming one damaged. As is so often the case, accounts from the opposing sides vary. No evidence exists to confirm that either jet was hit and two further claims were made by the *Luftwaffe* pilots, Büttner and *Feldwebel* Böckel each reporting the destruction of a Mustang. Only one such casualty can be traced, Flight Lieutenant Buckle's 2 Squadron machine failing to return from a sortie to Arnhem; certainly none were lost by the 353rd. On this date the 2 TAF fighters was again successful, Flying Officers R D Bremner and J R Stafford of 486 Squadron combining forces to destroy another Me262, on this occasion a *JG 7* aircraft in which *Feldwebel* Wilhelm Wilkenloh was killed when it crashed near Schwabstadt; he baled out, but his

Bleak Winter: December 1944 - January 1945

Above: John Wray, leader of 122 Wing, destroys his second Me262. (J B Wray)

Right: Wing Commander John Wray.

parachute failed. Spitfires of 411 (RCAF) Squadron, sweeping just east of Eindhoven, were bounced by a lone Me262. Flight Lieutenant J J 'Jack' Boyle recalled:

"He was upon us before the first warning shout came out of my earphones. Luckily, his fire missed everyone and, as he sped past us, he came right into my gun-sight and I fired a cannon burst instinctively. I saw a flash on his rudder that looked like an explosive strike but it could just as easily have been a sun flash. He raced away from us and was gone in seconds. After we landed, my No 2 confirmed that he had seen an explosion on the rudder. As a result of our Ops Report, I received credit for one 'damaged' enemy aircraft. I took quite a razzing from my squadron mates about 'seeing things' because none of us had really thought we could hit a jet. That was the first time I had seen an Me262 and just the sight of it was exciting." [34].

24th December, 1944:
On this Christmas Eve, another 7th Photo Recon Group F-5, flown by Lieutenant I J Purdy was intercepted by two jets over Nürnberg. Purdy, who was accompanied by another F-5 flown by Lieutenant Robert N Florine, reported:

> "We had taken off from airstrip A-83 near Valenciennes at 1130 hours. RAF Mosquito crews had told us six weeks earlier a rather eerie tale about an aircraft fast enough to keep circling them and attacking. Needless to say we were much impressed because we had little or no knowledge of jets at the time. Since we carried no guns, our one great advantage was that we could out-run most enemy aircraft at the time, if we saw them first.
>
> "The P-38 Lightning, such as we were both flying on this day, had a blind spot low and behind the pilot. This is where the Me262s hit us from, just as I started my camera run over Nürnberg. When on the mapping run it was necessary to keep the photo platform as steady as possible, so we were probably not watching as closely as normal; each pilot was supposed to cover his buddy's blind spot. But these guys came up so fast we never knew what hit us.
>
> "My aircraft was badly hit in the port wing and engine by cannon shells, and I was about to bale out when it seemed that the aircraft was still flyable. Lieutenant Florine's P-38 was not hit and he spent the next minutes keeping the two jets off my back by diving into them each time they tried to close and finish me: the most noteworthy aspect of his protecting action was the fact that his aircraft, like my own, was unarmed. There is little doubt that he risked his own life to save mine. I had now buckled myself back into the cockpit and headed for some ski-ing lessons in Switzerland."

Purdy found that his starboard engine was still functioning smoothly at high throttle settings, but as he headed south the German *Flak* gunners opened fire on him, one burst hitting his aircraft and forcing him off course. After another two *Flak* hits, he reconsidered his position and hearing other pilots talking to his base by radio, swung to the west and headed for France, determined to fly as far as possible:

> "After about two hours of single-engined flight, I finally received a vector from base. It looked to me that my gas supply might make it, so I continued. The visibility was very bad, so I received a vector every two or three minutes till I sighted base. Immediate landing was necessary; I landed at about 1530 hours, bellying the ship from west to east in the centre of the field. The ship slid about 270 yards and turned almost completely about. The right prop' was jerked off, and the right engine started afire almost immediately. I cut the switches and got out as fast as I could. The ambulance and what fire fighting equipment we had was standing by, and I was picked up immediately and taken to the dispensary. The ship burned

out and was a 100% total loss."

Florine, separated from Purdy, returned to base without further incidents. Ira Purdy's final comment was:

"Later that evening the events finally caught up with us, and I think I drowned my excitement in a bottle. I'm not sure how much we drank that nite [sic], but I still have an occasional headache from it!"[35].

25th December, 1944:
Even on Christmas Day there was no respite for either the jet fighter-bomber pilots or their opponents. At 12.30 hours on December 25th airmen at Heesch airfield were lining up for their Christmas dinner when an Me262 passed overhead. Flight Lieutenant Jack Boyle of 411 Squadron vividly recalled his second jet encounter:

"On Christmas morning, our entire Wing received orders to provide maximum air support in the American sector to the south, where the German had broken through our lines in what came to be known as the Battle of the Bulge. Our excitement was running high as we were briefed on

Pilots of 411 Squadron. Jack Boyle is kneeling, third from left. Dick Audet, another successful Me262-hunter, is in the top row, sitting, fourth from left. (R Bracken)

the extensive German fighter activity around Bastogne, and that our entire Wing, comprising five squadrons, would be taking off within the hour. Our squadron was the last to take off and it wasn't too long before we could hear the R/T chatter of those way up ahead reporting enemy aircraft sightings, and our sense of anticipation grew by leaps and bounds. In the midst of this, I couldn't believe my ears when I heard the voice of my No 2, calling to report a ropey engine that was running so roughly that he thought he shouldn't go on. Since a lame aircraft was never permitted to go home alone, this meant I would have to escort him back to base and miss out on all the activity going on just ahead of us. At first, there was some doubt in my mind about the seriousness of the engine problem because this was the very first operational trip for my No 2 and an 'early return' was usually examined for validity, to detect any inordinate combat nervousness. I decided we couldn't risk going on and reported to the C.O. that we were breaking off and heading for home. I was sorely disappointed by this turn of events and grumbled to myself all the way home, about bad luck and fickle fate.

"As we neared home base at Heesch, we were far too high and in an irritable mood, to get rid of the excess height, I stuck the nose almost straight down in a screaming spiral dive. As my speed shot past 500 mph, out of nowhere appeared a German jet Me262. It took only a second to set to my gun-sight and safety catch and then I was right behind him. My first burst of cannon fire hit his port engine pod and it began streaming dense smoke. He immediately dove for the deck as an evasive tactic, but with only one engine he couldn't outrun me. I scored several more hits before he clipped some tall tree tops and then hit the ground at an almost flat angle. His aircraft disintegrated in stages from nose to tail as it ripped up the turf for several hundred yards until only the tailplane assembly was left and it went cartwheeling along just below me at about my speed. Fire and smoke marked his trail. As I circled, Dutch farmers emerged from their barns and waved up at me.

"In the few minutes it took to return to base, I thought how fast the whole thing had happened, and realized I now seemed to be more excited than during the actual attack. After landing and pulling into my usual slot, my mechanics were waiting for me, almost jumping up and down in their welcome. When I had dismounted, the armourer came up and said he had always wondered, when he had to reload my guns, what the circumstances must have been when the guns had been fired, and what a thrill it had been for him to have actually seen his guns shooting down an enemy aircraft. As a matter of fact, most of the airmen in the entire Wing had witnessed the whole attack. Because it was noon on Christmas day, they had all been lined up for turkey dinner and at the sound of gunfire, they had hit the deck, facing upwards in case there was anything to see. On this day, it was an Me262 with a Spit' right on his tail. Later, everyone said what a thrilling spectacle it had been for them. For me too!" 36.

Jack Boyle was delighted to be told that he had scored the first 'solo' Spitfire victory over a '262. Sadly, Jack died two years ago following a long and courageous battle against cancer.

His opponent was a pilot from *I./KG(J)51*. *Oberleutnant* Hans-Georg Lamle was killed when his aircraft crashed near Erp, southeast of Heesch, making Jack Boyle the first Spitfire pilot to destroy a jet fighter unaided.

The next Spitfire engagement followed three hours later. The recollections from Squadron Leader J.E.Collier of 403 (RCAF) Squadron are both thoughtful and revealing:

"Four of my squadron were assigned to a front-line patrol along the Rhine River, which was then a part of the Battle of the Bulge. Our purpose was to discover and intercept any enemy fighter-bombers attempting an attack on our ground troops.

"While patrolling in our prescribed area, one of my sharp-eyed comrades spotted and reported three 'bogeys' about 2,000 feet above us and flying in close formation. Naturally we used full throttle to account for these three unidentified aircraft and climbed as fast as we could.

"Upon drawing up below them, it was obvious that they were '262s and we proceeded to engage them, with an advantage in that they had not perceived our presence due to our blind-spot position below them.

"Due to my position as leader of the group, I was out front and had the first chance at them. Maintaining our below level, we pulled up when in firing range and caught them completely by surprise since they were cruising much below their maximum speed.

"I fired my first burst at about 70 yards at the leader of the 'V' formation they were flying and obtained a hit on his starboard engine, which burst into flames. His two wing-men broke away in opposite directions, pursued by the other three of our flight, hampered by the tremendous acceleration of the '262. I followed my target down until I saw him bale out.

"That was a great moment in realising that I had shot down a '262, which was uncommon in those days. I was elated by the fact that I had destroyed one of their seemingly indestructible machines, but not with the fact that there was a human being (an enemy, of course) within it. I think the majority of fighter pilots very seldom thought of the human factor but just to remove that enemy machine from the battle. Of course there was always the possibility the he might return another day to kill me... but I don't think that this thought crept into fighter pilots' minds when in the midst of an air battle. I speak for myself but I think I express the feelings of most fighter pilots. It was the machine, not the man in it that you wished to destroy". 37.

This aircraft, '9K+MK' of *I./KG(J)51*, was flown by *Feldwebel* Hans Meyer, who was killed.

It seems possible that *KG(J)51* aircraft were operating further north, for Sergeant Jim Horan, tail gunner in a 390th Bomb Group B-17, saw several Me262s fly past his combat box in formation without attempting to attack. He remembered thinking that the Allies had nothing that could catch them.[11]

German records also indicate that a third Me262 was lost this, reportedly to an Allied fighter. The aircraft was from *I./KG(J)54*. There are no details of the pilot or the area of the action.

26th - 31st December, 1944

On the afternoon of 26th December RAF Bomber Command flew an escorted raid against St Vith in support of American ground forces. Flight Lieutenant E G Ireland of 411 (RCAF) Squadron reported:

> "I was leading Blue Section of 411 Squadron on a sweep west of Jülich, when on a course of 340 degrees an aircraft was sighted by our port section. As the aircraft was was crossing our course at right angles, our section was in position for attack. I closed and recognised the aircraft as an Me262, firing from 350 - 800 yards, angle off from 15 degrees to line astern. The port jet unit began to stream black smoke and Red 1 (Squadron Leader Newell) saw strikes on the aircraft. I continued to fire from line astern until my ammo was exhausted, at which time the enemy aircraft was 800 - 850 yards ahead. I then broke off the attack." [39]

This was claimed damaged, while Wing Commander Ray Harries, leading 135 Wing, made a similar claim against a second jet south of Stavelot. Next day (December 27th) Spitfires of 442 (RCAF) Squadron flew a sweep to Rheine, where an Me262 was claimed damaged by Flying Officer M A Perkins. An Me262 from *II./KG(J)51* crashed at Bunde, inujuring *Feldwebel* Walter Wehking, but it is not known whether this was the result of enemy action.

On the 28th, the Lightnings of the 82nd Fighter Group again tangled with Me262s while on a mission from Italy. North of Augsburg they were attacked by a single jet, which made firing passes on two P-38s without causing damage and was driven off by another American fighter pilot, who opened fire but made no claim.

Next day (29th), a jet was lost to AA fire, *Leutnant* Wolfgang Oswald of *I./KG(J)54* being reported missing from a combat sortie, but a success was reported by *III./JG 7*. *Oberfeldwebel* Büttner claimed a Mosquito destroyed, which is likely to have been a 544 Squadron machine piloted by Flight Lieutenant Olson DFC, reported missing on this date.

Bleak Winter: December 1944 - January 1945

Me262s of I./KG(J)54, showing a variation of the classic 'wave mirror' camouflage, which was widespread among Ju88 and Ju188 units during 1944/45.

On the final day of the year *Feldwebel* Baudach claimed another Mosquito, and again an RAF machine, NT231 of 464 Squadron, flown by Warrant Officer Bradley, failed to return.

The main objective for the 8th Air Force heavies on the 31st was oil and, during a heavy attack on the Rhenania Oil Refinery at Hamburg, a '262 swept in to shoot down B-17G 44-8632 of the 390th Bomb Group flown by Lieutenant R.J.Nash. Nash's B-17 had been hit by *Flak* and had dropped out of formation when the jet fighter pilot struck. One claim was made by the 8th Air Force, Captain A J Hawkins of the 339th Fighter Group saw another jet sweep in to shoot down the Mustang flown by Lieutenant James A Mankie in the same area, near Hamburg. This was again Helmut Baudach of *III./JG 7*, Hawkins turned in behind the jet and opened fire. Hits were seen and Hawkins unwisely chased it down. He too did not return and may have been a second victim to Me262s. A grim warning of things to come was reported by a 9th Air Force pilot however, when he sighted no less than, 'Twenty-four-plus Me262s flying in formation southwest of Trier'.

During December *Hauptmann* Georg-Peter Eder, *Kapitän* of *9./JG 7*, claimed his last jet 'kill', a B-17. The exact date is not known. This brought him to seventeen, with an additional eight 'probables', exceeding the total that would eventually be credited to Heinz Bär. It is clear that he had claimed 57 victories[40] by the time he joined *Erprobungskommando Lechfeld* and, adding the seventeen, his total was then 74. Yet he is credited with 78 victories. This must surely lead to the conclusion that four of his 'probables' were confirmed, actually giving him twenty-one jet 'kills' - all of them claimed before 1945.

While the majority of the Me262s sat on the ground during December, the *Luftwaffe* organisation had been busy; it had become abundantly clear that the only chance for Germany to negotiate with the western Allies would be if they could force a halt to the air offensive against German industry, airfields and particularly oil installations. The only weapon potentially able to achieve this was the Me262 fighter, and several more bomber units were ordered to prepare for conversion. Two new training *Ergänzungsgruppen*, *I* and *II.(Erg)/KG(J)*, were to be established to convert bomber pilots to the Me262, and *KG 6, 27, 30,* and *55* were earmarked to re-equip with the jets. The planned conversion was a logical progression, since the Allied bombing offensive had by this time deprived Germany of a high proportion of her oil resources: many of the bomber *Gruppen* existed in name only, for the available high-octane fuel was now being allocated almost exclusively to the fighter *Staffeln* of the Home Defence. Fuel for jet aircraft was still plentiful however, and thus the new and converted units were to be disposed as follows:

I.(Erg)/KG(J)	Pilsen
II.(Erg)/KG(J)	Neuburg
KG(J)6	Prague-Ruzyne
KG(J)27	Marchtrenk
KG(J)30	Smirschitz
KG(J)54	Giebelstadt
KG(J)55	Landau

This was a 'panic measure' and occurred far too late to be of any worth; Allied fighter-bombers were now haunting the skies and most of the proposed jet units, awaiting stores, equipment and aircraft, received little or nothing, as most of these supplies were destroyed by air attacks on the roads and at railway marshalling yards. The German land transport system was

Certainly a contender for the title of 'the most successful jet fighter pilot in history', the great Georg-Peter Eder, Kapitän of 9./JG 7.
(Georg-Peter Eder)

rapidly becoming paralysed and by the time of the surrender some units had received not a single jet aircraft. During late December, the few aircraft of *Einsatzkommando Braunegg* (soon to be redesignated *Nahaufklärungsgruppe 6*) were airborne again, reconnoitring the Allied airfields in Holland, Belgium and northern France. Their task was to help in the preparation for Operation *Bodenplatte* (Baseplate), which was carried out in the dawn of January 1st 1945.

1st - 4th January, 1945

Operation *Bodenplatte* took place when a force of some 800 *Luftwaffe* fighters struck at the major Allied airfields in Holland and Belgium, causing great damage to the Tactical Air Forces and an enormous shock to the Allied High Command. *I./KG(J)51* participated by putting up twenty-one Me262s to raid Eindhoven and Hertogenbosch in Holland, the largest number of jets known to have been employed by this unit in a single operation. The Me262s led the way to the two airfields, and their strafe was followed by the piston-engined fighters. One Me262 was claimed shot down and a second damaged by the AA defences at Gilze-Rijn. No evidence has yet been found to confirm a report that *I./KG(J)51* lost two Me262s during this operation. Another jet was engaged in the mid-afternoon by Spitfires of 401 Squadron. Flight Lieutenant J MacKay reported:

"I was flying as Blue 3 when I sighted an Me262 flying 7 or 8,000 below in the Rheine area. I attacked, closing to 450 to 500 yards and opened fire from dead astern. I saw strikes on fuselage - cannons packed up so I broke off attack." 29.

Flight Sergeant A K Woodill continued the chase, obtaining strikes on the wing and fuselage before the jet pulled away in a gentle turn to port. This aircraft was claimed 'shared damaged'.

Pilots of 442 (RCAF) Squadron reported two engagements; Flight Lieutenant J P Lumsden saw a lone jet at about 1,800 feet heading east towards Wesel. He closed in behind it, opened fire and saw strikes on the tail unit before his opponent disappeared into cloud. A second section from this unit - Flight Lieutenants K R Trumley and J N G Dick, Flying Officer W H Dunne and Pilot Officer E C Baker - were attacked head-on by another jet and all four Spitfire pilots opened fire. No hits were seen, but as it passed them smoke appeared to stream from it. The Spitfire pilots turned to give chase, but were easily out-distanced. On their return to base the pilots claimed a 'shared damaged', reporting that the German fighter had '...definite American markings on the fuselage, with crosses on wings, and swastika'. 41.

Later in the day, American heavy bombers flew out to attack the *Luftwaffe* airfields around Magdeburg. Escort was provided by Mustangs of the 20th Fighter Group. 'B' Flight of the 55th Squadron were flying top cover at 30,000 feet when, just before the bombers commenced their bombing run, two Me262s came through them like bolts of lightning. The Mustangs broke and Captain William Hurst fired a snap shot at one, seeing strikes as the jet raced past. The second section of the squadron, 4,000 feet below, was attacked and Lieutenant Thomas J Doody's fighter was damaged. The Messerschmitts hurtled away and were not seen again.42. The 4th Fighter Group were flying as withdrawal support and Lieutenant F Young claimed a jet shot down near Ulzen at 12.30 hours while Lieutenant Donald Pierine claimed another. Pierine's claim, though mentioned in the Mission Report, was not confirmed. Their opponents were undoubtedly fighters from *1./JG 7*. *Leutnant* Heinrich Lonnecker was shot down and killed, while *Unteroffizier* Detjens force-landed after combat west of Fassberg. A third aircraft, of *III./JG 7*, crashed near Ulzen, reputedly due to engine failure, but may also have been engaged with the US fighters.

Bleak Winter: December 1944 - January 1945

The weather was harsh in January 1945. Here, the 'black men' of II./KG(J)51 prepare the fighter-bombers for action. (via ARP)

Two days later, on 3rd January, *2./KG(J)51* sustained a loss when *Leutnant* Erich Kaiser was reported missing from a sortie in the Lingen/Ems area.[43] Next day, Typhoons of 439 Squadron flew an armed recce to the Almelo area. Fighter-bombers of *KG(J)51* were also airborne, and Flying Officer Hugh Fraser noted, '...bags of jet jobs about', but no combats resulted.

At this time *III./JG 7* moved base. *Major* Rudi Sinner, having replaced Erich Hohagen as *Gruppenkommandeur*, took the *Gruppenstab*, together with *Leutnant* Joachim Weber's *11 Staffel*, to Brandenburg/Briest, *Hauptmann* Georg-Peter Eder's *9 Staffel* went to Parchim, and *10./JG 7* commanded by *Oberleutnant* Franz Schall transferred to Oranienburg. At around the same time Johannes Steinhoff was removed from his post as *Kommodore* of *JG 7* and was replaced by the highly successful *Major* Theodor Weissenberger of *JG 5*. Adolf Galland had also been sacked. In an earlier meeting with Hitler, he and Goering had argued heatedly and when Galland tore the Knight's Cross from his throat and threw it upon the table, demanding that he be removed from his post and allowed to form a new jet fighter unit, Goering merely modified his tones, had grounded him, and had sent him 'on leave'. Now he was virtually an outcast, for no-one had been appointed to fill his position. 44.

13th - 14th January, 1945

Contacts with jets were rare until the middle of the month, but during a raid on Manderfeld by 2nd Tactical Air Force Mitchells on January 13th, a few Me262s were sighted in the target area at about the same time as one of the 320 Squadron bombers exploded for no apparent reason and a second went down in flames after bombing. On this day Lieutenant Walter J Konantz of the 55th Fighter Group attacked a *I./KG(J)51* jet shortly after it had taken off from Giebelstadt airfield, killing *Unteroffizier* Alfred Farber. Elsewhere, a Photo-reconnaissance Mosquito from the 25th Bomb Group was attacked by two *JG 7* aircraft, but escaped undamaged by executing tight turns into the attacks. Richard Kenney spent nine minutes evading their attacks then the two '262s pulled up alongside the Mosquito - at a distance - the pilots waved to Kenney, then the jets peeled off and disappeared! 45.

On January 14th Over 600 8th Air Force heavy bombers were sent out to attack the most precious reserve of the *Reich* - oil - and the *Luftwaffe* rose in force to oppose them. North of Berlin the 357th Fighter Group, sweeping ahead of the lead bomber Groups, surprised a large formation of FW190s. Battle was joined in which the Mustang Group claimed 56 German fighters destroyed, the highest total of air victories in a single mission that the USAAF was ever to claim. Lieutenant Dale E Karger remembered this sortie well, for a few Me262s of *JG 7* were sighted, but instead of engaging the bombers, they attacked the fighter escorts while FW190s stormed in and destroyed nine B-17s. Dale Karger was flying as 'tail-end Charlie' when it happened:

"I was on the left side, looking to the right when out of the corner of my eye I saw an Me262 very close into our formation behind the No 2 man. He had apparently pulled up quietly from the rear to look us over. I don't know whether he was firing at the No 2 man or the smoke was from his jets, but he was so close that I could see the pilot. I was so shocked to see him there that I could not get my brain working straight. The only thing I could think of was to slide over behind him to get a shot. I yelled over the radio (which was just starting to perk up with activity at this time) 'There's a jet job on your ass!' Of course, I didn't say who, so I guess everybody in the group had

The hunter becomes the hunted. This Me262 was hard on the tail of one American fighter when it was itself attacked by a Mustang. The camera-gun catches it shortly before its destruction. (USAF)

a fast look around at their rears.

"He was pulling up slightly and ahead rapidly as I got in behind him. An easy shot, no way could I miss: but I am a Christian now, and I'm sure that God had other plans for that German pilot than being shot down that day. We flew most of the time with our gun switches turned off as a precaution against blasting one of our own by accidentally pulling on the trigger while flying close formation. I knew these switches as well as I know my own name, but when I looked down to flip my gun switch I could see nothing but a mass of confusion.

"Until this day I think the Lord had a hand in this, because even at the Me262's speed, there is no way he could have outrun the bullets from my six .50 calibre guns. At this point I took to violently pounding myself on the side of the head to try to regain my thinking. When I finally came to my right senses, I fired a short burst, but he was well out of range straight ahead of me. To make matters worse, when I pulled up slightly, the rest of my squadron turned left, leaving me all alone, never even knowing what the last plane in the squadron was doing."[46]

Within a few minutes Karger caught a Bf109 and shot it down, but never forgot the jet fighter that was '...meat on the table but got away' - and always wondered why the German pilot did not shoot down one of the unsuspecting Mustangs. Within a few days however, Karger would enter combat with another of the jets.

Aircraft of the 353rd Fighter Group were escorting B-24s attacking Derben on this date. On the outward journey Red Flight sighted a pair of Me262s heading north at 10,000 feet and dived on them, attacking from the sun at around 500 mph. Lieutenant B J Murray was in the lead and hit the left-hand aircraft with a burst that travelled from the left to the right nacelle. The '262 pulled up sharply, and the pilot, *Unteroffizier* Detjens of *9./JG 7*, baled out. Lieutenants John W Rohrs and George J Rosen attacked the second Me262 and were shortly joined by Billy Murray. This jet was chased down and finally crashed into a field from an altitude of fifty feet; *Feldwebel* Heinrich Wurm, also from *9 Staffel*, was killed. Lieutenants M E Arnold and G E Markham shared another 'damaged' east of Hannover. Ten minutes earlier, at 12.50, Lieutenant K D McNeel had claimed a jet damaged over Perleberg, but it is not known whether it was a '262 or an Ar234. Major D S Creamer of the 55th Fighter Group claimed another damaged over Parchim airfield also at 13.00. Two further aircraft from III./JG 7 were lost; Oberfähnrich Hans-Joachim Ast was killed in a crash near Krivitz and a second pilot, flying 'Red 14' was shot down near Neuruppin. He is believed to have survived.

Pilots from the 359th Fighter Group had bounced a pair of jets on the way in to the target area, but scored no hits. Lieutenant Freeman F Hooker of this unit, after a dogfight with FW190s near the Dummer See (during which he claimed two destroyed), went down to strafe Hesepe airfield. He reported a jet damaged on the ground before his aircraft was hit by *Flak* and he baled out. During the course of operations against American bomber forces RAF Spitfires also claimed a success on the 14th when Captain Bolsted, of 332 (Norwegian) Squadron, caught the aircraft flown by *Unteroffizier* Friedrich Christoph of *II./KG(J)51* landing at Rheine and shot it down, killing the pilot. *I Gruppe* also lost a pilot when *Leutnant* Oswald von Ritter-Rittershain was shot down and killed by AA fire near Detweiler.

Another jet encounter was reported by the RAF when a photo-recce Spitfire of 16 Squadron was bounced by two Me262s. The pilot took violent evasive action and blacked out; when he recovered he saw a column of smoke and assumed that one of the jets had crashed.

Mustangs of the 10th Photo Recce Group also engaged jets when Lieutenants Logothetis and Franklin flew a mission to Diekirch, France. When over Bastogne, they were bounced by a lone '262 from dead astern but not hit, and as the jet overshot Franklin opened fire, followed by Logothetis, who chased it,

Bleak Winter: December 1944 - January 1945

'Red 3' of III./JG 7 taxies out. Particularly interesting are the twin rocket launchers mounted beneath the fuselage, given credence to their use by Kommando Nowotny early in November 1944. Also, the chevron on the fuselage is noteworthy, indicating that it was the personal machine of a senior officer, perhaps Hohagen or Sinner.
(via ARP)

blowing chunks from the wings, canopy and port engine and leaving it falling with pieces dropping away from the blazing tail section. This was credited as an 'He280 probably destroyed'.

15th - 17th January, 1945

On January 15th, Lieutenant Robert P Winks of the 357th Fighter Group found a lone Me262 over Schongau airfield. The jet was apparently 'beating up' the base and as it levelled out after performing a slow roll, Winks attacked, shooting it down at the edge of the airfield. Next day (16th) Mustangs of the 4th Fighter Group strafed Neuburg airfield, where Lieutenants Carl F Brown and Jerome E Jahnke jointly destroyed one of the jet fighters on the ground.

20th January, 1945

The jets were not seen again until January 20th, when American fighters flew many ground-strafing sorties. During these missions two Me262s were claimed shot down by the 357th Fighter Group. Lieutenant Dale E Karger was diving on a train near Munich, when:

> "I developed a runaway gun as I made my pass and I had to pull up to keep from hitting others in front of me. As I pulled up someone in the squadron reported two Me262s at about 8 to 10,000 feet directly above us. I still had my wingman with me and said, over the radio, that we would climb up to intercept. My one gun had expended its ammo by this time and we were

already a couple of thousand feet higher than the others. As we neared their altitude, the two Me262s headed east towards the city of Munich, descending slightly. By this time we were at full throttle and they were pulling away rapidly.

"As they approached the city, I could see only one Me262 (a mere speck by this time) making a left turn. I immediately turned north, in order to cut him off and intercept. Apparently he underestimated me and kept on coming around at a rapid rate now heading west, with me still heading north. As he closed, I started a left turn to line up for a shot. When I got him lined up in the computing gunsight, I could see him still slightly out of range and moving very fast at my altitude (about 3,000 feet). I led him about 1/8 of an inch with the computing sight and opened fire. Pieces of his canopy started blowing off, so I must have hit him close to the cockpit. A few seconds later the pilot baled out, and the '262 crashed into a wooded area; it did not explode but I did see smoke coming up from the wreckage. I also saw the German in his parachute land okay."[47]

At nineteen years of age, Dale Karger was to become the youngest American 'ace' in the European theatre, and ended the war with seven victories and another 'shared', plus four more destroyed in ground attacks. He regards the destruction of this jet aircraft as one of the high points in his combat tour. An Me262A-1 from *I./KG(J)54*, operating from Giebelstadt, was reported lost - a total write-off - with no details of pilot involved. This may have been Karger's opponent.

Meanwhile, Lieutenant Roland R Wright of the 357nd bounced a jet landing at Lechfeld, and shot it down in flames. One other jet loss has been traced for this date. *Unteroffizier* Karl Hartung of *III./EJG2* was killed when his aircraft crashed near Augsburg. *Unteroffizier* Heinz Kühn of *III./JG 7* had been reported as lost on January 19th. He was killed when his fighter crashed near Ingolstadt after having been shot down by fighters, but no such claim has been traced. It is more likely that an error of date has occurred and that he was involved in one of the actions related above.

21st January, 1945

Two jet encounters were reported by American aircraft engaged upon reconnaissance missions. The 355th Fighter Group despatched eight armed P-51s to photograph raid damage at the Politz oil refineries near Stettin. Captain Noble Peterson led his aircraft through the heavy *Flak* barrage, three of the Mustangs obtaining good photographs, but on the return flight two

Me262s attacked them near Steinhuder Lake at 14.30 hours. The P-51s broke into their pass, but Lieutenant Roscoe Allen became separated and managed to escape by continually out-turning them. He finally landed in France and returned to base next day. On this date however, the 25th Bomb Group lost another of its high-flying Mosquitos on recce duties over Germany. Meanwhile Mustangs of the 20th Fighter Group had a hair-raising experience whilst escorting Mosquitos to reconnoitre Merseberg. Jack Ilfrey wrote:

"Lieutenants Lowell E Einhaus, Robert H King and Garth L Reynolds of the 77th Squadron stirred up a hornets nest as they escorted their [25th Bomb Group] Mosquito over Stettin. Between 11.40 and 12.00 hours they mixed it up with what we believe is the largest number of jet jobs yet encountered at one time over Germany. Fourteen Me262s attempted numerous passes at the Mosquito and their [escorting] aircraft, but on each occasion the boys turned into them, and the jets broke off their attacks. None of these passes were successful, but because of the terrific speed of the jet jobs, it was impossible for our pilots to close in for a good squirt at them, although several shots were fired from out of range."[48]

The report above is inaccurate in that only four Me262s had engaged the little force. Richard Geary, flying the Mosquito, saw only one and broke hard as the Mustang leader called a break. Lowell Einhaus later wrote that,

"We encountered four Me262s flying our type of formation at our approximate altitude. They appeared to be heading for the Mosquito. We dropped our tanks and engaged the '262s in several 360-degree turns, firing at them on several occasions. No one was hit as far as I know. In the meantime, the Mosquito was heading west on a withdrawal course." [49]

22nd January, 1945

III./JG 7 sustained a serious blow when the Kapitän of 9 Staffel, the brilliant *Hauptmann* Eder was shot down as he came back from a mission:

"In January 1945, on the 22nd, I was shot down and wounded with a '262 when I made a normal landing in Parchim. I had to land because I was running out of fuel. I was shot at by several P-51s and P-38s. I broke both legs and came to the *Luftwaffe Lazarett* [hospital] Wismar and later to the *Luftwaffe* Lazarett Bad Weissee, where I was taken prisoner by the American army."[50]

23rd January, 1945

The RAF claimed several successes; 401 (RCAF) Squadron Spitfires had taken off at 09.50 hours to fly armed reconnais-

Flight Lieutenant R J 'Dick' Audet of 411 Squadron had a remarkable combat career. During his very first combat he claimed five victories and his total of ten plus one 'shared' included an Me262 shot down and a second damaged. On 3rd March he fell to Flak while 'train-busting'.

sances and several Me262s were seen taking off and landing on an airstrip north of Osnabrück. A warning was broadcast to any squadrons that might be in the vicinity and then the Spitfires attacked. Flying Officer Church and Flying Officer G A Hardy claimed one each, then the latter joined forces with Flight Lieutenant W C Connell to destroy a third. The pilots then strafed the airfield, claiming six more damaged. 411 (RCAF) Squadron took off for a similar sortie at 11.35 hours, patrolling Lingen and Münster, where an Me262 was seen and claimed destroyed by Flight Lieutenant R J Audet, who then strafed an airfield, where he claimed two more destroyed on the ground. Meanwhile, 56 Squadron Tempests flown by Flight Lieutenant E F McLeod and Flying Officer R V Dennis engaged another jet near Achmer. Frank McLeod remembered that action vividly:

> "Ron Dennis spotted one at ground level and, being at 7,000 feet, down we went. I remember checking my approach speed at 595 mph and saying to myself, 'Jesus Christ - I've never gone this fast in my life!'" [51].

Ronald Dennis remembers:

> "We were flying at 7,000 feet in the vicinity of Achmer airfield. Me262s were seen taking off, one of them flying low along the railway line in the direction of Hannover. I was flying No 2 to 'Casanova' McLeod and we were detached in pursuit. The sky was overcast with a light powdering of snow on the ground. At 3,600 rpm and maximum boost in a shallow dive we slowly overhauled the Me262, whose pilot did not appear to be aware of our

Bleak Winter: December 1944 - January 1945

Above: Frank McLeod proudly displays a painting of his encounter with Hauptmann Holzwarth's Me262. (E F McLeod)
Right: Frank McLeod when with 56 Squadron. The authors decided that it was ungentlemanly to enquire how he earned the nickname of 'Casanova'! (E F McLeod)

presence and continued to follow the railway line. As the pursuit continued I could hear a disembodied voice screaming with rage and hatred and suddenly, and rather shamefacedly, realised it was my own reactions! Suddenly the Me262 went into a gentle left-hand turn over Hannover airfield. 'Casanova' and I turned inside the enemy aircraft and opened fire. I found myself dead astern at about 300 yards. Following a burst of fire, flames poured from the enemy aircraft, which went into what appeared to be a controlled descent with the intention of a forced-landing. We slowed our speed and followed down. The enemy aircraft hit the ground at the far end of the field, lifted over a hedge and nosed into the ground beyond where it exploded in a ball of flames. The pilot never left the aircraft - I felt quite sad." [52.]

The two pilots had shot down the *I./KG(J)51* fighter-bomber flown by *Hauptmann* Hans Holzwarth, who was killed. Next day (January 24th) Dick Audet of 411 Squadron engaged another '262 over Münster, claiming it damaged.

In the meantime, a serious situation had been developing within the German Fighter Command, particularly concerning the use of the Me262. In mid-January, several officers had approached *Oberst* Günther Lützow and *Oberst* Johannes Trautloft, formerly Kommodore of *JG 54* and then successively on Galland's staff as Inspector of Day Fighters on the eastern front, then late in 1943, Inspector of Fighters. The two men were implored to make representations to Hitler himself to press for radical changes. This did not prove possible, therefore, on 22nd January, Lützow had arranged a meeting with Goering at Berlin in the *Haus Der Flieger* to discuss the situation. Lützow, spokesman for the delegation, began the meeting by asking for permission to speak without interruption for forty-five minutes, to which Goering agreed. There followed a damning indictment of the higher direction of fighter operations, ending with a demand that all Me262 fighter-bomber units should hand over their aircraft to Luftwaffe Fighter Command. Goering was furious. 'Did I not build the strongest air force in the world?' he roared. 'Yes', replied Lützow evenly, 'And it brought you many victories in the early years - but then you went to sleep!'

Goering roared 'This is a soldier's court! You're a bunch of mutineers, and I'll have you all shot!' Then he stormed out.

Goering had seen Galland, who was not present, as the instigator. He was ordered to report to present himself to the Chief of Personnel, where he was ordered to leave Berlin within twelve hours, but to hold himself in readiness for further orders. However, he returned to Berlin without permission and was ordered to the *Reichkanzlei* (Chancellery), where he was told that the Führer had only just been informed of Goering's actions against him and that they would stop immediately. He was then called to Goering's presence. The grounding order was revoked and he was told that his request to form a jet fighter squadron was granted, with Hitler's backing. In the opinion of many, the reason that Goering finally agreed was in the hope that the fiery Galland would be killed. Galland felt a certain irony in the situation. He had begun the war as a *Staffel* leader and now, as a General, would end the war as a *Staffel* leader. Lützow was banished to Italy, with strict orders not to communicate with Galland in any way. *Oberst* Gordon Gollob was given his job as Inspector of Fighters. [53]

Apart from the regular fighter *Geschwadern*, small fighter units had been established for the point defence of selected industrial complexes. These units, known as *Industrie Schütz Staffeln*, normally had on strength four to six day fighters, plus a couple of nightfighters. While they formed part of the overall *Reich* air defence, they operated independently for the sole purpose of defending their factories. Little is known about the activities of these units and indeed, some pilots were not regular *Luftwaffe* personnel. It is known, however, that at least one *ISS* had received a few Me262s since the *Luftwaffe* losses show one such aircraft damaged in an accident on February 2nd.

By early 1945, it was reckoned that the American fighter escorts were destroying one Me262 in combat for every ten missions flown by their Groups. This success rate was to improve dramatically as the pilots developed better tactics and received better equipment. The fighters, normally flying above the bomber formations, began to employ the 'split-S' (reverse Immelmann Turn), rolled onto their backs and carried out the second half of a loop as the jets approached. In this way, the escorts could often block an attack by attacking the Messerschmitts head-on. The pilots had now been issued with G-suits, and these, coupled with the K-14 computing gunsight, gave the Americans a personal advantage over their German opponents. By the war's end, the success rate would improve to approximately one jet destroyed for every four missions flown, due to tactics, technology and the increasing numbers of jet aircraft encountered.

Notes
29. Correspondence Col J W Garland - John Foreman.
30. *Adorimini*, by Steve Blake.
31. *Ibid.*
32. *Adorimini*, by Steve Blake.
33. Correspondence J.B.Wray - John Foreman.
34. Correspondence and telephone conversation Jack Boyle - John Foreman.

35. Correspondence Ira J Purdey - S E Harvey.
36. Correspondence Jack Boyle - John Foreman.
37. Correspondence J.E.Collier - John Foreman.
38. Reunion meeting; Jim Horan - S E Harvey.
39. Combat Report supplied by E.G.Ireland.
40. From *Die Ritterkreuzträger der Luftwaffe*, Ernst Obermaier, *JG 1/JG11* history by Dr. Jochen Prien and victory list of *II./JG 26*.
41. The Me262 File, Public Record Office.
42. Correspondence Paul C Roberts (flight surgeon 20th FG 1944-45) - S E Harvey
43. *Kampfgeschwader 51 Edelweis*, by Wolfgang Dierich.
44. *The First and the Last*, by Adolf Galland.
45. Correspondence from Norman Maylayney, Historian 25th Bomb Group.
46. Correspondence Dale E Karger - S E Harvey.
47. *Ibid.*
48. Correspondence Jack Ilfrey - S E Harvey.
49. Quoted by Norman Maylayney in correspondence with John Foreman.
50. Correspondence Rudolf Sinner, quoting a letter from Georg-Peter Eder.
51. Correspondence Frank McLeod - John Foreman.
52. *The Typhoon and Tempest Story* by C.F.Shores and Chris Thomas, quoted with the authors' permission.
53. Facts taken from *The First and the Last*, by Adolf Galland.

Chapter Five
Jets at Night: Kommando Welter

The idea of using the Me262 as a night fighter had originated as early as September 1944, when trials had commenced at Rechlin using a modified Me262A-1a, equipped with a four-pole *Hirschgeweih* (deer antler) antenna array and night interception radar equipment. The tests were carried out by *Oberst* Hajo Herrmann of *Jagddivision 30* (originator of the *Wilde Sau* single-seat night fighter tactics) and *Oberleutnant* Behrens from the *Erprobungsstelle Rechlin*. The principal object of this modification was to provide a means of intercepting the British Mosquitos that had long been a thorn in the side of the night defences. Their speed and manoeuvreability had made them practically invulnerable to interception and it was a rare night that these wooden aircraft did not visit the German capital city. Following the first successful trials, it was decided that the two-seat training model would prove more suitable as a night fighter and a new unit was established at Burg airfield, near Berlin; *10 Staffel* of *NJG 11*, under the command of *Major* Gerhard Stamp. Initial equipment was the single-seat model and it was to be March 1945 before the unit received a small number of the two-seat aircraft. One of the first to achieve success was *Oberleutnant* Kurt Welter, formerly an FW190 'Wilde

Major Gerhard Stamp flew over 300 sorties as a bomber pilot before converting to fighters. He flew with JG 300 by day and night before assuming command of the first Me 262 nightfighting test Kommando.

Sau' pilot with *II./JG 300*, who had already had thirty-four victories to his credit and had been awarded the *Ritterkreuz*. He went first to *II./NJG 10* and then, at the beginning of December, to *10 Staffel NJG 11*, equipping with the Me262. He would go on to become the most successful jet nightfighter pilot, claiming no less than twenty-nine kills, 25 Mosquitos and two heavy bombers at night and two more Mosquitos in daylight. This record undoubtedly makes Welter the most successful jet pilot of all time. [54.] Another successful jet pilot was *Feldwebel* Karl-Heinz Becker, who was to claim a total of seven victories, mostly Mosquitos, during February and March.

Details of these night operations are sparse. One of the earliest contacts occurred on the night of October 3rd, when an Me262 was sighted by a bomber crew, although no engagement occurred. Three weeks later, on the night of the 27th, a single Me262 was sighted near Nienburg by Wing Commander Voyce and Squadron Leader Galliene in a 139 Squadron Mosquito, but again no attack was delivered. Kurt Welter is believed to have claimed three night kills during December, including one of five Lancasters lost on the night of the 12th. On January 2/3rd he claimed a Mosquito, almost certainly a 139 Squadron aircraft flown by Flight Lieutenant Howard DFC and, three nights later, on 5/6th, he claimed another. Three aircraft were lost, two intruders and a 571 Squadron reconnaissance machine. It seems probable that the latter was Welter's adversary. Flying Officer Henry and his navigator baled out of their crippled aircraft after reaching Allied territory. Two nights later a '262 night-fighter was claimed shot down by one of the Bomber Command air gunners. Welter claimed another Mosquito on 10/11th January, but on this occasion no such losses were reported from units operating from the United Kingdom and it must be assumed that the aircraft came from Italy.

On the night of January 14th Lancasters of No 6 (Canadian) Group attacked Merseburg; there were many nightfighters about and a 434 Squadron aircraft flown by Flying Officer A Purnell was attacked by what appeared to be a jet. His gunners - Pilot Officer R McKay and Flight Sergeant J Barrett - opened fire, knocking pieces from this aircraft and setting it on fire. Members of the crew then reported seeing it explode on the

Possibly used by Kommando Stamp and Kommando Welter, a single-seat Me 262 experimentally fitted with a night interception radar array.

ground some 20,000 feet below. Two nights later an Me262 nightfighter was spotted over Zeitz and next evening (January 17th) a British Mosquito crew had an unnerving experience when their aircraft sustained cannon damage during a surprise attack near Magdeburg.

The jet nightfighter *Staffel* lost three aircraft and pilots in fairly quick succession, however. *Oberleutnant* Heinz Brückmann was killed when his fighter crashed on Wittstocker Heide on 21st January (probably 21/22nd), while *Oberfeldwebel* Paul Brandl and Oberleutnant Walter Eppstein both perished on the night of 4/5th February, Brandl in a crash near Briest and Eppstein north of Burg.

Another claim was submitted against these new interceptors on the night of February 7th, when Lancaster 'D' of 582 Squadron was returning from a raid:

"The rear gunner sighted a Me262 on the port quarter, attacking another Lancaster that was eventually shot down.

"The Me262 was seen to break away from the other Lancaster to starboard, and commence a curve of pursuit on Lancaster 'D' from the port quarter. Range was now approximately 500 yards, and the rear gunner opened fire. Me262 closed to 250 yards, but did not open fire. Rear gunner continued to fire until breakaway. By this time the enemy aircraft was burning furiously. Then at 250 yards went into a vertical dive and was seen to explode when it hit the ground. Mid-upper gunner opened fire at approximately 400 yards, but was unable to give a long burst because of the the tailplane of Lancaster 'D' obstructing his view."

Six nights later, on February 13/14th, a sighting of a single jet was reported south of Magdeburg during the Dresden fire raid, while next night Lancaster PB593 of 156 Squadron, flown by Flying Officer Wallace, was returning from Chemnitz when an Me262 nightfighter attacked. The gunners, Flying Officer J McRory (mid-upper) and Sergeant James Hayton (rear gunner) opened fire, reporting that one wing of the attacker had been shot clear away. During this operation Halifax gunners from No 4 Group claimed three further jets destroyed. One of the engagements was against an Me262 flown by *Feldwebel* Karl-Heinz Becker of *10./NJG 11*, whose aircraft was only damaged; he force-landed at Münster-Handorf, unhurt. Another jet crashed near Burg two night later, killing *Oberfeldwebel* Walter Bocksteigel. Me262 pilots of *10./NJG 11* claimed three Mosquitoes over Berlin during the night of February 20th, but no such casualties can be found in Allied records, and the date may be in error. Three nights later, on 23rd February, Bomber Command attacked Pforzheim. Lancaster 'S-Sugar' of 101 Squadron was engaged by an Me262 nightfighter, which was claimed destroyed by the gunners. It was seen to explode in mid-air. A jet landed at Prenzlau after being damaged in combat on this night

On 3/4th March, the night that the *Luftwaffe* flew its last great night intruder mission - *Operation Gisela* - against England, it is believed that another jet pilot was lost. *Oberfeldwebel* August Weibling was killed north of Magdeburg.

Another successful encounter was reported on the night of March 7th, when Bomber Command returned to Chemnitz. Lancaster 'O' of 428 Squadron was at 15,000 feet over the target when:

"Enemy aircraft seen crossing port quarter about to attack another bomber. Rear gunner fired a 3-second burst, the enemy aircraft burst into flames, turned hard to port and flew on for about thirty seconds, and then blew up. Both gunners saw a parachute go down, and then there was an explosion on the ground".

This nightfighter, clearly identified as an Me262, was claimed destroyed.

Karl-Heinz Becker, who had claimed a day victory over a P-38 on February 15th, came into his own during the latter part of March. On the night of the 21st he claimed his first Mosquito near Berlin; the 692 Squadron machine flown by Warrant Officer McPhee failed to return. Two nights later he claimed

Major Kurt Welter, possibly the most successful jet fighter pilot of all time. He claimed 63 victories and won the Eichenlaub to his Ritterkreuz. He was killed in a car accident on 7th March 1949.

another such aircraft, possibly a 139 Squadron machine piloted by Flight Lieutenant Searles. Next evening he claimed two and on the night of the March 27th, another Mosquito went 'into the logbook', and indeed five failed to return. Three further Mosquitos were claimed by unidentified pilots from *10./NJG 11*.

Oberleutnant Kurt Welter, now in command of the unit, claimed no less than four Mosquitos over Berlin during the night of the 30th, but just one aircraft has thus far been traced, Flight Sergeant Camprey's 692 Squadron bomber being reported missing. Next night Becker claimed another - his sixth - but the only loss was a 2 Group fighter, Flight Lieutenant Graham's 418 Squadron Mosquito crashing in Holland. Kurt Welter revealed after the war that interceptions of Mosquitos were made easier by the fact that the British invariably used one of three routes to approach Berlin. His pilots became so accustomed to this that they referred to them as 'platforms one, two and three', while the nightly Mosquito raids were known as 'the Berlin Express'.

On the night of April 3rd, two more RAF Mosquitos were lost. KB349 of 139 Squadron, flown by Squadron Leader Dow, is believed to have fallen victim to a jet. Five nights later an Me262 was claimed destroyed by a 4 Group Halifax crew on a mission to Hamburg. Jet nightfighters were certainly in evidence, for Flying Officer Wolstenholme's 9 Squadron Lancaster NG235:H was shot-up by a '262. He managed to bring the big bomber over Allied-held territory and ordered the crew to bale out before abandoning the aircraft himself. A 608 Squadron Mosquito crew managed a lucky escape on the night of 14th April when Flying Officer George Nunn and his navigator Pilot

Officer H.S.T.Harris flew the 'Berlin Express' carrying a 4,000 lb 'Cookie'. The target was found and bombed and they turned for home, observing a heavy Main Force attack on Potsdam. Harry Harris looked back, noted their own thick contrail and spotted a red and green light just above it. Harris had remarked that there was '...some idiot flying with is navigation lights on...' when several things happened practically simultaneously. Harris saw the lights gaining on them at an astonishing rate, yelled to his pilot to dive hard to starboard, and then saw the brilliant gunflashes as the '262 opened fire. Then they were suddenly caught in a 'cone' of some fifteen searchlights, which temporarily blinded Nunn, who flew for some minutes with his eyes closed, and recovered his vision to find that the Mosquito was at 1,600 feet over Berlin - flying inverted. When they eventually returned to Downham Market it was discovered that the aircraft had sustained two cannon strikes. One claim for a Mosquito destroyed was submitted by *10./NJG 11*. Although the identity of the pilot is not known, it is likely to have been *Oberleutnant* Kurt Welter. A further two Mosquitos from 613 Squadron failed to return from ground attack sorties.

The difficulties of jet night interceptions were tremendous, particularly when flying the single-seat model. Karl Heinz Becker, who became a member of a very exclusive 'club' - the jet night fighter aces - during March 1945 stated:

"Often our speed proved a great disadvantage, for it gave us no time to aim, and we would shoot past the target without even firing." [55.]

For a pilot alone in the darkness in an aircraft of such high performance the

The Me262-1a/U1 two-seat Me262s of Kurt Welter's 10./ NJG 11. During the last weeks of the war they operated from the autobahn between Lübeck and Leck, in Schleswig-Holstein

technical expertise needed merely to fly it was enough; to operate the airborne interception radar, locate the target visually and to deliver a successful attack, required skill, reflexes and a coolness far above the norm. Conditions were obviously easier with the two-seat version, but this arrived too late to have any significant effect. Only five sorties were flown with this model, during which three Mosquitoes were claimed destroyed. During the short operational life of *10./NJG 11*, seventy combat missions had been flown totalling 160 sorties, in which approximately fifty claims had been submitted both by day and night.

During the course of the war, the night bomber crews of the Royal Air Force carried out the longest campaign and sustained the heaviest losses of the RAF. Of 70,000 missing aircrew, over 55,000 were members of Bomber Command. Had the development of the Me262 not been so delayed, it is likely that the nightfighter version would have appeared earlier and that the nightly air battles over the Reich would have seen even greater slaughter. As with the day war, the Me262 could well have turned the tide in Germany's favour by halting the Strategic Night Air Offensive completely.

Notes

54. Victory totals taken from *Die Ritterkreuzträger der Luftwaffe*, by Ernst Obermaier.
55. Karl-Heinz Becker in *Wings of the Luftwaffe, the Me262*. (Video)

Chapter Six
Into the Jet Age: February 1945

1st February, 1945
III./JG 7 was still not fully operational: 'We still had a great deal of work to do regarding training, equipment, communications, ground organisation and the command structure', says Rudolf Sinner.[56] However some pilots and aircraft were combat-ready and *Leutnant* Rudolf Rademacher made his first claim with the jet by reporting a lone Spitfire destroyed near Brunswick. No Spitfire was lost in this area, but a 274 Squadron Tempest, flown by Flight Lieutenant G J Bruce failed to return. He force-landed near Krefeld where he was taken prisoner. A Spitfire of 313 Squadron was also lost, but Flight Lieutenant Pinney, who crashed near Monchen-Gladbach, was reported lost to accidental causes.

3rd February, 1945
The 8th Air Force attacked Magdeburg in strength and the jets of *III./JG 7* scrambled to intercept them. Fortresses were claimed by *Leutnants* Weber, *Schnörrer* and *Oberleutnant* Wegmann, while *Leutnant* Rademacher claimed two more. In addition, *Unteroffizier* Schöppler reported the destruction of an escorting Mustang. In total, 23 Fortresses and seven Mustangs

Rudolf Rademacher, highly successful with JG 54 on the Eastern Front, was another high-scoring jet Experte who was to die in a post-war accident. Sixteen of his 93 victories were claimed with JG 7 and he was killed in a glider crash on 13th June 1953.

were lost. One claim was submitted by the escorts when Lieutenant L V Andrew of the 364th Fighter Group reported an Me262 damaged south of Gardelegen. A *I./KG(J)54* fighter was reported to have crashed on landing, but this is unlikely to have been due to combat.

Lieutenants Jack F Brown and Leon Oliver of the 359th Fighter Group flew a PRU escort to the Berlin area during the day and the small formation was attacked by Me262s near Brunswick. Both American pilots fired, but no hits were claimed.

5th February, 1944
The 82nd Fighter Group, 15th Air Force, flew another photo-reconnaissance mission to Munich, one F-5 escorted by two P-38s of the 95th Fighter Squadron. As they headed home, Lieutenant Hartly Barnhart glanced behind and saw an Me262 closing fast on his wingman, Lieutenant Art Lewis. He called a break, but Lewis continued straight and level, taking a burst of 30mm that set his wing fuel tank ablaze. The German pilot, *Leutnant* Rudi Harbort of *III./EJG 2*, then tried to close on the F-5, but was driven away by Barnhart. Art Lewis, turned away with the fire spreading. He baled out near Lengeries as 12.30 hours and was captured unhurt.

8th February, 1945
The 82nd Fighter Group Lightnings had yet another skirmish with Me262s on the 8th, two jets turning clockwise behind them to make a stern attack. At once the five Lightnings broke hard to starboard, turning inside the jets and opening fire, closing to 100 feet. The rearmost American pilot managed to cut across and make a head-on pass at one of the jets, seeing strikes until it passed over him. The unnamed American pilot was credited with a 'damaged'.

9th February, 1945
Meanwhile, the German jet expansion programme was slowly proceeding. *KG(J)54*, designated as an all-weather unit, had received its first Me262s at Giebelstadt. The aircrew, all former Ju88 and He111 pilots, had considerable experience in foul weather instrument flying, but were inadequately trained in fighter techniques and tactics. When *I Gruppe* scrambled ten Me262s to oppose a raid by 1,500 American heavy bombers

With wheels and flaps down, an Me262 weaves low over the trees to escape the pursuing American fighter. (USAF)

escorted by a large number of fighters, the result was disaster. The jets intercepted the bomber force at 24,000 feet near Fulda; it was apparent that these were fairly inexperienced for initially only one pilot ventured an attack, but passed through the B-17s of the 94th Bomb Group without firing his guns. Eight others '262s, seen criss-crossing above, were reluctant to engage probably due to the heavy escort. The flight leader then came down a few moments later and, ignoring the 94th, managed to score hits on a Fortress from the lead Group. The bomber crashed in flames after six parachutes were seen. Three more jets then attempted to attack stragglers, but were forced away by the Mustang pilots. A little later a lone Fortress of the 94th, which had lost an engine prior to reaching the target and had bombed an alternate, was attacked by a lone jet that failed to press home its advantage and soon made off. During these engagements *Major* Ottfried Sehrt, the *Grupppenkommandeur*, claimed a B-17 shot down plus a *Herausschuss* and similar claims were submitted by unnamed pilots. These jets, flown by bomber pilots who had never fired their guns in anger, quickly became as lambs to the slaughter for the battle-hardened Mustang escort pilots as they attempted wide sweeping turns that allowed the American escorts to close in. Six Me262s were claimed shot down; Captain Donald H Bochkay and Lieutenant John L Carter of the 357th Fighter Group claimed two and another fell to Lieutenant S C Ananian of the 339th Fighter Group near Fulda. Carter had chased one jet that easily outdistanced him, then saw another apparently already hit by gunfire. He closed in and, as he opened fire, the canopy flew off and the pilot baled out. This was possibly *Major* Sehrt who landed near Frankfurt, the only known survivor of the six that fell. Carter fired on another jet that was claimed probably destroyed.

Lieutenant William E Hydorn of the 78th Fighter Group claimed one probably destroyed and another was claimed damaged by Major Robert W Foy of the 357th. Captain E H Miller of the 78th reported:

> "An Me262 was approaching the box of bombers, which we were escorting. I called the bounce from approximately 22,000 feet, diving on the Me262, which was flying 14,000 feet below. I began firing at extreme range, knowing that he would out-distance me the moment that my wingman and I were spotted. So on the first long burst the right engine began to smoke and the jet rolled over, falling through a cloud bank, and we were unable to follow and confirm the victory. This was considered a 'probable', which appears on my record".

Three more jets attempted to attack stragglers from the bomber formation, but were beaten off by fighters from the 364th Fighter Squadron. The *Geschwaderkommodore*, *Oberstleutnant* Volprecht Riedesel Freiherr zu Eisenach, was one of the five missing pilots, perishing when his jet exploded on the ground at Limburg. Other losses included *Oberleutnant* Günther Kalher, who was killed near Neuhof and *Oberleutnant* Walter Draht, who died in his aircraft near Meerholz. The final two casualties were aircraft that crash-landed at Giebelstadt after this fight, both pilots unhurt.

Meanwhile, in an action over Berlin, Me262s from *III./JG 7* stormed a Fortress formation. *Leutnant* Rademacher claimed two victories over the capital while *Oberleutnant* Wegmann claimed another. Again a single escort fighter was reported destroyed, *Leutnant* Schnörrer claiming a Mustang - possibly that flown by Captain Browning of the 357th Fighter Group - that failed to return. Later in the day Mustangs of the 339th Fighter Group flew a sweep during which a single Me262 was sighted. This was chased and claimed damaged by Lieutenant J J Sainlar at 17.00 hours. He actually shot down 'White 18' of *III./EJG 2*, *Unteroffizier* Heinz Speck dying when this fighter crashed at Zusmalthausen.

Oberstleutnant Volprecht Riedesel Freiherr zu Eisenach, Kommodore of KG(J)54, was one of the casualties on 9th February. Although the former bomber pilots under his command fought bravely, the lack of adequate fighter training negated the technical superiority of their aircraft.

11th February, 1945

Eight Tempests of 274 Squadron RAF flew an armed reconnaissance of the Paderborn - Hannover area. A lone Me262 was sighted by Squadron Leader D C Fairbanks, who chased it through scattered clouds for some twenty miles before catching it in the landing circuit at Rheine and shooting it down in flames. Although it has been postulated that his opponent was an Ar234B of *1.(F)/123* flown by *Hauptmann* Hans Felden, it seems unlikely that the highly experienced 'Foob' Fairbanks would have made such a mistake, especially after such a long chase. It is more likely that his adversary was an Me262 flown by *Major* Hans Grözinger, *Staffelkapitän* of *11./JG 7*. Grözinger survived, but died four days later after contracting virulent polio. (Fairbanks would become the leading Tempest 'ace' before being shot down and made prisoner on February 28th).

14th February, 1945

The British scored again when *KG(J)51* flew 55 fighter-bomber sorties against Allied ground targets in the Kleve area. Seven Spitfires of 41 Squadron flew a 'Rat Catching' patrol to Rheine, where several Me262s were seen in the circuit. These were covered by FW190Ds of *III./JG 54*, which kept the Spitfires at bay at the cost of two of their number. A little later, Spitfires from 610 Squadron patrolled over Rheine, finding some Ar234 jet bombers, which used their speed to escape. Flight Lieutenant F A O Gaze left his wingman below cloud in the hope that the latter might catch the Arados returning to land and climbed up

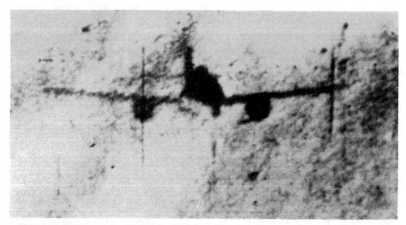

Feldwebel Richard Hoffmann's '9K+NL' just seconds before destruction; a frame from Tony Gaze's camera gun. (British Official)

through the overcast to allow the sunlight to clear ice from his windscreen. Suddenly a flight of three bomb-carrying Me262s shot past the Spitfire XIV and Gaze applied full power to catch them, using cloud cover to hide his approach. The jets were cruising along and the Australian pilot, with just his cockpit cover and fin poking through the cloud like a metallic shark, was able to take them unawares. Centring his gunsight on the starboard aircraft, he opened fire. Pieces flew off the starboard engine, which caught fire at once. The fighter-bomber dived straight into the clouds and was seen by Tony Gaze's wingman as it emerged below, on fire. It dived straight into the ground near Emmerich, with no sign of a parachute. This was '9K+NL', a machine of *I./KG(J)51*, flown by *Feldwebel* Richard Hoffmann who was killed. The other two Me262 pilots, now aware of the danger, opened up their throttles and accelerated away from the pursuing Spitfire pilot.[57]

At around the same time, a section of Typhoon pilots from 439 (RCAF) Squadron were flying near Coesfeld, on the German/Dutch border. The fighter-bombers had been engaged upon ground attacks below cloud and were re-forming at 7,000 feet when Flying Officer L.C.Shaver sighted two Me262s 4,000 feet below them. The German aircraft were carrying bombs and were

Into the Jet Age: February 1945

Above: Lyall Shaver (2nd from rt, half obscured) examines pieces of Me262 brought back in his aircraft. (M Peters)

probably the two survivors from Gaze's attack. Lyall Shaver's subsequent combat report read:

"I was leading a section of four aircraft of 439 Squadron on an armed recce in the Coesfeld-Enschede area. While flying west at 7,000 feet at approximately twenty miles from Coesfeld, I observed two Me262s line abreast flying west at 3,000 feet. I informed the other pilots and dove to attack. I came in line astern slightly below the enemy aircraft and opened fire with a short two-second burst at 100 yards. No strikes were observed. I raised my sights slightly, closed to 50 yards and again opened fire with a two-second burst. The enemy aircraft exploded in mid-air. I flew through the blast of the exploded aircraft and saw the other Me262 break off to port. I fired two two-second bursts from quarter position but did not observe any strikes. I then saw Red 3 (F/O Fraser) attacking from above and to the rear of the second enemy aircraft. Both the enemy aircraft and Red 3 disappeared below cloud, I observed a plume of black smoke bulging above cloud".

Hugh Fraser, flying as Red 3, will never forget that particular day:

"At 6,500 to 7,000 feet I was joining up on Lyall Shaver and our other two aircraft weren't yet visible. From memory I was coming up on his port side about 100 feet away and a couple of lengths behind. While we were looking for our own third and fourth aircraft we both spotted two Me262s break through the cloud cover climbing in the same direction (west) as we were headed. Lyall reported them on the R/T at 2 o'clock almost directly below us and ordered the attack. We turned over and dove down on them at sixty degrees angle or more. Halfway down they spotted us and broke down to port heading for the cloud cover about 1,500 feet below them. At 400 yards Lyall was abreast of me about 200 feet to starboard. The Me262s were also about 200 feet apart and the starboard aircraft was trailing the other one by 200 feet. We were doing over 500 mph and my aircraft was vibrating badly. I fired at the port aircraft and saw no hits. Lyall must have firing at the other one, which was now only 100 yards ahead of me and 200 feet to the right; we were closing on them very fast. I was firing again and at this moment Lyall's target exploded in a black cloud about 200 feet across. Later Lyall said he had flown through it and had picked up some pieces in his radiator. By now I was 100 yards from the other one, firing, and saw hits on the port wing and fuselage. My last burst was from 50 yards and the port engine came off and went by just under me, as well as a section of wing, which had folded up from the engine nacelle outward, came off, and went under me flat, not looking like much. I pulled up to avoid colliding with the Me262. The moment I pulled up we were into cloud, and out the bottom of it, a couple of seconds later, still in a 45 degree dive. I recovered and pulled up in a circle to 1,500 feet and saw the Me262 burst into flames as it hit the ground, without a ripple from any bomb it might have carried. When the one that Lyall got exploded neither of us saw anything at all come out of the far side of the black cloud, nor anything fall out underneath. We later figured that it had completely disintegrated.

"I then continued climbing still at about 400 mph up to 8,000 feet and the first thing I saw was the large black circular cloud left by the '262 that Lyall had destroyed and then I passed a parachute just above the cloud top with something burning at the harness end; not the pilot. We re-formed, just Lyall and I, and went home to Eindhoven. The armourer said I had only half a dozen round of ammo left. Also I had lost two wing access panels and the radio panel on the port side of the fuselage. At extremely high speed the aircraft was vibrating badly and crabbing sideways, which is why I wasn't hitting the '262, and why the hits finally were all on the port side. Firing the four cannons added to the vibration shaking the panels off. Lyall and I both figured we were fortunate that our own aircraft hadn't fallen apart while firing at over 500 mph as they were shaking so badly. The Typhoon vibrated a lot anyway, which is why camera guns never worked, the image on film looked like at least two aircraft in the picture. Ground crews gave up on them.

Right: Hugh Fraser, pictured after bringing down two FW190s on 1st January 1945.
(Public Archives of Canada)

"Everybody thought that the Me262 was the fastest and best aircraft anybody had in the air. The two we saw must have broken out of cloud climbing and doing about 400 mph to have reach 1,500 feet above cloud in half a minute or less and in the next minute or so they were both destroyed. Scary when you think about the logistics". [58]

In this, the first successful encounter between the big Typhoon fighter-bomber and the jets, both were confirmed from German records. *5./KG(J)51* reported the loss of two Me262s in this area, together with their pilots, *Leutnant* Hans-Georg Richter and *Feldwebel* Werner Witzmann. A little later, Typhoon pilots from 184 Squadron engaged Me262s near Arnhem, where Captain A F Green DFC of the South African Air Force claimed one damaged as it streaked past him. Initially this was claimed as the first such jet to be hit by Typhoons, but the honour had already gone to 439 Squadron just a little earlier. On this date also, Squadron Leader D C Fairbanks of 274 Squadron had his second encounter with a jet, this American Tempest pilot claiming one damaged over Rheine airfield.

Meanwhile the 8th Air Force had despatched a strong raid across northern Germany. Six jets of *III./JG 7*, accompanied by a couple from the newly-formed *I Gruppe*, engaged Fortresses between Lübeck and Neumünster, *Leutnant* Rademacher, *Unteroffizier* Schöppler and *Unteroffizier* Engler each claiming a B-17 destroyed. One Messerschmitt was shot down, the pilot baling out safely. Nine Fortresses failed to return from this raid. Mustang pilots of the 20th Fighter Group engaged Me262s near Stuttgart, one being claimed damaged by Captain J K Brown and Lieutenant K D McNeel. A fourth aircraft from *I./KG(J)51* was lost, the pilot baling out safely, while two machines from *II Gruppe* crashed on landing, all possibly as a result of the several engagements described above.

15th February, 1945
A jet kill was reported from the Eastern Front. Colonel Ivan Kozhedub of the Russian Red Air Force, the leading Red Air Force 'ace' and commander of the 176th Guards Fighter Air Regiment, patrolled along the battle front and spotted a movement over some pine woods. The aircraft was well camouflaged and would have escaped detection had it not been for snow on the ground. Kozhedub dived to investigate and identified it as an Me262, the first to be seen on the Eastern Front. He closed in, seeing the turbo-jets pour out black smoke as the German pilot opened up the throttles, but it was too late, for the Russian pilot in his Lavochkin La-7 was well within range. Cannon shells struck home and the jet scythed into some fir trees and exploded, giving the pilot no chance of survival.

One claim was submitted by the 8th Air Force, Lieutenant D M Amoss of the 55th Fighter Group claiming a jet shot down near Amberg at 12.15 hours. Two losses in action were reported by *I./KG(J)54*. One pilot, *Unteroffizier* Litzinger - apparently Amoss's opponent - baled out near Obergrasheim while on a training flight. A second machine force-landed at Mandelfeld. A third jet from this unit crashed near Giebelstadt, cause not known, killing *Unteroffizier* Kurt Lange.

16th February, 1945
Me262s of *III./JG 7* rose to engage ten-fifteen Mustangs over Hannover. In this combat *Leutnant* Rademacher claimed a P-51 destroyed. His opponent was a 325th Fighter Group aircraft flown by 1st Lieutenant B T Crosby, who was killed in the crash. During the course of the day, Mustang pilots of the 339th Fighter Group reported a fight with jets. No claims were submitted, but the aircraft flown by Flight Officer Cohen was shot-up and he crash-landed at base.

III./KG(J)54 sustained three Me262s damaged during an Allied fighter-bomber attack on Neuburg airfield and another was strafed and destroyed at Obertraubling.

17th - 19th February, 1945
I./KG(J)54 reported losing a jet to fighters, *Oberleutnant* Franz

Major Theodor Weissenberger, reported wounded on 19th February, was possibly involved against A-26 Invaders of the 386th Bomb Group. (via ARP)

Theeg being killed near Wolkshausen, The only Allied claims involved P-47s of the 365th Fighter Group, Lieutenants T B Westbrook and C E Buchanan each claiming an Me262 damaged east of Würzburg, the latter credited as 'unconfirmed'. *Stab./JG 7* recorded a casualty on February 19th, although it is more likely to have been a day earlier, *Major* Theodor Weissenberger force-landing slightly wounded following an attack upon Fortresses. However, the 386th Bomb Group of the 9th Air Force had recently exchanged its B-26 Marauders for A-26 Invaders and, on the 19th, Major Myron L Durkee out-turned an attacking '262 and claimed it probably destroyed - which may have been Weissenberger.

21st February, 1945

III./JG 7 took on American fighters near Berlin and although no successes were claimed, demonstrated a high degree of skill and tenacity. At 11.30 hours, P-51s of the 479th Fighter Group were attacked and the American group leader reported:

"We were flying in an easterly direction when we were 'bounced' from the three o'clock position by four Me262s. Our flight broke into the jets, which crossed in front of us, going straight up and away. At that moment four more came in at us from above and to our rear. We again turned into them and they broke away in a high speed climb. The first flight of jets then came at us again and once more we turned into them. This was repeated again and again by the German pilots 'til 1210 hours when the jets broke off combat. Other P-51s in the area were also attacked by two other jet flights of four aircraft, each in much the same fashion. No aircraft were lost as neither us or the German pilots could get into a firing position. The German pilots in both actions were aggressive and experienced; they made sure they were not caught in a turn. If they did get into such a position, they rolled out and climbed away. We found it impossible to climb with them and used much fuel trying. Action finished up around 25,000 feet". [59]

One Me262 of *II./KG(J)51* flown by *Oberfähnrich* Gerhard Rohde was lost on this date however, Lieutenant H E Whitmore of the 356th Fighter Group claiming an Me262 destroyed near Stettin at 15.30 hours while on escort to a photo-recce aircraft. The German aircraft had made a pass at the F-5, but passed directly in front of the Mustangs flown by Whitmore and Lieutenant Russell H Webb, the latter firing but claiming no hits before Whitmore fired two bursts from 400 yards, blowing the jet up. An engagement was also reported by an RAF Spitfire pilot when Flight Lieutenant L A Stewart of 412 (RCAF) Squadron attacked a jet, saw black smoke plume from one engine and claimed it damaged before his target accelerated away. Finally, an F-5E of the 7th Photo Recce Group was reported missing, believed to have fallen victim to an Me262.

Giebelstadt airfield was again strafed by American fighters and two Me262s from *I./KG(J)54* were damaged.

22nd February, 1945

The Allies despatched more than 3,000 combat aircraft in support of *Operation Clarion*. Some fifty jets, operating in small formations, were seen again by American escort fighters over central Germany when Me262s from *III./JG 7* at Parchim attacked near the target areas of Salzwedel and Ludwigslust; they were driven off, only one B-17 being lost:

> "The 20th Fighter Group led by Major Robert J Meyer (A Group) and Major Merle B Nichols (B Group) escorted three combat groups of 1st Air Division B-17s from the Zuider Zee to the targets at Salzwedel and Ludwigslust and back to the German-Holland border. Escort was uneventful except for five Me262 twin-jet planes, which were seen in the target area and driven away from the bombers. Major Meyer (79th Squadron) chased one to the deck but was outdistanced and couldn't get close enough to hit it. Captain Ronald K Howard (55th Squadron) turned into another with his flight and got some strikes before the jet job ran away". 60.

Howard was credited with a ·damaged'.

III./JG 7 had put up 34 Me262s on this day. *Oberfeldwebel* Hermann Buchner and *Oberfähnrich* Heinz Russel discovered a B-17 formation near Stendal, but as they prepared to attack they sighted escorting Mustangs of the 352nd, 363rd and 364th Fighter Groups. The 364th Fighter Group had 61 P-51s airborne on escort duties and these were in a position to interfere with the attack; Buchner quickly changed his plan and swept in on

Francis X Radley, a Mustang pilot from the 364th Fighter Group. He was killed in action on 22nd February during an attack by Hermann Buchner.. (L Rasse via H Buchner)

the fighters instead, coming in fast behind Lieutenant Cliff Hogan's section and shooting down the aircraft flown by Lieutenant Francis X Radley. Hogan reported:

"At approximately 12.15 our Squadron was heading 40 degrees to intercept the bombers. We had just rolled out of a turn when two bogies were called in at three o'clock in the sun. I checked my flight's position and, finding it good, looked into the sun. Then I was looking back to my left, seeing Radley's ship on fire and the Me262 in range and with its nose pointed at me. I called a break to the whole squadron. The Me262 passed under me, I made a turn and came back in.". [61.]

Radley's Mustang was last seen spinning down in flames at 10,000 feet and with the canopy still in place. The 364th lost two further Mustangs, possibly to jets. Lieutenant Frederic Ross was captured and Lieutenant Edward Kortendick was killed. Pilots of the 352nd Fighter Group saw four '262s hit the bombers, shooting down two Fortresses.

Captain S C Phillips and Lieutenants G O Warner and S J Price of the 364th each claimed a jet damaged in this combat - Price's opponent having just destroyed a B-17. Major E D Duncan and Lieutenant C E Goodman of the 352nd and Lieutenants R L Hunt, W E Randolph, L H Phipps and L L Lefforge of the 363rd were also credited with jet 'kills'. A little later Lieutenant C B Kirby of the latter unit claimed a 'probable' near Wittstock. In other combats, *Oberleutnant* Günther Wegmann claimed a P-51, which was not confirmed, *Unteroffizier* Hermann Nötter two B-17s and *Leutnant* Hans

Waldmann, of *9 Staffel*, claimed the destruction of two Mustangs. One B-17 that definitely fell to a jet fighter was from the 398th Bomb Group. It crashed near Altendorf, Thuringia.

The 353rd Fighter Group flew a free-lance patrol to Berlin and were warned of jet activity near Brandenburg. When northeast of the city, Major Wayne K Blickenstaff's Mustangs met four Me262s, Blickenstaff chasing one that broke to the southwest and took the Mustang right over Berlin. Then another '262 was seen below and Blickenstaff abandoned his first quarry and dived upon the newcomer, but this was quickly lost in the haze. He climbed to 8,000 feet heading northwest and then sighted a third Me262, flying east. Managing to close on it, he opened fire; after wild evasive action the jet slowed up, taking more hits before the pilot baled out. Meanwhile Captain Gordon B Compton had attacked the fourth jet in the original formation, which burst into flames; this German pilot also took to his parachute. Other claims by 8th Air Force Fighter Groups on this date were: Lieutenant Charles D Price of the 352nd one near Wahrenholz and Captain R W Stevens and Lieutenant Clarence B Kirby of the 364th Fighter Group, one shared near Wittstock. *Oberfeldwebel* Helmut Baudach of *10./JG 7*, one of the original *Erprobungskommando 262* jet pilots, was shot down near Schönwalde/Niederbarin. He baled out, but struck his head on the tail unit and subsequently died of his injuries. Several further *JG 7* jets were lost; of the *Geschwaderstab*, *Unteroffizier* Nötter belly-landed near Stade and a second jet was shot down in this area, the pilot baling our. In addition to the loss of *Oberfeldwebel* Mattuschka of *III./JG 7*, who baled out near Hagenow, another pilot crashed near Döberitz, after engine failure, and was killed, while a fourth was shot down near Lärz, the pilot baling out. Two more force-landed with battle damage, one at Oranienburg and the other at Lärz. Additionally, one *I./JG 7* aircraft force-landed at Kaltenkirchen with battle damage. These high losses had been suffered for relatively little gain, for only three B-17s were lost, although twenty-two Mustangs failed to return.

Meanwhile, P-47 Thunderbolts of the 365th Fighter Group, 9th Air Force, flying close-support sorties from Metz, were having their own 'jet party' near Aachen, where Me262

Into the Jet Age: February 1945

A fine shot of an Me262 fighter-bomber, probably from KG(J)51, showing clearly the underslung bomb load. The sighting arrangement was primitive, however, causing the effects of an attack to be more a matter of luck and experience than to technical invention. (via ARP)

fighter-bombers were strafing American troops on the Düren highway close to the German-Belgian frontier. P-47s of the 388th Squadron arrived on the scene at 5,000 feet to find two of the Rheine-based *KG(J)51* jets attacking the troops. The American pilots put their Thunderbolts into steep dives and flames spurted from the jet engines as Leutnant Kurt Piehl began to pull away from Red Flight. Lieutenant Oliven T Cowan, leading White Flight, reported:

> "When the jet started to pull away from Red Flight, I took my Number Two, leaving Three and Four as top cover, and started down. I pushed everything forward and went down with water injection. At Approximately 5,000 feet we were doing 530 miles per hour. I do not believe the jet pilot saw me until too late. I shallowed my dive, pulled my nose through and gave him a burst from my guns. He then dropped out of my sight at 300 feet." [62]

Cowan dropped the nose of his Thunderbolt and watched the big puff of smoke as the Messerschmitt hit the ground; Piehl was killed. The other P-47s pursued the second, but failed to catch it. While the 365th Fighter Group were so engaged, P-47s of the 48th Fighter Group were bounced by three Me262s near Wittstock. No Thunderbolts were hit and the jets pulled away after Captain M F Mason had claimed strikes on one of them. A little later Thunderbolts of the 366th Fighter Group sighted another fighter-bomber near Aachen, which was claimed shot down by Lieutenant D B Fox. A final claim was made by a reconnaissance Mustang pilot, Lieutenant W A Grusy of the 361st Recon Squadron reported damaging an Me262 near Jülich at an unrecorded time. One German loss was 'B3+GS' of *8./KG(J)54*; *Obergefreiter* Jurgen Brink died when his Me262 was shot down by a fighter near Landsberg.

Jagdverbände 44 had begun to form at Brandenburg/Briest, near Berlin on February 22nd, initially taking over FW190s from *IV./JG 54* prior to receiving the first jets. One *Staffel* of FW190Ds, commanded by *Leutnant* Sachsenberg, was retained for local air defence. Johannes Steinhoff had at once volunteered for Galland's unit as did Günther Lützow. Quickly many of the top aces were clamouring to join him, some coming from hospital with wounds yet unhealed; Galland welcomed them all. Although realising that the end of the Third Reich was but weeks away, they were all determined to demonstrate to everyone - and particularly their own High Command - just what a small group of expert fighter pilots could do when equipped with the most formidable fighting aircraft in the world. It soon became a standing joke that the 'badge' of *JV 44* was now the *Ritterkreuz*.

Conversion to the Me262s began quickly, but few jets were available; indeed, the unit could seldom muster more than fifteen Me262s when fully operational. Apart from the 'aces', there were some volunteers with no combat experience at all. One such pilot, *Leutnant* Blömert, had come straight from flying school, having been trained on Ju88 bombers. He was selected by Steinhoff for a training sortie towards the Russian Front in mid-February. Blömert was briefed on the sortie: 'We will most probably meet Russian fighters. Do as I do', ordered Steinhoff and they climbed into their sleek fighters.

Soon they were airborne, sweeping around Berlin and heading north towards the River Oder, where a ferocious land battle was underway. Steinhoff lost height to observe the ground situation, when suddenly a Russian Yak fighter slid across the sky in front of them, so close that Steinhoff almost rammed it. He climbed hard to position himself for an attack, but on glancing behind, saw another Yak coming up behind,

Johannes 'Macki' Steinhoff served with JG 26, JG 52, JG 77, JG 7 and JV 44. He was credited with 176 victories including six with JV 44, won the Eichenlaub and Schwerter and later rose to the rank of General with the new Federal German Luftwaffe, serving with distinction at NATO headquarters. He has recently died.

cannon blazing. Steinhoff continued his climb, shaking off the Russian with ease and looked around for Blömert - but sighted instead a gaggle of Russian fighters. These had either seen the '262s or had been warned, for they were taking constant evasive action. Steinhoff decided to withdraw and then make a high-speed surprise attack when he spotted Blömert low and to port. Moving into the eye of sun, Steinhoff opened his throttles and dived, building up speed rapidly and opening fire on one of the Yaks, but the vigilant Russians broke in all directions as the jet sped through them. Down to 3,000 feet, Steinhoff abandoned all hope of destroying one of the agile fighters and headed back across the Oder, sighting a flight of heavily armoured Ilyushin Il-2 *Shturmovik* ground attack aircraft strafing and dive-bombing German troops on the Berlin-Frankfurt autobahn. Blömert slid into line astern formation and the two jets dived on their opponents, opening fire in turn on the rearmost bomber. The Il-2, normally notoriously difficult to shoot down, offered little resistance to the 30mm cannon fire however. It glided downwards leaving a thick black smoke trail, finally bellying in on the deep snow beside the autobahn. As the two jets flew over, the German pilots saw one of the Russian crew scramble from the wreckage and run for dear life towards nearby woods. With fuel getting low, Steinhoff led Blömert home, both landing safely after their eventful training flight.[63]

23rd - 24th February, 1945

On February 23rd, RAF Mustangs were in action over northern Germany whilst escorting Bomber Command aircraft on *Ramrod 1474*, a claim for an Me262 damaged being submitted by Warrant Officer H A Pietrzak of 309 (Polish) Squadron. The 55th Fighter Group also reported a fight, during which 1st Lieutenant Thomas M Love's Mustang was hit and he crash-landed near Oldenburg to become a prisoner.

During the day, Neuburg airfield was strafed. One jet from *III./KG(J)54* was destroyed and five more were damaged.

Next day *III./JG 7* pilots reported an engagement with American bombers, in which a B-17 and a Mustang were claimed destroyed by *Leutnants* Rademacher and Weber respectively; one B-17 of the 94th Bomb Group failed to return, as did ten Mustangs.

Meanwhile, 274 Squadron Tempests flew a 'Rat Catching' patrol to Rheine, where Flight Lieutenant R C Kennedy attacked and damaged an aircraft of *II./KG(J)51*. The severity of the *Flak* prevented the Tempests from inflicting further damage.

25th February, 1945

This day was to prove a black day for the German jet units. Thunderbolts of the 365th Fighter Group, 9th Air Force, had been ordered to seek out ground targets near Köln and at 08.40 hours, Lieutenant John H Rodgers (leading a flight from the 386th Squadron) sighted a formation of sixteen Me262s near Düren. The jets were at 11,000 feet, some way below the Thunderbolts and heading east. Apparently these aircraft were from *KG(J)51* operating out of Rheine/Hopsten. The jet pilots clearly saw the Thunderbolts approaching and immediately made a half-turn, opening up their throttles and heading back west. With a bomb slung beneath each wing, the P-47s stood no chance of catching them in a dive and Rodgers ordered his pilots to maintain course. A few minutes later, Lieutenant Longo reported a loss of power and was ordered home, but as he crossed the Ruhr river an Me262 suddenly appeared on his starboard quarter, coming at him with cannon blazing. Longo broke hard to port, away from the attack - against the established principles of air fighting. In this case his tactics

Into the Jet Age: February 1945

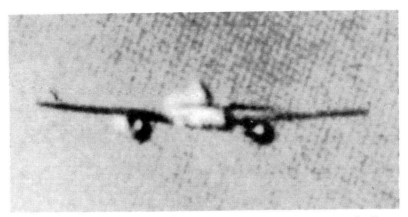

This Me262 pilot foolishly allowed his speed to drop in a shallow climb, allowing an American pilot to close in for the kill. (USAF)

proved correct, for the jet fighter overshot and he was left in a perfect position for a quick shot. He fired a long burst, seeing pieces fly off before the jet fighter stood on its tail and rocketed up into the clouds. Longo returned home to Metz without further incident, but said, 'I kept looking over my shoulder all the the rest of the way home!'

Curiously, Longo is officially credited with three Me262s 'unconfirmed damaged' on this date.

Meanwhile Rodgers' depleted flight had continued their outward journey, but within a few minutes they too were attacked by Me262s. Bombs were jettisoned as the P-47s broke wildly. Lieutenant J L McWhorter spotted two jets closing on him from astern and used his superior rate of turn to change the situation into a head-on attack, seeing strikes on both before they passed him, too fast to catch. Like Longo, McWhorter is credited with two 'unconfirmed damaged'.

The Thunderbolts reformed and headed for home. An Me262 was sighted low down over the Allied positions, but this flew off before the American pilots could intervene. Shortly afterwards three more were seen, turning below them over Düren. Captain C Ready and Lieutenant L Freeman managed to get close enough open fire, each claiming strikes as the jets accelerated away, the one attacked by Freeman leaving a smoke trail. When they were but specks in the distance a violent mid-air explosion was seen, indicating the possibility that the damaged jet fighter had blown up. Both pilots were credited with an 'unconfirmed damaged'. For the third and last time this flight spotted more jets, two of which were seen strafing Allied troops, but again they left the scene at high speed before the P-47s could engage.

Aircraft of the 366th Fighter Group, 9th Air Force, twice encountered two jets on separate sorties; at 10.20 hours two were claimed damaged near Gladbach by Lieutenants M R Paisley and J T Picton. Meanwhile P-47s of the 405th met Me262s east of Erkelen, Captain R W Yothers claiming one damaged at 10.40 hours. The last 9th Air Force engagement occurred ten minutes later, when P-47s of the 373rd Fighter Group engaged jets between Linnich and Jülich, Lieutenants E P Gardner claimed one damaged and Lieutenant D D A Duncan reported hits on two more.

In the late morning the P-51s of the 4th Fighter Group flew a strafing mission near Leipzig. Lieutenant Carl G Payne of the 334th Squadron reported:

> "We were ten minutes southwest of Leipzig at 8,000 feet, when I spotted a Me262 at about 4,000 feet at our one o'clock. I peeled off on him, calling in at the same time. I closed to about 400 yards and opened fire, holding it until about 100 yards. I hit him and knocked out his left jet."

Lieutenant Arthur A Bowers had followed Payne and, when the latter overshot and turned for another pass, Bowers opened fire:

> "I slipped in behind him and began firing short bursts for about two miles, but I was excited and it was the first jet I'd seen and my sights were set wrong; I was shooting too far in front and missing".

Payne saw his companion's error and bored in again:

> "On my next pass I was not hitting him as I should, so I moved up to 10 to 30 feet behind him and began firing. He exploded and covered me completely with flames. This jet flew darned fast even on one unit and the pilot hugged the contours of the ground. But all the time his starboard unit kept pulling him in a gradual right bank." [64]

It is likely that his opponent was *Oberleutnant* Josef Bohm of *III./EJG 2*, shot down and killed near Debendorf.

The Mustang pilots reformed and carried out their airfield strafe at Rohrensee, near Dessau, where six conventional aircraft were destroyed. After a strange encounter with FW190s that formated on them instead of attacking, brought their

Into the Jet Age: February 1945

Pilots of the 4th Fighter Group pictured after the 25th February mission (l to r) Lieutenants Carl G Payne, Gordon A Denson, Arthur R Bowers and Captain Thomas R Bell. Payne was credited with an Me262 shot down, probably a III./EJG 2 fighter. Apart from the jet, these pilots claimed a further six aircraft destroyed by strafing Rohrensee airfield. (via S E Harvey)

fighters safely back to Debden where they found that their air and ground claims had brought the score of the 'Debden Eagles' to 800.

Meanwhile, sixteen Me262s of *I* and *II./KG(J)54* began a mission with their new jets, taking off from Giebelstadt and climbing through the thick clouds to emerge below the P-51s of the 55th Fighter Group. The result was again a disaster. Captain Donald O Penn ordered, 'Drop tanks and engage!' Instantly the air was filled with diving Mustangs, dropping like hawks upon the inexperienced jet pilots below. Penn, diving at 500 mph, closed on one Me262 obviously trying to get back to the airfield, which was now plainly in view. The jet was making a shallow turn to port with its wheels down as Penn closed to 300 yards, opened fire and watched it roll onto its back and dive into the ground. Meanwhile Captain Donald M Cummings and Lieutenants Milliard O Anderson, Donald T Menegy, John F

O'Neil and Billy Clemmons had each accounted for a jet. A few minutes later, Cummings caught another *KG(J)54* jet on the landing approach and destroyed this to become the second American pilot to shoot down two Me262s in a single action. In total, six Me262s were lost in this battle, against American claims for seven; those flown by *Leutnants* Hans-Georg Knobel (B3+AN), Josef Lackner (B3+BN) and *Feldwebel* Heinz Clausner (B3+DP) of 5 *Staffel* were all shot down and the pilots killed. In *I Gruppe, Feldwebel* Felix Einhardt was killed, *Leutnant* Wolf Zimmermann baled out wounded and a third pilot was shot down on approach to Giebelstadt - probably by Cummings - and crash-landed on the airfield. A further five Me262s were destroyed and three damaged at Giebelstadt later in the day by strafing American fighters and two more were lost in accidents; the *Gruppe* never recovered from this blow. At this time a new *Kommandeur, Major* Hans-Georg Baetcher, was appointed to take over *III./KG(J)54*, arriving to discover that his unit had only twenty Me262s left.

Meanwhile two engagements were reported by RAF Spitfire units, Flight Lieutenants K S Sleep and B E Innes of 402 (RCAF) Squadron claimed damage to an Me262, while Pilot Officer L E Spurr of 416 (RCAF) Squadron got strikes on another before it escaped.

27th - 28th February, 1945
Leutnant Rademacher of *III./JG 7* reported further success when the American 'heavies' attacked Halle and Leipzig, being credited with the destruction of a B-24 Liberator, one of the six reported missing on this date. Next day (28th) the 78th Fighter Group patrolled over the Hersfeld-Fulda area, where Lieutenants Wayne F Bechtelheimer and James E Parker jointly claimed an Me262 damaged.

The situation regarding supply of jet aircraft to the units was now becoming increasingly severe; the German aircraft industry was naturally one of the prime targets for Allied air attack and during the month at least one hundred Me262s had been destroyed either on the production lines or whilst in transit by rail or road. March would prove to be worse, yet the jet pilots of the *Luftwaffe* would still show to the world what 'might have been'.

Notes

56.	Correspondence Rudolf Sinner - John Foreman
57.	Australian War Memorial records.
58.	Lyall Shaver's Combat Report and the personal account from correspondence Hugh Fraser - John Foreman.
59.	*The Mighty Eighth*, by Roger A Freeman.
60.	Correspondence Paul C Roberts MD (flight surgeon 20th FG) - S E Harvey
61.	Cliff Hogan's Personal Encounter report supplied by Hermann Buchner.
62.	*The 9th Air Force*, by Kenn C Rust.
63.	*Im Letzter Stunde*, by Johannes Steinhoff.
64.	Correspondence Col Gordon Denson USAF Retd - S E Harvey.

Chapter Seven
Jet Crescendo: March 1945

1st March, 1945
American fighters flew large scale sweeps across Germany in the early afternoon. Near Ingolstadt, Mustang pilots Lieutenants John K Wilkins and Wendall W Beaty of the 355th Fighter Group shot down two Me262s of *I./KG(J)54*. *Leutnant* Hans-Peter Haberle crashed to his death south of Giebelstadt while *Feldwebel* Josef Herbeck fell east of Treuchtlingen, also losing his life. In the same general area Major F B Elliott and Captain C W Getz III of the 2nd Scouting Force each claimed a 'damaged', while at the same time Major H H Kirby of the 355th Fighter Group claimed another damaged near Donauwörth. Two American Mustangs were lost to the jets; Captain J H Beckmann of the 355th crashed near Neuburg, while Flight Officer W W Montague became one of the few victims to *I./KG(J)54*. His P-51 crashed near Wertheim at 15.45 hours. Both American pilots were killed. A second victory to *KG(J)54* was credited as a B-17 near Treuchtlingen and was possibly claimed by Herbeck.

2nd March, 1945
The Thunderbolts of the 365th Fighter Group, having recently moved from Metz to Florennes/Juzaine airfield in Belgium, met their old adversaries *KG(J)51* over northwest Germany. In all, four attacks were made upon the Thunderbolts during the mornings' dive-bombing operations; at 10.05 hours Lieutenant Archie F Maltbie's flight (388th Squadron) was bounced from astern by three jets, forcing the P-47s to jettison their bombs and abandon the sortie. Ten minutes later a flight led by Captain Russell L Gardner (387th Squadron) was still over Belgium at 9,000 feet when a lone Me262 dived straight through the formation and disappeared. At 10.20 hours Lieutenant Warren J Jahnke's flight (387th Squadron) was bounced

when climbing away from their target, a factory at Niederhausen. Again no American aircraft were hit and the lone jet made no attempt to re-engage. Finally at 11.05 hours, Lieutenant Robert Rollo (386th Squadron) was reforming his flight after bombing railway yards at Gladbach when a pair of Me262s were sighted over Köln. The jets were 4,000 feet below, coming up at them fast, Rollo ordered his pilots to attack, but the Me262s broke away, heading back across the city. After a few minutes Rollo ordered the chase to be abandoned, saying later, 'It was like rhinos chasing gazelles'. It seems from these events that the bomber pilots of *KG(J)51* were now mastering their machines and were becoming increasingly willing to engage American fighters as 'targets of opportunity' once their bombing sorties had been completed. The jet unit lost one Me262, *Hauptmann* Fritz Abel, *Kapitän* of *5 Staffel*, being shot down and killed near Nijmegen. It seems that he was engaged by a Mustang of the 107th Recon Squadron, west of Köln at 10.15 hours, and his aircraft was claimed probably destroyed by Lieutenant F T Dunmire.

The 354th Fighter Group (9th Air Force) was at this time flying Mustangs from Meuthe-et-Moselle, France. Captain Bruno Peters, Lieutenant Theodore Sedvert and Flight Officer Ralph Delgado from this unit sighted four Me262s near Kassel while on a mission over the front. Giving chase they each reported the destruction of one Messerschmitt, but only Peters' claim was allowed - as an 'unconfirmed destroyed'. *I./KG(J)54* sustained two known casualties. *Feldwebel* Günther Gorlitz baled out and *Feldwebel* Heinrich Griem was reported missing after an action near Würzburg. Both these events occurred at around 12.35 hours. A further claim for an Me262 damaged was submitted by Lieutenant F T O'Connor of the 364th Fighter Group, fifteen miles northeast of Frankfurt. One further Me262, from *I.(E)/KG(J)*, was shot down by a fighter near Dillingen. *Oberfähnrich* Horst Metzbrand was killed.

3rd March, 1945
Action began to 'hot up', when *III./JG 7* despatched 26 Me262s to oppose American heavy bombers attacking Magdeburg, Hannover, Hildesheim, Brunswick and other minor targets. The B-17s of the 493rd Bomb Group, targetted on Hildesheim, were

Jet Crescendo: March 1945

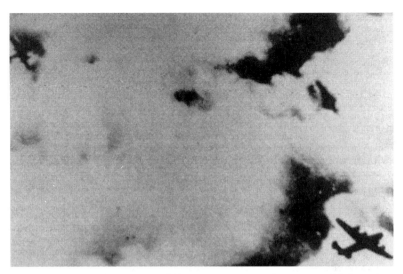

High over Germany, a lone Liberator, apparently separated from its combat box, become the target for an Me262 (top right corner). (USAF)

intercepted just south of Hannover as they began their run-up to the target. *Umbri'ago*, flown by Lieutenant Wayne E Dorsett, was in the thick of it; the toggelier (non-commissioned bomb-aimer) on this flight was Staff Sergeant Lawrence B Bird, who recalled:

"We were around 21,000 feet altitude. After checking my bombardier panel, I started to keep my eye on the lead plane ready to drop my bombs when he dropped his. Moderate Flak was bursting ahead of us. Suddenly three black sleek-looking planes with underslung engines on their wings appeared in front of me at 11 o'clock, attacking head-on in what appeared to be a 'company front' attack. As they whizzed by I saw white crosses on their fuselages (this all happened in seconds). I recall catching a quick glimpse under our No 1 and 2 engines of the Fort' on our left falling away with a large flame. Just as this was happening, our co-pilot shouted over the inter-phone, 'Bandits! Bandits! We're under attack!' While this was going on, all four of our engines 'ran away' from us. Simultaneously we were attacked by three Me109s from our right front, which made a fast pass at us. Our pilot manoeuvred out of formation, which made us easy prey for enemy fighters. In all this confusion I managed to release our bombs with our Squadron (863rd) when they dropped theirs up ahead.

"In the meanwhile, the jets disappeared behind us. Our pilot got the plane under control and we were trying to catch up with our Squadron, but as we were nearing the Squadron one '262 came in on our tail out of the sun. Again our guns rattled....." 23.

Technical Sergeant Paul F Sink was the tail gunner in Dorsett's B-17 and also remembered that day well:

"At 10.30 hours, we were attacked by three Me262 jets over Hannover.... the leader passed within 25 feet of my position in the tail of our B-17 and I saw them pass at speed through our low Squadron of B-17s, a few thousand feet below us. We were at the same time being attacked by German piston-engined fighters. The Me262s returned and flew a course just out of range, to our right for about 1,500 yards, then they came back through our Squadron from the front in a firing pass. Two made a 180 degree turn as they passed our B-17 - the last in the flight - and the other kept going away at speed. I opened fire on what I thought was their flight leader from 750 yards range as he closed; the jet exploded in mid-air and, a few seconds later, the second jet also exploded, having been hit by fire from a B- 17 to my left. Later I heard that they had shot down two of our Squadron's B-17s as they passed them head-on. I also found out later that it was Carl V Eneff, the top turret gunner of the other Fortress who had hit the second jet." 66.

Larry Bird continued the story:

"When we pulled up into our squadron we noticed another B-17 pulling up to the right of us with its left wing smoking. Suddenly the wing burst into flames; the pilot dropped his ship out of formation, did some dips and dives to try to fan the flames out, but suddenly the whole plane burst into flames and disappeared into a cloudbank below. Each man kept a sharp vigilance over his section of sky, the bomber in front of us had lost its left stabiliser. The enemy fighters had all disappeared. The enemy fighters had flown through their own Flak to reach us and must have been very desperate. I respect their bravery. During this mission we had been 'C' Squadron - last Squadron of the Group over the target."

On the way back Bird wondered why the American escorts had been absent during this action, but discovered that the Mustangs, sweeping ahead, had broken up a large formation of *Luftwaffe* fighters some miles away. The relative handful of jets and Bf109s that had been engaged were the few that had broken through. Apart from the two 493rd Bomb Group Fortresses mentioned above, the 95th, 100th and 487th Bomb Groups each lost one B-17 to fighters during these raids. The 487th Bomb Group aircraft was 43-39108 flown 2nd Lieutenant H E Webb Jr and was attacked by a '262 over the target. Nos. 1 and 2 engines were hit and began to 'windmill', the aircraft dropping out of formation and losing height. The bombs were dropped at 8,000 feet and Webb headed west, with an escorting

Mustang. An hour later, a fire broke out in the cockpit and Webb ordered the crew to bale out. Four jumped at once and Webb and the remainder finally baled out over the front lines, the bomber crashing between Wesel and Köln. Additionally, two B-17s from the 452nd Bomb Group were heavily damaged by Me262s but managed to get back.

B-24s were also engaged by jets near Rathenow, two bombers from the 448th Bomb Group colliding whilst taking evasive action (one hit by 30mm cannon fire) and a further two from the 445th Bomb Group were shot down.

The first attacks were delivered by *9 Staffel* of *JG 7*, which stormed into the bomber stream between Braunschweig and Magdeburg. Four B-17s were claimed in this area, by *Hauptmann* Gutmann, *Oberfeldwebel* Lennartz, Oberfähnrich Russel and *Leutnant* Schnörrer, while *Oberleutnant* Wegmann claimed a Liberator and a Mustang. *Oberfeldwebel* Hermann Buchner remembered:

"I flew as a *Schwarmführer*. *Hauptmann* Gutmann was on my right side as we attacked the bomber formation in line astern formation at about 6 - 7,000 metres altitude. We broke through the fighter escorts but then found ourselves under massive defensive fire from the turret gunners aboard the bombers. When we were about 1,000 metres from the bombers Gutmann's cockpit flashed with fire and his fighter sheered away from our formation and dived away vertically. I think that he must have been killed outright, anyway he did not attempt to bale out." [67]

Stab, 10 and *11./JG 7* then attacked near Magdeburg, harrying the bombers as far as Berlin. *Major* Sinner saw a combat box of Liberators. He later wrote:

"After judging the tactical situation, I attacked with my wingman *Leutnant* Müller and we made a head-on pass. After a short burst at around 800 metres with my four MK.108 cannon using mainly incendiary shells, I had great difficulty getting through the bomber formation without hitting any of them. I did see a flash on the wing of my B-24, near the fuselage. Müller was certain that he had missed his target.

"I reported this combat to *1 Jagddivision*, without believing that I had been successful. After a few days, Müller and I received notification from *1 Jagddivision* concerning the destruction of two B-24s. A *Flak* battery had seen the fight and had seen two Liberators crash. A few men from the aircrews were taken prisoner. After the war I received the MACR (Missing Aircrew Report) from friends in the USA and it brought additional information. The B-24 that I hit rammed another 'plane from the formation. Only one of the crew members reported that this event had been brought

Rudolf Sinner's combat on 3rd March shows the sheer speed of jet combat. He brought down two Liberators, but was too busy avoiding collisions to see them. (via ARP)

about by a jet attack." [68.]

His targets had been the combat box of Liberators of the 448th Bomb Group, attacked near Rathenow (noted above). *Oberfeldwebel* Heinz Arnold accounted for a Fortress and a Thunderbolt.

American fighter pilots were able to make six claims for Me262s damaged during these missions. Captains J L Sublett and I L Maguire of the 357th Fighter Group claimed one near Magdeburg and the second near Brunswick respectively. Colonel E W Stewart of the 4th Fighter Group claimed another near Gardelegen and Lieutenants R G Johnson, W S Lyons and J E Frye of the 355th Fighter Group each made a claim in a running fight between Brunswick and Hamburg. One 78th Fighter Group pilot, Lieutenant Marvin C Bigelow, had a disappointing engagement whilst escorting B-17s. He was flying an old P-51B and gave chase to one of several attacking Me262s, following it down in a high speed dive from 20,000 feet. Although his airspeed reached almost 600 mph he could not close to firing range. Pulling out of the dive with the wings 'shaking like a wet puppy' he discovered that the Mustang was in a bad way and found difficulty keeping it airborne. He managed to return and landed safely, but subsequent inspection by the ground staff found it to be 'Category E' - fit only for scrap.

During the course of the jet interceptions, twenty pilots from *III./JG* 7 had reported *Feindberührung* (contact with enemy units) and a total of seven heavy bombers and two escort

Pierre Clostermann of 274 Squadron discovered that, even with one engine functioning, the Me262 could outrun a Tempest.

fighters were claimed shot down. The US units admitted the loss of six fighters and seven bombers. In addition to Gutmann's loss, five more jets were shot down, but no further details are known.

439 Squadron sent Typhoons out to attack the Wesel-Haldern line, where a couple of Me262 were sighted. Flying Officer Hugh Fraser, who had become the second Typhoon pilot to destroy a '262 on February 14th, was keen for further action. He was disappointed, recording, 'Two jets followed us home from Wesel. No joy'. [69.]

7th March, 1945

The Allies had gained an important foothold in Germany when the Ludendorff Rail Bridge at Remagen was taken almost intact by the US 9th Armoured Division after desperate hand-to-hand fighting. The Germans had attempted to destroy this vital river crossing in the early hours of the morning, but the explosive charges had been sufficient only to damage it; the *Luftwaffe* was given the task of completing the destruction. American engineers were already on the bridge, clearing debris and strengthening it for the passage of tanks, when eight Ar234B jet bombers from *KG 76* attacked, covered by thirty Me262s believed to have been from *I./KG(J)51*. RAF Tempests of 274 Squadron, sweeping the area, broke up the main attack. Flight Lieutenant P H Clostermann found an Me262 just north of the bridgehead and opened up the big Sabre engine to get in close. He made a firing pass from astern, seeing his 20mm cannon score hits on the port engine, from which black smoke poured, then watched in disbelief as the German pilot opened up his starboard engine and steadily accelerated away from the

Tempest.[70.]

Jets from *III./JG 7* scrambled from Briest at 13.04 hours, *Major* Rudi Sinner finding a Mustang formation near Jüterbog airfield. He attacked and claimed a P-51 shot down in flames. Meanwhile, *Oberfeldwebel* Heinz Arnold increased his personal tally to three by claiming a P-51 near Wittenberge. One P-51 from the 7th Photo Recce Group failed to return.

9th March, 1945

JG 7 lost one of its 'old hands' when *Oberfähnrich* Heinz Russel scrambled to intercept a reconnaissance aircraft over Kiel Bay, he reported 'enemy contact', but radio contact was abruptly lost and he failed to return. His aircraft is presumed to have crashed into the sea near Laaland Island, but the cause remains a mystery, for no Allied claim has been traced. Russel was, however, credited with a confirmed victory. A 541 Squadron reconnaissance Spitfire failed to return from a sortie during the day and it is possible that Russel had collided with it while attacking. No trace of RM631 or its pilot, Flight Lieutenant Platts, was ever found.

One Allied crew did report an engagement in this area when a photo-recce Mosquito (MM283) was chased by three jets over Peenemünde, but escaped into clouds. Another jet pilot, *Hauptmann* Engleder of *III./EJG 2*, was credited with a victory over a B-26 Marauder, one being reported missing by the 344th Bomb Group, 9th Air Force.

One claim was submitted by the 8th Air Force, Lieutenant J F O'Neill of the 55th Fighter Group reporting an Me262 damaged near Giebelstadt airfield at 10.45 hours. This was almost certainly B3+HL of *2 Staffel KG(J)54*, which was damaged by a P-51 over the airfield. *Leutnant* Bernhard Becker broke away from his attacker, outpaced it and finally crash-landed at Kitzingen. The pilot was unhurt, but his aircraft was severely damaged.

During the next nine days there was to be bitter fighting around and above the Remagen Bridge as the Germans strove to retake or destroy it. *Oberstleutnant* Robert Kowalewski's Arado jets from *KG 76* flew many bombing sorties, but most were caught by Allied fighters and shot down or driven off before they could get close. Following the failure of the initial

Jet Crescendo: March 1945

An Me262 on the flight line. Note the Reichsverteidigung band and the position of the 'White 3', indicating that it was possibly an aircraft from III./EJG 2 at Lechfeld.

attack, Goering called the *Gruppenkommandeur* of I./KG(J)51, asking for volunteers to ram the bridge. It is believed that two pilots stepped forward for this suicide venture, but the sortie was never flown, due to the increased intensity of Allied defences around the area. On 17th March, having allowed Allied aims to establish a firm footing across the Rhine to be fulfilled, the bridge at Remagen collapsed into the river.

12th March, 1945

Main cover for the Remagen bridgehead had been supplied by Lightnings of the 474th Fighter Group. Pilots from this unit sighted Me262s at 12.40 hours but were unable to engage them. In the evening, two Spitfires 401 (RCAF) Squadron took off in answer to a cry for help from Army units west of Wesel. Flight Lieutenant L.N.Watt remembers:

> "At this time the Army was preparing for the Rhine crossing and we received a call telling us that an Me262 was bothering them. The weather was very poor, with a heavy overcast and a ceiling down to about five hundred feet. I took off from Heesch with my wingman and headed for the area. It was of course very difficult to see anything and the Army had a habit of shooting at everybody.
>
> "When we arrived in the area, the jet - which we later understood to have been photographing the Army positions and had been dropping down below the cloud to take a couple of photos before taking cover again - suddenly

appeared, coming down from the clouds at a slight angle to me, right above my head. I pulled up the nose and opened fire, hitting him at once and he began to pull away and started to turn. I followed, firing short bursts and hitting him again. Then the Army opened fire, but as usual they were shooting too far behind, which meant they missed the '262 and myself but hit my wingman, who managed to get back to base. The jet then went down and crashed and was confirmed by the Army." [71.]

Meanwhile, a comparatively uneventful mission was flown to Berlin by the Americans, during which Lieutenant F G Rudd of the 356th Fighter Group bounced a '262 near Wesermünde, claiming it damaged. Jet pilots from *III./EJG 2* intercepted an American bomber formation, *Hauptmann* Wilhelm Steinmann claiming a Fortress destroyed; two were actually lost.

13th March, 1945

Another Canadian Spitfire pilot gained success when Flying Officer H C Nicholson of 402 (RCAF) Squadron engaged an Me262 near Münster after excellent vectoring by ground control. It is likely that his victim was a *III./KG(J)51* machine that crashed near Coesfeld after his attack, injuring *Oberfeldwebel* Georg Schabinski.

The capture of the Remagen bridge had now made the airfield complex at Rheine/Hopsten untenable for the *Luftwaffe,* since it would soon be overrun by advancing Allied armoured spearheads.

On 13th March *I./KG(J)51* commenced moving out to Giebelstadt, en route for Leipheim in the south. It seems that part of the unit was intercepted on its way to Giebelstadt by P-47s of the 365th Fighter Group operating from Florennes. Lieutenant Archie F Maltbie led his aircraft into German airspace at 09.35 hours, heading northeast of Köln. Maltbie, leading White Flight, was at 16,000 feet with Blue and Red Flights 4,000 above, to afford top cover, when suddenly four Me262s passed in front of them, heading southeast. Maltbie warned his squadron by radio, whereupon the two top flights at once went into power dives; however the watchful *Luftwaffe* pilots, unwilling to fight, opened up their turbines and left the Thunderbolts far behind. While climbing to their original position, Lieutenants Frederick W Marling and Henry Dahlen of Blue Flight then spotted a lone Me262 on the same course as the other four, some 7,000 feet lower. Marling at once rolled his

Wilhelm Steinmann, who served firstly as a bomber pilot and then with JG 27 and JG 4 and was credited with 40 'kills'. He then flew with III./EJG 2, claiming four victories with the Me262 and ended the war with JV 44.

aircraft into another steep dive, followed by his wingman. The German pilot was taken by surprise as the two Thunderbolts hurtled down from the blinding eye of the sun, Marling delivered a rear starboard-quarter attack from 400 yards, closing to 600 feet. Strikes were seen all over the wings and fuselage, followed by an explosion near the cockpit; the jet then rolled over and dived into the ground. The pilot was not seen to bale out and would appear to have been *Oberfähnrich* Jürgen Höhne, one of two *KG(J)51* pilots lost near Xanten during the day. Höhne was killed, but *Oberleutnant* Harald Hovestadt survived, albeit badly wounded, after crash-landing. His heavily damaged machine was subsequently discovered by advancing troops and was inspected by Allied Intelligence teams.

Lightnings of the 82nd Fighter Group flew a photo-reconnaissance mission to Munich. They were jumped by a lone Me262 that came out of cloud behind them. It was 1,000 yards behind the last P-38 pilot when it was spotted and the Americans broke hard. The jet accelerated out of range and did not return.

14th March, 1945

P-38s from the 474th Fighter Group patrolled the Remagen bridgehead and succeeded in bouncing three jets from *KG(J)51* engaged in bombing the bridge in the late afternoon. All three Me262s were claimed damaged before they made off, by Lieutenant J J Kozlik, Lieutenants G G Clark and W H Barker (one shared) and by Lieutenants C H Darnell and D F Lloyd (one shared).

Lieutenant R S Keeler of the 56th Fighter Group took part in a fighter sweep to Holzwickede, some miles in front of the bomber formation. They were near the Muritz Lake, to the north of Berlin, when:

> "An Me262 passed less than 100 feet beneath our flight while we were orbitting at about 22,000 feet. I called the bounce and led the flight after the German jet. The Jerry spotted us coming in and began to pull away. We were ready to break off the chase when he started a turn. He continued in the turn until I had closed the distance between us to less than 200 yards. I fired a long burst and saw the right wing of the Me262 explode. The jet snapped [sic] and plunged downward in flames."

A second jet, apparently flying in line astern some distance behind, then bounced the strung-out P-47s, damaging that flown by Lieutenant Dawson before breaking away. Keeler's claim was apparently not confirmed however.

The 2nd Scouting Force claimed its second success when Lieutenant C R Rodebaugh reported an Me262 destroyed near Koblenz in the afternoon.

Meanwhile, *Leutnants* Weber, Ambs and *Unteroffizier* Giefing of *III./JG 7* had scrambled from Brandenburg/Briest. A few minutes after take-off two Mustangs were sighted heading west. Ambs took one in a head-on firing pass, claiming that his target had blown up, while Weber claimed the second destroyed. These were possibly two fighters lost by the 325th Fighter Group from Italy.

15th March, 1945
The American 'heavies' raided Zossen and Oranienburg. Due to serviceability problems, *JG 7* could put up only a handful of Me262s to oppose them, but four claims were made. *Leutnant* Weber reported two Liberators shot down, *Unteroffizier* Schöppler claimed another and *Oberfähnrich* Pfeiffer and *Fähnrich* Windisch each claimed the destruction of a Fortress. A few jets from *III./EJG 2* were also in evidence, *Hauptmann* Steinmann claiming another B-17 shot down. The 8th Air Force reported the loss of thirteen B-17s and three B-24s, while two more B-24s were reported missing from 15th Air Force units. Mitchells of 2 TAF flew a sortie to Dorsten during the day, sighting a few Me262s that did not attack; these were probably some of the remaining *KG(J)51* fighter-bombers.

16th March, 1945
A P-47 was claimed destroyed by *Leutnant* Wilhelm Batel from

This Me262 taxiing out carries a figure '4' on the nose below the JG 7 crest and also flashes on the fuselage, indicating that it was possibly Major Theodor Weissenberger's personal aircraft.

I./KG(J)51, while *Major* Theodor Weissenberger, *Kommodore* of *JG 7*, claimed a Mustang shot down north-west of Eberswalde at 16.04 hours. Two were lost, one from the 354th Fighter Group during a heavy combat with Bf109s near Limburg, while the 10th Photo Recce Group reported the loss of an F-6C, which was probably Weissenberger's victory. On this date a new jet fighter Gruppe, *II./JG 7*, was established under *Major* Hermann Staiger, but this unit would not become in any way operational until late in April, when it moved to Prague.

17th March, 1945
The Americans raided Ruhland, Böhlen and Cottbus. Again only a few *JG 7* aircraft were scrambled, pilots from this unit claiming four of the nine bombers lost by the Americans; *Oberleutnant* Wegmann and *Oberfeldwebel* Göbel were each credited with a B-17, while *Unteroffizier* Köster claimed two. Lieutenant Kühn of the 354th Fighter Group attacked one of the jets, claiming it damaged near Koblenz at 16.15 hours.

An important step towards automated warfare was taken by the *Luftwaffe* when the already-formidable armament of the Me262, four MK 108 30mm cannon, was supplemented by the R4M rocket. This was an air-to-air folding fin missile designed by Kurt Heber and was manufactured by *Deutsche Waffen und Munitions Fabrik* at Lübeck, Schleswig-Holstein. The 55mm rocket weighed 8.8 lbs and the thin-walled shell contained 17.6

oz of Hexogen (Cyclonite) explosive, giving it a considerable blast effect. The batteries of twelve rockets were mounted on wooden racks carried outboard of the jet nacelles. Firing was effected electrically, either as an instantaneous salvo or 'ripple-fired' in quick succession, from a range of 800 yards, well out of range of the bomber defences. The effect was that of a giant shotgun, which could be discharged whilst the jets were travelling at high speed. Normally, a reduction in speed was necessary to allow the cannons to be sighted, leaving the aircraft vulnerable to both fighter attack and defensive gunfire from the bombers. German technology had again taken a stride into the future and at a stroke the firepower of the Me262 had more than doubled. When the *DFW* factory at Lübeck was finally overrun by advancing British troops, it was found that the missiles were being produced at a rate of 25,000 per month. Had this production been available in 1944, it is likely that 8th Air Force raids would have sustained even more horrifying casualties than had been the case.

18th March, 1945
III./JG 7 rose in strength to oppose heavy raids by the 8th Air Force. The jets made good use of the hazy cloud persisting over northern Germany and for the first time the deadly R4M rockets were employed. Three bomb divisions had despatched 1,327 heavy bombers to attack targets around Berlin and 37 Me262s were scrambled to intercept in the target area. Here aircraft of the 1st Air Division were engaged by ten jets of the *Geschwaderstab* and *III./JG 7,* which swept through them like a whirlwind, knocking down two B-17s and damaging several more in the first pass. They then returned to cause further mayhem, the 1st Air Division losing four further B-17s in these attacks. The first two Fortresses to fall were credited to *Major* Weissenberger, at 11.09 and 11.10 hours. Meanwhile ten to fifteen more Me262s engaged B-17s of the 3rd Air Division as they neared Salzwedel, south of Hamburg. Four Me262s picked on the Low Squadron of the 100th Bomb Group, which were badly strung out and an obvious choice. The Group lost one Fortress during the first pass, this was *Skyway Chariot* (43-37521) flown by Lieutenants Rollie King and Jack Williams. The left tailplane was shot away and it went down, under

Jet Crescendo: March 1945

The raison d'etre for Jagdgeschwader 7; the destruction of the American heavy bombers. Caught by German combat film, a B-17 Fortress banks away with the flashes of cannon strikes all over it. It was estimated that three strikes from the MK108 30mm cannon were sufficient to dispose of an American 'heavy'. (via ARP)

control. Then a '262 swept in and delivered the coup de grâce, seven men baling out before it exploded. Six minutes later, at 11.14 hours, *Sweet Nancy II* (43-38861) came under attack. Lieutenants Edward Glynn and Donald Reichel struggled to hold the aircraft steady as the crew began to bale out. Then the Fortress nosed up, the tail unit fell away, and it went down with The pilots and two further crewmen unable to escape. The tail gunner, Sergeant Joseph Greigo, was fortunate to get out of the severed tail unit.

Then, at 11.20 hours, the jets turned their attention to Fortress 44-8717, the lead ship. This was flown by Lieutenants Paul DeWeerdt and Bill Thompson, and also had the Group's Command Pilot, Captain Rodger Swain aboard. The first pass destroyed the No.1 engine and ignited the wing tanks and at once the crew began to bale out. With one man still aboard, another jet hurtled in, blowing the tail off. The stricken B-17 rolled onto its back and dropped away. The crew of Fortress 44-6295 were incredibly lucky. Lieutenants Merrill Jensen and Charles Kemp were holding it steady behind and below the lead aircraft when the attack developed and were engaged at the same time. The 30mm shells blew away five feet from the port wing, exploded inside the fuselage destroying several parachutes, hit the Nos. 2 and 3 engines and clipped the propeller of the No. 4 engine. At this moment the lead aircraft, on fire, turned into them and Jensen hauled hard on the control to avoid a collision, seeing 44-8717 slide beneath them burning furiously. The Fortress now had difficulty in maintaining altitude and Jensen nursed it down to 9,000 feet, heading east. They crossed the River Oder and managed to force-land at Kostian in Poland, in Russian hands. 'The Bloody Hundredth' had again lived up to its grim reputation.

It is likely that these were the bombers claimed by *Major* Weissenberger - his third on this sortie - *Oberfeldwebel* Lübking, *Leutnant* Rademacher and *Leutnant* Sturm. Oberleutnant Schall then engaged a Mustang, which he claimed to have destroyed, probably that flown by Lieutenant Norman E Jentz of the 361st Fighter Group, who baled out. Meanwhile B-17 crews of the 457th Bomb Group, having first sighted some jets over the Zuider Zee (which made no attempt to attack) were engaged some 65 miles from the target by small groups of Me262s, which caused damage but no losses until the Initial Point was reached, some fifteen miles from Berlin. One group had swung wide to avoid turbulence and excessive contrails and four Fortresses became detached. These were instantly pounced on by four Me262s, attacking from dead astern. Lieutenant John Schwikert's bomber spun out of formation and went down with its starboard wing blazing, while that flown by Lieutenant Craig Greason sustained a huge hole ripped across the rear of the port wing. With one engine crippled and numerous other strikes, Greason brought his bomber home. The B-17s flown by Lieutenants Cantillon and Castanias, shielded by the contrails, escaped unscathed. Four 'jet' claims were confirmed to 457th gunners; Staff Sergeants Frank Humphries, Ralph Ingraham, Technical Sergeant Martin Norsic (probable) and Staff Sergeant Harold Buhrow (damaged).

It was in this area that Mustang pilots of the 359th Fighter Group sighted ten Me262s. Lieutenant Theodore J Urban was the only American to score, claiming one damaged before the jets outdistanced their pursuers, but his claim was disallowed.

Meanwhile six Me262s had scrambled carrying the first of the R4M rockets, *Oberleutnants* Wegmann, Seeler, *Oberfähnrichs*

Jet Crescendo: March 1945

*Above: The deadly R4M folding-fin air-to-air missiles mounted on wooden racks beneath the outer wing sections of the Me262. They could be fired in salvoes, or 'ripple-fired' in waves. One hit was usually sufficient to destroy a four-engined bomber.
Right: Karl 'Quax' Schnörrer claimed a B-17 on 18th March using R4Ms. He was forced to bale out wounded on 30th, losing a leg. His war was over.*

Ullrich, Windisch, *Leutnant* Schnörrer and *Fähnrich* Ehrig engaging Fortresses near Rathenow. Günther Wegmann made one attacking run to fire his R4M rockets saw a B-17 go down, then turned for a second pass. He attacked another B-17, saw cannon hits on the starboard wing, but was caught in crossfire from the formation that shattered his cockpit canopy and instrument panel and wounded him in the right knee. Disengaging, he nursed the crippled aircraft towards Parchim, but as he descended to 13,000 feet, in a shallow dive, his starboard turbine exploded into flame and he smartly abandoned the aircraft, landing safely near Wittenberge. Fortunately, a Red Cross nurse was nearby and treated him before he was taken to hospital. He never flew operationally again; his right leg, knee

Hans Waldmann flew with JG 52 in the east, JG 3 in the Reichsverteidigung and then with JG 7. He was credited with 134 victories, two of them with JG 7. His Eichenlaub were awarded on 1st March, but he died in a mid-air collision on 18th March.

shattered by the heavy .50 calibre bullet was subsequently amputated. Further victories over B-17s were claimed by Schnörrer, Ehrig, Seeler, Windisch and Ullrich. Additionally, these pilots were each credited with one *Herausschuss*, as was Wegmann (above). In all, the 3rd Air Division reported nine B-17s shot down over Germany and two more that crashed into the Channel on the return flight.

Wegmann was not the sole casualty during the March 18th battle. *Oberleutnant* Seeler was last seen diving into the bomber stream over Berlin, but then radio contact was lost. It is thought that he too fell victim to the turret gunners, his aircraft exploding under concentrated fire; no trace of aircraft or pilot was ever found. *Oberfähnrich* Günther Schrey was also shot down; he baled out, but his body was later found riddled with bullets and it was believed that he had been shot whilst parachuting. Earlier, *3./JG 7* had lost two aircraft when *Oberleutnant* Hans Waldmann and *Leutnant* Hans-Dieter Weihs collided whilst climbing through thick cloud shortly after take-off from Kaltenkirchen. Hadi Weihs baled out unhurt, but Waldmann, a high-scoring *Experte* and Knight's Cross holder, was killed. [72]

Escort for the bombers had been provided by more than 600 American fighters, but only one claim for a 'damaged' was made, by Flight Officer W V Totten of the 353rd Fighter Group near Prenzlau. Two American Mustangs were claimed shot down by *Hauptmann* Steinmann of *III./EJG 2*.

Claims by *III./JG 7* pilots totalled twelve heavy bombers and three escort fighters; the Americans had lost twelve B-17s and one B-24. Fifteen further bombers were classified as 'write-offs' after returning, while ten more from the 3rd Air Division flew on east to crash-land in Soviet-held territory; a massive total of 714 bombers had sustained battle damage of one sort or another. American gunners had claimed eight Me262s destroyed, but only three were actually lost in combat. In addition to the heavy bomber losses, a further 21 fighters, including ten Mustangs, failed to return.

19th March, 1945

The 2nd Air Division despatched 125 B-24s to attack the Me262 training base at Neuburg, where some eighty aircraft were found, all but ten of them jets. The attack, delivered from

Liberators of the 2nd Air Division hit Neuburg on 19th March. An indication of the uncertain state of the German air defences is given by the fact that only one aircraft was lost.

15-21,000 feet caused severe damage to runways, hangars and buildings. Sixteen of the jet aircraft were claimed damaged and this figure was confirmed by air reconnaissance next day. *III./KG(J)54* sustained one write-off and fifteen more damaged, ten of them heavily. One B-24 of the 44th Bomb Group was shot down during the raid. Subsequent attacks on 21st and 24th March by 15th Air Force bombers increased the damage at Neuburg and a final raid on 9th April 9th left the base a total ruin.

Mustangs of the 355th Fighter Group, flying escort to the above mission, made one jet sighting when Captain C H Spencer surprised a jet over Geisenheim airfield. He opened fire at extreme range and the '262 was seen to go down and crash at Kitzingen airfield at 16.45 hours.

Meanwhile, B-17s of the 3rd Air Division were engaged north of Chemnitz by Me262s of *III./JG 7*. Due to bad visibility, only 28 of the 45 airborne jets found the American bombers, but for the same reason the Mustang escorts had become detached from their charges and their first indication of *Luftwaffe* jet intervention came via the bombers' radio. When the P-51s eventually found the Fortresses, six had already fallen to R4M rockets (One from the 96th Bomb Group, one from the 385th and four from the 452nd, one of these crash-landing in Russian line; four more were damaged beyond repair). Claimants on this occasion were *Oberfeldwebel* Lennartz, *Oberleutnant* Schall, *Oberfeldwebel* Arnold and *Leutnant* Schnörrer (new Kapitän of *9./JG 7* following Wegmann's incapacity). *Oberfeldwebel* Reinhold had achieved a *Herausschuss* and two unnamed pilots had forced another pair of Fortresses from the defensive screen. *Leutnant* Rademacher claimed a Mustang. The 357th Fighter Group P-51 pilots reported sighting three waves of twelve Me262s, the 363rd Fighter Squadron beating off the second and third waves. Captain R S Fifield claimed one shot down while Major Robert W Foy saw several jets chasing a flight of P-51s. The Me262s passed over his section apparently without seeing them; Foy pulled up the nose of his fighter He opened fire at the leading jet from a range of 600 yards and the Messerschmitt did a 'split-S' before it crashed into the ground. Major Niven K Cranfill, leading the 368th Fighter Squadron of the 359th

Jet Crescendo: March 1945

Fighter pilots were often superstitious. The number thirteen was usually shunned, but Heinz Bär habitually flew 'Red 13'. His FW190 with 5./JG 1 carried this number as did his personal Me262 when with III./EJG 2, pictured above. He flew operationally from 1939 until 1945 and survived the war with 220 victories. For him, '13' was indeed lucky. (via ARP)

Fighter Group, spotted three Me262s near Leipzig, but then saw ten more approaching the bombers. One of the jets attempted to engage a lone P-51, but Cranfill intervened, scoring hits and driving it off. He then got behind another, firing until it went down to explode on the ground. Cranfill's wingman Lieutenant Clifton Enoch, did not return and is presumed to have fallen victim to one of the jets. Meanwhile, Captains J L Carter, A G Manthos and Lieutenant J W Cannon had each claimed a 'damaged' between Chemnitz and Leipzig. while a reconnaissance pilot, Lieutenant N A Thomas of the 15th Recon Squadron, claimed one damaged over Darmstadt. Two Me262s actually failed to return, *Oberfeldwebel* Heinz Mattuschka of *10./JG 7* and Leutnant Harry Meyer of *11 Staffel* both being shot down and killed near Eilenburg. It seems likely that these fell to Foy and Fifield of the 357th Fighter Group. Lieutenant Ayer's section of P-51s from the 4th Fighter Group was bounced by two Me262s near Lechfeld, but none of the Mustangs were hit. Aircraft from the 1st Air Division, which were attacked in the same area, lost one B-17 of the 384th Bomb Group; two more were classified as 'write-offs' on return. These were possibly attacked by aircraft from *I./JG 7*, *Gefreiter* Heim claiming one confirmed and *Unteroffizier* Koning a *Herausschuss*. *Oberstleutnant* Heinz Bär of *III./EJG 2* claimed a P-51 during the course of the day. This was from the 52nd Fighter Group, 15th Air Force, which he shot down near Ingolstadt, killing 2nd Lieutenant B H Nippert.

Unnamed pilots from *I./KG(J)54* claimed a B-17 and a *Herausschuss* at around 15.00 hours.

One Fortress crew was lucky. This aircraft, returning from Plauen, sustained engine trouble and was quite alone, nearing the Allied lines when three Me262s climbed up from the haze and delivered three attacks, all of while missed. Lieutenant Kirkland brought his aircraft safely home.

20th March, 1945

Hamburg was the target for the 1st Air Division and 22 Me262s of *JG 7* were in the air, intercepting over the target area at around 16.00 hours. Two jets engaged the 358th Fighter Squadron (355th Fighter Group) and Lieutenants Peterson and Roberts were repeatedly attacked, only escaping by means of their superior maneouvreability. Two B-17s of the 303rd Bomb Group were among the first of nine to fall to the jets' rocket and cannon fire. 43-39160 had its fin shot off on the first pass and, on the second attack, the starboard wing caught fire and it exploded. 43-38767 also blew up during a jet attack. The 100th Bomb Group also attracted attention. B-17 44-8613 flown by Lieutenants Bernard Pointer and Charles Higginbotham was engaged and shot down near Plauen, only Pointer surviving. Lieutenant Billy Birtle, under attack from another jet that damaged the No.4 engine and blew the wingtip from his Fortress, saw Pointer's B-17 blow up and also reported seeing the attacking '262 explode.

Claims for B-17s destroyed were submitted by *Fähnrich* Ehrig (three), *Feldwebel* Pritzl (two) and *Oberfähnrich* Pfeiffer, *Oberfeldwebel* Heiser, *Fähnrich* Christer and *Oberleutnant* Sturm, while *Oberfeldwebel* Buchner reported a *Herausschuss*. Surprise had been complete and the P-51 escorts were able to intervene only as the jets were departing. Lieutenants Vernon N Barto and Robert E Irion of the 339th Fighter Group each claimed the destruction of a Messerschmitt, four of which were lost. *Unteroffizier* Hans Mehn's 'White 7' of *1./JG 7* was damaged initially and was finally shot down on the approach to Kaltenkirchen; *Obergefreiter* Fritz Gehlker of *10 Staffel* died

Jet Crescendo: March 1945

The American attacks were destroying many of the jets on the ground, thus every possible measure was taken to hide them. Here an Me262 sits under camouflage netting, probably rearming for the next sortie.

near Bad Segeberg, *Oberfeldwebel* Erich Büttner of the latter unit was shot down and baled out slightly wounded near Kiel and a fourth jet was shot down, but the name and fate of this pilot are not recorded.

Major Merle B Nichols, leading the close escort 20th Fighter Group reported:

"Big Friends and Little Friends arrived in the target area at 16.10 and, shortly after, the jetters started a big fuss. twelve to fifteen Me262s commenced attacking the 2nd and 3rd Combat Groups of the 1st Division. Four bombers were seen to go down. Our boys beat off several attacks by turning into the jets and did their best to overtake and destroy those that did press home their attacks, but generally the '262s were able to speed away and escape.

"Two of our mighty midgets, Lieutenant John Cowley of the 77th Squadron and Lieutenant Charles 'Charley' Nicholson 55th Squadron did get in good swipes however, and each claimed a blow job damaged. Lieutenant Cowley out-guessed his victim by swinging into a turn before him and cutting him off. Lieutenant Nicholson pursued his number through a heavy haze in a 20 degree dive and got in good bursts with his sights dead on him." [73].

There is no record of any victory credit being awarded to

Nicholson, but further claims on this Hamburg mission numbered four jets damaged; one by Lieutenant K V Berguson and two by Lieutenant R S Hill, both of the 339th Fighter Group and another by Lt Edward G Rudd of the 356th Fighter Group, all in the target area.

Meanwhile, B-24s of the 2nd Air Division had struck at Baumenheim, near Munich, bombing a factory believed to be involved in jet aircraft production. The raid was effected in clear weather with no intervention from enemy fighters and, for a pleasant change, the bombers returned without damage or casualties. Not quite so fortunate was a 25th Bomb Group Mosquito crew. Roger Gilbert was intercepted by an Me262 that blew four feet from his port wing. He struggled back to Watton, where he found that the aircraft became uncontrollable below 180 mph; with the aileron jammed, it simply rolled hard to port. However he made a safe landing, no doubt reflecting upon the firepower of the enemy jet.

On this same day, the 82nd Fighter Group, 15th Air Force, flew another reconnaissance mission to Munich. The five aircraft (four P-38s and an F-5) were attacked first by two jets, then by one. No gunfire was seen from the jets on either occasion, but the Americans opened fire, seeing possible strikes on the singleton, but no claim was made. Later in the day a bomber escort was flown to Vienna, where Me262s were seen, but no engagements took place.

21st March, 1945
The American forces despatched heavy raids to south and eastern Germany. Thirty-one Me262s were scrambled by *JG 7* and were many combats took place. One bomber formation, targetted on the motor works at Plauen, were intercepted over the River Elbe near Wittenberge, some twenty minutes from the target. Three Me262s streaked in and carried out successive attacks upon B-17s of the 94th Bomb Group. Their prime target was the lead aircraft, which took many hits and fell from the sky. Meanwhile, a stronger force of jet fighters assaulted B-17s of the 490th Bomb Group in the same stream, American crews reported that some '262s closed to a range of five yards before breaking away, determined to score hits. One jet pilot was seen to shoot down a Fortress, then attacked another from the 850th

Jet Crescendo: March 1945

Lieutenant C S Needham's 388th Bomb Group crew had an eventful mission on 21st March. (C S Needham)

Bomb Squadron. The rear gunner, Staff Sergeant W H Cole engaged it, apparently hitting the pilot, for the jet half-rolled over the B-17 and smashed straight into a Fortress above, both aircraft falling as balls of fire. A further two B-17s fell to R4M rockets before the Messerschmitts turned on aircraft of the 100th Bomb Group, destroying one with cannon fire.

One of the successful jet pilots was *Leutnant* Hans-Dieter Weihs, from *3./JG* 7. He cut a Fortress from the formation and his wingman, *Leutnant* Tangermann, saw it explode, still with its bombs aboard. [74] Return fire was heavy and 'Hadi' Weihs was forced to belly-land near Crimmitschau, Saxony, due to hits in both engines. *Gefreiter* Heim, also from *I./JG* 7, claimed another Fortress.

Another B-17 was attacked as it neared its target at Reichenbach, south of Leipzig. Lieutenant C S Needham's crew from the 560th Squadron, 388th Bomb Group, were on their 33rd mission. The pilot recalled:

"We had briefing on target at 03.00 hours. I sure wished we could get a couple of short ones for a change. We got all the way to the Initial Point with no trouble. At this point I got the No 2 engine knocked out by Flak and several other holes in the aircraft, including the hydraulic system shot out.

Because of the heavy bomb load, I had to lag; we dropped two bombs and that did no good, so we dropped two more. I still could not catch up with the formation, so I had to abort. The prop on my No 2 engine would not feather, this causing more drag. After I got rid of my two wingmen, we were hit by two jet jobs...." [75].

Sergeant Duane A Sears, crouching beneath in the ball turret, had already seen four jets attacking another lagging Fortress in the distance, which suddenly burst into flames and fell out of control:

"Since we were also on our own then, we thought that we would be next. Sure enough, we were hit by two of them, one off the left wing and one off the right, when they made their pass at us. I was never so surprised, though. Aircraft without props; the first jet planes I had ever seen. They didn't stay long and must have been short on fuel and ammo after their attack on the other B-17. It was lucky for us, if not for the other crew." [76].

Lieutenant Needham finally got the No 2 propeller feathered and, by over-boosting the three remaining engines, caught up with his formation. Once the attack was over, his B-17 dropped back and was given an escort of four P-51s right back to the lines. He would have been less confident had he known just how difficult it was for a section of Mustangs to protect a lone Fortress. On this day the 482nd Bomb Group had sent a single B-17 out with an escort of P-51s to attack a target near Frankfurt/Main with a new kind of bomb. *Leutnant* Fritz Müller of *III./JG 7*, patrolling near Dresden with his wingman, sighted this small formation some miles behind the main American bomber stream, heading for Plauen and Reichenbach. They swept in to attack. The P-51s were above and behind the Fortress, but were taken by surprise as the two jets dived beneath them and opened fire on the B-17 from 300 yards. Hits were gained on the fuselage and engines and, although the tail gunner threw back a hail of gunfire, it was to no avail. The jets hurtled past the stricken bomber and the German pilots glanced back to find the P-51s coming down at full throttle while the stricken Fortress exploded and spun down. Although the Mustangs were travelling at well over 500 mph, the jets outdistanced them with ease.

By late March 1945, the high octane fuel shortage was preventing many of the *Luftwaffe* conventional fighters from opposing American attacks; B-24s of the 448th Bomb Group, raiding the Me262 assembly plant at Kitzingen, near Augsburg, escaped interception, all bombers returning safely.

The 78th Fighter Group enjoyed a field day whilst escorting B-17s to the Ruhrland synthetic oil factory. Lieutenant John A Kirk III, then a 20-year old Flight Leader remembers:

> "We were positioned at 28,000 feet and to the right of the bomber stream. Thus I was about 3,000 feet above the bombers as they neared the target. The first sighting of an Me262 came when I saw a B-17 being attacked and bursting into flames. The jet broke off and went into a 45 degree dive straight ahead. I had peeled off and dove just about straight down as I was slightly ahead of him. My wingman followed me. The airspeed indicator rapidly advanced until it was in the red line. As I remember, it indicated that the plane was flying at about 550 mph That must have been terminal velocity, however I had no problems handling my aircraft. He was in my K-14 gunsight, but out of range of my six wing guns. As we dove down to about 15,000 feet I knew I was not gaining on him, but he was not pulling away either. I decided to lob some bullets at him, although it was forbidden to fire your guns when your speed was in the red line as vibration would tear the wings off.
>
> "Having great faith in the strength of the Mustang, I pulled up the nose so that the gunsight was about one radius above the Me262. One quick burst and a check on the wings showed them to be all right, so another fast burst was fired. My bullets must have hit his right engine, as smoke appeared. He slowed up and I anticipated his next move. I then pulled up from my steep dive, hoping to gain on him when he levelled out. He pulled up from his dive and we closed fast. Soon I was in perfect firing range. The guns were fired in long bursts as soon as he was centered in my gunsight. Strikes appeared all along his fuselage and wing roots. Suddenly the pilot seemed to 'pop out' of the cockpit and flew back very close to me. I could see him very well. To record the kill, I took a camera shot of the plane crashing in a ball of flame and the German pilot floating down on his parachute." [77.]

Five further jets were claimed by the 78th Fighter Group on this mission, Lieutenants Walter E Bourque, R H Anderson and R D Anderson each reporting one Me262 destroyed while Lieutenants Alan A Rosenblum and W H Brown shared another. These were caught at low level after taking off from Giebelstadt at 12.15 hours. Captain Edwin H Miller, who had scored a 'probable' during the battle of 9th February, spotted a '262 'leap-frogging' through the bombers near Wittenberge, shooting two of them down. As the jet made a wide turn to come back again, Miller and his wingman closed in. Miller opened fire and the jet dived for the ground, with the two Mustangs in hot pursuit:

> "We broke through a scattered undercast and I was sitting right on his tail until my guns were completely empty. By that time I knew he was a 'Dead Duck' and veered off to the left just as he crashed into the ground."

Lieutenant Richard I Kuehl is believed to claimed a seventh.

Lieutenant Harry M Chapman of the 361st Fighter Group, escorting B-17s near Dresden at 09.55 hours, was at 20,000 feet and flying as No 4 in a flight of Mustangs slightly higher and to port of the bomber stream when four Me262s came down on the Fortress from astern:

> "When the jets started their dive we turned into the bombers so as to intercept, but the manoeuvre was somewhat hopeless since their speed was such that they could have hit the bombers and gotten clear away before we could get there. For some unknown reason the jets turned into our flight instead of continuing their dive, thus putting their number 4 man and myself in a head-on confrontation.
>
> "At about the same moment we both started firing. His nose lit-up first, which was probably his guns firing. My K.14 sight pip was right on his canopy as I opened fire a second later. His entire left wing and left side of fuselage burst into flames and then the jet came past me so close that I could see the pilot in his seat and so fast that for a moment I thought it was another P-51 Mustang, except for the lack of prop'; the head-on silhouette was very similar, the P-51 drop tanks and the Me262 engines were placed about the same." [78]

Both Lieutenant Homer G Powell, leading Yellow Flight, and Lieutenant Carl W Wolfe (Red Two) saw this jet go spiralling down in flames and finally explode just above the ground, confirming Harry Chapman's jet kill, bringing US claims to seven on this mission.

The main opponents of the bomber force were *Stab* and *III./JG 7* and many claims were submitted by the jet pilots; B-17s were claimed by *Oberfähnrich* Pfeiffer, *Leutnant* Schnörrer, *Oberfeldwebel* Arnold, *Leutnant* Weber and *Gefreiter* Heim from *III Gruppe*, with *Unteroffizier* Giefing claiming two. *Leutnant* Ambs claimed three. He attacked from above, his first victim spinning down in flames. Zoom-climbing, he caught another that fell away with one wing blown off and then continuing his climb, sighted a third leaving thick condensation trails. He attacked this also, again claiming to have blasted one wing away. He was then hit by gunfire and wounded, baling out safely.

Above: 'Death Angel'. Harry Chapman's 361st Fighter Group P-51 at the Little Walden dispersal. (H Chapman)
Right Harry Chapman, who destroyed an Me262 on 21st March. (H Chapman)

Major Weissenberger and *Major* Ehrler of the *Geschwaderstab* also claimed a Fortress each. Further *III Gruppe* claims were submitted by *Leutnant* Müller (B-24) *Oberleutnant* Schall (P-51, possibly Lieutenant Cornelius C Howard of the 364th Fighter Group, lost near Achmer) and *Unteroffizier* König (P-47). *Oberstleutnant* Heinz Bär of *III./EJG 2* claimed a B-24 destroyed during these operations and *Leutnant* Bell of the same unit is believed to have scored a victory over a 15th Air Force P-38 on this date. The 8th Air Force lost a total of eight Fortresses and thirteen fighters, while two B-24s were lost from 15th Air Force operations over Germany.

On the same day the fighter-bombers of the 9th Air Force, which had already begun a heavy ground strafing programme, made a concerted effort to destroy a large part of the *Luftwaffe* jet fighter force on the ground, by hitting many airfields in southern Germany known to be operating Me262s. It was almost certainly a Thunderbolt from this force that strafed a staff car on the Leipheim autobahn bridge, killing four officers from *I./KG(J)51*, including the newly-appointed *Gruppenkommandeur*, *Oberstleutnant* Halensleben. Other fighters, striking at Giebelstadt airfield, caught three Me262s landing. All three were shot down. The pilots, *Hauptmann* Eberhard Winkel, *Leutnant* Erwin Diekmann and *Unteroffizier* Heinz Erben, were killed. Winkel, formerly a Ju88 pilot with *III./KG 51*, had previously flown with distinction on the Eastern Front. On one occasion during the winter of 1943/44 he had landed his bomber in a snow-covered field behind Russian lines to rescue a shot-down comrade and his crew. On 21st March he died from a single bullet, striking him in the back of the head. Ironically, within a few days Me262 units would begin to receive cockpit armour plating to protect pilots against just such attacks. No claims for jets in these circumstances by P-47 units have been found, but at 15.00 hours Captain T W Sedvert, a Mustang pilot from the 353rd Squadron, 354th Fighter Group caught one at 500 feet, opened fire and watched it belly in with a great cloud of white smoke near Osthoven, but his claim was downgraded to 'unconfirmed'. The 4th Fighter Group, strafed Achmer, where Captain William O'Donnell claimed a jet destroyed. Captain J S White of the 12th Recon Squadron made the last American claim, reporting an Me262 damaged over Ludwigshafen at 14.30 hours.

Bombers from the 15th Air Force attacked Neuburg airfield in strength. Me262s from *III./KG(J)54* were taxiing out for take-off as the bombs came down and none left the ground. 7 *Staffel* lost *Unteroffizier* Rolf Dahlmann and *Unteroffizier* Heinz Klewin (both killed) and *Feldwebel* Rudolf Suchert (wounded), while *8 Staffel* lost *Obergefreiter* Lothar Martius and *Hauptgefreiter* Clemens Kippke (killed) and *Feldwebel* Bruno Borg and *Unteroffizier* Gerhard Bauer (wounded). *Unteroffiziers* Josef Biebel and Josef Traumüller from *9./KG(J)54* were also wounded. One aircraft of *I./KG(J)54*, flown by *Unteroffizier* Willi Ehrecke, managed to scramble from nearby Steinbrücken airstrip, but was shot down and killed near Giessen as he attempted a pass at B-17s.

The 'grinding machine' of Allied air power slowly drained the Luftwaffe of its best pilots. Joachim Weber, one of the 'old originals', fell on 21st March.

The raid on Neuburg had resulted in twelve jets being totally destroyed, 38 more being damaged.

III./JG 7 lost two fighters in combat near Dresden; *Leutnant* Joachim Weber, one of the original cadre of *Erprobungskommando 262* pilots, who had claimed seven victories whilst flying the Me262, was shot down and killed, as was his wingman, *Unteroffizier* Kurt Kolbe, who fell near Tharandt. From the aggressive manner in which the Me262 pilot engaged Harry Chapman's Mustang, it seems likely that it was flown by Weber. Kolbe is likely to have fallen to two 339th Fighter Group Mustang pilots when Lieutenant Billy E Langohr claimed an Me262 destroyed jointly with Lieutenant Nile C Greer near Würzburg at 10.45 hours. *JG 7* lost two further jets during the course of the day, both pilots surviving with wounds, these possibly the fighters engaged by the 78th Fighter Group.

22nd March, 1945

Mustang pilots from the 78th Fighter Group claimed two more jets destroyed while on bomber escort sorties; Lieutenants E L Peel and M B Stutzman shared one near Ulm at 13.00 hours, while Captain H T Barnaby claimed another over Giebelstadt thirty minutes later. Aircraft of the 15th Air Force were also operating, striking northward from Italy; the 31st Fighter Group flew a sweep over the Ruhland area at midday, where some 25 - 30 Me262s were engaged in a running fight that lasted for over an hour. One '262 was claimed shot down by Captain W J Dillard, who caught one attacking bombers and chased it down to ground level:

"I never did see any strikes from my bullets, but some pieces flew off and his left engine caught fire. The pilot flubbed his jet around a bit and then flipped over and bailed out."

Claims for jets damaged were submitted by Captain Hugh D Naumann and by Lieutenants Bobby J Bush, Robert R Blank, Claude E Greene and Norman R Hodkinson, all from the 31st, while Lieutenant J W Cunnick of the 55th Fighter Group claimed another shot down at Lechfeld and Captain F E Birtciel of this unit got a 'damaged' over Schwabisch-Hall airfield. Additionally, an unnamed pilot from the the 27th Fighter Group claimed a 'damaged' at 11,10 hours. At least seven Me262s were actually lost in air combat; *Oberleutnant* Hans König from *Stab./KG(J)54* scrambled with others from Würzburg airfield and soon after was engaged by P-51s. He was shot down and killed. *Unteroffizier* Adalbert Egri of *I/KG(J)54* baled out wounded near Giebelstadt, clearly victim to Barnaby of the 78th Fighter Group. *Fähnenjunker-Oberfeldwebel* Helmut Reckers of *III./EJG 2* was killed when his fighter crashed onto the southern perimeter of Lechfeld airfield - obviously Cunnick's opponent. *Feldwebel* Franz Eichmer of *11./JG 7* was shot down and killed by a fighter near Altdobern, while two unidentified *JG 7* pilots were also shot down and killed, while a third baled out wounded.

Ground strafing attacks on the German bases were carried out, mainly by 9th Air Force Thunderbolt pilots, who claimed two Me262s destroyed and sixteen more damaged during strafes of Giebelstadt and Kitzingen. At Giebelstadt, several jets from *I./KG(J)54* were taxiing prior to taking off when the Americans hit them. *Oberfeldwebel* Paul Overbeg was wounded and *Unteroffizier* Ernst Franke was killed, while a third jet became a 'write-off' and ten more suffered damage. Nine more Me262s were hit at Kitzingen, *Hauptgefreiter* Gustav Ponopp being killed. The Americans were not alone in these operations, for two Mosquitoes of the Fighter Experimental Flight flew a Day Ranger patrol to Neuburg airfield, where Flying Officer R E Lelong and Flight Lieutenant H C Craft claimed two Me262s destroyed and one damaged, plus an FW190 destroyed and two more damaged.

Many victories were claimed by the jet fighter pilots. Fortresses were reported destroyed by *Major* Weissenberger and *Major* Ehrler of *Stab./JG 7* and by *Leutnant* Schnörrer, *Oberfähnrich* Petermann, *Oberfähnrich* Windisch, *Oberfähnrich*

Hit in the starboard wing and turbine, this Me262 attempts to evade the pursuing American fighter (USAAF)

Pfeiffer, *Oberfeldwebel* Lennartz, *Oberfeldwebel* Buchner, *Leutnant* Ambs, *Oberfeldwebel* Arnold, *Unteroffizier* Köster and *Oberfeldwebel* Lübking of *III Gruppe*. *Leutnant* Schlüter claimed another as a *Herausschuss*, while *Oberleutnant* Schall claimed a P-51 and *Leutnant* Lehner a P-51 *Herausschuss*.

23rd March, 1945
The RAF despatched a strong force of bombers on a daylight raid to attack a vital bridge over the River Weser, to prevent the escape of trapped German troops. This force was heavily escorted, mainly by British Mustang IIIs, but as the bombers made their run-in, some fifteen to twenty Me262s attacked, going through the bombers at high speed and shooting down two Lancasters of 101 Squadron, flown by Flying Officer Little and Flight Lieutenant Patterson, before the Mustangs could intervene; a third Lancaster was damaged. The German fighters then headed back north-east, but one of the jets - almost certainly a *I./JG 7* aircraft from Kaltenkirchen, near Hamburg -

lagged behind, probably having been damaged by return fire. Flying Officer A Yeardley, of 126 Squadron, got in close to the diving jet and opened fire. He saw strikes on the fuselage and the Messerschmitt nosed over into a steeper dive from which it failed to recover; the pilot was not seen to escape. Meanwhile Flight Lieutenant G H Davis of 129 Squadron attacked another, saw white smoke emerge and pieces of metal fly off and claimed it damaged. Mustang pilots from 118 Squadron were also involved. They were some twelve miles south-southwest of Bremen at 19,000 feet when, at 10.10 hours, Flight Lieutenant J L Evans reported:

> "I was flying the same level as the bomber stream when two Me262s approached the bombers from the starboard above, made an attack and turned to port in front of me. The first enemy aircraft was going too fast to attack but I turned inside the second enemy aircraft. I then jettisoned L.R.tanks and fired a two-second burst at extreme range and observed a flash half-way up the Me262's port wing. I fired another two-second burst but was unable to close the range and the enemy aircraft dived away to the E, going very fast."

Meanwhile Flight Lieutenant K M Giddings, leading Flycatcher section, saw several more:

> "As we were leaving the target (Bremen) I led my section down on an Me262. I fired very short bursts as this and two other Me262s in the same area at extreme range, observing no strikes.
>
> "As we turned to rejoin the bombers I dived on another Me 262 which was turning below me and fired a two - three second burst from 700 to 500 yards, seeing a couple of strikes and a part of his starboard wing root fly off; this is confirmed by Drumhead 4. It was impossible to close the range of these attacks."

Flight Lieutenant W Harbison, Giddings' No.3 was also in the thick of the fight:

> "I followed Flycatcher Leader down on an Me262 at which I fired a short burst at very long range, observing no strikes. We chased this Me262 for a short period and then turned to rejoin the bombers. After flying for approx five minutes I saw another Me262 in a left-hand turn, at 10 o'clock below. I dived on his tail and fired a four-second burst closing from seven hundred to four hundred yards. A long column of white smoke came out of the starboard motor. Flycatcher leader also saw strikes on this aircraft."

All three pilots claimed one Me262 damaged.

One further bomber, Flying Officer Gilbert's 466 Squadron Halifax, force-landed in Belgium, possibly as a result of this

Negro pilots of the 332nd Fighter Group won the respect of the bombers they escorted by their tenacity. On 24th March they claimed at least three Me262s shot down and received a DUC.

action. Another Mustang III pilot, Sergeant Aleksander Pietrzak of 309 (Polish) Squadron, engaged an Me262 over Bad Bayerhausen, claiming it damaged. Meanwhile bombers of the 15th Air Force flew north to attack oil refineries at Ruhland and were engaged by *Stab./JG 7* near Chemnitz. *Major* Ehrler claimed two Liberators shot down and *Oberfeldwebel* Reinhold a Fortress probably destroyed. The Americans recorded that three bombers had fallen to jet fighter attacks.

24th March, 1945

The Allies executed *Operation Plunder*, the crossing of the Rhine near the Reichswald Forest, accompanied by a huge paratroop drop and glider assault. Meanwhile, 'heavies' of the 15th Air Force flew their first raid against Berlin, under heavy fighter protection. As the bombers neared their target thirty Me262s attacked, but most were held at bay by the Mustangs. One of the American escort Groups engaged was the 332nd, the only USAAF operational unit to be composed entirely of negro pilots and ground staff. One of the pilots, Lieutenant Roscoe C Brown, gave chase to a Messerschmitt after its firing pass, but lost it in cloud soon afterwards. As he was climbing back to his escort position, he glanced back and saw the Me262 swooping down onto his tail. As he broke hard to port, the jet swept past him and the tables were turned. Brown sighted quickly, pressed the triggers and hit his opponent hard, slowing it down and allowing him a second, longer burst. Something flew off the aircraft - presumably the cockpit canopy - and the pilot baled out. Lieutenant Earle R Lane chased another down to 6,000 feet, firing short bursts that finally set the Messerschmitt on fire. Flight Officer Charles V Brantley attacked another, but lost sight of it after hits were seen. Other pilots saw this jet fighter go down to crash and he was credited with its destruction. Lieutenant Richard Harder claimed two Me262s damaged, Lieutenant Vincent I Mitchell joined forces with Captain Thomas to damage another. Two unnamed American pilots claimed 'probables'. The 332nd Fighter Group received a Distinguished Unit Citation for this mission, but three P-51s were shot down, Captain McDaniel and Lieutenants Ronald W Reeves and Robert C Robinson all failing to return. Lieutenant Hannibal Cox, with a one-foot length shot off one wing of his Mustang, succeeded in returning to Italy at low level. Lieutenant Leon W Spears was at first reported missing, but was later found to have crash-landed his crippled Mustang in Russian-held territory. One of the missing Fortresses was seen to spin away with its starboard wing torn off by 30mm cannon fire while one of the P-51s also had a wing shot off by an Me262, but the pilot baled out safely. Lieutenant J Lanham later reported:

> "I heard Lieutenant Schell say 'McDaniel just got shot down!'. Someone said 'There he goes'. Then I heard Walter Manning say 'Here's a whole bunch of them!'. A jet came in at 90 degrees to attack the bombers. We made a 180 degree turn, but the jet went over the horizon before we could get to the attack point."

The 31st Fighter Group was also engaged and claimed five more of the 25 jet attackers destroyed. Colonel William A Daniel attacked one at the rear of the German formation, which snap-rolled and blew up. Lieutenant William M Wilder caught another lining up for an attacking run on the bombers:

> "I hit the right engine and a lot of smoke began to come out. The German baled out."

Captain Kenneth T Smith's opponent baled out as the Mustang pilot was still firing on him, while Ray D Leonard caught another firing on a bomber:

> "My shots started it smoking and it pulled up in a slight climb to the left. I kept shooting and pieces flew off, both engines caught fire, and the pilot baled out."

Hermann Buchner of III./JG 7 was a former fighter instructor who flew close-support missions in Russia, using his fighter training to protect his less companions. He scored 46 victories in the east before joining Kommando Nowotny. (H Buchner)

Lieutenant Forrest M Keene Jr claimed an Me262 destroyed during this action, whilst claims for jet fighters damaged were submitted by Lieutenants James C Wilson, William H Bunn and George E Erichson.

The jets were mainly from *JG 7*, the German pilots reporting two separate engagements. Elements of the *Geschwaderstab* and *III./JG 7* intercepted bombers near Wittenberge. *Oberfeldwebel* Arnold and *Leutnants* Rademacher and Lehner each claimed B-17s, as did *Major* Ehrler of the Stab on this occasion. During the second engagement, four-engined bombers were claimed destroyed by *Oberleutnant* Kulp, *Oberleutnant* Sturm, *Oberleutnant* Schall, *Oberfeldwebel* Pritzl and *Oberfeldwebel* Buchner. *Oberleutnant* Ernst Worner of *9 Staffel* cut a bomber out of the formation, but his fighter was then hit and set ablaze. He baled out wounded near Northeim. *Oberleutnant* Kulp was caught by a P-51 pilot and he also baled out wounded. A pilot from *10 Staffel*, *Unteroffizier* Ernst Giefing, was wounded, but succeeding in force-landing safely. *Leutnant* Alfred Ambs, after a brief but successful career with *11 Staffel*, was shot down near Wittenberge and baled out wounded. *III./EJG 2* jets were also in action, *Oberstleutnant* Heinz Bär claiming the destruction of a Liberator and a Mustang. To the north, *Oberleutnant* Walter Schuck and *Leutnant* Hans-Dieter Wiehs, his wingman from *3./JG 7* patrolled near Neumünster, sighting a P-38 Lightning and a pair of Mustangs. The two jet pilots attacked, Schuck claiming both P-51s shot down while

Weihs claimed the Lightning. 'Hadi' Weihs remembered, 'Shuck had considerable difficulty, in spite of his *Eichenlaub* to the *Ritterkreuz*. Major Erich Rudorffer, *Kommandeur* of *I./JG 7*, was also successful. He found RAF Tempests near Wesel and bounced Flight Lieutenant J B 'Bob' Stark of 274 Squadron, who was shot down and killed.

Neuburg was attacked again and on this occasion no less than sixty Me262s of *II* and *III./KG(J)54* were destroyed by the bombing.

The day's fighting had cost the Americans dear; in addition to a considerable number of transport aircraft lost during the Rhine crossing some 29 heavy bombers and fourteen fighters of the 8th and 15th Air Forces had been shot down, plus five Thunderbolts and several medium bombers of the 9th Air Force.

25th March, 1945
During the morning B-24s of the 2nd Air Division were briefed to raid Buchen, some thirty miles east of Mannheim. One squadron of the Liberators from the 448th Bomb Group had became separated from the rest of the stream and was sighted by elements of *III./JG 7* west of Ulzen, heading north towards Lüneburg. *Leutnant* Rademacher led the attack, storming in from astern and cutting a Liberator out of the formation. *Leutnant* Müller shot down a Liberator in flames at 10.25 hours, but his aircraft was then hit in the wing and he force-landed spectacularly at Stendal, rolling into a hangar at speed and hitting five Ju88s. Meanwhile, *Feldwebel* Taube had claimed a B-24 over Rheinsehlen, but was then caught by P-51s and died when his aircraft exploded, almost certainly shot down by Lieutenant Raymond H Littge of the 352nd Fighter Group, who had seen a B-24 shot down by a '262 and destroyed its attacker. *Oberfeldwebel* Hermann Buchner claimed another Liberator near Hamburg and escaped unscathed. *Oberfähnrich* Windisch and *Oberfähnrich* Ullrich were not so fortunate; both claimed Liberators shot down, but Windisch was attacked and his fighter badly damaged by a Mustang, again probably from the 479th, Lieutenant F W Salze claiming a 'damaged' in this area. More than thirty hits were counted in Windisch's Me262, which was described as being 'like a sieve!'. Ullrich was shot down and killed by Mustangs while landing, as was *Oberleutnant* Schatzle.

The latter had probably fallen victim to Lieutenant Eugene H Wendt of the 479th Fighter Group, who claimed a jet fighter as it was landing at Rechlin. Against the claims for seven bombers, four were actually shot down outright from this formation. A fifth B-24 was badly damaged and headed north towards Sweden, but was either ditched or abandoned short of the neutral coast. Eight of the crew were later rescued from the Baltic Sea. At least one Mustang fell to the jets, pilots from the 339th Fighter Group seeing a 352nd machine, flown by Lieutenant Wesley Roebuck, destroyed. This Me262 was then attacked and claimed damaged by Major Schaffer. Two P-51s were actually claimed, these by *Oberleutnant* Franz Schall and *Leutnant* Schnörrer of *III./JG 7*.

When south of Lüneburg, pilots of the 56th 'Wolfpack' had seen six or seven Me262s appear from the north, flying a loose line-astern formation. The jets had charged into the rear combat box, shooting down two Liberators before splitting up. A few of the attacking Me262s sped away eastwards, pursued by P-47s of the 63rd Fighter Squadron. The jets soon disappeared, but Captain George E Bostwick decided to take his Thunderbolts on towards Parchim airfield, just a few minutes flying time to the east. As they neared the base, Bostwick's No 4 man reported a Me262 in the landing circuit and, using cloud cover, the P-47 pilots stalked it. At that moment four Me262s were seen, orbiting very low down, and at once the American pilots broke formation and attacked from their superior position. Bostwick picked out his target, a jet apparently about to land, but as he closed on it he saw that its undercarriage was still retracted. It flew down the runway at low level, passing just above another Me262 that appeared either about to touch down or to have just taken off. At that moment the latter German pilot saw him, broke hard to port and instantly dug his port wingtip into the ground, the aircraft breaking up as it cartwheeled across the airfield. Bostwick continued after his first opponent, now accelerating as it climbed away. He gave one burst at extreme range, seeing strikes on the tail unit, before it pulled away and escaped. Bostwick glanced around to find the sky empty. The wreckage of the crashed '262 lay beside the runway. There was no fire, indicating that it had probably been landing with almost dry fuel tanks. Bostwick returned claiming one Me262 destroyed without firing a shot. A second 56th Fighter Group pilot, Lieutenant Edwin M Crosthwait, also claimed an Me262 in the same area. It is believed that *Leutnant* Günther von Rettberg of *10./JG 7*, was Bostwick's opponent, while Ullrich fell to Crosthwait. Ullrich succeeded in abandoning his machine, but was found dead.

One casualty was sustained by the RAF when Mosquito MM285 of 544 Squadron flown by Flight Lieutenant Stuart S. MacKay was intercepted and shot down by a Me262 over Peenemünde. The aircraft was ditched in a lake and both MacKay and his navigator Flying Officer A S Lobban were taken prisoner. Both men had narrowly escaped falling victim to Me262s on previous occasions, Lobban on July 25th and MacKay on 19th November 1944. The identity of their attacker is not known, but is likely to have been an aircraft from *JV 44* based at Briest. Other losses were sustained by RAF Bomber Command (see 27th).

26th March, 1945
One Allied aircraft fell to a jet fighter this day, when a 5th Photo Recce Group F-5E flown by 2nd Lieutenant H P Panch was engaged south of Munich, possibly by a JV 44 aircraft. The Lightning managed to disengage, flew southwards for a short distance and finally spiralled into the ground.

27th March, 1945
Me262s of *III./EJG 2* were reportedly scrambled to oppose a raid on Lechfeld, *Oberstleutnant* Heinz Bär claiming three P-47s, while *Oberst* Walther Dahl claimed two and *Feldwebel* Rauchensteiner one. *Leutnant* Heckmann of *10./JG 7* claimed a Lancaster. *Leutnant* Hans-Dieter Weihs of *3./JG 7*, flying with *Major* Rudorffer, claimed a four-engined type and is unsure of the date, but believes that his action took place on the 27th.

"This was quite interesting, because I noted that this, my third victory, was also the 1,000th [sic] victory of the *Staffel*! And twenty-six hits in my Me262!." [79]

None of the above claims appear to accord with the losses sustained by the Allies. It is possible that these combats actually occurred on March 25th when both the RAF and the USAAF sustained losses over Germany that may relate to these

Without question one of the greatest fighter pilots the world has ever seen, the legendary Heinz 'Pritzl' Bär. He fought on every front and in every major campaign - west, east, North Africa and Reichverteidigung and ended the war with 220 victories. He has always been ranked with Colonel Joe McConnell (USAF in Korea) as the top-scoring jet pilot, but their score of 16 has, it is believed, been surpassed by Rademacher, Eder and Welter. Like so many others, he survived the war to die in an accident, being killed in a light aircraft crash on 28th April 1957.

claims.

28th March, 1945

B-17s of the 3rd Air Division, returning from a mission to Berlin, were attacked near Brunswick. A flight of Me262s hurtled through the formation, shooting down a Fortress of the 303rd Bomb Group and one from the 401st. A third machine, also from the 401st, was severely damaged and was subsequently abandoned over Belgium, while five more were classified as 'damaged beyond repair' on return to England. *Oberfeldwebel* August Lübking of *11./JG 7* lost his life when a B-17 that he was attacking, exploded, sending the jet fighter down out of control, presumably during this interception. Claims were submitted by *Oberleutnant* Stehle of *2./JG 7* for a B-17 and a Mustang, while another Mustang was claimed by *Oberleutnant* Schuck of *3 Staffel*.

30th March, 1945

Jagdgeschwader 7 scrambled thirty Me262s to defend Wilhelmshaven, Bremen and Hamburg against heavy attacks by the 8th Air Force. *Leutnant* Karl Schnörrer and *Oberfähnrich* Viktor Petermann intercepted bombers over the latter city, Schnörrer claiming two B-17s and Petermann one, but the former's machine was hit by crossfire and he broke away. On the way back to base a flight of P-51s came down on him hard and fast. Realising that he could neither outrun nor out-fight them, he flipped the fighter onto its back, jettisoned the canopy, released the straps, and fell out. As the abandoned aircraft went past him, he was unlucky enough to be struck by the tailplane. Although in great pain, he managed to open his parachute and land safely. When he arrived in Ulzen hospital it was found that his leg had been fractured; for another Me262 pilot the war was over. At the same time *Major* Erich Rudorffer led eight Me262s of *I Gruppe* away from Kaltenkirchen, to engage American bombers over Hamburg. *Flieger* Reiher claimed a Fortress destroyed while his comrades were engaged by the escorts. *Fähnenjunker-Feldwebel* Janssen's Messerschmitt was shot down in flames, but *Major* Rudorffer claimed two unidentified fighters and *Gefreiter* Heim a P-51. Between Hamburg and Bremen *Feldwebel* Geisthovel discovered a Mosquito, which he claimed to have destroyed. He was then attacked from above by three fighters and crash-landed in a field, escaping from his aircraft before the P-51s came down to strafe it. It is likely that his attackers were from the 339th Fighter Group, Lieutenant C W Bennett claiming a jet shot down and another damaged near Lübeck. This Group lost a Mustang when Lieutenant Everard L Wager fell to a '262 northeast of Hamburg. He baled out, but his parachute failed to open.. Three further Me262s of *I Gruppe* returned with combat damage. A Mosquito was indeed lost this day, RF971 of 544 Squadron failing to return from a reconnaissance mission to North Germany.

The 3rd Air Division lost three B-17s during the attacks, one from the 486th Bomb Group and two from the 493rd, with two more damaged beyond repair. The 1st Air Division lost one from the 381st with one more 'written-off' on return.

The American fighters had not been idle. A flight of Mustangs from the 339th Fighter Group, 'Rat Catching' over Kaltenkirchen, surprised a pair of *I./JG 7* Me262s taking off to chase bombers that had passed overhead a few minutes earlier en route for Hamburg. The P-51s jumped the jets shortly after they had left the ground; Lieutenant R F Sargeant attacked the closest and the port turbine belched smoke. *Leutnant* Erich

Two Experten of I./JG 7.
Left, Major Erich Rudorffer, the Gruppenkommandeur. He claimed 224 victories, 86 in the west including twelve with the Me262.
Right Oberleutnant Walter Schuck, Kapitän of 3 Staffel was credited with 206 victories, seventeen in the west including eight while flying Me262s with JG 7.

Schulte baled out at below 400 feet and was killed. The precise cause of his death remains a mystery; one report states that his parachute failed to open fully and he died on hitting the ground as his fighter crashed in flames a few hundred yards further on, while a second states that he was strafed by the Mustangs whilst helpless in his parachute. The second German pilot accelerated away and vanished towards the east.

Further 'confirmed' claims on March 30th were submitted by Colonel John D Landers and Lieutenant Thomas V Thain of the 78th Fighter Group, who shared one between them near Rendsburg while Lieutenant Kenneth J Scott of the 361st claimed a jet in the same area. Lieutenant P L Moore of the 55th found another '262 landing at Lübeck, claiming this destroyed, while Lieutenant J C Hurley of the 352nd claimed another north of Magdeburg. Lieutenant J B Guy of the 364th claimed another, sharing this victory with an unidentified

Mustang pilot, also near Magdeburg. Meanwhile, Colonel J B Henry, leading the 339th, had claimed a 'probable' southwest of Hamburg and Captain G T Rich and Lieutenant S C Ananian of this unit each claimed one damaged north of Lüneburg. Henry's claim appears to have been rejected however, for no credit was awarded. Lieutenant P A Erby of the 55th and Lieutenant R L Hunt of the 364th had each claimed a 'damaged' south-west of Lübeck and near Brandenburg respectively. This brought US claims to seven destroyed, one probable and five damaged against a known loss of four, with three more damaged.

It was on this day that the first Me262 was captured intact by the Allies. The factory at Neuburg had completed its final twenty Me262s in late March and Hans Fay, a Messerschmitt test pilot, was flown to Schwabisch-Hall to help ferry them out before the base fell into the hands of the rapidly advancing Americans. Fay was, above all things, a realist. Knowing that the end of the Third Reich was but a few weeks distant, he climbed into an unpainted Me262A-2a fighter-bomber *Werke Nummer* 111711 and took off from Schwabisch-Hall, heading west. He landed safely on Rhein-Main airfield, where he surrendered to the occupying American Forces. At last the Allies had an undamaged jet fighter in their possession! Those Messerschmitts left at Schwabisch-Hall were eventually blown up shortly before the Americans captured the base, but it was too late. Fay's defection had ensured that none of the Me262's secrets would now be denied to the Allies.

That night (March 30/31st) a Mosquito night fighter pilots of RAF Bomber Command's 100 Group claimed success when Pilot Officer L G Holland of 515 Squadron, claimed one Me262 destroyed and two more damaged during a ground strafe.

Meanwhile an Air Sea Rescue OA-10 Catalina had set out at dusk to seek a missing American fighter pilot. Lieutenant Daniel L Myers of the 357th Fighter Group had suffered engine failure and landed in the sea some five miles north of Schiermonnikoog, off the north German coast. Lieutenant John V Lapenas set out in the late afternoon, making rendezvous with a P-51 escort as the location was close to the German-held coast. It was 18.55 hours and getting dark as they saw flares sent up by the fighter pilot and Lapenas put the big PBY

Leonard K 'Kit' Carson of the 357th Fighter Group (right) was annoyed that his 31st March opponent could not be caught. Nearly forty years later he was amazed to learn that his adversary that day had been traced and was Hadi Weihs of I./JG 7.
(Via R Freeman)

Teamwork 75 down ten minutes later into a six-foot swell. The landing was heavy and the starboard engine-oil line broke. Although they were only 100 feet from Myers' dinghy. the wind and the heavy swell forced them to drift apart and they lost sight of him. Lapenas, using his port engine, managed to taxy a few miles westwards, but it was now dark. They waited for morning.

31st March, 1945
Early in morning of March 31st Lieutenant John A Carroll, flying PBY 'Teamwork 70' flew out to locate Daniel Myers. meanwhile Lapenas' PBY had been covered by RAF Warwicks until shortly before noon, when Major L K Carson led three Mustangs of the 357th out to the area to cover the rescue aircraft. 'Kit' Carson later wrote:

> "A few minutes later two Me262s came storming out from the mainland at a much lower altitude than ours, possibly a thousand feet off the water. They took no time to scout the situation; obviously they were informed before arriving. Their course was dead into the Catalina."

As the two jets slid beneath them, Carson yelled a warning to his wingmen and dived flat-out. He saw the nose-guns blazing as both jets opened fire on the PBY, but even diving at full power he could not close sufficiently to drive the jets off course. By this time he too was shooting at the leading '262 at extreme range.

> "The '262s peeled off to the right and made a wide, high speed circle back to

the mainland. Certainly not wishing our troops in the Catalina any bad luck, I was hoping that bastard in the lead '262 would tighten up his turn and try to come back, because if he had I was going to nail his ass. I had the throttle through the gate at seventy-two inches of mercury and 3,000. My speed was up and I had a 3,000 foot altitude advantage, so I could easily have reached 400 mph, maybe more. If I could get my sights on him for three seconds at 200 yards, that's all I needed. He do it though, and there wasn't anything I could do about it." [80]

'Kit' Carson and Lieutenant M A Becraft each reported hits and the Me262s fled.

Warrant Officer Tommy Dykes was flying one of the 280 Squadron Warwicks during the rescue. His tail gunner, Gus Platte remembers:

"I was dividing my time between searching the sea for any signs of life and the air for any sign of sudden death, when suddenly the intercom erupted, 'Christ! An aeroplane, coming like the clappers of Hell!' The voice was Vince Keeley's, the mid-upper gunner. 'Where? Call it out' retorted the skipper, Tommy. 'It's coming like the clappers!', came the reply. "Call it out, where is it? Who is that?'

"None of us had any idea where the enemy aircraft was coming from. I searched the sky in every direction. The late sun was over the nose and the front gunner would be looking up there. We are talking about fractions of a second. Some instinct told me the attack would be out of the sun. I gambled and depressed the guns, half-standing, braced, and looked below. If it had been a head-on or beam attack, we could have been in trouble. I could hear the mid-upper guns crackling and the enemy cannon. And suddenly there he was. He was so far below and going so fast I couldn't believe it. I hosed the air around him, but my tracer seemed to be slower than he was, and he seemed to be leaving it behind. An optical illusion, of course, but our apparent relative speed from which a gunner bases his his calculations was about 875 mph! His fuselage seemed to be triangular in section, with low wings and two underslung engines. His black silhouette sliced away towards his homeland without returning for a second attack. Whether he had a problem, or was hit by our bullets, we would never know. The skipper was very upset that he hadn't been able to take evasive action, saying that any advice to weave port or starboard would have been preferable to 'like the clappers of Hell!'

"Back at Beccles an inspection of the Warwick revealed not a scratch. At de-briefing I drew the silhouette of the aircraft I saw. Vince said it didn't have propellers. I drew the shape of a Messerschmitt 262. 'They are flying their jets', said the de-briefing officer as he shook his head. 'Now we are for it!'" [81]

Clearly this crew had seen one of the two jets after the attack on the Catalina, running for home.

John Lapenas, in the stricken PBY. reported:

"262s made two passes at us. Tail of the PBY completely shot off. Port float all but shot away. Port wing damaged. PBY listed to port and began sinking. Lots of hole in the aircraft. None of the crew hit. Abandoned ship."[82]

The crew took to their dinghy, finally being rescued on April 4th; Meanwhile John Carroll had landed his PBY close to Myers, but was fired on from the shore and forced to abandon the rescue. Daniel Myers finally drifted ashore where, alive but weak, he was taken prisoner. *Leutnant* Hadi Weihs of *I./JG 7*, who took rueful exception to Carson's 'rather rude' description of himself, remembered:

"I was flying the leading Me262 on that day, but I'm not sure who was my wingman. It may have been Oberleutnant Grünberg. I strafed the Catalina and we got away from the Mustangs without being hit." [83]

During February and March 1945, RAF Bomber Command had undertaken an increasing number of daylight bombing raids over northern Germany, since the daylight defences had become less effective than those at night. Thus on March 31st, 428 Lancasters and Halifaxes from Nos 1 and 6 Groups, led by the Pathfinders of No 8 Group, struck at the Blohm und Voss works at Hamburg. *JG 7* scrambled 38 jets to meet this attack and it is believed that some Me262s were also sent up by *10./NJG 11*. The Lancasters and Halifaxes from No 6 (Canadian) Group had arrived too late to effect rendezvous with their RAF Mustang escorts over Holland and unwisely pressed on unprotected. The British crews had no experience of the tight formation flying required to establish an effective defensive crossfire and thus the huge straggling mass of bombers became easy prey for the fast jets.

Meanwhile twenty more Me262s had been scrambled in some haste by *I./JG 7*. *Oberleutnant* Stehle led ten of these aircraft towards Bremen whilst *Oberleutnant* Grünberg led eight more to Hamburg, both formations encountering British bombers.

433 (RCAF) Squadron bore the brunt of the attacks, sixteen separate engagements being reported. The aircraft flown by Squadron Leader P D Holmes was attacked by two Me262s. Warrant Officer E J Ash (rear gunner) together with Warrant Officer V M Ruthig (mid-upper gunner) opened fire on the first jet, which dived away pluming smoke and dropping debris; this

was claimed destroyed. Ruthig assisted his pilot in evading five further attacks and was later awarded the Distinguished Flying Cross. Flying Officer D Pleiter's bomber was attacked by a jet, which was claimed probably destroyed by his gunners, Flight Sergeants C H Stokes and M A Graham. The 431 (RCAF) Squadron Lancaster flown by Flying Officer E G Heaven was attacked by three fighters, but Flight Sergeant W Kuchma in the rear turret claimed to have shot one down, this aircraft veering sharply to starboard as the complete tail assembly flew off, forcing the fighter into a spin. One further '262 was claimed damaged. Another jet was claimed by Flying Officer D M Payne's 428 (RCAF) Squadron crew, Flight Sergeants R C Casey and A E Vardy reporting one shot down in flames. 434 (RCAF) Squadron reported ten separate engagements, resulting in one jet claimed probably destroyed by Flight Sergeant R Spratt and Flight Sergeant R Taylor in Flying Officer J Dawson's crew, while two more were damaged by Flying Officer F Hawes' gunner Flight Sergeant Lambert and by Pilot Officers J Baxter and E Cowlin, gunners in Flying Officer M Isenberg's crew.

429 (RCAF) Squadron aircraft had nine combats. Flying Officer A M Humphries aircraft was attacked and the Me262 was engaged by his gunners. Flight Sergeant D H Lockhart's guns jammed after twenty rounds had been fired, but Flight Sergeant R Jones, in the mid-upper turret, continued firing until the jet dived away apparently out of control, shedding lumps of metal from the starboard wing. One 429 (RCAF) Squadron gunner, Flight Sergeant J O Leprich had all the turret electrics shot away over Hamburg, but continued firing one-handed, hand-cranking the turret with the other until three Mustangs arrived, by which time an attacking jet had been driven off trailing smoke. Flying Officer R P Pike brought the bomber home safely and Leprich was awarded an immediate Distinguished Flying Medal for his coolness and courage under fire. One 424 (RCAF) Squadron aircraft was attacked by two jet fighters, Flight Sergeant Howes in the mid-upper turret engaging one abeam, while Flight Sergeant S J Robinson fought off a stern attack. Howes' guns jammed, but Robinson continued firing until the attacker spiralled away with flames spouting from beneath the fuselage. Flight Lieutenant J L Storms' 427

The abiding fear of all Me262 pilots was to be caught in the landing pattern. There was no time to raise the gear and open up to escape, since the turbine response was so slow and a flame-out was a real danger. This jet pilot, caught by a Mustang low down, is doomed.
(USAF)

Oberfeldwebel Pritzl each claimed a Fortress. *Leutnant* Rademacher reported another P-51 *Herausschuss*, bringing the *Geschwader*'s victory total to seventeen confirmed claims for the day. One P-51 from the 361st Fighter Group is likely to have fallen to either Ehrler or Rademacher; Flight Officer Deane E Jackson was last seen in combat with Me262s and did not return.

Crews from the 466th Bomb Group sighted seven Me262s, which attacked the 3rd and 4th squadrons, but no hits were recorded. Gunners claimed one destroyed and two damaged. Mustangs from the 353rd Fighter Group were escorting B-17s to Derben, when between ten and twelve jets were sighted and chased away, Lieutenant H B Tordoff attacked one, hitting it and continuing pursuit until the port engine burst into flames and the pilot baled out near Dessau. Meanwhile, further 8th Air Force units, sweeping across central Germany, reported further combats. Lieutenant W L Coleman of the 78th Fighter Group claimed a jet destroyed near Stendal and fighters from the 361st engaged jets near Brunswick, where two were claimed damaged by Lieutenants G R Stockmeier and E E Tinkham. Lieutenant R I Bromschwig, of the 479th, claimed another jet damaged near Braunschweig and a Thunderbolt pilot, Lieutenant F H Barrett of the 56th, got another 'damaged' over the Steinhuder Lake, after pilots from the Group had seen two Fortresses falling to jet attack. One 9th Air Force pilot, Lieutenant P M Hughes of the 358th, claiming yet another damaged over the River Main. Jet pilots from *I./KG(J)54* were also involved in combats near Halle, unnamed pilots claiming a B-24 shot down and another as a *Herausschuss*. One of their jets fell in this area, when *Oberleutnant* Dr Heinz Overweg, *Kapitän* of 2 Staffel, was shot down and killed.

A pair of Mustangs from the 2nd Scouting Force were attacked by Me262s near Brunswick at 08.10 hours, but succeeded in turning the tables on the jet pilots, Lieutenant M H Castleberry claiming one shot down, while Captain Richard W Nyman reported heavy damage to a second.

Units of 1 TAF (Prov) were flying medium bomber escort missions throughout the day and at 10.20 hours P-47s of the 371st Fighter Group sighted a jet taking off from Giebelstadt. Captain William T Bales Jr, of the 404th Fighter Squadron, dived on one, caught it at 900 feet and shot it down in flames.

During the course of the above engagements, *JG 7* reported the loss of four Me262s; one pilot was killed, two more missing and the fourth is believed to have baled out safely. It is likely that the two missing pilots fell to the RAF gunners near Hamburg.

The situation regarding jet bases had by now become acute for the American campaign of airfield attacks, directed particularly against those bases thought to operate Me262s, was causing great destruction. Between March 21st and 31st, it was reckoned that no less than 34 airfields had been devastated. Jet units, including *10./NJG 11*, now began to operate from *Autobahnen* in increasing numbers, using the wide roads as impromptu runways and utilising the thick pine forests that flanked them as dispersals. Few could doubt that the end was now in sight.

Notes

65. Correspondence Lawrence Bird - S E Harvey.
66. Correspondence Paul Sink - S E Harvey.

67. In conversation with the authors.
68. Correspondence Rudolf Sinner - John Foreman.
69. From Hugh Fraser's logbook.
70. *The Big Show*, by P H Clostermann.
71. Correspondence and conversation L N Watt - John Foreman.
72. Hitherto, it was always believed that Waldmann and Schrey had collided. However Hadi Weihs has corrected this for the authors.
73. Correspondence Paul Roberts MD (flight surgeon 20th FG) - S E Harvey.
74. Documents Hans-Dieter Weihs.
75. Via Larry Bird to S E Harvey.
76. Correspondence Duane Sears - S E Harvey.
77. Correspondence John A Kirk III - S E Harvey.
78. Correspondence Gen. Harry Chapman USAF - S E Harvey.
79. Documents from Hans-Dieter Weihs.
80. *Pursue and Destroy*, by L K Carson. Text supplied by Hadi Weihs and quoted by permission of L K Carson.
81. Correspondence Gus Platte - S E Harvey via Malcolm Holmes.
82. Records of 5th Emergency Rescue Squadron USAAF.
83. Interviewed by John Foreman in Steyr, Austria, in 1991.

Chapter Eight
Bloody Twilight: April 1945

By the beginning of April, most of the the fighter-bombers of *KG(J)51* were firmly boxed into Bavaria, its *Staffeln* occupying the bases at Riem, Fürth and Memmingen, later moving to Linz in Austria. Elements from *KG(J)51* would shortly move to the great airfield complex at Prague/Ruzyne, joining remnants of *I* and *II./KG(J)54* and the few aircraft received by *KG(J)6* to form *Gefechtsverband Hogeback* under command of *Oberstleutnant* Hermann Hogeback, *Kommodore* of *KG(J)6* and holder of the Knight's Cross with Swords and Oak Leaves. Soon this Combat Group would be reinforced by aircraft from *JG 7* and *JG 1*, the latter operating the He162 *Volksjäger*. *I./JG 7* was ordered to evacuate Kaltenkirchen and transferred its three *Staffeln* to Briest, Burg and Oranienburg, although it is clear that a small number of *JG 7* fighters remained in the north, operating independently until the surrender.

From mid-February, many of the great *Experten* had joined Galland's embryo *JV 44*. Johannes Steinhoff, dismissed in January from leadership of *JG 7*, *Leutnant* Herbert Kaiser, recovering from wounds sustained with *JG 1*, and *Major* Erich Hohagen, (who had been succeeded in January by Rudolf Sinner as *Gruppenkommandeur III./JG 7*) were among the first. They scoured the hospitals and rest homes, later bringing *Oberstleutnant* Gerhard Barkhorn and *Major* Walter Krupinsky (known throughout the *Luftwaffe* as 'Count Punski') Most of the pilots had never flown the Me262, but quickly became familiar with it. The unit would soon begin to receive more fighters, principally from *IV.(Erg)/KG(J)51* at Neuburg, from whence several junior pilots also came. Conditions at Brandenburg were fast becoming impossible however, and on 31st March the unit moved to join *KG(J)51* at Munich-Riem. The twelve serviceable Me262s left Brandenburg and headed over the Härz Mountains and the Valley of the Golden Lea, thence over Lichtenfels, Erlangen,

Nürnberg, Ingolstadt and on to Munich. The 300-mile flight, carried out at low level to avoid detection by Allied fighters, took under an hour and Galland was relieved to find that there were no lurking fighters around Riem airfield, all twelve Me262s landing safely.

April 1st 1945

The first day of the month saw an engagement between *I./JG 7* and American heavy bombers when a few Me262s intercepted twenty Fortresses near Stendal. Only *Oberleutnant* Stehle penetrated the escorting fighter screen and claimed a B-17 destroyed. During the course of this day *Unteroffizier* Köster of *III./JG 7* claimed a lone Spitfire, apparently a reconnaissance machine, most likely an F-6C of the 111th Tactical Recon Squadron. P-51s of the 162nd Recon Squadron were engaged near Bad Mergentheim at 18.00 hours, Lieutenants J W Waits and W R Yarbrough each claiming a 'damaged' before the jets vanished.

On both 2nd and 4th April, jets from JG 7 again intercepted American bomber formations that were raiding the U-boat pens at Kiel and airfields - principally Wesendorf, Parchim, Hoya, Fassberg and Eggebeck. Ten bombers were lost during these raids, but on the 4th, American escorts, sweeping ahead to cover the known jet airfields, accounted for several Me262s.

April 4th 1945

At 09.15 hours, a flight of 339th Fighter Group Mustangs flew a sweep over Rechlin airfield, finding a flight of Me262s from *III./JG 7*, led by *Major* Rudi Sinner, emerging from the clouds after taking off. *Oberfeldwebel* Hermann Buchner wrote:

> "I flew as leader of the second *Schwarm*. Sinner started first with the first *Schwarm* and I followed a few minutes later with the second. Over the airfield the cloudbase was down to about 100 metres and, as I pulled up the wheels and flaps and began to climb i heard Sinner over the radio reporting enemy contact, but when we emerged from the clouds no American fighters were in sight. I led my flight towards Hamburg." [84]

Major Sinner, the *Gruppenkommandeur*, had been warned of enemy fighters in the vicinity, flying at 24,000 feet, but this was wrong - they were much lower. After circling the airfield and joining up with seven other members of his flight he climbed through the clouds.

Wolfgang Späte, who took command of III./JG 7 after Sinner was shot down.

"Climbing up through the cloud I saw four enemy aircraft in formation above me and against the sun (Thunderbolts). I climbed steeply but could not catch them, then one of the Thunderbolts dived steeply at me. I learned later that these enemy aircraft were Mustangs. My rockets would not fire and the rest of the Gruppe had no luck.

"I tried to out-run the Mustangs, but saw four Mustangs behind me in an attacking position. I dived and turned sharply but was hit from behind and damaged. Then I tried a series of evasive manoeuvres bit I could not throw off the Mustangs as I was now too low. I was now running from eight Mustangs, which were shooting at me. I tried to find some cloud cover in the hope of losing my attackers and attempted to fire my rockets, but two of the Mustangs followed me closely. I did not see my rockets fire.

"As I pressed the rocket firing switch my cockpit began to fill with dense smoke and I saw that my left wing was on fire. The fire soon reached the cockpit and I decided to bale out. The air speed was 700 km/hr when I baled out, but I struck the tail in doing so. I realised that my parachute was not open and that my right leg had become entangled in the harness." [85]

Sinner's aircraft was hit by the combined fire from Captains Kirke B Everson and Robert C Croker. With badly burned face and hands he tumbled earthwards. To his surprise the parachute opened at the last possible moment, but was not fully deployed and he was hanging by just the left strap as hit heavily in a ploughed field and was dragged sideways into a barbed wire fence. He reported that two Mustangs then came in low, opening fire upon him. He lay still, feigning death and, as the Mustangs pulled away he staggered away from the parachute and dropped into a deep furrow.

Eventually the Americans departed and he was given first aid by the crew of a nearby *Freya* radar site before being taken to hospital. For another of the jet pioneers the war was over. His position as *Gruppenkommandeur* was at once taken by *Major*

Wolfgang Späte, who had formerly flown Me163B rocket-powered fighters with *JG 400*.

The Americans deny having strafed Sinner on the ground, but there is no reason to doubt his account. It had become policy for this type of event to happen, particularly by the USAAF, since jet pilots were clearly an important asset to the *Luftwaffe*. They were far more valuable than their aircraft, which could be easily replaced and it is no secret that American pilots were under orders to kill jet pilots in their parachutes. Some obeyed, more did not. In this case it is best left as a difference of opinion.

Meanwhile, *Oberleutnant* Franz Schall, one of the 'originals' from *Kommando Nowotny*, had engaged a Mustang, which he claimed destroyed. He was then shot down and forced to bale out - one of the few to survive two bale-outs from Me262s. Two further jets were claimed by 339th Fighter Group pilots, Lieutenant Nile C Greer and Captain Harry R Corey. At 09.40 hours, B-24s of the 2nd Air Division were over Schwerin, approaching their target of Parchim at 18,000 feet, when eight Me262s attacked. Captain Robert H Kanaga of the 4th Fighter Group reported:

"While flying at 20,000 feet as Green Three, I observed two Me262s, one of which had completed an attack on the bombers. I selected the Me262, which was moving into position to fire on the bombers again and closed to within a thousand or eight hundred yards. He discontinued his pass at the bombers and headed away under them in a gentle dive. I followed dead astern at 18,000 feet and fired most of my ammunition at him, using my K-14 sight. The Hun presented a very steady target and range did not change noticeably during the engagement. Strikes were observed on this aircraft with my first tracers, he dipped twice sharply, emitting considerable black smoke forward of the blowers. He was beginning to break up, so I discontinued the attack, levelled off, and was able to locate an Arado 234 for my wing-man (I was short of ammunition). I told him to go get him - that I would fly on his wing. In the meantime my wingman, Lieutenant Denson, observed my Me262 roll twice and go into the deck vertically through the thin transparent veil of cloud at 500 mph." [86]

Five minutes later Lieutenant Raymond A Dyer got a second jet, south-east of the target. Soon, three further Me262s came in fast near Stendal, one being chased away and shot down over Ludwigslust by Lieutenants Michael Kennedy, Donald P Baugh, Harold H Fredericks and William H Ayer. (Only Kennedy and Frederick were awarded credit for this shared victory however).

George Ceuleers with his Mustang 'Constance'. On 4th April he chased an Me262 for 182 miles before getting within range for a 'kill'.
(via R Freeman)

Meanwhile, Lieutenants C W Harre and H H Frederick each claimed a '262 damaged. In another combat near Parchim, Lieutenant Colonel W C Clark, leading the 66th Fighter Wing, also claimed one damaged.

In the meantime, the B-24s came under attack by six jets over Hamburg. The 448th Bomb Group lost three 'heavies' in quick succession; Captain John Ray's Liberator, flying with the High Right Squadron, exploded, while two from the Lead Squadron were shot down. Lieutenant James J Shafter's crew abandoned their crippled aircraft *'Miss-B-Having'* after the one engine had been shot out and a fire started in the nose began to spread. Lieutenant Bob Mains' bomber was last seen going down with two engines on fire. Only Technical Sergeant Charles E. Cupp, the radio operator, escaped to become a prisoner. He was sucked through a gaping hole in the fuselage and his parachute opened only a short distance from the ground.[87] One from the 93rd Bomb Group was also seen to fall to a jet while several further bombers were badly shot-up in the rocket attack. A jet was reported shot down by the 446th Bomb Group formation, but unfortunately this was later ascertained to have been a Mosquito flown by Colonel Troy Crawford, the 446th Group Commander. As the P-51s came down, the jets sped off in all directions. Major George Ceuleers of the 364th Fighter Group got behind one as it flew south in a shallow dive, pushing his Mustang to the limit as he chased it for 180 miles. He finally caught up with it at low level near Dessau, and shot it down from 500 feet. Lieutenant J S Rogers from this unit claimed an Me262 damaged over Fassberg airfield.[88]

Another flight of Me262s took on 150 bombers near Nordhausen. These raiders had apparently become separated from their fighter escorts on the way in and the jet pilots had a field day, claiming ten destroyed with many more grievously damaged. Aircraft from *III./JG* 7 had assembled near Stendal and intercepted American bombers south of Bremen, shooting down three. *Leutnant* Fritz Müller after taking off from Lärz airfield, together with several other jets, sighted P-47s near Bremen. They ignored the American fighters and carried on, soon making contact with B-24s heading southeast, almost head-on with the German aircraft. Müller attacked in a descending right turn, coming in from the starboard quarter and firing his rockets into their midst. His missiles struck home on one bomber, which reared up and then fell away. As Müller turned back towards the formation he saw the American pilot somehow get the bomber steady enough for six men to bale out before it began to break up. With all four engines running, it plunged vertically into the cloud layer below. Further victories were claimed by *Leutnants* Schenk and Rademacher, *Feldwebel* Pritzl and *Oberfähnrich* Pfeiffer, all for Fortresses.

Jets from *I./KG(J)54* had also been scrambled, Fortresses being engaged near Hannover in the mid-morning. *Leutnant* Becker of *2 Staffel* was credited with one victory and a second was credited to an unnamed pilot. The 361st Fighter Group was engaged between Hamburg and Berlin in a running fight that resulted in many claims for Me262s damaged; Lieutenants L F Gendron and W H Street claimed four and two respectively, while single aircraft were reported damaged by Lieutenants E Jungling, R J Farney, H A Euler, L L Jewell and H S Dixon.

Three further American claims were submitted by the 56th Fighter Group; 1st Lieutenant Russell Kyler claimed one destroyed, downgraded to a 'probable', while Captain W D Clark and Flight Officer J W Kassap each claimed an Me262 damaged near Salzwedel and Hamburg respectively and Lieutenant E H Sims of the 479th Fighter Group reported damaging another north of Lüneburg.

Mustangs of the 355th Fighter Group flew a free-lance support mission to the above attacks, Mustangs of the 354th Fighter Squadron dropping below the 1,000-foot cloud base to

Bloody Twilight: April 1945

Ripped in half by an R4M rocket, a 448th Bomb Group Liberator spins away. This is believed to be that brought down by Leutnant Fritz Müller on 4th April. (USAF)

take a look at Ludwigslust airfield. Two were shot down, Lieutenant Goth in a head-on pass by a FW190D of the *JG 7* airfield protection Staffel, while Lieutenant Truell crashed taking evasive action. A third - Lieutenant Gray - fell to *Flak*. One Me262 was claimed damaged by Lieutenant R.W.Cooper during this mission.

Two more jets were claimed damaged by other units, one by Lieutenant W H Bancroft of the 2nd Scouting Force during an engagement south of Parchim at 09.35 hours, and one by Lieutenant L B Alexander of the 474th Fighter Group, 9th Air Force at 11.00 hours.

Fighters of the 15th Air Force and from 1 TAF (Prov) ranged across southern Germany in the late afternoon when two American units engaged jet fighters in the area of Munich. Lieutenant Andrew N Kandis of the 324th Fighter Group made one 'confirmed' claim while Lieutenants J W Haun and R T Dewey claimed a 'probable' (subsequently upgraded to 'confirmed destroyed') and a damaged, respectively, the former after a solo fight with four Me262s. Meanwhile at 16.20 hours 325th Fighter Group pilots engaged jet fighters, Lieutenant William N Clark claiming a 'probable' and Lieutenant W K Day a 'damaged' over Munich. A jet pilot was successful in this area when at 11.20 hours P-38J of the 14th Fighter Group was caught by a '262 near Höhenlinden, Bavaria. 2nd Lieutenant B Randle was captured.

One RAF 2nd Tactical Air Force crew had an unnerving experience when an artillery-spotting Auster, of 652 Squadron, was jumped at low level by two Me262s. The pilot evaded by using the tiny turning circle of the aircraft until the jets flew away!

The *Luftwaffe* had scrambled some 47 Me262s to oppose the various raids and 44 of the pilots had reported engagements. Eight jets were lost and five more returned to their bases with battle damage. One of the jet pilots lost that day was *Major* Heinrich Ehrler of *Stab./JG 7*, who had been removed from his post with JG 5 for failing to defend the battleship *Tirpitz* against the deadly attack by Lancasters of 617 and 9 Squadrons, in which the capital ship had at last been sunk. Ehrler had entered combat near Berlin, and was shot down near Schaarlippe after claiming two B-17s destroyed. (Recent evidence, including a note in Helmut Lennartz's logbook, that Ehrler was lost on April 6th does not appear to be in accordance with the fact that although he is known to have been killed whilst intercepting American bombers, no contact with jets was reported on that date. The authors are convinced that his loss indeed occurred during the engagements on April 4th, as has always been believed). The *Geschwaderstab* also lost *Oberfeldwebel* Gerhard Reinhold, who was shot down and killed near Neu-Chemnitz, while *11 Staffel* lost two pilots in combats near Leipzig; both *Leutnant* Alfred Lehner and *Unteroffizier* Heckmann were killed. JG 7 claims totalled ten; in addition to those already noted, *Major* Weissenberger of *Stab./JG 7* claimed a B-17, *Leutnant* Stehle and *Gefreiter* Heim of *I./JG 7* also claimed Fortresses, and *Leutnant* Weihs of *3 Staffel* reported a Mustang destroyed near Bremen and later a Thunderbolt in the Schleswig-Holstein area, while *Oberstleutnant* Heinz Bär of *III./EJG 2* claimed a P-51. It seems likely that mistakes in recognition had occurred, B-24s being misidentified for B-17s. Apart from the American bomber losses already noted, a further fifteen were severely damaged, but succeeded in reaching Allied

Bloody Twilight: April 1945

Left: Heinrich Ehrler had been blamed for failing to prevent the destruction of the battleship Tirpitz by RAF Bomber Command. He died in the cockpit of his Me262 on 4th April and his body was never found. By the time of his death he had been credited with 208 victories, eight of them with JG 7.

Right: Charles M Bachmann and his 379th Bomb Group crew were lucky to escape when their combat box was hit by Me262s on 5th April. (C M Bachmann)

territory. Additionally, a 323rd Bomb Group Marauder was shot down south of Frankfurt-am-Main by another.

5th April, 1945

Heavy bombers of the 8th Air Force formed up over Paris and headed south-east to attack targets in central and southern Germany. Five Me262s from *JV 44* scrambled from Riem to intercept, the German pilots claiming two Fortresses destroyed. One B-17 of the 379th Bomb Group was shot down by an Me262 near Karlsruhe and two more were damaged so severely that they were 'written off' on return. One of the P-51 escorts also failed to return. A formation of B-24s was also attacked by jets and Charles M Bachman, who was a B-24 pilot with the 389th Bomb Group, recalled:

"I was not flying with my own crew on this mission to central Germany. I was an instructor with a new crew who had no previous combat experience. We called this the 'Dollar Mission' for new crews. I was in charge of their B-24 Liberator as First Pilot. We flew bucket lead on this mission, and were well into German airspace when a fighter suddenly went past our aircraft from the rear, very fast. 'What the Hell was that?', my co-pilot exclaimed. 'Messerschmitt 262', I replied. 'Jet fighter'. Three B-24s went down in the first seconds of the attack, and could never have known what hit them. Gunners reported another flight of the jets coming in; where the Hell were our escorts? I felt my aircraft shake as our gunners opened fire, and the stench of cordite filled the cockpit. One jet passed only feet above our heads as the guns rattled out. The jet got smaller by the second to our front, leaving us as if we were standing still in the air. This jet suddenly exploded, and disintegrated in front of the formation. Our upper gunner later reported that he had raked the jet's belly with his guns as it overshot us, and was later given credit for destroying it. The formation lost two more B-24s from the second wave of jets. Almost fifty of our airmen lost their lives that day."[89].

The 379th Bomb Group lost three B-24a to jets and the 388th and 453rd Bomb Groups one each - probably all to *JV 44* pilots. Two Fortresses also were lost by the 3rd Air Division, with two more heavily damaged machines crashing in Allied-held territory during their return journey.

The escorts were largely ineffective, due to the scarcity and elusiveness of the targets. Lt Ralph C Butler of the 354th Fighter Group claimed a 'damaged' in the Nordhausen-Leipzig area at 08.30 hours, and three hours later the 56th Fighter Group, - part of the escort to B-17s - was near near Regensburg when Me262s were sighted coming in. One shot down a Fortress of the 401st Bomb Group before Captain John C Fahringer closed on it, opening fire before the '262 slipped into cloud. Fahringer stayed with it, chasing through the cloud and scoring more hits before the German pilot baled out. Lt G Z Schroeder of the 364th claimed a 'damaged' in the same area and Lieutanant S C Ananian of the 339th scored another 'damaged' near Böblingen. Bomber crews were also successful; Staff Sergeant W E Adler of the 453rd Bomb Group, and Sgt W L Reckland of the 388th each being credited with one destroyed. Two Me262s of *JG 7* were reported as lost on this date.

7th April, 1945

The *Luftwaffe* High Command perpetrated the final madness; volunteers had been requested for a special operation, and more

Robin Olds of the 479th Fighter Group had his first engagement against a jet on 5th April 1945. Twenty-seven years later he was still fighting jets, leading F-4 Phantoms against MiGs over Vietnam, where he became one of the leading MiG-killers. (USAF)

than a hundred pilots had stepped forward to become part of *Sonderkommando Elbe*. Their task was to ram the American bomber formations. Most of the pilots were no more than boys, scarcely able to control their FW190s and Bf109s, and predictably the result was catastrophic. Me262s were involved as fighter cover for the *Rammjäger*, but when battle was joined against American formations over the Dummer and Steinhuder Lake areas the Mustang pilots had a field day; 59 German fighters were claimed destroyed, while bomber gunners claimed about 40 more. Some piston-engined fighters managed to penetrate the escort screen, but no more then eight bombers actually fell to ramming attacks. In the words of one gunner, 'It was a turkey shoot!' Only fifteen conventional German fighters eventually returned to their bases, so the American claims are substantially correct. The jets of course were harder to engage. One flight charged through the 100th Bomb Group, knocking down two Fortresses, while another flight that attacked the the 390th Bomb Group, destroyed one more; the 357th Fighter Group, on escort duties near Parchim, reported that a total of five B-17s had fallen to the jets. Only two *JG 7* claims against bombers are known; *Oberfeldwebel* Göbel claimed a B-17 over Parchim, and *Unteroffizier* Schöppler a B-24 near Bremen. A B-24 of the 389th Bomb Group was lost, accidentally rammed over Lüneburg by an unrecorded *JG 7* pilot. However, it is believed that aircraft of *JV 44*, equipped with R4M rockets, made an attack upon Fortresses over Thuringia, several being shot down. [90.]

A short while later, Me262s of *JG 7* attacked in some strength, but on this occasion took on the escorts. The American fighter pilots, normally ignored by jet pilots, were taken off guard as the '262s stormed in and victories over two Mustangs were claimed by *Oberfähnrich* Neumann and *Oberfähnrich* Pfeiffer of *III/.JG 7*. (*JG 7* pilots are believed to have claimed a total of 28 escort fighters during this operation, but no further details are available). In return Lieutenants Hilton O Thompson and Captain Verne E Hooker of the 479th Fighter Group claimed one jet apiece between Lüneburg and Bremen, while Lieutenant Richard G Candelaria claimed a 'probable' and Major Robin Olds a 'damaged'. Captain George E Bostwick of the 56th Fighter Group saw a '262 approaching the bombers and turned into it, driving it off and claiming it damaged over the Krummel area. The 4th Fighter Group was escorting Liberators that were attacked by four Me262s north of Steinhuder. The jets made a swift firing pass, bringing down one bomber before the German piston-engined *Rammjäger* attacked. The 453rd Bomb Group on its 255th mission of war, were engaged by two Me262s. Lieutenant Da Garcia, in one of the leading aircraft, spotted a '262 coming in at 11 o'clock and warned Staff Sergeant Willard Adler in the nose turret. At that moment another Me262 appeared, only 150 feet away and Adler opened fire, seeing .50 strikes in the cockpit, left wing and left engine. Then other members watched as it climbed away trailing smoke, then caught fire and dropped away into a vertical dive, vanishing into the clouds at 3,500 feet over Bremen. Adler was credited with a 'damaged'.

Oberfeldwebel Hermann Buchner was airborne and remembers:

> "I flew with my Schwarm as fighter escort to Operation *Elbe* in the area of Bremen-Hamburg-Hannover. Afterwards we had to land at Wiesmar, since Parchim was screened by Mustangs. We returned to our base that same evening." [91].

More Mustang units were involved in large combats between Bremen and Celle; Flight Officer J J Rice, and Lieutenants P E Petitt, O K Bigg, L M Carter and C M Mason of the 339th Fighter Group each claimed a Me262 damaged, Lieutenant R V Blizzard claiming one probably destroyed and another damaged. Lieutenants Reiff, Griswold and Hartzog of the 355th shared one 'destroyed' (no victory credit actually awarded) and Lieutenants Kouche and R V Finnessey of this unit damaged two

Trappings of an Experte. Hermann Buchner's decorations included the Ritterkreuz (top), The Deutsches Kreuz in Gold, (centre left), Frontflugspange (mission clasp) showing 600 sorties and his pilot's badge. (H Buchner)

more south-east of Bremen. Lieutenant Percy C O'Quinn of the 356th damaged another north-east of Steinhuder Lake while four other pilots from this unit - Captain Samuel P M Kinsey, and Lieutenants Thomas K Epley, Eldon L Slanker and Jerome S Thorough - jointly claimed another damaged, but again no victory credit has been traced. It seems that the Americans had underestimated the effects of their fire on this occasion, for whilst only two confirmed claims were submitted, *JG 7* reported the loss of five Me262s on this date.

The *Gruppen* of *KG(J)54* were now operating mainly from grass airstrips, but thirteen managed to get airborne from Hagenow airfield. They found a formation of B-17s and hurtled through them, three being claimed destroyed and another as a *Herausshuss*. Hauptmann Werner Tronicke, having reported the destruction of one B-17 and the *Herausschuss* of a second, was chased back to Hagenow by Mustangs, where he was shot down and killed flying 'B3+White 8'.

The 30th Recon Squadron of the 9th Air Force lost two Lightnings; in one of these Captain William T Heily was busy photographing a section of autobahn near Seesen when he was bounced by two Me262s of *3./JG 7*. *Oberleutnant* Walter Schuck shot out both engines and Heily baled out to become a prisoner. He was rescued by advancing troops eight days later.

8th April, 1945

RAF Lancasters attacked Hamburg and were intercepted by fifteen Me262s. Mustangs IIIs from 126 and 165 Squadrons were providing escort on this occasion and none of the bombers were lost, although one was claimed by *Oberleutnant* Stehle of *2./JG 7*. *Leutnant* Weihs, from *3 Staffel*, claimed a Lightning north of Berlin, having taken off from Oranienburg. *Feldwebel* Geisthovel of *III./JG 7* intercepted a section of four Mustangs near Cottbus, making one fast firing pass and claiming two of the American fighters shot down. *Oberfeldwebel* Hermann Buchner of *III./JG 7* had an interesting experience:

> "I flew a *Rotte* operation (two aircraft) in the Hamburg area. At about 8000 metres over the city I spotted a Spitfire, 1,000 metres lower, flying north. I looked for bombers, and awaited instructions from ground control. A few minutes later this aircraft, which appeared to be a reconnaissance aircraft, returned, heading northwest towards the Elbe. Since I was in a good tactical position, I was able to close very fast on the Spitfire from behind without being seen. It was going very fast, and in the final moment I believe that the Tommy was able to turn his aircraft to come at me head-on. Then I made a mistake; instead of opening fire, I broke to the left, so hard that my aircraft flicked over and went down out of control. I was momentarily terrified and then had my hands full trying to get the aircraft back to normal flight. By this manoeuvre I lost my wingman, and thus we returned to Parchim separately. I was richer from this experience, although no success was granted to me. I believe also, that our nerves were unduly stressed." 92.

Over southern Germany two jets were claimed destroyed, one by Lieutenant J J Usiatynski of the 358th Fighter Group, 9th Air Force, over Nordlingen at 14.15 hours, while little later Thunderbolts of the 50th Fighter Group, 1 TAF (Prov), engaged jets over Crailsheim, unrecorded pilots claiming one shot down and another damaged. American reconnaissance units were also engaged against Me262s; Lieutenants R A Rumbaugh and P Reavis of the 162nd Recon Squadron claiming a 'probable' and a 'damaged' respectively near Gunzburg at 07.45 hours, while Lieutenant R K Wylie of the 111th Recon Squadron claimed a 'damaged' at 16.45 hours.

It is possible that the 358th Fighter Group combat had been engaged with *JV 44* aircraft, for the experienced pilots of the *Gruppe* had commenced an intensive training programme for

Supervised by Leutnant Neumann, ground staff manhandle a JV 44 Me262. Note the small '8' and dark-to-light dappled camouflage.
(via ARP)

the relative novices. It is believed that on this date *Oberst* Johannes Steinhoff had led *Major* Krupinski and *Leutnant* Fährmann out on one such flight. The two jets had travelled only a short distance from Riem when a flight of P-38s passed beneath them. Steinhoff climbed and turned, hoping that Fährmann would follow; he had already warned the young pilot of the vulnerability of the '262 whilst turning. The jets were travelling fast; Fährmann was left behind as Steinhoff instinctively reacted and the inexperienced pilot's aircraft disappeared from view. Steinhoff made a fast dive at the P-38s, opening fire with his cannon, but the American pilots broke hard, evading the attack. They went down in fast dives, but the experienced German refused to be drawn; to follow could prove fatal. He had retained his R4M rockets and, as Fährmann suddenly appeared again on his port wing, the fighter controller reported a bomber formation approaching Regensburg. With fuel for only fifteen minutes remaining, Steinhoff decided to make one pass at the bombers before returning to Riem. He headed for the American formation with Fährmann closed in tight on his wing and very soon the enemy appeared, the sky filled with aircraft. He switched his rockets to 'live' and the two jets went down through the fighter cover at high speed, taking the American fighter pilots by surprise. As the Mustangs and Thunderbolts scattered, Steinhoff lined up on a box of Liberators and hit the firing button, but the R4Ms remained in their racks; the mechanism had failed. So great was his closing speed, that by the time he had selected his cannon, the plunging jet had overshot the target and the B-24s were above and behind him. Pulling back on his stick he climbed steeply, delivering an attack from below, cannon blazing as he again hurtled through the bombers at over 500 mph. Glancing backwards he saw one B-24 dragging a thick banner of black smoke. Fährmann had vanished again, and Steinhoff headed for Riem at speed. On landing he discovered that his wingman had been shot down. Fährmann, hit during the first pass, had then been set upon by four Thunderbolts as he nursed his crippled fighter away. He tried to reach cloud cover on his one functioning turbine, but bullets then hit his cockpit, slamming against the back armour and demolishing his instrument panel; he released the canopy and undid his harness. Later he told *JV 44* pilots that the air had hit him like a brick wall as he was literally sucked out of his seat, throwing his arms and legs in all directions; he then felt a sharp pain as his parachute opened, checking his wild descent a few hundred feet over a small wood. Bavarian farm workers extricated him from a tree and told him that his jet had plunged into the nearby River Danube. From these details, it is likely that Fährmann had fallen to Usiatynski's Thunderbolt. According to Steinhoff, Fährmann had accounted for two Fortresses during this engagement. [93]

The 100th Bomb Group were lucky on this occasion, for when four jets from *JV 44* attacked them, Mustangs intervened, driving the attackers off.

I./KG(J)54 pilots were again in action, four bombers being claimed destroyed and several more damaged by unnamed pilots.

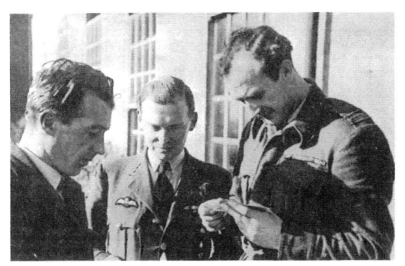

In April, RAF Bomber Command daylight attacks increased in number but the escorts rarely met jets. Flight Lieutenant Michel Gorzula of 309 Squadron (centre) was one RAF Mustang III pilot who got into the action on 9th April during Ramrod 1521 to Hamburg.
(via S E Harvey)

9th April, 1945
RAF Bomber Command returned to Hamburg in the afternoon, again escorted by Mustang IIIs. Flight Lieutenant M Gorzula of 309 (Polish) Squadron remembered *Ramrod 1521* very well:

"We flew across Hamburg, heavily veiled in writhing clouds of smoke reaching close to 10,000 feet. The stragglers in the bomber stream dropped their precious loads and we turned for England, base and beauty. We had barely left the target area when my earphones vibrated, and I heard 'Hello escort Leader, this is bomber Leader. Some jets about - over'. I looked all round carefully, but could see no Jerries. Then a green flare went up from the bomber stream, a second followed, and then a third.

"Things began to hum now, as order after order came through. I gave my engine more revs and more boost. I then saw six aircraft about 2,000 yards away diving towards the bomber formation. I dropped my supplementary fuel tanks and dived into the attack with other Mustangs from my flight. As we got closer I recognised the German aircraft as Me262s; twin-jet fighters. The jets levelled out after hitting the bombers and began to speed away, but one peeled off to make a second attack on one of the bombers that was losing height after their attacking run. I closed on the Me262 from above his tail; my airspeed was 500 mph at this time, and my engine was whining away at top pitch. At that moment he saw me, and was pulling away, 1,000 yards out from me, but I boosted my engine once more and got a little closer. Getting my sights on him I gave him a short burst, added a little correction, and gave him a longish burst and then another. My tracer was right on him, and the next moment he began to slow up. As I closed, I gave one last long burst of gunfire; there was a flash and the Me262 broke in two and began to spin, bursting into flames. One of its engines broke away and spun crazily downward. I then saw, as I rapidly closed, the pilot's parachute opening amidst the wreckage. Next moment the fabric burst into flames; he had 'bought it', falling from the sky with a blazing parachute." [94.]

Three further Mustang pilots, Squadron Leader J Zulikowski of 306 (Polish) Squadron, and Flight Lieutenant Jerzy Mancel and Warrant Officer Anton Murkowski from Gorzula's squadron also claimed Me262s shot down during this engagement, the latter pilot also claiming one damaged, as did Flying Officer A D Woodcock of 64 Squadron. 309 Squadron reported two more combats; Flight Lieutenant Jan Mozotowski engaged another jet but was unable to claim hits, while Pilot Officer Jan Lewandowski fought two more without success. The jets had attacked just as the bombers were leaving the target area. Flying Officer Greenfield's 61 Squadron Lancaster (RF121) took hits, reared up, and exploded. A 50 Squadron Lancaster (NG342) flown by Flying Officer Berriman was also shot down. Sergeants E Bestwick and J Huck, mid-upper and rear gunners in another 61 Squadron aircraft, opened fire on the Messerschmitt that had destroyed Greenfield's Lancaster, hitting it as it came abeam and seeing black smoke belch forth as it nosed over into a vertical dive.

JG 7 had scrambled 29 Me262s to defend Hamburg, and Lancasters were claimed by *Oberleutnant* Schall of *III./JG* 7 and by *Unteroffizier* Engler, *Leutnant* Zingler and *Gefreiter* Müller of *I Gruppe*. Additionally, in a separate combat against American fighters, *Leutnant* Müller of *11 Staffel* claimed the destruction of a Thunderbolt.

While the Lancasters were punishing Hamburg, the 'heavies' of the 8th flew the long haul down to Munich, and again jets were encountered. On this occasion it was Mustang pilots of the 55th Fighter Group that claimed the honours. Major Edward B Giller (now Major General Giller, USAF ret.) wrote:

{While we were escorting the 'Big Friends' to Munich, they flew into a small high cloudbank north of the city, just before the target. I pulled south at

24,000 feet to miss the cloud, and stumbled across an Me262 at 24,000 feet in a gentle right turn. I observed two P-51s chasing him, so I dropped tanks and turned left hoping to cut him off. I lost him for a minute and was about give up when I saw him at 20,000 feet, still being chased. Having altitude, I started chasing him south and east, staying the same distance behind him (about 1,500 yards). This went on for ten minutes with the jet doing a very gentle left turn and losing altitude. Finally we started back over the southern end of Munich - the jet at 1,000 and I at 7,000. I lost him again for a minute, then discovered him making for Munich-Riem airfield. I didn't know if he was going to land or try to drag me over some Flak. Going 'balls out', I caught him at fifty feet just over the perimeter track. He was going west to east about 100 yards to the right of the runway. I fired several bursts and observed strikes on the left wing root and fuselage. I noticed his wheels were not down, and his air-speed was about 250 mph. As my airspeed was about 450, I overshot rapidly and pulled up. When I looked back I saw him crash or belly-in on the field 100 yards to the right of the runway in a large cloud of dust and flying pieces. He did not burn, which I believe was due to the fact that he was out of fuel. The aircraft was completely wrecked." [95]

This success was confirmed by Giller's wingman Lieutenant Ernest E Leon, who stayed with his leader throughout the action. It is believed that the Me262 was one of Galland's *JV 44* aircraft. A second jet is believed to have been claimed on this mission by Lieutenant Grady Moore, also of the 55th Fighter Group, but was possibly unconfirmed, as no details are known. One further engagement took place when an unrecorded pilot from the 86th Fighter Group, 1 TAF (Prov), reported damage to another jet fighter.

The tactical bombers of the 9th Air Force were also in action on April 9th, 40 B-26s of the 387th Bomb Group attacking Amberg-Kummersbrück ordnance depot. Shortly after 10.00 hours, two Me262s made a line astern attack, shooting down one the Marauders flown by 2nd Lieutenant J D Stroud nine kilometres southwest of Amberg and badly damaging a second, but defensive fire hit one of the jets as it returned for a second pass. It was seen to go down in flames, exploding into a wood after the pilot had baled out. It is likely that these fighters were from *III./EJG 2*, *Oberstleutnant* Heinz Bär claiming two B-26 Marauders destroyed.

Meanwhile, 8th Air Force fighters were out over Germany in strength and reported several successful engagements against jets. The first was at 10.00 hours, when Mustangs from the 361st Fighter Group were engaged west of Berlin, where

Lieutenant J T Sloan claimed one Me262 destroyed and a second damaged. In the mid afternoon a long-range sweep was flown to Leipzig. Major H F Hunt and Lieutenant L M Orcutt of the 339th Fighter Group each claiming one jet damaged between Leipzig and Halle at 15.30 hours. An hour later, Me262s were claimed damaged near Augsburg by Captain M F Boussu and Flight Officer R C Muzzy of the same unit, the latter sharing a third 'damaged' with Lieutenant F Rea Jr. Fighters of 1 TAF (Prov) were also operating, Lieutenant J O Peeples of the 324th Fighter Group claiming a 'damaged' in the area of Augsburg during the morning, while an unidentified pilot from the 86th Fighter Group claimed another in the late evening. Lieutenant M W Geiger of the 162nd Recon Squadron also claimed a jet probably destroyed between Nürnberg and Augsburg. One Me262 from *3./JG 7* is known to have been lost, *Unteroffizier* Köhler perishing, but no details are known. *Leutnant* 'Hadi' Weihs of *3./JG 7* had scrambled from Oranienburg and met Mustangs south of Berlin. His own aircraft was damaged and he force-landed at the factory airfield at Dessau with a damaged undercarriage.

Operating from the south, the Lightning pilots of the 82nd Fighter Group had their last encounter with Me262s on another reconnaissance mission to Munich. The jet came up from below, approaching the lead element. The vigilant Americans saw it coming, dropped their external tanks and dived, opening fire. The German pilot then opened up his throttles wide and dived away.

10th April, 1945
Jagdgeschwader 7 sent off the largest number of jet fighters the Germans were ever to employ in a single mission; 55 Me262s from all three *Gruppen* were airborne, accompanied by the meagre reserves of piston-engined fighters to face more than 2,000 Allied aircraft; almost all the jet pilots reported engagements.

At least fifteen Messerschmitts got through to the B-17s of the 1st Air Division as they neared targets at Oranienburg, northern Germany. The jets used the same tactics as had been employed on previous occasions, breaking into pairs and going through the bomber stream from astern. Five B-17s from the

Bloody Twilight: April 1945

Aircraft and buildings burning after one of the three heavy USAAF raids on Parchim during April. These photos could well have been taken during the raid on 10th April. (H Buchner)

379th and 384th Bomb Groups were shot down before P-51s of the 20th Fighter Group intervened to prevent further destruction. Me262s were claimed destroyed by Captain John K Brown, Lieutenants Walter D Drozd, Albert B North and Captain John K Hollins, while Flight Officer Jerome Rosenblum and Lieutenant John W Cudd shared a fifth. Further jets were fired on and claimed damaged by Captain Douglas Michel and Lieutenants Robert W Meinzen and Glen R Hall. Some had been chased and shot down on landing, one other was brought down directly over Berlin where it was seen to fall into the heart of the city. Another was shot down with a 90 degree deflection shot, difficult enough against a conventional aircraft, almost unbelievable against a jet, even when using the remarkable K-14 computing gunsight.

Despite the intervention of the Mustangs, further B-17s fell to the jets. The 303rd Bomb Group lost Lieutenant R E Murray's 44-8427 over the target and the 100th lost two more. Fortress 43-38963 went down during an attack by seven Me262s at 14.05 hours and 43-38840 was shot down near Hannover at 14.15 hours. This Group lost another, which managed to return to England with severe damage and was scrapped after crash-landing.

It is probable that these attackers were from *I./JG 7*, the jet pilots claiming ten victories; *Oberleutnants* Schuck (four) Grünberg (two), Stehle, Bohatsch, *Oberfähnrich* Neuhaus and *Flieger* Reiher one each. Walter Schuck was shot down and baled out unhurt.

The Fortresses of the 351st, 401st, 457th and 487th Bomb Groups from the 3rd Air Division were briefed to bomb jet bases at Brandenburg/Briest, Parchim, Magdeburg and Lärz, and were bitterly opposed. For Engineer/gunner Frank M Mead Jr. of the 487th Bomb Group, the mission to Lärz was one he will never forget:

"We were approaching the German airfield, and we were caught out of formation with engine trouble by a flight of four Me262s. They made several passes at us with their nose cannon blazing, and we suffered severe damage. They shot the roof of the bomb bay right off with 30mm cannon shells and the large life raft that was stowed in the roof of the bomb bay automatically inflated and was sucked out of the hole torn in the top. It wrapped itself around our stabiliser fin at the rear, which set up a severe and unpredictable vibration right through the aircraft. With petrol leaking from damaged fuel lines, and with one engine dead, we went down out of control for all of 8,000 feet.

Almost down to tree-top height, this Me262 pilot desperately tries to escape the pursuing Mustang. (USAF)

"Our pilot, Lieutenant Orchard, and his co-pilot fought with the controls all this time and skilfully pulled the B-17 out of its death dive. One hour later he made a wheels-down landing at St. Trond air-field in Belgium. After we had all recovered from this experience, we looked over our damaged 'Fort'. We found whole panels shot off all over the wings. If a fire had started we would never have made it out of Germany. The B-17 was a write-off, and never flew again." [96].

Crews from this formation later reported that the attacking jets had guns beneath their wings, outboard of the engines. What they had in fact seen were the R4M missiles as the rockets were ripple-fired from the racks.

As the 457th Bomb Group turned away from their target, more jet fighters attacked. Captain Rod Francis' bomber, flying lead, took the main weight of the first pass. It broke formation and headed eastwards towards the Russian lines - and was never heard of again. Meanwhile that flown by Lieutenant Thompson nosed down and dived vertically into the ground. 2nd Lieutenant Edward Sells' *'Queen of Hearts'* (44-6913) had lagged behind the formation as they approached Brandenburg and was attack from astern. 30mm cannon strikes were seen in the fuselage, but for some minutes the B-17 maintained station. Then it slowly turned away and was last seen near Celle. All this crew survived to be taken prisoner. Two further Fortresses from the 487th were attacked simultaneously over the target at

15.14 hours. Seven of Flight Officer Max Hauenstein's crew baled out 44-8702 caught fire. Then the wing came off and the B-17 crashed near the Elbe. 1st Lieutenant L H McGinnes was flying 44-8808 was shot down in flames near Gardelegen. Eight men managed to bale out, the co-pilot, 2nd Lieutenant Murray Brill, later being forced to bury the badly burned bodies of the pilot and the engineer, Technical Sergeant J V Henderson, in a cemetery near Gardelegen. [97.]

Also on the 10th, the 100th Bomb Group was engaged, seven Me262s making determined attacks near Magdeburg airfield at 14.15 hours. Lieutenant Delbert Reeves' 43-38840 had a wing shot off and went down in flames with one man baling out, while 43-38943, already out of formation with engine trouble, became an easy target. Nos. 3 and 4 engines were hit and burst into flames, four men parachuted and the aircraft went down carrying Lieutenants James Dotson and Lawrence Bazin (the pilots) and the rest of the crew. Lieutenant Griswold Smith's Fortress was badly shot-up by the jets, but he returned with the rest of the Group, one jet being credited to a gunner. These attackers were possibly from *I./KG(J)54*, which had scrambled 21 Me262s. *Leutnant* Paul Palenda claimed a Fortress and a *Herausschuss*, *Leutnant* Rossow another Fortress and scored hits on a fourth, while *Leutnant* Becker destroyed a fifth. One further B-17, a B-24 and a P-51 were claimed by unnamed pilots. Palenda and Rossow were then shot down and killed by P-51s near Genthin, while *Leutnant* Bernhard Becker was caught on finals at Berby by another Mustang. He managed to bale out of 'B3+Yellow 9', but was strafed and badly wounded on the ground. The *Gruppe* suffered one further loss when *Oberleutnant* Beck was caught by American fighters near Böhmen, where he was shot down and killed. Total claims for *I./KG(J)54* were reported as twelve confirmed and three *Wahrscheinlich* (probables) during several actions. Several Me262s force-landed, but there are no available details of these.

Meanwhile further Mustang units had been engaged. The 55th Fighter Group encountered jets between Lübeck and Burg, where two were claimed shot down by Lieutenants K R McGinnis and K A Lashbrook; two more were reported damaged by Lieutenants D D Bachmann and C S Chioles. At the same time Thunderbolts of the 56th Fighter Group arrived over Muritz Lake, where Lieutenant W J Sharbo claimed an Me262 shot down, the pilot baling out. Captain W Wilkerson and Lieutenant E W Andermatt were credited with strikes upon two more. A short while later the 352nd Fighter Group engaged more of these fighters near Berlin. Lieutenant Colonel Earl D Duncan shared one 'kill' with Major Richard G McAuliffe, Duncan reporting that his gunfire was hitting the '262 even while the pilot was attempting to bale out. He considered that the pilot could not have survived. Lieutenants J W Pritchard and C A Ricci shared a second near Neuruppin, and Lieutenant C C Pattillo got a third east of Ulzen airfield, while a 'damaged' was credited to Lieutenant K M Waldron.

Mustangs of the 353rd Fighter Group were flying escort to B-17s that were bombing Zerbst and Briest, and encountered single Me262s near Dessau. Captain Gordon B Compton claimed one shot down at low level and Captain Robert W Abernathy fired on another at 18,000 feet and saw the pilot bale out after it had caught fire, while Lieutenants Jack W Clark and Bruce D McMahan sighted a third, flying at low level over the town. Clark recalled:

"I made an ess and went down on him. We were in range before he could turn on his jets. Lieutenant MacMahan and I both shot long bursts into him. I saw Lieutenant MacMahan get hits on the right jet and wing, and he saw me hit the left jet and wing. The E/A was in a 60 degree climb when our combined fire knocked out both of his jets. He fired a red-red flare, rolled over, and baled out."

During the day the 353rd Fighter Group also flew ground attacks, strafing *JV 44*'s base at Riem, claiming three jets destroyed and a similar number damaged.

Mustangs of the 4th Fighter Group, flying Penetration Support, engaged jets near Lübeck, where, at 14.45 hours, Lieutenant Willmer W Collins claimed one destroyed. The 356th Fighter Group, engaged over Oranienburg at 15.15 hours, Lieutenant W C Gatlin claiming one shot down and Lieutenant T M Mauldin another probably destroyed while Lieutenant E W Schrull claimed one damaged.

On the 10th also, Mustangs of the 359th Fighter Group flew out to Gardelegen, catching several jets in the circuit. Two were claimed shot down by Lieutenants H Tenenbaum and R J

Franz Schall died on 10th April and was buried at Parchim. His grave is still carefully tended.
(H Buchner)

Guggemos, while Captain W V Gresham and Lieutenant J T Marron, hunting near Lübeck, claimed to have inflicted damage upon two more, and Lieutenant R R Klaver adding another damaged north-west of Berlin. Finally at around 16.00 hours Captain D J Pick and Lieutenant H C Schwartz of the 364th Fighter Group reported an Me262 shot down over Staaken airfield, west of Berlin.

Although the 8th Air Force Mustang units had borne the brunt of the fighting, Thunderbolts of the 9th, operating in the tactical rôle, met jets on one occasion; Lieutenant R B Manwaring of the 358th Fighter Group claimed a 'damaged' over Crailsheim at around noon.

One *Luftwaffe* pilot, *Leutnant* Walter Hagenah of *III./JG 7*, had been on his first operational flight with the Me262 that day, although he had previously seen considerable action whilst flying the FW190. He and his wingman were engaged by Mustangs before reaching the bombers and the inexperienced No 2, having never been in combat before, panicked. He was at once shot down. Hagenah acted coolly, outran his pursuers, then turned hard for a firing pass. He fired off his rockets into their midst, bringing down one Mustang before speeding away to land on an airfield that was under attack by other Mustangs; he was fortunate to get down without being hit. On April 10th Hagenah was one of the lucky ones.

III./JG 7 was also heavily engaged; one Fortress was reported destroyed by *Fähnrich* Pfeiffer, Mustangs by *Oberfeld-*

webel Lennartz, *Leutnant* Rademacher and *Oberfeldwebel* Greiner, whilst *Feldwebel* Pritzl claimed a Thunderbolt.

During this operation *JG 7* lost 27 jets, more than 50% of its available strength and considerably more than were claimed by the US escorts. Eight of the pilots are known to have survived to fight again and five were reported killed. These included *Oberleutnant* Walter Wagner, *Kapitän* of *1 Staffel*, who was shot down by P-51s near Stendal. The remaining fourteen were posted as missing - either dead or prisoners. Eight more Me262s landed with battle damage. *10./JG 7* suffered a grievous loss when its *Staffelkapitän*, the brilliant *Oberleutnant* Franz Schall, force-landed in a field beside Parchim after claiming a Mustang destroyed. His Me262 rolled into a bomb crater and exploded, killing him instantly. At the time of his death he had claimed sixteen confirmed jet victories. A third Staffel leader, *Oberleutnant* Walter Wever, of *7./JG 7*, was shot down and killed by a fighter near Neuruppin. *Gefreiter* Heim, of *1./JG 7*, was shot down near Berlin as was *Feldwebel* Schwarz. Both were killed. It seems probable that most of the *JG 7* losses noted above were suffered during engagements with the 20th, 56th and 356th Fighter Groups near Oranienburg. Many of the jets were destroyed near their airfields as they sought to land, while others had been overwhelmed by the bomber escorts. 815 American escort fighters were operating. Burg airfield was attacked, and here ten jets were destroyed - four from *10./NJG 11*, three from *2./JG 7* and three more from *Nahaufklärungsgruppe 6*. Aircraft from 9 and *10./JG 7* had been scrambled from Parchim at 14.15 hours, but Thunderbolts were lurking nearby and the jets flown by *Oberfähnrich* Windisch and *Unteroffizier* Vigg were shot down. Both pilots survived, although wounded.

It was a blow from which the jet fighter force would never recover. Never again would jets rise in such strength to give the American pilots such a wealth of targets. With the steel ring now closing steadily around the shrinking *Reich*, time was running out. *Leutnant* 'Hadi' Weihs of *3./JG 7* wrote:

"April 10th 1945 was the blackest day for the Me262. Oranienburg was, like many other airfields - ploughed up by several attacks; I went through that on the ground." [98.]

After the bitter losses of April 10th, orders came for *JG 7* to move again, to Plattling, Mühldorf, Landau and Prague/Ruzyne and the transfer was effected during the next few days. Thus *JG 7* was largely absent from the Home Defence (*Reichsverteidigung*) for several days. The most complete *Gruppe, III./JG 7*, moved to Prague/Ruzyne airfield on 11th April, when it would be joined by the remnants of *KG(J)54*.

11th April, 1945
A section from *III./JG 7* arrived at Prague/Ruzyne. The airfield was reported clear of enemy aircraft, but as *Oberleutnant* Hans Grünberg approached, he was attacked by American fighters and shot down, baling out safely. Two claims were made on this date, Lieutenant Colonel James G Thorsen of the 31st Fighter Group claiming a Me262 damaged near Simbal, while a similar claim was made north of Halle by Lieutenant C W Staats of the 107th Recon Squadron, this latter credited as 'unconfirmed'. Meanwhile Tempests of 222 Squadron set out to strafe Fassberg airfield, where Squadron Leader E B Lyons attacked a Me262 on the ground. As his pilots reformed, a jet was seen to take off and climb away from the base on fire. It reached 2,000 feet where the pilot baled out. It was considered probable that this was the aircraft that Lyons had just damaged.
It was also time for *I./KG(J)54* to leave Alt Lonnewitz and Brandis. It too went Prague/Ruzyne, where it joined *JG 7*.

April 12th 1945
At 02.00 hours infantry elements of the British 2nd Army occupied the town of Westen, on the River Weser, some 30 miles southeast of Bremen. Shortly after daybreak Sergeant J Baker, serving with the Royal Engineers, saw a number of jets come in low, raking Westen with cannon fire. Royal Artillery Bofors batteries opened fire, shooting down one of the aircraft nearby.[99.] Far to the south *JV 44* was in action again over Bavaria; *Oberstleutnant* Heinz Bär, who had recently transferred from *III./EJG 2*, claimed another Marauder shot down. During the afternoon, elements of *3./JG 7* engaged twenty P-47s over Dresden and here *Flieger* Reiher claimed a confirmed success.

14th April, 1945
After a quiet day on April 13th - at least as far as jet activity

concerned - elements of the 2nd Army moved forward along the west bank of the River Weser to discover that the railway bridge at Rethem had been destroyed by the retreating German forces. Royal Engineers laboured to throw a Bailey pontoon bridge across the river, and when General Neil Ritchie, the Corps Commander, visited the site to check on the progress of the work, more Me262s came over at low level, strafing the bridge and troop positions on the west bank.[100]

There were several jet engagements on April 14th, three involving 9th Air Force units. The first occurred at 15.30 hours when Lieutenant A J Richey of the 354th Fighter Group claimed an Me262 damaged, north of Halle. Fifteen minutes later Captain Clayton K Gross of this unit found a lone Me262 of *9./JG 7* at around 3,000 feet near Alt Lonnewitz airfield; he attacked and shot the Messerschmitt down, killing *Oberleutnant* Erich Stahlberg. At 16.20 hours aircraft of the 353rd Fighter Group, 8th Air Force, encountered another near Riesa, which was claimed destroyed by Lieutenant Lloyd J Overfield. This was probably that flown by *Feldwebel* Arno Thimm of *II./JG 7*, who baled out wounded - possibly the first operational casualty of the *Gruppe*. During the course of this day elements from *Gefechtsverband Hogeback* are believed to have engaged American heavy bomber formations. P-47s of the 27th Fighter Group, 1 TAF (Prov), were also attacked over southern Germany, Lieutenant Almond being shot down by an Me262. One further American claim was submitted, Lieutenants R M Kollar and E B Scott of the 162nd Recon Squadron claiming a 'damaged' near Ansbach, at 17.00 hours. A third Me262 was lost, flown by *Unteroffizier* Ludwig Ehrhardt of *9./KG(J)54*. He had managed to take off from the desolation that was Neuburg airfield, but was engaged by Mustangs and shot down. He too baled out wounded. His opponent was obviously one of the 354th Fighter Group pilots mentioned above.

15th April, 1945
Thirty-four Marauders of the 394th Bomb Group raided the Gunzburg marshalling yards; near Lake Constance, three Me262s attacked from astern at around 13.00 hours, scoring no hits; two were claimed damaged by turret gunners. Meanwhile in the north, jets attacked British Army positions as Otersen,

After a disastrous start to operations in 1943, the remarkably streamlined B-26 Marauder went on to become a very effective medium bomber, well-liked by its crews and respected by its opponents. (C Ellis)

and returned to strafe the Bailey Bridge at Rethem. Although Bofors gunners put up a heavy barrage, no successes were claimed. During this attack both jets and piston-engined aircraft were seen, and bombs were dropped, indicating that on this occasion the jets were probably providing cover for conventional fighter-bombers. RAF Tempests from 56 Squadron flew an armed reconnaissance between Kiel and Oldenburg in the morning, where at 10.10 hours Flight Lieutenants J A McCairns and N D Cox spotted a jet aircraft to the north-east, near Kaltenkirchen airfield. The two pilots dived, McCairns catching the jet in a climbing turn to port and delivering a one-second burst at 600 yards:

> "I closed the range to 300 yards and gave a three-second burst, closing to about 100 yards from dead astern. I observed strikes on the fuselage and starboard wing."

He broke hard to starboard and Cox attacked:

> "I closed in astern to 200 yards, closing to 75 yards and firing all the time.... I saw strikes on the fuselage, wing roots and starboard power unit."

As Cox broke away McCairns watched the jet dive into a house four miles to the south-east of the airfield. Although they claimed an Me262 'shared destroyed', their opponent is believed to have been an Ar234 bomber. For the second day in succession

Mustangs from the 162nd Recon Squadron were engaged by jets, and again the American pilots proved equal to the challenge. Lieutenant W P Simpson claimed two damaged near Nordlingen at 16.00 hours, while Lieutenant G B Gremillion claimed damage to two more north of Nürnberg five minutes later.

16th April, 1945

JV 44 rose in some strength to engage B-26 Marauders, known to the Germans as the *Haifisch* (Shark). *Generalleutnant* Galland attacked one formation and claimed two destroyed with his rockets. Although this action is reported to have taken place on April 15th, an error of one day appears to have occurred, for no Marauders were lost on that day, but on the 16th two B-26s of the 322nd Bomb Group, and another from the 387th were lost.

In the afternoon, the 8th Air Force despatched a heavy bomber mission to Rosenheim, south of Munich. Major Louis H Norley of the 4th Fighter Group was leading 'Cobweb' Squadron (334th) as 'B' Group:

> "We gave our box of bombers close escort from rendezvous through the target and back to Ulm, and safe airspace, where we broke off escort and set course back to the target area. We cased a previously-planned area, which was an autobahn running south-southeast from Munich. In a section of the wooded area adjacent to the autobahn we found approximately seven fires burning, and eight to ten aircraft parked on the north edge of the woods still intact. We reduced altitude from six to four thousand feet and checked them, however the light Flak was too accurate and intense to warrant an attack, so we drove on north to Munich to look over Gablingen airfield seen previously. The aircraft parked on this field numbered approximately 15; Dornier 217s, a couple of Me262s, plus a single Royal Air Force Halifax bomber, which must have force-landed there.
>
> "The *Flak* was too vicious to warrant an attack. While we were orbiting, an Me262 passed two thousand feet above us heading southeast. I despatched one flight from our group to attempt an engagement, the jet seemingly attempting to land at the aerodrome we were orbiting. The jet managed to escape destruction." [101].

The 8th Air Force 'heavies' did not escape without some jets intervening, for the 483rd Bomb Group lost three Fortresses over Ruhland to jet action.

Twelve P-47s of the 368th Fighter Group, 9th Air Force, found a dozen Me262s taking off from an airfield west of Prague, in

A dappled grey Me262 of JG 7 taxies out. The camouflage is very different from the JV 44 aircraft pictured earlier in this chapter.
(via ARP)

the afternoon. Two were claimed destroyed by Lieutenants Harry A Yandel and Vernon O Fein. Other P-47 Groups strafed airfields, claiming a further six destroyed and three damaged. Meanwhile, the 55th Fighter Group, 8th Air Force, visited Hörsching airfield where, at 15.30 hours, an Me262 was sighted and claimed destroyed by Major Eugene E Ryan; *JG* 7 recorded the loss of one Me262, the pilot of which was killed.

17th April, 1945
Both *I./KG(J)54* and *JV 44* pilots opposed another raid by heavy bombers on Munich. Nine Me262s led by Adolf Galland lifted off from Riem and headed for the city. They arrived just as the first bombers were turning away after their bombing runs. Clouds of smoke rolled up from the suburbs and factories, punctuated by the flashes as the heavy *Flak* batteries put up a concerted fire that shot one Fortress from the sky.

The jet pilots waited until the leading bomber Groups had escaped the box barrage and then they dived. Several other B-17s had been hit by gunfire and as the Me262s closed, one disappeared in a blinding explosion. Nearby bombers were rocked by the blast, losing their tight formation just at the moment that the jets attacked, firing off their R4Ms like giant shot-guns. *Oberst* Steinhoff hit the rocket button, but the firing mechanism failed. He then saw a jet ahead of him collide with a Fortress, the wing slicing the bomber's tail unit clear away; the Messerschmitt spun down with the outer section of one wing missing while the B-17 rolled over and plunged vertically downward. The the destruction of this jet was credited to Technical Sergeant Murdock K List, gunner aboard a 305th Bomb Group Fortress and of the stricken bomber, all of Lieutenant Brainard H Harris' crew were killed.

Steinhoff hit the rocket release button and for the second time the mechanism failed; as he charged through the scattering formation he saw the escorts diving from above and decided to join his companions now speeding away. They had enough fuel to divert to Feldkirchen, if American fighters were lurking around Riem, but when they neared that base they found nothing but destruction; other American bombers had raided the airfield in their absence, leaving the fuel dump and workshops in flames.

The jets landed and were quickly dispersed into their blast pens. The sole missing aircraft was that involved in the mid-air collision. It was assumed that *Unteroffizier* Edward Schallmoser had perished on his first combat sortie with the jet. Later in the day, however, he appeared at Riem having baled out unhurt, and was instantly christened 'The Jet Rammer of *JV 44*'. Seven B-17s were lost.

The *KG(J)54* Me262 pilots claimed six B-17s destroyed and three *Herausschüsse*.

During the course of the day 9th Air Force fighters had flown massive airfield strafes, claiming 124 German aircraft destroyed and damaged, including four Me262s.

On the same day B-17s of the 1st Air Division were intercepted south of Berlin by aircraft from *III./JG 7*, which shot down one Fortress of the 305th Bomb Group with cannon-fire; this aircraft, *The Towering Titan*, was the last 1st Air Division Fortress to fall to fighter action. The 357th Fighter Group reported that jets hit the bomber stream just as it turned at the Initial Point and headed for the Chemical works at

Aussig. Seven Me262s came in, but were beaten off by Mustangs. One cut power and attempted a tight turn, but Lieutenant James A Steiger did a wing-over and got behind it. He opened fire, seeing strikes all over it, following which a wing flew off and the fighter crashed. Lieutenant Colonel Jack W Hayes claimed a 'damaged'. The escorts chased the jets south, straight onto the guns of 20th Fighter Group Mustangs, which were supporting another raid on Dresden. Lieutenant Robert M Scott and Flight Officer Jerome Rosenblum from this latter unit reported hits on Me262s as they swept past, the latter claiming that he might well have destroyed one had not a section of Mustangs from another Group blocked him. Two further jets were claimed destroyed by Captains Robert J Frisch and John C Campbell of the 339th Fighter Group, part of the Aussig raid escort Frisch's opponent was obviously already badly damaged. As he and his wingman swept down, the German pilot hurriedly baled out. The subsequent claim was not credited. Campbell pursued his quarry for many miles, finally catching it as it neared Prague/Ruzyne airfield, where two jets were also claimed destroyed on the ground by pilots of the 357th. *Oberleutnant* Grünberg of *I./JG 7* had led three of his pilots back to Prague, where all four were shot down while landing; only Grünberg baled out safely. One these victims may have been *Unteroffizier* Fick of *3 Staffel*, reported shot down and killed by a fighter near Prague. Another pilot reported missing during the day was *Oberfeldwebel* Heinz Arnold of *11./JG 7*, who had claimed 42 victories on conventional fighters and had added at least seven more on jets; he may have been Lieutenant Steiger's victim.

The 4th Fighter Group, flying a free-lance sweep in the Prague area, found a single Me262 that was chased down to ground level. Before the Mustang pilots could close sufficiently to open fire, the German pilot crash-landed his jet, and no claim was made. The 364th Fighter Group was also supporting these raids and engaged jets between Dresden and Prague. Captain R W Orndorff claimed one shot down over Prague, Lieutenant W F Kissel claimed a second on the ground near Falkenst, and Captain W L Goff a third over Pilsen. Lieutenant S V Price reported one damaged near Dresden. Aircraft of the 324th

Fighter Group, 1 TAF (Prov), engaged jets ten miles north of Halle, where Lieutenants K E Dahlstrom and J V Jones each claimed a 'probable', Lieutenant R Pearlman claiming a damaged and Lieutenants D L Raymond and T N Theobald sharing another 'damaged'. The 358th Fighter Group, 9th Air Force, patrolled near Nürnberg, Lieutenant T R Atkins claiming a 'probable' while Lieutenants E E Heald and F C Bishop shared a 'damaged' during a separate engagement. Finally, Major Hewitt of the 78th Fighter Group caught an Me262 landing at Kralupy and reported it destroyed, but his claim was disallowed.

One of the 1st Air Division Wing Commanders, Brigadier General William Gross, was airborne in a B-17 operating as a 'command scout'. Although such aircraft did not normally accompany the main force further than the French coast, Gross decided on this occasion to follow the bombers to their target at Dresden. His intention was to observe the results of each bombing wave in turn, but as he left the first wave and orbited, waiting for the second, an Me262 appeared from nowhere, opening fire on the lone Fortress. So fast was the attack that the gunners had no time to open fire; fortunately only one shell hit the bomber, turning the empty bomb bay into a shambles. Before the '262 could attack again, Gross got the B-17 tucked in tightly with the next bomber formation - and stayed with them all the way home!

On the same day B-26 Marauders of the 17th and 320th Bomb Groups from the 1 TAF (Prov) were engaged by Me262s:

> "Two missions were flown today...... On mission two, six of our ships bombed Alt Dettelsau ammo' dump with fair results. Two jet fighters jumped the 17th Bomb Group formation damaging one ship, others damaged two B-26's of the 320th Group also on this second mission."

Sergeant James A Valimont of the 34th Bomb Squadron was awarded the Distinguished Flying Cross for courage displayed during this operation, as described in the following citation:

> "On April 17 1945, Sergeant Valimont served as a tail gunner in a formation of B-26 Marauders attacking Dettelsau in Germany. As the bombers approached the target area, a total of six jet aircraft suddenly jumped from a layer of clouds, attacking the Marauders in an aggressive manner. The tail section of Sergeant Valimont's plane was shot away, and his left leg was severely cut. Recovering his position with only the framework of the tail

remaining intact, Sergeant Valimont resolutely manned his guns, and on the next attack so badly damaged the fighter aircraft that the attack was diverted without further action." [102].

Another B-26 gunner, Sergeant Chestnutt, submitted a claim for a jet fighter destroyed during this combat.

Eight Mustangs of the 354th Fighter Group, 9th Air Force, flying an armed reconnaissance near Karlsruhe at 13.45 hours, found a lone Me262 at 1,500 feet, which was attacked and claimed destroyed by Captain Jack A Warner. Later that afternoon P-47s of the 371st Fighter Group (another 9th Air Force unit), flying co-operation for the XX Army Corps, found a jet at 6,000 feet near Eger. Lieutenant James A Zweizig managed to bounce it, and claimed to have shot it down - the fifteenth jet aircraft to be destroyed by 9th Air Force fighters.

The great airfield strafes continued, with American fighters ranging deep into the last bastions of the Reich. The bases at Ruzyne, Saaz and Pilsen were all attacked, nine Me262s being damaged amongst hundreds of other aircraft.

Jet pilots also submitted several more claims. *I./JG* 7 engaged Fortresses near Dresden, where three were claimed by *Hauptmann* Späte, *Oberleutnant* Bohatsch and *Oberleutnant* Stehle. *III Gruppe* entered claimed four more over Prague, credited to *Leutnant* Müller, *Oberfeldwebels* Pritzl and Göbel, and *Unteroffizier* Schöppler.

Meanwhile in the north, jets again attempted to destroy the British 2nd Army river crossings west of the River Elbe. Me262s attacked on the evenings of 17th and 18th April; during one of these attacks Bofors gunners scored strikes on one aircraft, which limped away on one engine after a spurt of flame was seen to erupt from the other nacelle.

18th April, 1945
During the morning the Luftwaffe fighter control plotted a strong bomber force entering the Stuttgart area. The target was estimated to be Regensburg, and at once Galland was contacted at Riem. Six Me262s were readied, Galland leading the first three-aircraft *Kette* and *Oberst* Steinhoff the second. Other pilots flying that day included *Oberstleutnant* Heinz Bär, *Leutnant* Fährmann and *Leutnant* Hein Wübke. The latter had been shot down four times in four missions, each time returning to Riem by train. He had now taken to painting *Ich Fliegen für*

Bloody Twilight: April 1945

Top: The wreckage of Steinhoff's Me262 at Riem. (via ARP)

Above: Don Bochkay brings his Mustang in to land at Leiston. (via R Freeman)

Right: Don Bochkay, one of the very few Allied pilots to destroy two Me262s. His first was on 9th February, his second on 18th April. (via R Freeman)

Das Reichbahn on the fuselage of his Me262 - 'I fly for the railway!'

The first flight took off with no problems, but as Steinhoff accelerated hard down the runway he suffered the one misfortune that every jet pilot feared; an engine flame-out at the point of take off. With only 150 yards of runway remaining, the result was inevitable. The jet, weighed down with fuel and rockets, skidded sideways and, with a long trail of flame erupting from the faulty engine, hit an embankment. The wheels ripped away and the aircraft leapt into the air before smashing back down and bursting into flames. Eye-witnesses saw only a funeral pyre, but suddenly the figure of the pilot staggered out, dreadfully burned; he was rushed to hospital. Although Steinhoff's war was over, he began another battle as medical staff fought to save his life. He survived to attain high rank with the Federal German *Luftwaffe*, but to the day he died he remained terribly scarred, a bitter legacy of the Me262.

The 357th Fighter Group was flying on area support duties in the vicinity of Prague, where two jets were seen taking off from Ruzyne. One escaped, but Major Bochkay attacked the second, shooting it down in flames. A short while later four more were seen, apparently attempting to land. One of these was claimed destroyed by Captain Charles E Weaver, but the other three also escaped. Mustangs from the 356th Fighter Group flew a similar sortie to Ingolstadt, engaging jets attacking bombers. One was chased right through the bomber formation and claimed damaged by Lieutenants W C Gatlin, G W Seanor and L B Proctor, while Lieutenant O L Burwell was credited with damage to a second. At the same time Major L K Carson claimed two jets damaged over Ruzyne airfield while Lieutenants F A Dellorta and R H Bradner shared another 'damaged'. The 339th Fighter Group was also operating far to the east, Lieutenant Colonel Joseph L Thury reporting a Me262 damaged near Tabor.

Aircraft from the 15th Air Force were again sweeping over southern Germany. Mustangs of the 325th Fighter Group patrolled near Riem where, at 10.50 hours, a jet was sighted taking off by Major Ralph F Johnson. He dived from 10,000 feet to ground level, his gunfire beginning to hit the jet as it left the runway. The German pilot made a gentle climbing turn to the left, Johnson maintaining contact and firing in short bursts until the two aircraft reached 3,000 feet. His victim then rolled onto its back and the pilot dropped out.

B-26s of the 322nd and 387th Bomb Group were also engaged by jets and despite the P-51 escorts, one Marauder of the 387th flown by 1st Lieutenant E L Walker was shot down near Donauwörth and another damaged. Finally, during the mid morning period, two Mustangs of the 162nd Recon Squadron took off from Hagenow, near Strasbourg, for a sortie over Nürnberg. Lieutenants Newman and Walter P Simpson had just passed over the city at 8,000 feet through a partial undercast but with clear sky above. They saw a large land battle taking place nearby, but Newman then noticed something of greater interest:

"At that moment I spotted an Me262 heading south in a shallow descent, about a mile ahead of me and at 12 o'clock to my position. I called him out to my leader and this being my first air-to-air engagement I foolishly made a high side-curve of pursuit full throttle pass at this jet, which turned out to be a decoy.

"My leader, luckily for me, fell in behind to cover my tail. As I closed on the jet, getting near to firing range, he picked up speed and accelerated away from me. Despite his half-windshield lead on me, I fired a burst which was limited to a desperate 'hope-I-hit-him' shot. As I fell into trail behind him, out of range and getting further behind by the second, my leader's voice came over the ear-pieces of my flying helmet: "Break!"

"I immediately turned hard to port, noticed black puffs in the air where I had been a second before and also around Lieutenant Simpson's plane as he followed me round. At the same time I saw the source of the puffs; 30mm cannon fire from a second Me262 which had attacked from the rear as soon as we had committed ourselves to the bait. I continued my turn to come round onto this jet aircraft as he sped by and managed a quick deflection shot on him as he accelerated down through the undercast. I have no idea if I got any hits on him as my gun camera failed that day. We did not see either of them again after this engagement. The second jet got one or two hits on Lieutenant Simpson's aircraft, but he got back to base okay. The only damage I had was to my ego. I was 'Green and Lucky' that day."[103].

These jets were either from *JG 7* or *JV 44* - probably the latter. During the course of the day *Oberstleutnant* Heinz Bär claimed two Thunderbolts shot down.

The Me262 Combat Diary

19th April, 1945
One of the last-known engagements between the Me262s of *III./JG 7* and 8th Air Force bombers took place when B-17s of the 3rd Air Division raided railway yards at Aussig, Czechoslovakia. B-17s of the 490th Bomb Group were over Prague, turning for their run in to the target when four Me262s dived out of the high cirrus cloud. Two made a head-on pass, shooting down a Fortress from the leading formation. These jets were chased by 'B' Group of the 357th Fighter Group right back to Ruzyne airfield where both were claimed destroyed, one by Lieutenant James P McMullen, and the second shared by Captain Ivan L McGuire and Lieutenant Gilman L Weber. McMullen, on his second combat mission, had found himself 1,000 feet above and behind an unsuspecting jet pilot, who quickly baled out when attacked at 1,500 feet. Meanwhile the other two Me262s went through the high and low squadrons of the 490th, bringing down three further bombers. These two German fighters were chased through the bomber formation by Mustang escorts and one was claimed shot down by Captain Robert Deloach of the 55th Fighter Group.

A few moments later, a single Me262 attacked aircraft from the 447th Bomb Group in the same general area, shooting down the B-17 flown by Lieutenant Robert Glazner, who baled out with his crew. All were captured, but were liberated by advancing Allied troops within a week.

In total, six bombers fell to Me262s on this date. *Hauptmann* Späte, *Unteroffizier* Schöppler, *Oberleutnant* Bohatsch and *Oberleutnant* Grünberg of *I Gruppe* each claimed one success, whilst a fifth fell to *Oberfeldwebel* Göbel of *III Gruppe*. The price was again heavy; four further Me262s were claimed by the pilots 'A' Group of the 357th Fighter Group who had swept ahead of the bombers, arriving over Prague at 11.50 hours and catching aircraft from *III./JG 7* as they took off from Ruzyne airfield. Lieutenant Colonel Jack W Hayes waited, circling his Group up-sun until sixteen jets were airborne, and then led his Mustangs down. Hayes chased one across a river south of the city outskirts, where the pilot tried to avoid his fire by diving behind a large building, but misjudged his height and crashed into the ground. Credits were awarded to Hayes, Captain

Bloody Twilight: April 1945

Leo Schuhmacher started the war in 1939, flying Bf110s with ZG 76. He later flew FW190s with Heinz Bär in JG 1 and finally ended up with JV 44, getting one confirmed victory to bring his score to 23. Despite his relatively 'low' score, he received the Ritterkreuz, clearly due to his worth against the American 'heavies', ten four-engined bombers falling to his guns.

(via ARP

Robert S Fifield and Lieutenants Paul N Bowles and Carroll W Ofthsun. Claims for Me262s damaged were submitted by Lieutenants W J Currie, G A Zarnke, F A Kyle and D C Kocher, the latter near Dresden. The *Gruppe* lost at least four Me262s during these engagements, while *I./KG(J)54* lost *Unteroffizier* Bruno Reischke, who was shot down and killed while taking off from Ruzyne He was probably the only caught by Robert Fifield, who dived on a jet pulling away from the airfield. The '262 had not yet gained much speed and Fifield, diving flat-out, quickly caught up. He opened fire until he overran the Messerschmitt, pulled up, then went down again for a second attack. The port turbine caught fire and the jet rolled onto its back and went straight in from 2,000 feet. *Leutnant* Mai managed to get into a B-17 bomber stream and claimed one destroyed before he too fell to a Mustang at Klotsche, near Dresden.

This was the end for *III./JG 7* in the west. Never again were its aircraft engaged by American fighters. A few jets were seen over Ruzyne in the last days of the war, but these avoided combat. Most British and American raids had ceased by 25th April and the Germans, in a desperate last-ditch effort to deny more of their territory to the Russians, threw their last reserves into actions on the eastern front. No information relating to this aspect of the war has ever been forthcoming from the Soviet Union however, but it must be assumed that *III./JG 7* was from that time almost exclusively employed against the Red Air Force. *JV 44* had also been operating on April 19th, *Oberstleutnant* Heinz Bär claiming a pair of P-51s over southern Germany.

Medium bombers of the 9th Air Force reported two engagements. A pair of Me262s attacked the low flight of the 394th Bomb Group near Ulm at 10.04 hours, damaging one B-26. In the afternoon, however, a larger fight took place when Marauders of the 322nd Bomb Group raided the Donauwörth Railway Bridge. Ten Me262s attacked the second 'box' at 16.20 hours, just after the bombing run, and before the bombers had a chance to reform. The jets came in fast from astern and continued attacking for some minutes before P-47s of the 404th Fighter Group could intervene. Two B-26s were badly damaged, but turret gunners claimed damage to two Messerschmitts, while one more was claimed damaged by Lieutenant B F Baylies, one of the P-47 pilots. Meanwhile, in the north, the British 2nd Army was still encountering Me262s. Royal Engineers removing a surplus trestle bay from the bridge at Westen were strafed during the morning; after the trestle had been moved to a new position at Niederaverbergen in the late afternoon, the jets returned and attacked again.

Between 18th and 22nd April the Me262s of *I./KG(J)51* flew the last recorded jet fighter-bomber sorties against the western Allies by attacking bridge-heads at Dillingen, on the River Danube north-west of Augsburg.

20th April, 1945
During the morning 48 B-26s of the 323rd Bomb Group set out to attack the marshalling yards at Memmingen, but at 11.00 hours, just as the Group was nearing the objective, fifteen Me262s delivered a concentrated attack that shot down three Marauders, damaged another beyond repair, and slightly damaged ten more. Sergeant Edward S Tyszkiewicz, a Marauder gunner, received a Silver Star for this action:

> 'As top turret gunner on a B-26 type aircraft, Sergeant Tyszkiewicz served with particular distinction when his flight was attacked by Me262s. He quickly opened fire on the hostile aircraft and displayed brilliant marksman-

ship and determination, Sergeant Tyszkiewicz destroyed one of the jet propelled fighters. Subsequently another Me262 executed an attack against his aircraft and in a series of aerial tactics Sergeant Tyszkiewicz destroyed a second enemy plane. When enemy fire severely damaged his aircraft and wounded (him), despite the pain and constant attack by the enemy, he manually operated his turret thwarting their attacks and allowing his aircraft to bomb the objective." [104]

These were the only claims by the bombers, but P-51s of the 370th Fighter Group soon arrived, engaging the jets. Captain M P Owens and Lieutenant Caldwell each claimed a 'probable' and a 'damaged' for the loss of one Mustang, which subsequently belly-landed. One aircraft from *12./JG 7* was shot doen by a Marauder, the pilot baling out.

The veteran 354th Fighter Group, 9th Air Force, was sweeping near Nürnberg in the morning, where Lieutenants L R Blumenthal and J E Carl shared credit for an Me262 damaged at 10.00 hours.

British fighters were also out on patrol, Spitfire pilots of 41 Squadron sighting a Me262 near Oranienburg, north Germany. This was attacked by Warrant Officer J Rossow, who forced the German pilot to belly-land.

On the 21st a Spitfire patrol from 403 (RCAF) Squadron sighted five Me262s on Hagenow airfield, but these were not attacked due to the intervention of two Bf109s, both of which were shot down. Whilst this engagement was taking place a lone Me262 made a single pass, but did no damage and disappeared at once. On this date also, another jet pilot ended his war. *Major* Gerhard Barkhorn, who had arrived with Galland's *JV 44* on 15th April, suffered engine failure and crash-landed. He was badly injured when his unlocked cockpit hood slid forward and smashed into his neck.

22nd - 23rd April, 1945

American armoured units overran the airfield at Strasskirchen, in southern Germany, where Staffeln from *II./KG(J)51* were based. A number of jets led by *Oberleutnant* Wolfgang Baetz took off as the American troops fought their way onto the base. These landed at Landau airfield a few miles to the south. At Erding. a few jets from *III./KG(J)54* were based. One attempted to take off and was shot down by unidentified fighters. The pilot, an Unteroffizier, was killed. No claim has been traced from the Allied records; possibly it was a Russian fighter.

On the following day (23rd) Me262s from *I./KG(J)51* moved from Memmingen to Munich/Riem, where many of the aircraft were taken over by Adolf Galland to supplement the dwindling strength of *JV 44*. April 23rd also saw Thunderbolts of the 27th Fighter Group patrolling over the 7th Bridgehead over the River Danube, where Me262s attacked them; one was claimed damaged by Lieutenant Bill V Ackerman. The RAF's Fighter Experimental Flight was again successful when Flight Lieutenant P S Compton attacked Neuburg airfield this Mosquito pilot claiming a jet fighter destroyed and a second damaged on the ground.

24th April, 1945
B-26s of the 17th Bomb Group flew three escorted sorties to attack ammunition dumps at Schwabmünchen. The first mission was abandoned due to bad weather. The second flight of five aircraft experienced no fighter opposition, but the third mission by just three Marauders, with escort provided by P-47s of the 365th Fighter Group, met trouble. The fighters were flying in three flights, Blue Flight at 20,000 feet while Green Flight covered the Marauders at 17,000 feet and White Flight was below the bombers. At 15.25 hours four Me262s of *JV 44* hit the bombers from low astern. Pilots of Major Hill's White Flight saw them coming, and being unable to match the '262 in a climb, radioed to Lieutenant O T Cowan's Green Flight to engage them. Cowan moved his flight down to protect the Marauders but the jets went through the bomber formation like lightning, passing beneath the noses of the diving P-47s. Cowan was the only American fighter pilot within range and opened fire. He saw strikes on the wings of the rearmost aircraft, but could not stay with the jet as it accelerated away with the Thunderbolts of Green Flight in futile pursuit. One of the German pilots made a complete circle to deliver a second attack on the bombers, but failed to spot Captain Jerry G Mast's Blue Flight coming down from the top cover position. It was only at the last moment that the German pilot sensed danger, saw the Thunderbolts and rolled into a steep dive into the clouds with Mast close behind. White Flight was below the cloud and Lieutenant William H Myers, flying as wingman to Major Hill, suddenly saw the jet

Oberst Günther 'Franzl' Lützow was one of the great early fighter leaders of the Luftwaffe, serving with and later commanding JG 3 until he was grounded after gaining his 100th victory on 24th October 1941. He then undertook staff positions until, following the 'mutiny' in January 1945, he was allowed to join Galland in JV 44. He claimed two victories with the jets but was lost in action on 24th April.

emerge with Mast's Thunderbolt still close behind. The Luftwaffe pilot pulled a tight turn in an attempt to shake Mast off - and then saw the P-47s of White Flight dead ahead of him, with Lieutenant Myers preparing to engage him in a head-on pass. The jet abruptly dived and Mast doggedly chased it down to ground level, where it went out of control and dived into the ground at a speed estimated to have been almost 600 mph. Mast nearly followed suit, his wings brushing the tree-tops as he pulled out. Myers had apparently also fired, for he was credited with a half-share in this victory.

Meanwhile, another Me262 had made a firing run on the bombers. Lieutenant Byron Smith Jr of Blue Flight managed a fleeting shot as the German took sharp evasive action. Smith saw strikes on the wings before the jet disappeared into cloud cover, not to be seen again. Lieutenant Dale L Seslar was also credited with a 'damaged' in this engagement. Two B-26s of the 34th Bomb Squadron flown by Lieutenant Fred Harms and Lieutenant Leigh Slates were shot down in this action. From these crews only one gunner - Staff Sergeant Edward F Truver -survived to be taken prisoner. Slates' aircraft crashed near Unterschönegg and Harms' Marauder at Oberoth. Two P-47 pilots of the 27th Fighter Group, also on escort duties to the Marauders, claimed Me262s damaged by Lieutenants R E Prater and J F Lipiarz, but lost Lieutenant Hack, who baled out but was killed at Betlinshausen. Later this unit participated in airfield strafes, claiming two jets destroyed on the ground.

Other 9th Air Force fighters were engaged on this date when Lieutenant D S Renner of the 358th Fighter Group claimed a pair of Me262s damaged near Odelzhausen at 10.20 hours.

It is possible that the Me262 chased by Mast and Myers had been flown by one of the great *Experten* of the *Luftwaffe*. Oberst Günther Lützow of *JV 44* failed to return from a sortie against American bombers in this area and his body was never found. Lützow had been admired and respected by his comrades and had been the chief spokesman at the 'Mutiny of the Aces' in January 1945. The *Luftwaffe* would not long survive his death.

Notes
84. Correspondence Hermann Buchner - John Foreman
85. Combat Report Rudolf Sinner.
86. Correspondence Col. Gordon Denson (4th FG) - S E Harvey.
87. Records of 448th BG, USAAF.
88. *The Mighty Eighth*, by Roger A Freeman.
89. Correspondence Charles Bachmann - S E Harvey.
90. *Horrido!*, by Trevor J Constable and Raymond F Toliver P.295. The authors state that 'twenty-five kills were scored in a few minutes', clearly a vast over-estimate, for fourteen B-17s and three B-24s were lost in total by the 8th AirForce and none at all by the forces operating from Italy. Thirteen fighters were also lost, but not all during escort operations. The date given (7th) may be in error.
91. Correspondence Hermann Buchner - John Foreman
92. Correspondence Hermann Buchner - John Foreman
93. *Horrido!*, by Trevor J. Constable and Raymond F.Toliver P.75
94. Polish squadron records via Mrs H.J.S.Pietrzak.
95. Correspondence Gen Edward B Giller USAF retd - S E Harvey.
96. Correspondence Frank M Mead Hr - S E Harvey.
97. MACR
98. Documents from Hans-Dieter Weihs
99. Correspondence J S Baker - S E Harvey.
100. *Ibid.*
101. *Escort to Berlin*, by Jeffrey Ethell.
102. 17th and 320th BG records via Howard P Husband.
103. Correspondence Gen. Stanley F H Newman USAF retd - S E Harvey.
104. Via Howard P Husband.

Chapter Nine
'Too Little And Too Late'
The Final Collapse

25th April, 1945
Early in the morning the Mustangs of the 4th Fighter Group set out for their last mission of World War Two, the target was *KG(J)51*'s airfield at Prague/Ruzyne. and fittingly, perhaps, the last success for the 'Debden Eagles' was to be over a jet. Lieutenant W B Hoelscher reported:

> "I was flying Cobweb Blue Three. When we got to Prague at 08.00 hours, I broke to get out of a *Flak* barrage and saw an Me262 that apparently had just taken off from an aerodrome. I broke onto his tail, missed with my first burst and then started getting hits all over him. I kept firing three-second bursts at a range of about 500 yards, getting hits as I chased him all around the aerodrome. My indicated airspeed was 375 mph and altitude around 1,000 feet. During the chase I had been hit by Flak in the wingroot and half of my tail was blown away but I kept firing short bursts. Then I saw the Me262 go out of control and begin to burn and smoke. It rolled over on its back."

As he was beginning to overshoot, Hoelscher broke away and headed his crippled Mustang away. After about fifteen minutes flying at 130 mph, he realised that the aircraft would go no further and abandoned the Mustang at 300 feet near Milestin, Czechoslovakia. Lieutenant G A Denson had witnessed the combat:

> "Immediately afterwards I saw a large explosion near the edge of the aerodrome under us, where the Me262 went down out of control on his back." [105.]

Hoelscher was credited with a 'probable' as a result of this engagement. His opponent may have been an aircraft that crashed on landing at Ruzyne during the day. *Oberleutnant* Sturm rushed up on a motor cycle to assist the pilot, but was himself badly injured when the aircraft exploded. Six more jets were seen in the landing pattern, but the *Flak* defences put up a tremendous barrage, keeping the rest of the Mustangs away. Some thirty minutes later P-47s of the 358th Fighter Group swept the Munich area, Lieutenant Leo D Volkmer claiming a '262 probably destroyed and Lieutenants Michael M Esser and Charles G Dickerson sharing a 'damaged' over Neubiberg airfield.

In the afternoon medium bombers of the 9th Air Force flew sorties against the airfield at Erding and also attacked ammunition depots. B-26s of the 344th Bomb Group were near Erding at 17.45 hours when eight or nine Me262s approached, but were driven off by P-51s of the 370th Fighter Group. Lieutenants Richard D Stevenson and R W Hoyle jointly claimed one destroyed, the seventeenth and last Me262 to be shot down by 9th Air Force fighters. Four more were claimed damaged by Lieutenants C L Harman, I B McKenzie, M M Deskin and S H Banks.

Thunderbolts of the 27th Fighter Group, 1 TAF (Prov), flew a sweep over southern Germany during the day. On the way out the formation was jumped by three Me262s. Major Weihardt's P-47 was chased, but escaped. That flown by Captain Herbert A Philo was hit, but he returned safely.

The RAF claimed several successes in the north; Spitfire XIVs of 41 Squadron flew a sweep to Lübeck/Blankensee, where four Me262s were seen and chased. Flight Lieutenant Peter Cowell DFC remembered:

"I got a few hits on one and then they split up. The one I had hit attempted a downwind emergency landing, while another tried to get down from the other end and ground-looped to avoid colliding with the first. I was right in the middle." [106]

He was credited with one destroyed and another damaged. One of the German pilots was seen to jump from the aircraft while it was still rolling. Fighters from 2 TAF also visited Lübeck during the day and another Me262 was shot down in flames whilst landing by Flying Officer K A Smith, a 486 Squadron Tempest pilot. A further success was claimed by 130 Squadron Spitfire pilots when Flight Lieutenant Stowe and Warrant Officer Ockenden, claimed a 'shared probable'. 403 (RCAF) Squadron strafed Hagenow, three '262s being claimed damaged by Squadron Leader H P M Zary and Flight Lieutenants R Morris and E O Doyle.

Fighters from III./JG 7 were ordered to attack Fürstenfeldbrück airfield, recently occupied by the Americans. One pilot

A rare bird in Switzerland. Hans-Guido Mütke's Me262 after he force-landed at Dübendorf due to fuel shortage.

airborne was *Oberfähnrich* Hans-Guido Mütke who found himself separated from his comrades after the low level attack. Lost, and with fuel getting short, he headed for the nearest airfield - Dübendorf in Switzerland. Moments later he performed a fast emergency landing, much to the astonishment of Swiss Air Force personnel. It was the first jet aircraft to be seen in Switzerland and both pilot and aircraft were interned. In 1957 the jet became the only one captured ever to be returned to Germany and now rests in the *Deutsches Museum* in Munich.

During the day, the Marauders of the 17th Bomb Group returned to Schwabmünchen and were again intercepted by a few jets, but on this occasion the American escorts were able to prevent any attacks from being delivered.

I./JG 7 was still active, reporting an action against B-17s during which successes were claimed by *Major* Späte (three), *Unteroffizier* Schöppler, *Oberfeldwebel* Göbel, *Leutnant* Kelb and *Unteroffizier* Engler. *JV 44* aircraft were also in action, when *Unteroffizier* Köster, who had recently left *JG 7* to join Galland's unit, claimed two Mustangs.

In the north, Lancasters and Halifaxes of No 6 (Canadian) Group RAF flew a daylight mission to raid Hamburg under heavy Spitfire and Mosquito escort. As the bombers were leaving the target area a lone Me262 attacked. Two Lancasters of 431 (RCAF) Squadron, flown by Flight Lieutenant Emmet and Flying Officer Baker, then collided and fell away locked together; one had apparently been hit by gunfire and collided with the second as it fell. The jet fighter, its work done, peeled away and disappeared.

It seems likely that this day saw the last combat sortie for *Oberfeldwebel* Hermann Buchner of *III./JG 7*. His logbook for April was, like so many others, stolen by American troops and thus he is unsure of the date, originally believing it to have been in mid-April between the 14th and 16th. Subsequent research into Army records places the date as being certainly later than 22nd April and is likely to have been on or around the 25th. He recalls:

> "We flew an operation against four-engined bombers in the area of the Steinhuder Lake. We broke through the heavy fighter escorts and attacked the B-17s with our guns, saw hits, but then the Mustangs dived on us and we had to break away and try to escape. Our formation broke up and so I tried to find an airfield in the north. The flight time remaining for my return flight compelled me to fly to Bremen.
>
> "I reached Achym, near Bremen, but as I flew over it I saw that the base had been overrun by British troops and armour. I then headed east, and reached Rotenburg airfield on my last drops of fuel. I could not see any Allied fighters in the area. In any case, I was fully occupied with my landing and was about to touch down when I was surprised to see gunfire hitting my right wing. As I landed the fighter hit my engine nacelle. The fighter was going fast and flew over my aircraft. The engine began to burn as I tried to bring the aircraft to a halt. As it stopped, the flames reached above the canopy. I had difficulty in getting out of the right-hand side of the cockpit and, when I had reached a safe distance from the aircraft my strength gave out and I collapsed and was then taken to hospital. It was not serious, just the initial shock. I was 'lucky' again; The Ami or Tommy pilot was either going so fast or had been surprised by my appearance that he had no chance to deliver a 100% decisive attack. I survived, and that was my last combat sortie in World War Two." [107]

It is possible that his attacker was either an aircraft from 130 Squadron, Warrant Officer Ockenden and Flight Lieutenant Stowe claiming a 'probable', or from 403 Squadron, claimed as a 'damaged' on the ground'. However, Hermann Buchner's flying career with the Luftwaffe was over. Shortly afterwards Buchner took the ground crews out to Prague/Ruzyne airfield, but the situation was so chaotic that as he has stated, he never again had the opportunity to fly the Me262 in action.

'Too Little and Too Late' The Final Collapse

On 13th May 1990, Peter Cowell and Hermann Buchner met at the RAF Museum - and promptly exchanged ties! (J Foreman)

In 1990, at the RAF Museum in Hendon, Hermann met an RAF pilot who had been in action against Me262s on that day, Peter Cowell, then a Flight Lieutenant with 41 Squadron. Peter returned to Surrey wearing a tie with a Bf109 on it, while Hermann took a *'Spitfire Society'* tie back to Austria and, due to Peter Cowell, the former Me262 *Experte* is now an honorary life member of that organisation.

26th April, 1945
During the early morning, *Generalleutnant* Galland led a formation of five Me262s from *JV 44* off from Riem. One turned back with engine trouble, while the remaining jets were vectored towards Ulm, where a 1 TAF (Prov) raid had been reported. B-26 Marauders of the 17th Bomb Group, escorted by Thunderbolts of the 27th and 50th Fighter Groups, had been briefed to bomb Lechfeld. The jets met them almost head on, the opposing forces passing in a flash. Galland turned his section in a wide sweep and came in fast from the 8 o'clock position. Taking a bomber in his gunsight, Galland opened fire with cannon, causing it to blow up in mid-air. Quickly he pressed the

rocket release, but there was no response; he had quite forgotten the safety catch! As he hurtled through the formation he had just time to deliver a quick burst of cannon at another Marauder, seeing hits as he steep-turned away, but at that moment his jet was struck by fire from this B-26's guns. Howard P Husband was a navigator with the 95th Bomb Squadron on that mission:

> "As we approached our target for the day in southern Germany, German jet fighters came at us almost head-on at 12 o'clock. I was in a leading B-26 as they shot past without firing, two going right under our ship. A few seconds later I heard explosions and two Me262s shot past our B-26 very close. One jet looped in front of us and our crews saw him shoot down one of our P-47 escort fighters. Also a total of three B-26 bombers were seen to go down from the formation. We were in bad weather at the time the jets appeared, about to turn back to base in France." [108]

Galland, with his machine's fuel tank damaged by the return fire, had pulled away from the bombers; as he did so a 50th Fighter Group P-47 flown by Lieutenant James Finnegan dived on him, bullets from the Thunderbolt smashing into the cockpit. Galland was protected by his seat-armour, but as his instrument panel exploded before his eyes, debris smashed into his right leg. His engines were running well and he accelerated hard away from the P-47. Meanwhile, Captain Robert W Clark of the 50th Fighter Group attacked a second jet, shooting it down and watching the pilot bale out. Finnegan was credited with an Me262 damaged during this engagement, as was a pilot from the 523rd Fighter Squadron, 27th Fighter Group.

With his instruments now useless, Galland returned to Riem by following an Autobahn, but found the base under attack by Mustangs. He was bleeding heavily and his aircraft was very short of fuel, but had no choice other than to land during the attack. The throttle controls had gone and he virtually threw the aircraft down onto the grass by cutting the engines at the last second and sliding it in. He scrambled out and crawled into a nearby a bomb crater until the Mustangs had departed, miraculously leaving his fighter intact. It did not matter, Adolf Galland, fighter pilot from 'first to last', had flown his final sortie. His place was at once taken by *Oberstleutnant* Heinz Bär. Meanwhile *Oberst* Walther Dahl claimed a success, a P-51 near Dillingen, for his 129th and last combat success of the war. On

Generalleutnant Adolf Galland, the fiery commander of JV 44. As General of Fighters he had fought many battles against the Luftwaffe beaurocracy for fighters with which to defend Germany. On 26th April 1945, a fighter pilot from 'first to last', he fought his last battle in the air.

this mission he is believed to have been flying with *III./EJG 2*.

During the engagement three Marauders had indeed been lost, one from the 34th Bomb Squadron and two from the 95th, these flown by 2nd Lieutenant K L Bedor, 2nd Lieutenant E E Reeves and 1st Lieutenant A P Shatto, all crashing in the target area. A fourth B-26, presumably that damaged by Galland, returned to Allied territory and was crash-landed. were killed, Thirty-five minutes later, at 07.55 hours, more P-47s from the 27th Fighter Group sweeping near Munich, engaged jets - presumably from *JV 44*. Captain Herbert A Philo, who had been roughly handled the previous day, obtained his revenge by claiming a jet fighter shot down. This Group had its last contact with jet fighters at noon, when one more was claimed damaged by an unidentified pilot.

On this day RAF Typhoons enjoyed a rare success when four aircraft of 263 Squadron carried out a rocket attack on a train in Niebull station. Pilot Officer D E Morgan's aircraft was hit by *Flak*, but as he went down to force-land, two Me262s attacked. Morgan's No 2, Warrant Officer H Barrie, at once opened fire and, joined by Flight Lieutenant W J Fowler and Pilot Officer J W Shellard, carried out a second attack upon one of the jets. The '262 rolled onto its back in flames and dived into the ground from 3,000 feet, crashing some two miles northeast of Niebull.

The second jet broke away and smartly disappeared. This was the third Me262 and the last German aircraft to be credited to Typhoons.

Most of *JG 7* had by now arrived at Prague/Ruzyne and had begun to engage the advancing Soviet ground forces, the fighter pilots turning their hands to the hazardous business of ground attack.

With Galland in hospital and the Allied armies closing in fast, *JV 44* made its final move, to Salzburg in Austria. The end was near for the *Luftwaffe Jagdverbände* in the south however. Almost all fighter-bomber Staffeln had moved to Prague/Ruzyne by April 30th. *JG 7* had found this base well stocked with vast amounts of fuel and R4M rockets. This allowed the unit to continue in the ground attack role, strafing Russian armour moving along the Guben-Cottbus road en route for Berlin. *Oberfeldwebel* Otto Pritzl well remembered the low-level sorties against the heavily armoured T-34 tanks. The jet pilots found that their R4Ms were deadly; the attacks, delivered at low level and high speed, meant that results could not immediately be seen, but on subsequent sorties the awesome results were apparent. He recalled, 'We saw the total effect of our rocket attacks was massive'.

The pilots of *JG 7* were ordered to avoid combat with Russians, but:

"Naturally there was the occasional skirmish with Russian fighters, but they seemed unaware that we could easily withdraw from the area." [109]

Pritzl flew ground attack sorties to Brestau and Tschenstochau in Poland (now Wroclau and Czestochowa) and flew a round trip of 400 miles to the latter area five times in one day. On one of these sorties he strafed the nearby airfield of Airokopra (sic) where hundreds of Soviet aircraft were parked. It is likely that the Russians considered the base, so far behind their own lines, safe. 'We left many hundreds of planes burning after we left the area that day', says Pritzl.

As the Russians advanced, *JG 7* was forced to move again, finally arriving at Mühldorf in Bavaria on April 27th. For this unit the war was practically over and there it would remain until the advancing American forces captured the airfield. A few pilots had elected to remain at Ruzyne with *Gefechtsverband*

The diminutive Wilhelm Herget of JV 44. Originally a Bf110 pilot, he transferred to nightfighting duties. His 73 combat successes included 58 at night and one with the Me262. He was chosen by Galland to parley with the Americans on 2nd May, but his aircraft was shot down, destroying the hopes of taking JV 44 intact. He died on 27th March 1973.

Hogeback and continued ground attacks against the advancing Russians.

27th - 28th April, 1945

JV 44 put up several jets on April 27th, *Oberstleutnant* Heinz Bär claiming two Thunderbolts destroyed, *Leutnant* Köster two and *Major* Herget one. It is probable that these pilots were actually involved against Russian aircraft (see below). A little further east, elements of *JG 7* strafed Russian road transport, claiming sixty-five trucks destroyed. Shortly afterwards some twenty Il-2 *Shturmovik* ground attack bombers were the sighted and six were claimed destroyed - five by *JV 44* pilots (above) for the loss of two Me262s.

Next day (April 28th) *Leutnant* Ernst-Rudolf Geldmacher of *JG 7* was shot down and killed whilst taking off from Ruzyne. No British or American claim has been found and it is possible that he fell to Russian fighters. The unit, now operating exclusively against Russian forces, was to find the task of ground attack exceedingly dangerous; between April 28th and May 1st, approximately ten Me262s failed to return from such operations. One engagement was recorded by *JV 44* when *Oberstleutnant* Heinz Bär claimed a Thunderbolt over Bad Aibling, bringing his confirmed score to sixteen.

29th April 1945

Me262s were still being seen in the north. On this date jets blasted a pontoon bridge over the River Elbe, killing ten men from the Royal Engineers. Sandbags were blown onto Sapper Fred Read, who was the sole survivor. Also, ten P-47s of the

86th Fighter Group discovered aircraft dispersed on a section of autobahn near Augsburg. The Thunderbolt pilots carried out a strafe, claiming nine Me262s destroyed and seventeen more damaged. Meanwhile, in the east, a few remaining aircraft of I and II./KG(J)54 were now also operating exclusively against the advancing Soviet armoured columns. Several from *II Gruppe* were lost in such operations on the 29th. As one group took off from Prague/Ruzyne airfield, *Hauptmann* Kornagel crashed and was killed. Another, 'B3+Red 3', was among several that took off from Fürstenfeldbrück. It failed to return. More left from Erding, again to attack advancing Russian armour. Two of these, 'B3+Red 2' and 'B3+Red 4' were lost, flown by *Hauptmann* Spadiut and *Leutnant* Paukner.

For *Leutnant* Hadi Weihs of *3./JG 7*, the war in the air ended on the 29th:

> "On 13th April, we came overland to Prague/Ruzyne. On the 21st, we went overland as *Vorkommando* of *JG 7* firstly to Lechfeld and from there on to Mühldorf on the Inn. On the 29th, came the final roll-call at Mühldorf." [110]

30th April, 1945

One claim was submitted by the 358th Fighter Group, 9th Air Force, during an early morning sweep, Captain James H Hall and Lieutenant Joseph Richlitsky claiming a jet fighter 'shared damaged' at 08.35 hours. This was almost certainly flown by *Leutnant* Fritz Kelb from *I./JG 7*. He was killed when his jet crashed shortly afterwards. He had formerly flown with *JG 400*, the Me163B unit and had been credited with two victories while flying the remarkable rocket fighter

I./KG(J)54 lost another jet during a ground attack mission to the east, shot down by Russian AA fire. However a pilot from this unit was able to shoot down an Il-2 *Shturmovik*. Two more of this type fell to *Oberfähnrich* Wittbold and a Yak-9 to *Oberleutnant* Schlüter of *JG 7* during the last days of April, but regrettably the precise dates are not known.

2nd - 8th May, 1945

In the late evening of May 2nd, American armoured units reached the outskirts of Salzburg where they halted for the night, awaiting the dawn before making an assault on the airfield. *JV 44* had arrived at Salzburg on their last drops of fuel and, even had replenishment been available, they had

Fritz Kelb of I./JG 7 was one of the very few German pilots to fly the rocket-powered Me163 Komet in combat, serving with JG 400. He is pictured boarding one of the 'Power Eggs' prior to a sortie. he fell in combat on 30th April. (via ARP)

nowhere to go. Adolf Galland decided that his aircraft would be handed over to the Americans. He was even prepared to have his jets flown to the nearest airfield under safe conduct and ordered that a Fieseler *Storch* be painted with surrender markings to take his proposals to the US forces. *Major* Wilhelm Herget volunteered for this mission and departed to speak with the Americans. However, the mission proved to be fruitless, for his little aircraft was engaged and shot down by American tank gunners and he was wounded, captured and hospitalised. The hand-over of the Me262s never happened.

Next morning the *Luftwaffe* ground crews pushed the jets out onto the field and waited for the end. American fighters appeared, but made no move to attack, merely circling the airfield out of range of the light *Flak* gunners. They had strict orders to take the jets intact if possible but it was not to be. As the first American tanks rolled slowly onto the field, the ground crews opened the fuel cocks and put the jet fighters to the torch. No Allied pilot ever flew an Me262 belonging to *JV 44*. Around sixty Me262s were torched on the airfield, many having been delivered by fighter-bomber pilots, who clearly felt that JV 44 could do more good with them.

Units in the north obviously still had a little fuel remaining for, on May 2nd, as British 2nd Army units were crossing the River Elbe near Hamburg, two Me262s appeared, strafing the pontoon bridge before engaging a section of patrolling Spitfires; the Spitfires disappeared smartly, with the jets chasing them. It is possible that the troops had witnessed the beginning of a engagement during which Flying Officer G N Smith of 402 (RCAF) Squadron claimed a Messerschmitt damaged. Meanwhile Tempests of 3 Squadron undertook an airfield strafe, Pilot Officer J I T Adams claiming a '262 destroyed on the ground.

During the first week in May, *I./KG(J)54* recorded another loss when *Unteroffizier* Andreas Rupprecht failed to return from a close support mission against Soviet forces,

The last recorded combat between jet aircraft and the western Allies took place on May 4th, when aircraft of the 365th Fighter Group chased three Me262s over Prague-Ruzyne airfield at 11.00 hours. Two were claimed damaged by Lieutenants A G Sarrow and A T Kalvastis, although airfield *Flak* gunners damaged one of the Thunderbolts.

KG(J)51 fighter-bombers operated until the last day of the war, flying close-support sorties around Prague with the few jets remaining to them. Seven pilots had volunteered for this desperate last ditch action, commanded by *Hauptmann* Rudolf Abrahamczik. On May 6th, *Leutnant* Schimmel perished when his jet was shot down into the very streets of the city and, on May 7th, the day that the formal surrender document was signed, *Leutnant* Strothmann and *Feldwebel* Pöhling, who had earlier gone to *JV 44* for a few days, met the same fate.

Meanwhile elements of the Vlassow Armoured Division moved onto Prague-Ruzyne airfield and destroyed the last reserves of fuel. Otto Pritzl and his remaining comrades had flown out earlier that day to Saaz airfield to the south and there awaited the cease-fire. Several Me262s of *KG(J)51* were at Zatec, north of Prague. When the surrender details were announced four of the pilots, unwilling to become guests of the Soviet Union, decided to make a run for Germany. *Hauptmann* Abrahamczik led *Leutnants* Batel, Haeffner and Fröhlich (the latter actually shown on the strength of *JV 44*) off towards the west, Abrahamczik and Haeffner landing at Munich-Riem at about 1440 hours, where they surrendered to the Americans. Fröhlich flew on to Fassberg, giving himself up to British forces at 14.50 hours. Fröhlich's aircraft, Werke Nummer 500200, was

With the end of the war in sight, an Me262 of JG 7 sits in a hangar awaiting a repair that will probably never happen.

to be one of three brought to the Royal Aeronautical Establishment, Farnborough between October 5th and November 16th, it was flown nine times by British test pilots before being sent to Australia where it now resides.

Wilhelm Batel was the last of the four to reach his destination, arriving over Lüneberg at 15.28 hours after a flight of some 300 miles. His fuel was almost exhausted and he found the nearest aero-drome clogged with Allied aircraft. Finally he belly-landed the jet on Lüneberg Heath, not far from his home village. He hid in a small wood until dark, then went home, avoiding the British troops in the village. A few days later he gave himself up and went into captivity. He was one of the lucky ones; in just ten months of operations, his unit had lost 134 aircrew.

Two pilots from *I./KG(J)54* also decided that American captivity was to be preferred to Russian imprisonment. On 8th May they too flew out from Czechoslovakia to the west, one landing safely at Innsbruck and the other crash-landing.

In the north, many units had arrived at Leck in Schleswig-Holstein. As well as many 'normal' day and night fighter Gruppen, there were the Me262 nightfighters of Kurt Welter's *10./NJG 11* and also the He162 *Volksjäger* jets from *JG 1*. On 6th May the aircraft were lined up as if on parade and, next day, the ground crews began to disable them by removing propellers, rudders and all ammunition in preparation for the surrender to the British forces. In all, around thirty to forty jet fighters were among the hundred or so combat aircraft immobilised on the airfield when the British armoured speaheads took the surrender, which was signalled to all German military formations on May 8th, but several Me262s flew on that date from bases in Czechoslovakia. Probably the last fighter claim of the war was made by the *Luftwaffe* when at 16.00 hours on May 8th *Oberleutnant* Fritz Stehle, *Kapitän* of *1./JG 7*, shot down a Russian Yak-9 fighter over Czechoslovakia whilst flying one of the last airworthy Me262s from *Gefechtsverband Hogeback*.

Staff Sergeant A A Raidy was with the 47th Troop Carrier Squadron of the 9th Air Force and on V-E day he was en route to Stavanger with British paratroops and Free Norwegian government officials in order to effect the German surrender of Norway:

> "We headed across the North Sea at a pre-arranged altitude and compass heading that had been agreed with the Germans, as a two- aircraft element. As we neared the Norwegian coast we saw what we thought was an aircraft on fire. It was trailing smoke and approaching our two transports at a high rate of speed and, a few moments later, was circling our aircraft. It was then that we could all see its German markings and that it was jet powered. It circled us at such a speed that we felt as if we were standing still in the air. Then it flew off, back toward the coast.
>
> "Later, after we had landed at the large Luftwaffe base, I came across this one jet in a hangar, apparently the same one that had flown out and looked us over. None of the Germans, officers or other ranks, would say who had flown the jet out." [111.]

With the final surrender came the inevitable post-mortems and interrogations, together with test reports on the most formidable fighting machine of the war. The *Luftwaffe* had lost the aerial battle, overwhelmed by sheer weight of numbers, but the jet pilots had written a page into history that would change the whole course of air fighting.

The operational record of the jet units has, in the past, been treated with some scepticism, many historians believing that no more than a hundred victories had been claimed. More recent research, provides the following figures:

Unit	Victories	In Text
Stab and *III./JG 7*	427	252
I and *II./JG 7*	80 approx	66
IV.(E)/JG 7	30 approx	nil
III./EJG 2	25 approx	22
JV 44	56	31
Ekdo Nowotny	35	34
10./NJG 11	50 approx	24
I./KG(J) 51	5 approx	1
I./KG(J) 54	50 approx	44
Ekdo 262	25 approx	21
Ekdo Lechfeld	3+	1
Total	**781**	**496**

Even allowing for the 'normal overclaim' rate of one third, this still represents the not inconsiderable figure of around 520 aircraft destroyed by a relative handful of fighter pilots.

Notes

105. *Escort to Berlin*, by Jeffrey Ethell
106. Interview Peter Cowell and John Foreman
107. Conversation and letters to the authors.
108. Correspondence Howard P Husband - S E Harvey.
109. Correspondence Otto Pritzl - S E Harvey.
110. Documents Hans-Dieter Weihs
111. Correspondence Augustine A Raidy - S E Harvey.

Chapter Ten
The Phœnix Rises

Although the Me262 had fought its last over the dying embers of the Third Reich it was, like a Phœnix from the ashes, to rise once more.

As soon as hostilities ended, the Allied forces had an important priority. The German military technical developments had always been more advanced than those of the British or Americans - except perhaps in the field of radar - and those German secrets needed to be studied carefully. For the Allied air forces, priority number one was the Me262.

The British had assumed responsibility for the area of northwest Germany and most of the captured German jets were gathered at Fassberg and Leck. One RAF pilot, Flight Lieutenant Clive Gosling, had a remarkable experience when he became the first Allied pilot to fly the *Schwalbe* successfully:

> "With the 'outbreak of peace' in May 1945, my unit, No.616 Squadron equipped with Gloster Meteor III jets, transferred to Lübeck. Like all pilots with little to do - apart from routine patrols along the Danish border - we relaxed in the evenings with (wine) spirited parties.
>
> "During the morning of 27th May, my CO (Squadron Leader Schrader), came to my room and told me that he and I were to go to Fassberg to pick up a pair of Me262s. It seemed inevitable for me since, after my first tour on operations, I had gone to Supermarines as a test pilot, flying with the famous Jeffrey Quill. There I had flown the Spitfire, Seafire, Hurricane, Typhoon, Tempest Mustang and Mosquito. Also the little Walrus and Sea Otter flying boats. Therefore I had, in two years test flying, achieved over 1,000 hours flying time, far more than the normal operational RAF pilot.
>
> "Therefore I had a cup of coffee, picked up my flying equipment and reported to the ops officer. We were to travel from Lübeck to Fassberg in an Airspeed Oxford, the 'maid of all work' of the RAF. I never welcomed being flown by other pilots, except for top test pilots. And due to a severe headache, I made it very clear that only I would fly the aircraft and no-one else. I believed that this would be the only way to guarantee a peaceful flight, with no dramatic events to spoil it.

"We arrived at midday and our first task was to have a beer and lunch. In the afternoon, my CO had another little drink with some friends, while I went over to landing area to try to familiarise myself with the Me262. Already waiting were a few *Luftwaffe* ground crewmen, an RAF interpreter, a few RAF ground crew and a young *Luftwaffe* officer, about 25 years old, who had flown one of the aircraft to Fassberg.

"There were six aircraft ready and the German ground crews had selected two of them as the most airworthy. I selected number '17' and, while I climbed into the cockpit, the interpreter and the *Luftwaffe* pilot climbed onto the left wing. Firstly, I had to familiarise myself with the cockpit layout and the systems. Then I asked the first question to the interpreter, which he repeated to the German pilot. It was some time before the interpreter managed to get the answer back and it was immediately clear to me that this method would take a great deal of time before I was thoroughly conversant with the aircraft and its systems. In short, this was going to hold up the flight considerably. As the day drew to an end, I realised that I not learned that much. We then left, to spend the night in Fassberg, planning to return next morning to carry on. I hoped that, next morning, I would have learned enough to make the flight. I also wanted to know about the German pilot and his opinion of the aircraft, whether he was a spirited type, or was he one of the careful ones. Had he any doubts about it? In short, I wanted to be able to talk to him 'pilot to pilot'.

"Before the evening meal, I checked out the German pilot and found that he was under guard. I requested that I be permitted to take him for a meal and a drink and this was granted, but with the condition that he remained isolated with his guard and had to leave the Mess with him. So it happened. He came in, I bought him a beer, he took his food, then left.

"In view of the problems that awaited me next morning, I went to bed early.

"After a pleasant breakfast, I returned to the airfield to continue my instruction. The German pilot was there already with the others. A 'Good Morning' came from the German pilot and it was at once clear to me that he spoke fluent English. My questions were suddenly answered 'pilot to pilot'. He was very formal and a little reserved, but this was understandable in this situation; the idea that a former enemy was about to take over his aircraft. His conduct was absolutely correct. He gave nothing of his own free will, but answered every question faultlessly. It would have been so easy for him to have given false information and so cause cause a catastrophe for me, but I could not conceive that any fighter pilot would do such a thing.

"After the briefing, I was convinced that I could now fly the Me262. I believed that the little act of humanity of the previous evening had convinced him that the 'Englander' was not such a bad type.

"Now I had to brief my Squadron Commander. I hoped that he had understood it all exactly, but subsequent events showed that he had not. He

Me262s at Fassberg

Top: *Leutnant Hans Dorn's 'Yellow 17', 500210, flown to Lübeck by Clive Gosling, with Unteroffizier Günther Engler's 'Yellow 7' 112372, now exhibited in the Aerospace Museum at RAF Cosford.*

(via R.Bracken)

Centre: *(l to r) 'Yellow 17'; 'White 5', 111690, believed to have been surrended by Oberleutnant Fritz Stehle and was another flown to England; 'Yellow 5', 500443, the mount of Unteroffizier Anton Schöppler. (via R.Bracken)*

Bottom: *The fighter-bomber surrendered by Leutnant Fröhlich at Fassberg W.Nr. 500200. This aircraft was test-flown in England and later taken to Australia, where it now resides. Behind it can be seen the fin of Anton Schöppler's 'Yellow 5'. (via R.Bracken)*

was to take off first. The friendly ground crew assisted him to get going and he taxied to the take-off point. Soon after, I saw him whistling over the field in a slight climb and it was plain that it would be a near thing. He cleared the trees at the end of the field by a hairs breadth and disappeared towards the horizon.

"I had noted all this very carefully. Now, with the friendly mechanic stood by the wing, I climbed into the cockpit and strapped in. The starter for the left turbine wouldn't operate, so the mechanic sprang forward, pumped CO_2 in, and the turbine started up at once.

"All the engine dials rose to their designated levels and, with the mechanic still at the left wingtip, I taxied to the take-off point. It was important that I had the greatest possible length of runway and when I reach very end of the runway, the mechanic called to me, then left the wingtip and ran back to check the engines. He gave me the 'OK' signal and I closed the hood and opened the throttles to 8,700 rpm. The acceleration was not breathtaking. I don't say that it was weak, but it was not as good as the Meteor. I was almost at the end of the runway when I attained take-off speed, raised the nose slightly, and lifted off. I realised that I had the bird almost in the trees. Hardly had I raised the flaps and undercarriage, when I felt the cockpit fill with red hot air. 'My God! I've got a fire at sixty feet in a strange aircraft!' That was my first thought. A glance at the instruments told me otherwise. Then I noticed the cockpit heating lever was fully open and realised that the mechanic had played a little joke on the English pilot.

"I was now climbing at 8,400 rpm and as I reached 7,500 feet I levelled out. The stable handling and the clean balanced rudder of the Me262 were impressive. Cruising at 640 kph I began to try some manoeuvres, beginning with steep turns and wing-overs. It dropped very fast, and climbed easily. With full throttle I brought it up to 800 kph and then reduced speed to try its low-flying characteristics. 'What a fine aircraft', I thought, 'a really great fighter'.

"I had no more time for further exploration of its handling. That had to wait for another time. Meanwhile a slight problem had arisen. As I reached for the trimmer at cruising altitude, the trimmer-lock jumped out and refused to work. So I had to make the rest of the flight with it in its original position.

"When I reached Lübeck and prepared for landing, I saw the other Me262 in the middle of the runway with a collapsed nosewheel amid a carpet of foam. I had already been airborne for forty minutes and the fuel gauges were slowly approaching critical. I flew low across the airfield, seeing mechanics attempting to move the wrecked '262 off the runway and, after a few more circuits, It became clear to me that I had to land soon. To force-land beside the runway would be impossible, since it would cause a certain catastrophe. I made another circuit and realised that, in theory, the runway was wide enough for me to get down without hitting the wrecked Me262. I made a right turn into the downwind leg of the circuit, dropped

Clive Gosling of 616 Squadron was the first Allied pilot to fly an Me262 successfully.
(C.Gosling)

the undercarriage and lowered the flaps to twenty degrees. The work on the runway suddenly became hectic. I turned crosswind, noting that the runway had now been cleared and that the small pieces from the wreckage had also been removed. Flaps fully down, I turned in for final approach, smoothly, speed over the perimeter over 220 kph and a smooth touchdown. I couldn't lift the nose, making aerodynamic braking impossible. The brakes were reliable however, and I rolled to the end of the runway.

"After taxiing to the dispersal area, I shut down the turbines and climbed out of the cockpit, pleased with myself and the flight. My CO complained to me that his nose-wheel would not lock down. I asked him how fast he had been travelling when he attempted to lower the wheels and he replied '500 km/h!' He should have been grateful that he hadn't killed himself. One flight had gone well, the other ended in disaster.

"However, this wasn't the end of the story. Next day 2 Group issued instructions that the Me262s were to be 'grounded'. In other words, no more flights with this bird. Had I known that the 004 turbines were so unreliable. I would never have become involved in this adventure.

"Now, what was the Me262 like in comparison to the Meteor? It was 80 kph faster, the critical Mach number was higher and the rate of climb roughly similar. The rudder balance was smooth and the view from the cockpit was definitely not so good. It was rather more difficult to fly and the turbines were less reliable. I had flown two hundred hours in the Meteor with only one engine failure. The armament was essentially heavier than the Meteor, the rate of turn less good and, with this one short flight and the few manoeuvres I had attempted, the amount of fuel remaining led me to believe that the consumption was much higher than the Meteor and that the Me262 could have had only a short combat radius and would have had to return to base much earlier." [112].

Many years later, Clive made an acquaintance with Ottomar

Kruse, formerly a fighter pilot with *8./JG 26*. Clive had often wondered about the young pilot who had so expertly briefed him for his flight in '17' (formerly flown by *Leutnant* Hans Dorn of *JG 7*). If he was still alive he would very much like to contact him. And so Kruse undertook to search for him in Germany. He found that the man was Friedrich-Wilhelm Schlüter, nicknamed 'Tim', who had formerly been a reconnaissance pilot and who had almost certainly flown the '262 in the photo-recce rôle. The story had a sad ending, however, for when Ottomar Kruse finally located the Schlüter family he found that 'Tim' Schlüter had died just months earlier.

The British managed to gather nine airworthy Me262s three examples each of the fighter, fighter-bomber and two-seat nightfighter versions. They were brought to Leck airfield in Schleswig-Holstein, where they were test-flown before being flown to England. The pilots involved were Squadron Leader A F Martindale, Flight Lieutenants T Melhuish and P Arend and Captain Eric Brown CBE, DSC, AFC of the Fleet Air Arm. The three nightfighters were flown directly to Farnborough and were the first to undergo trials, while the rest went first to Manston in Kent. Captain 'Winkle' Brown was very impressed the jet:

"It was in my view unquestionably the foremost warplane of its day; a hard hitter, which out-performed anything that we had immediately available but which, fortunately for the Allies, was not available to the Luftwaffe in sufficient numbers to affect drastically the course of events in the air over Europe. It was a pilots aeroplane that had to be *flown* and not just heaved into the air. Basically underpowered and fitted with engines sufficiently lacking in reliability to keep the adrenalin flowing, it was thoroughly exciting to fly, and particularly so in view of the lack of an ejector seat." [113].

Three of the single-seaters were flown to Farnborough and were there in September 1945, but only two of them were test-flown. One of the two-seaters, an aircraft from *10./NJG 11* (*Werke Nummer* 110305), was flown from Farnborough to Ford on 6th July 1945 by Squadron Leader Gonsalvez, who had been a successful Mosquito intruder pilot with 85 Squadron. He had a mishap when landing however, damaging the aircraft when it overshot the Ford runway. After repair, it went via No. 71 MU (Maintenance Unit) at Slough to No. 47 MU at Sealand and thence by road to Birkenhead.

To the victors the spoils. Curious American G.I.s examine some of the hundreds of wrecked Me262s discovered on airfields and in forests throughout southern Germany.

Here, in late February 1946, it was loaded aboard SS *McRae* bound for South Africa. It arrived on 7th March 1947 and now resides in the Johannesburg War Museum, still complete with the *Hirschgeweih* radar array. The other two nightfighters are believed to have been 'reduced to produce' (scrapped) at No. 6 MU in 1947. Two of the single-seaters, one fighter and one fighter-bomber, were shipped out to Canada in late 1946, but their fates are not known. The sad fact is, that of the original nine, only one survives in Britain. This is 112372, which was believed to have been from *KG(J)51* and is painted in that unit's markings. However, when the authors took Hermann Buchner to see the aircraft, a curious thing happened. He clambered up into the cockpit and settled in, glancing around the instruments. Then he said 'The markings are wrong. This is not a fighter-bomber. I can tell at once from the weapons switches. It must have come from my old unit, *Jagdgeschwader 7*!'

Another fighter-bomber (*Werke Nummer* 500200) was the aircraft that was surrendered to British forces by *Leutnant* Fröhlich of *II./KG(J)51* on 8th May. This aircraft was taken to Australia and exhibited at Point Cook before reaching its final destination in the Australian War Memorial, Canberra.

The American programme started shortly after the surrender, when Colonel Hal Watson, of the Technical Intelligence Department, was given a simple brief. Form a specialised unit to to scour Germany, seeking out aircraft and technical documentation covering the latest developments in *Luftwaffe* military aviation.

1st Lieutenant Robert C. Strobell was one of the first American fighter pilots inducted into the operation. He had served with the 353rd Fighter Group and was now with 1 TAF (Prov) Headquarters at Vittel, France. He had worked with Watson for some time and, when Watson walked into his office carrying a file marked *Top Secret*. *Operation Lusty,* he had no idea that he would be the first American pilot to fly one of the German jets. Watson told him that the '262 was top of the 'wanted' list, ordered him to draw field rations and told him to fly to Lechfeld, where a further six officers would eventually join him. Thus he became part of what was to become known as 'Watson's Whizzers' and was catapulted head-first into the jet age.

Meanwhile, ten top USAAF crew chiefs had been recruited to to the project:

Technical Sergeants: Edward J. Thompson
                                      Ernest C. Parker
                                      Noel D. Moon

Staff Sergeants: Charles A.Barr
Charles L.Taylor
Robert H.Moore
John G.Gilson
Archie E.Bloomer
Donald J.Willcoxen
Everet T.Box

Bob Strobell arrived at Lechfeld during the last week in May 1945. He found extensive Allied bomb damage on the airfield, one of the Messerschmitt offices was ransacked and there were around thirty Me262s scattered around the field. Many of the fighters were damaged, others pillaged, but some seemed intact and merely abandoned.

He entered one of the main hangars to find four American crew chiefs already at work on a small batch of '262s, assisted by 26 former Messerschmitt employees, who had been hired by

'Watson's Whizzers' (l to r) 1st Lieutenants James K.Holt, William V.Haynes, Robert J.Anspach, Colonel Harold E.Watson, Captains Kenneth E.Dahlstrom, Fred I.Hillis, 1st Lieutenants Robert C.Strobell and Roy W.Brown. This photo was taken at Melun in June 1945, during the ferrying of Me262s from Lechfeld to Cherbourg.
                                                                          (R.C.Strobell)

the Army of Occupation. Usefully, one man, Gerhard Caroli, spoke good English as did two former test pilots, Karl 'Pete' Baur and Ludwig 'Willy' Hoffmann, who had also volunteered their service to the team.

Strobell's first night at Lechfeld was not comfortable. He lay in a sleeping-bag on the second floor of a wrecked building near the hangar. There was no glass in the windows, no doors in the frames, and Strobell spent a restless night in the building with a Colt .45 pistol beneath the kit bag that served as a makeshift pillow. Liberated forced-labour prisoners had been reported roaming the area looking for old scores to settle with their former captors.

The four crew chiefs spent the night sleeping on the hangar floor to guard the jets in their charge. Soon, however, tents were provided by the Army unit on the far side of the base, who also found cots for the enlisted ground staff, who elected to remain in the hangar. Also, mess facilities were set up by the Army field kitchen for both enlisted men and officers, replacing the boxed field rations, which they had lived on for the first few days.

By the first few days of June, all the crew chiefs and officers were working on the jet fighters, learning all they could from the co-opted German technicians. For the pilots, the first task was cockpit familiarisation and the task of developing a detailed check list. One '262 that could not be made airworthy was towed to the hangar area and anchored down for engine trials. It was imperative that the pilots should become familiar with the temperamental engines, particularly the throttle handling. The engines were run in this static test-bed to allow pilots to master emergency drills and flying procedures. Difficulty was found in mastering the German instrument layout and finding switches etc., but this was eventually mastered. In addition, the engines were run at maximum power, were deliberately flooded with fuel and forcing them to overheat in order to discover the tolerances and limitations.

It was assumed that, once a jet was flown, it would behave as any other aircraft. However, the pilots were to find that the '262 was to have its own peculiar traits.

One of the Me262s taken by the Operation Lusty team. a single-seater inscribed 'Lady Jane IV'. (R.C.Strobell)

during that first week of June, the first Me262, checked and double-checked by Gerhard Caroli and pronounced airworthy. The German test pilots concurred - just as well, since Bob Strobell decided that the first test flight would be given to 'Pete' Baur. This was not due to any distrust of the Messerschmitt staff, but sheer common sense. It seemed prudent that the first flight should be in the hands of the most experienced Me262 test pilot present.

The fighter was fueled with a half-load and rolled out. 'Pete' Baur clambered aboard as he had done so many times before, then took off, disappearing from sight for several minutes before reappearing, to make several circuits of Lechfeld as Bob Strobell and two of the crew chiefs drove out in a jeep to the end of the runway to await Baur's return.

Baur had been airborne for fifteen minutes before sweeping down to a perfect landing. He taxied to a halt beside the waiting jeep and Strobell climbed up to take his place in the cockpit, to taxi the jet back to the hangar area. Back in the hangar, it was refuelled and a guard placed on it, allowing none but American personnel to approach it. They had worked with their former enemies to to get the aircraft airworthy, but they were still occupying German soil. The possibility of sabotage was ever-present and they could not afford to take chances.

1st Lieutenant Robert Strobell was now ready to take his first flight in the legendary Me262. He wanted 'to see what this blowtorch could do'. He was in for some surprises:

"I did not make a normal take-off. I held the nose too high and spilled air through the slots, gaining speed slowly. At mid-runway, it became obvious that I was not going to fly! I then lowered the nose wheel down to the runway, gained speed rapidly and hauled it off the ground at the end of the airstrip. This was 'Lesson One' learned.

"The next event startled me. The slots along the leading edge began to blink, moving in and out, slamming shut momentarily due to air turbulence. I expected them to be either open or shut, but they blinked until the jet gained enough speed to close them. 'Lesson Two' learned.

"After levelling off from the climb out of the airport, I became aware of the smooth, no-vibration, effortless flight. Upon reaching cruise speed, over 400 mph, I got another surprise - the aircraft thumped and bumped through air turbulence, sharp thumps, not like the P-47 that lumbered and rolled in rough air. After a 180 degree turn, I flew back over the airfield and was again surprised at the unbelieveable speed even at cruise settings. 'Lesson Three' learned.

"When it came time to land, after fifteen minutes flight as planned, I failed on the first attempt! Two events happened. On the downwind leg, I pulled the throttles back to 6,000 rpm required for landing, but nothing happened. The jet simply went streaking past the airfield showing no signs of slowing down. While the airfield disappeared from sight, I was trying to figure out how to slow the screamer down. The trick was simple. I came back around the airfield at 500 feet, pulled the throttles back again to 6,000 rpm and zoomed up a couple of thousand feet, where the speed dropped below 250 mph - safe speed to pop the gear. With the landing gear down it was necessary to add more throttle to hold speed at 250 mph in the landing pattern. 'Lesson Four' learned.

"I got another surprise on this manoeuvre. When the jet slowed to 250 mph whilst I was zooming up, I dropped the gear and the nose pitched up abruptly. Not violent, but worrysome, because I was already in a climb attitude at low speed. When the gear locked down the aircraft resumed level flight. Lesson Five.

"The landing pattern was not normal, because I was at high altitude and had to extend the downwind leg and base leg to kill off altitude. The landing was smooth and uneventful and I taxied back to the hangar area. When I climbed out of the cockpit, two of my pilots were waiting for me, Lieutenants Ken Holt and Bob Anspach. They came over and broke the propellers of my Air Force lapel insignia, saying that I would not need them any more. Classy touch.

"We could not fault the Messerschmitt test pilots for not alerting us to

One priority for the Americans was to get at least one trainer version airworthy to allow their test pilots a safer means of flight familiarisation. This is a rare shot of the single-seat trainer model, with an indecipherable inscription on the nose. It is likely that this was later exhibited in the USA, with the (incorrect) name of 'Der Schwalbe'.
(R.C.Strobell)

these five lessons. After all, they were test pilots, not instructors, and their familiarity with these experiences were common and may not even have entered their minds. I learned a lot from this flight and all our pilots were briefed on it." [114]

During the following days at Lechfeld, the American pilots came to trust the Germans. They found them to be 'gentlemen', rightly proud of the Me262. They were all craftsmen, without any military stigma.

An Me262 two-seat trainer was the next aircraft to reach flight status. This allowed Karl Baur and Willie Hoffmann to act as instructors to the rest of the American pilots. Restoration of the other jets proceeded quickly, assisted by a keg of Bavarian beer, which the mechanics consumed in the late afternoon on hot days.

Lieutenant Bob Strobell test-flew each jet as it came out of the hangar. One was the model equipped with the six-foot 50mm cannon built into its nose. It proved to be nose-heavy on take-off but, once airborne, Strobell found that, 'It could be waved around as easily as a sucker stick'.

Spare parts were required to keep the aircraft flying and, with the help of the German staff, they drove drove out into the countryside, miles from Lechfeld. 'We picked up six brand-new Jumo 004 jet engines, still in their crates, stashed in a farmer's barn under the hay'. Truck loads of spare parts were recovered in this way from other farm building and even private homes. They had been dispersed during the closing weeks of the war to protect them from Allied bombers.

With nine Me262s restored to flying condition at Lechfeld, it was time to move them west. On 10th June, all nine were flown out to Melun airfield in France, some of the pilots using this trip to solo on the jets. The weather was fine, but even so, cruising at a fuel-efficient 10,000 feet without radio and navigating by Air Force maps, they did well to bring all nine '262s to Melun without mishap.

The jets remained at Melun for three weeks until the 27th and, during this time, Lieutenant Strobell, Colonel Watson and Karl Baur flew in the units C-47 transport to Schleswig to recover a pair of Ar234s and another Me262. Strobell was to bring the '262 back via Holland, but on this occasion the trip did not go as planned. The trip down to Holland for a pre-arranged refuelling stop was uneventful - until the landing. He had been warned that the runway was quite short and recalls:

> "My landing approach was set to hit the end of the runway. An instant before I touched down, I felt a heavy thump, the airplane touched down and all hell broke loose. The jet swerved to the right, violently shuddering and thumping, down the runway. I managed to keep it on the runway 'till it came to a halt. After I mopped my face, I checked the landing gear and found the right scissor broken, the wheel turned 45 degrees and dragging the tyre sideways as it came to a rest. Remembering the pre-landing thump, I went back to the end of the runway and found a foot-high mound of dirt from a drainage ditch, with two tyre grooves six inches deep across it. The tricycle landing gear saved my neck and the airplane." [115]

A new wheel strut was brought in on a C-47. After installation, Strobell flew the jet on to Melun without further incident.

General Carl 'Tooey Spaatz visited Melun on 27th June to review the aircraft, pilots and crew chiefs. Colonel Watson escorted the General through the review, then Lieutenants Strobell, Holt and Captain Hillis took three of the Me262s out to the runway for a demonstration.

After take-off, the three pilots went into line-astern and made diving high-speed passes across the airfield in front of the reviewing party. Strobell performed a 'victory roll' during the

On 27th June 1945, General Carl 'Tooey' Spaatz and General Curtis LeMay visited Melun. (l to r) General Spaatz, Colonel Hal Watson and General LeMay take a close look at one of the Jumo 004 turbines.
(R.C.Strobell)

demonstration and was later informed by Willie Hoffmann that this was a very dangerous manoeuvre that often caused the engines to flame-out. He had been lucky to get away with it.

As Tooey Spaatz walked away from the demonstration, he was heard to mutter 'Wicked, wicked'. At last he had witnessed at first hand the nightmare fighter that his bomber crews had faced.

The jets were then flown on to Cherbourg. On this leg of the journey, Willie Hoffmann was chosen by Strobell to fly the '262 with the 50mm cannon, a particularly prized aircraft. Part way to the destination, however, disaster struck when the starboard engine turbine blades failed. Hoffmann heard it, like a small explosion, followed by violent vibrations throughout the aircraft, bouncing the trim lever into a noise-down position. The jet had lost no speed and Hoffmann did the only thing possible. He jettisoned the canopy, rolled the '262 onto its back and was thrown out of the cockpit. He had believed that he was fairly close to the ground and pulled the ripcord early, before his body speed had slowed and stabilised.

Next day, Bob Strobell visited him in hospital. He was groggy, but coherent and pointed to his parachute, lying in the corner of the room. When Strobell inspected it, he found that three cores were ripped apart near the apex. Two of them were three feet long and the other six feet long. Additionally, six of the shroud lines had broken! Willie told him that he owed his life to the Irvin parachute and was certain that the German 'chutes would have totally disintegrated under the shock of that opening. Indeed, no-one believed that any of the American pilots could have survived such a bale-out.

Bob Anspach's flight to Cherbourg was eventful for another reason. Flying above the clouds, he made a let-down towards what he thought was Cherbourg but, to his surprise, found only open sea beneath him. Fuel was getting low, so he turned 180 degrees and found the island of Guernsey. He made a normal landing there, but it was to be some hours before the worried team discovered his whereabouts. Two drums of fuel were sent out to him in a C-47 and the fuel was hand-pumped aboard, allowing him to fly out from Guernsey to re-join the team next day.

During the days following, the jets were prepared for shipment by sea to the United States. They were loaded aboard the Royal Navy aircraft carrier HMS *Reaper*, which departed for Newark, New Jersey on 20th July, arriving eight days later. *Operation Lusty* was over.

Bob Strobell was not there to see the completion of the program, however. On 4th July, Independence Day, he had flown a war-weary P-47 Thunderbolt back to Germany to pick up his personal possessions and equipment and was carrying with him twenty-five rolls of film and all his records of the Me262 test program.

It was a warm day, the Thunderbolt was fully fueled and, with a raised railway bed with pole wires at the end of his take-off run, he opened the throttle wide for maximum power. He cleared the obstruction, climbed to around 1,000 feet - and then an induction manifold blew out, which filled the engine

'Happy Hunter II', the spectacular-looking Me262 with the 50mm cannon, which was lost en route to Cherbourg. The German test pilot, Ludwig Hoffmann, survived injured. (via ARP)

compartment and cockpit with raw vapourised petrol. He slid the canopy back, cut the switches and began an emergency glide back to the airfield with the airscrew windmilling. Suddenly the engine backfired, setting off a flash fire like an explosion. He recalls:

> "I baled out by sheer instinct, so close to the ground that the airfield personnel did not see the parachute open."

The P-47 dived into the ground and with it went the priceless film and his records of the jet program. Strobell himself hit the ground hard and was to spend the next 45 days recovering in the base hospital.

Back in the US, the Me262 test program continued in the hands of US Air Force and Navy pilots until spares finally ran out in 1946.

Looking back on *Operation Lusty*, the American pilots considered that they had been lucky. German records showed that many Me262 crashes had been caused by lack of pilot training on the type. A third of ground accidents had been due to undercarriage failure. Indeed, the nosewheel assembly was so fragile that, under ground towing, the stress on the unit needed to be eased by means of cables attached to the two main oleo legs to spread the load. Another third of crashes were due to engine failures.

The final tribute to the test program is that the '262s flown by Strobell and Holt survive today. Strobell's in at the US Air Force Museum at Wright Patterson AFB, Dayton, Ohio. Holt's is on show at the National Air and Space Museum, Washington DC.

Notes
112. Account provided by Clive Gosling and first published in *Flugzeug* magazine.
113. *Wings of the Luftwaffe* by Eric Brown.
114. Correspondence Robert C Strobell - S E Harvey.
115. *Ibid.*

Chapter Eleven
Post Mortem and Remembrances

The Me262 was gone, but not forgotten. Indeed, some went into service again as front-line fighters, this time with the Czech Air Force, where the few on strength were known as Avia S-92s.

American test pilots flew the *Schwalbe* in mock combat sorties against B-17s, when they discovered that the time elapsed between entering the field of fire of the bomber defences and the break-away after delivering an attack was just six seconds. If the jet pilot maintained maximum combat speed, the Bendix power-operated turrets were incapable of traversing fast enough to track the fighter at all, making a deflection shot impossible. There is little doubt that, had the Me262s and the R4M rockets been available earlier, the American daylight strategic bombing campaign would have been seriously hampered, if not halted altogether.

The sheer speed of the Me262 could not be matched by any Allied service aircraft for some years. On 7th September 1946, a

One of Kurt Welter's nightfighters from 10./NJG 11 in British markings. The 'Hirschgeweih' radar array can just be seen forward of the gun ports. This may have been the aircraft later sent to South Africa and still displayed there.

modified Gloster Meteor (EE549) was flown to a speed of 616 mph by Group Captain E M Donaldson. Even so, it was short of the 624 mph attained by the 12th prototype Me262 in July 1944! The Meteor, the first operational Allied jet fighter, came into service with 616 Squadron at approximately the same time as the Me262 and was employed first against the V-1 flying bombs and later on ground attack duties in Holland and north Germany. No engagements took place between the opposing jet fighters but, had this occurred, it seems probable that the German aircraft would have proved the superior machine.

During its short but effective service career, many variants of the fighter had been tested. Some models, known as the 1-1b variant, were those intended to carry the R4M missiles. It had been planned for 24 rockets to be mounted beneath each wing, but test trials showed that 17 was the maximum possible. A plan to carry a Mauser MG213 multi-barrel cannon (similar to the later American Vulcan high cyclic rate gun) did not proceed further than the drawing board. A cannon that could have proved extremely effective was the Rheinmetall BK-5, a 50mm cannon experimentally fitted to three Me262s designated as the Me262la-U2. This massive weapon projected some seven feet from the nose and was tested in the only one of the three to fly (*Werke Nummer* 130083). In ground trials, 27 out of 30 rounds hit the target, but when tested against American heavies by *Major* Wilhelm Herget it was found that the high G-forces experienced in combat caused the weapon to jam.

Survivors

Top: Hans Fay's aircraft, now preserved in the Air Force Museum at Dayton, Ohio. (via ARP)

Centre: Avia S-92 served with the Czech Air Force from 1946 until 1948. It was then displayed in the National Technical Museum, Prague until the early 1980s. After a full repaint, it was moved to the Czech Air Force Museum at Kbely, where it remains.

Bottom: Strikingly painted in 1945-style grey-blue wimter camouflage, the Me262 trainer displayed at Willow Grove. Either the photo negative has been reversed or the swastika on the fin has been incorrectly applied.

Post Mortem and Remembrances

As has already been mentioned, surviving Me262s can be found in England, Australia and South Africa, while of the several examples taken to the United States, four still survive. One is an Me262A-1a fighter, which is to be found in the Planes of Fame Museum at Buena Park, California. This aircraft, beautifully restored and maintained, was bought shortly after the war by the billionaire Howard Hughes, who offered to enter it in the Bendix Air Race, where it would compete against the latest American combat fighters. His offer was turned down. Many thought that the German jet would put its more modern competitors to shame and would not risk what they felt would be a 'national disgrace'! Another Me262, test-flown by Bob Strobell, is in the National Air and Space Museum at Wright-Patterson Field, Washington DC., the A-2a fighter-bomber surrendered by Hans Fay is at the USAF museum at Dayton, Ohio. The last aircraft, originally believed to have been a two-seat nightfighter, is a trainer. It resides at the Naval Air Station, Willow Grove, in Pennsylvania and is one test-flown by Ken Holt during *Operation Lusty*.

Additionally, Hans-Guido Mütke's aircraft was returned to Germany by the Swiss Authorities and stands in the Deutsches Museum, Munich, while a Czech Air Force Avia S-92 is kept at the Air Force Museum at Kbely - a total of nine. However, these may not be the last the world will see of the Me262; in recent years many replica warplanes have been produced, notably the World War I replicas built for the film industry. Now plans are afoot in America for replica Me262s to be built - hopefully with more reliable engines - to keep its history alive. The authors hope that these plans will indeed come to fruition.

As people walk past the still and silent survivors in the quiet of museums, few realise the true significance of the aircraft and the turmoil it caused both within the Allied High Command and the ranks of the aircrews who had to face it in combat. Neither is there any appreciation of the courage of those young *Luftwaffe* pilots who flew it, many of whom had only rudimentary jet training before being sent to face staggering odds. Nor are people conscious of the awe with which the jet was regarded by those who fought against it.

When the Me262 is mentioned to ex-aircrew, however, the consensus of opinion seems to be that, 'only a handful were ever used and they were too few in number to be a serious threat'. They are amazed when told that a total of 1,294 Me262s were built, of which between a half and three-quarters entered unit service. In that context, the loss rate in combat was not that high. Some 160 were claimed by American fighter pilots, about half over or near their airfields; some 30 more were reported destroyed by British and Commonwealth squadrons. Claims by the Russians are not known, but may amount to only one in aerial combat. Setting these against the reported claims of nearly 800 by Me262 units, it is clear that the jet gave a rather better account of itself than it has ever been given credit for.

The *Luftwaffe* jet fighter pilots were the true pioneers of the jet age. Their machines were never thoroughly tested and evaluated before entering service and the high-speed tactics were evolved under combat conditions. Although its speed was awesome, it could also prove a disadvantage when attacking much slower aircraft. Pilots would reduce their throttle settings in order to allow more time for aiming, but this instantly put them at a disadvantage against the slower but more agile Allied fighters. A jet pilot attempting a bale-out was also presented with a major problem, for no air brakes were fitted and a bale-out at speeds in excess of 250 mph often caused the pilot to be struck by the high tail unit. Had ejector seats been fitted, as in the He219 *Uhu* nightfighter, many lives would have been saved.

The *Schwalbe* could be flown with safety up to 570 mph, but between 585-630 mph (speeds varying due to differences in individual airframes) an Me262 could become uncontrollable. Gerd Lindner, the Messerschmitt test pilot, flew one to Mach 0.86 at high altitude, noting the the nose pitched down progressively, requiring more and more strength to be applied to the control column to prevent a flat-out vertical dive totally out of control. Indeed, *Luftwaffe* instructions were, that 596 mph should not be exceeded below 26,250 feet and above that no aircraft should exceed 560 mph. In the heat of combat and aircraft could quickly reach 'critical' speed and it is easy to understand that many crashes were caused by the inadvertent exceeding of these 'speed limits', giving the pilots no means of escape.

The main moments of vulnerability were take-off and landing. Engines could flame-out without warning if the throttles were mishandled and a stall would occur below 175 mph if a tight turn was attempted with the undercarriage down, which often occurred if attacked. Landing speeds were high - 115 to 125 mph - and great care had to be taken to hold the nosewheel off the runway until the last possible moment due to the risk of oleo collapse (as Squadron Leader Schrader of 616 learned to his cost at Lübeck - Chapter 10). Landing accidents were also caused when pilots, seeing an Allied fighter approaching, tried to get their aircraft down too quickly.

The endurance of the aircraft was very limited. High speed flight would allow a pilot to remain airborne for approximately forty minutes but, by careful use of throttles, an experienced pilot could increase this to sixty - seventy minutes, even longer at high altitude where turbines became more efficient.

The Germans opted for a complicated solution when an Me262A-1a was fitted with a Walter R11-211/3 rocket motor was installed in the rear fuselage and vented below the modified tail unit. This aircraft (*Werke Nummer* 130186), known as the Me262C-1a, was tested on 27th February 1945 by Gerd Lindner and attained 38,000 feet in 4.5 minutes from a standing start. This was improved on in March, when Karl Baur flew the only test flight of the Me262C-2b *Werke Nummer* 170074, modified with lower-rated BMW 003R turbines of 1,760 lbs thrust (as opposed to the service Jumo 004 of 1,980 lb thrust), but incorporating a BMW 718 rocket motor of 2,700 lbs thrust. The rocket motor was automatically ignited when the aircraft reached 100 mph and reached 25,000 feet in just one and a half minutes from a standing start. It was planned to put the Walter-powered C-1a *Heimatjäger* in production, carrying fuel for the rocket in disposable tanks beneath the nose. Both motor and tanks would be jettisoned after combat altitude was reached, the motor being fitted with a parachute for re-use. Again, it was too late, the surrender taking place before any production could be started. It is puzzling that small drop-tanks never seemed to have been considered for the fighter intercep-

Former enemies could become close friends. Georg-Peter Eder (right) and Urban L. 'Ben' Drew visit the South African War Museum in 1989 and pose before the resident Me262 nightfighter. It was the first occasion that Eder had seen one since 1945. (U.L.Drew)

tors. They would not have affected 'scramble time' appreciably, could have been jettisoned before combat was joined, and could have extended the 'time in combat' enormously.

The Allied bombing campaign against the German aircraft industry had been particularly severe but, by an almost superhuman effort, construction facilities had been widely dispersed. During 1945, Me262 production was moved to forest areas at Horgau, near Augsburg and to Obertraubling, near Regensburg, the latter being a 'finishing' site.

These dispersed factories produced some 200 Me262s a month and the Horgau site was a closely guarded secret and indeed, the Allies were unaware of its existence until the area was overrun by American forces during the last few days of the war. As the American troops advanced through the forest areas, they discovered that the woods were packed with completed Me262s awaiting delivery to combat units that no longer existed. The Obertraubling plant had been detected by the Allies, however, and the camouflaged factory had been heavily bombed during March.

Professor Willy Messerschmitt was arrested by British troops as his beautiful villa at Oberammergau. The British, French and Americans all sought to obtain his services, but he refused all offers. The brilliant designer, who had produced two of the most outstanding combat aircraft of the war and had employed some 81,000 workers, then slipped into obscurity - for a short time; the post-war German aircraft industry needed his remarkable talents. In the late 1950s the new concern of Messerschmitt-Bolkow-Blohm (MBB) was established and Willy Messerschmitt became a director. He worked there until his death in 1978 at the age of 80.

Fittingly, the last words should be from those who witnessed the Me262 in action.

Major John C Meyer, who had been one of the first Allied pilot to be outrun by jets, saw another when on bomber escort duties to Berlin. Answering a desperate 'May-Day' call from a damaged Fortress, Meyer's eight Mustangs arrived to find the 'Big Friend' under attack from a '262. The Mustang pilots formated on the bomber, turning into each attack and forcing the German to continually break away. From this experience, Meyer determined that one Me262 was equal to eight P-51s.

Those who bore the brunt of the Me262 attacks were, of course, the heavy bomber crews. Frank Belasco was, in 1944, a B-24 navigator with the 376th Bomb Group, 15th Air Force. He remembers:

"On three or four occasions in late summer 1944or early fall of that year, we flew missions to Austria or southern Germany and saw Me262s flying above our formation. They would approach the formation by diving on it from fairly high altitude, taking care not to come within range of our fifty calibres, as I recall. About 600 yards out, they pulled up and climbed back to high altitude, where they did S-turns over the formation.

"We were escorted on these missions by P-38s, P-47s and P-51s, and I recall on at least one occasion watching P-47s trying to chase the jets, but the Germans left the P-47s standing. I assume that, because the Germans did not attack our bomber formation, and German FW90s and Me109s were attacking in great numbers, our fighters did not go after the jets other than that one time - the first time I saw an Me262.

"As I recall, there were only two, three or four Me262s in a flight, and I only saw one flight on each occasion. Our identification of these 'planes was confirmed by reference to our aircraft identification material after the first sighting, and was confirmed by subsequent sightings of the the same type of airplane on later missions.

"We flew combat missions to France, Yugoslavia, Czechoslovakia, Hungary and Rumania as well as to Austria and Germany during this period, but the only places I observed these airplanes was Austria and Germany. We were told that they had only 45 minutes to one hour's fuel and they would not attack us. Whether this was official information or rumour I don't remember, but it seemed to be reliable with respect to the attack." [116.]

Frank Belasco was lucky, as was another navigator, formerly with the 413th Bomb Squadron of the 96th Bomb Group, flying in B-17s from Snetterton Heath, England. Leo Freedman flew 35 missions between July 1944 and February 1945, retiring with the rank of Major. He recalls:

"My limited experience with the Me262 was that on a few occasions they came up to scout our altitude and strength. During one mission I saw an Me262 in the distance. Two P-51s dived on him from above - by the time the P-51s were at our altitude, the Me262 was on the ground and the pilot was probably eating his lunch. But I was never fired on by an Me262 in that time." [117.]

Major Erich Rudorffer, last *Kommandeur* of *I./JG 7*, had previously served with great distinction in France and Africa and then moved to the east with *JG 54*, claiming 212 victories before transferring to the jet fighters and adding a further twelve kills to his score. When interviewed post-war, he remarked:

"The aircraft was the best we had at the end of the war, but we had too few of them and too few good pilots left for the jet *Staffeln*."

He confirmed that the P-51 was the aircraft most feared by the jet pilots as it could out-manoeuvre the Me262, although the German pilots could usually outrun them, but he saw many young *Luftwaffe* pilots shot down by the seasoned American fighter pilots. On at least one occasion he saw a German bale out, only to be followed by a P-51 and strafed while hanging helplessly in his parachute. It made him and his comrades feel sick but, he said, that at that stage of the war, pilots on both sides who knew no better were doing the same thing. It is known that some American units were specifically ordered to kill parachuting jet pilots, since they were more valuable to the *Reich* than their aircraft, which could more easily be replaced. Many American pilots, quite naturally, refused to participate in this foul practice, but some relished it. As one said 'It was a rough war!' Another remarked, 'If we did not do it, he would come up at us next day in another aircraft. We would not all do this.' The old chivalry of the air, invented in the First World War and displayed in some measure in the early years of the Second, was finally dead.

Another Me262 pilot, commenting on the unreliability of the jet engines, gave a graphic picture of those last, desperate days in one simple sentence:

> "The engines were rated for twenty-five hours but, since the average combat life of an aircraft was only about seven hours, what did it matter?"

The Me262 had been designed not only as the perfect fighter, but also for ease of maintenance under combat conditions. Bob Strobell, chief test pilot of the Operation Lusty team, recalls:

> "One of the the things that you want to be able to do in combat, is to keep the maximum number of aircraft in operation. To do that, you oft-time have to change engines on them. Well, changing an engine on a Thunderbolt is at least a full day's job, if not two or three, even under the best conditions. And yet I know for a fact that you can change a jet engine on a '262 in thirty minutes."

His commanding officer Colonel (later General) Hal Watson, did not fly the jet in Germany, but did so later. He remembers:

> "Of all the airplanes I've flown, it was the most exciting, the most combat-worthy, and you could do anything in it."

The only British fighter pilot to destroy two Me262s was John Wray. In the winter of 1944 he flew as Wing Leader of 122 Tempest Wing and made some very pertinent comments as to the differing operational conditions prevailing between the RAF and American units and especially regarding the British tactics:

> "The Me262s that we met were used principally in the bombing rôle. They were used to drop anti-personnel bombs on our airfield causing damage to both personnel and aircraft.
>
> "The aircraft had a very short endurance and obviously, the more power that was used, the shorter that became. Our radar picked the jets out fairly easily because the 'blip' was travelling so much faster than the others."They operated from only two airfields in our sector, Achmer and Rheine, both

near Osnabrück. So far as I can recall, this was due to fuel and spares problems.

"We tried to deal with them in two ways. Firstly by intercepting them and secondly by patrolling their bases in order to make it difficult for them to take-off or land. German AA was both accurate and pretty lethal, and they spared no effort in defending their airfields. So the second tactic had its drawbacks!

"No Allied fighter had the speed or acceleration to deal with the Me262 in level flight and so advantage had to taken of height and surprise. This allowed us to build up sufficient speed to get into firing range and hold the target long enough either to kill him or slow him down so that a further attack could be carried out. Unless one could get close enough without being seen, his acceleration was usually sufficient to get him away safely.

"Unless one was airborne at the time and in the vicinity of the jet, interception was not easy. Their sorties rarely lasted for more than some thirty minutes or so, therefore they were exposed to us over our own territory for a very short time. So, interceptions were largely a matter of chance. The American experience was possibly slightly different because they, additionally, had the jets attacking their escorted bombers and therefore offered themselves more easily as targets.

"One tactic that was used - rather in desperation - was to try to make the jet 'weave' by firing at him even if he was out of range. If he knew you were firing, and particularly if tracer was used, he would often start to make evasive manoeuvres which, in turn, slowed him down. It depended upon how close one was at the time and what the speed differential was.

"I was also interested in the head-on attacks by the '262s. The Germans were already using this form of attack with their '109s and '190s when the US fighter escorts became so large and were able to go to the target and back.

"The problem was always to get far enough in front of the target to get into position to launch a successful attack, which often meant the attacker not being able to see the target, thus arriving at an angle.

"After the war, we tried to perfect the head-on attack, using Meteors against USAF B-29s, but we were being positioned by radar, so one was lined up and put on the right course. However, the closing speed was such that the attacks were 'hairy' in the extreme., bearing in mind that this was peacetime, and mid-air collisions were not acceptable! Finally, a Meteor clipped the the top of the fin of a Superfort and that was the end of that. Even though little damage was done to either aircraft, I suspect bowels were loosened a bit!"

John Wray, who retired with the rank of Group Captain, also recalled how the jets would approach the Nijmegen bridge, trying to draw the covering fighters away. He also remembered that the 'Rat Catchers' were often disappointed when jets did not return to the airfields from which they had departed. At the time, Tempest pilots believed that the *Luftwaffe* were using nearby *Autobahnen* as make-shift satellites for the jets.

An 80 Squadron Tempest pilot, John Garland, destroyed a '262 on 3rd December 1944, but had seen jets on several previous occasions:

> "We had been bombed at Grave and Volkel and were well aware of their high-speed capability. I also saw from the ground a low-level combat between a '262 and Spitfires. This was between Nijmegen and Grave. From this brief sighting it appeared that the Spitfires had a considerable manoeuvring advantage. I hear later that a Canadian squadron had shot down a '262 about this date.
>
> "Twice in October and November, three '262s had attacked our squadron while on patrol (probably at about 10,000 feet). They had dived from above and astern. When we turned towards them, they made no attempt to engage, but continued diving at a speed that made any thought of pursuit out of the question. My feeling was that we had little hope of success against the jets at altitude, but could cope at ground level."

The action that John Garland had witnessed had been the epic fight between Hans-Christof Büttmann and the 401 Squadron Spitfires, about which Rod Smith added the final comments:

> "We received our combat films within about a week after the '262 went down. I recollect that John MacKay's film showed two or three strikes on the trailing edge of the wing alongside an engine nacelle, and also showed the strange-looking smoke beginning to issue from the place where those strikes had been. Tex Davenport's showed fire streaming from alongside the engine nacelle and also showed my Spitfire between Tex and the '262. My film was white for the first few seconds, due to the fact that the steepness of my climb brought the glare of the sun into those frames, but when it cleared it also showed fire streaming from the same place. I am fairly sure that the fire beside the engine nacelle was where John MacKay's first strikes had been. I wonder whether those strikes might have caused the fire that eventually brought the '262 down. However, because the smoke had stopped issuing out of it and it had been able to sustain such a long near-vertical climb just before the end of this action, and because of all the confusion, we shall never know who did exactly what to the '262. A little later I heard that the barrel from one of the four 30mm cannon with which our '262 was armed had ended up at 127 Wing at Grave. I drove over and asked Johnnie Johnson, the 127 Wing Leader, if I could have the barrel for 401 Squadron as a souvenir. He graciously handed it over. I gave it to 401 Squadron's adjutant and told him to treasure it. I left the squadron in early December and some time after that it disappeared, to the disappointment of squadron members of later years.

"We learned after the war that Hitler, in his infallible wisdom, had decreed that the Me262, although designed as a fighter, was to be used as a bomber. It was a superb fighter but a very poor bomber. This insane decree probably cost poor Büttmann his life. He showed he could throw an aeroplane around the sky very well and that he had great fighting spirit, but he had been sent to fly a fighter in an enemy fighter's sky."

Jack Boyle, who was delighted to discover that he was the first Spitfire pilot to single-handedly shoot a jet down, recalls the initial apprehension felt by fighter pilots flying piston-engined fighters:

"With a top speed in excess of 500 mph it could quickly out-distance the 400-plus of the Spitfire IX and, since their main tactic seemed to be to attack out of the sun from above, we felt quite defenceless against them. With such speed, their one passing attack would only take seconds and, since it was so difficult to spot them right at the outset, we always felt exposed and vulnerable."

Troops who face the jet fighter-bombers of KG(J)51 also remember them. Hubert J Hammett served in Holland with No.2875 Bofors Battery, RAF Regiment, in the winter of 1944/45. He saw no jets during the New Year's Day attack, but:

"On the following and consecutive mornings, they came over our position at first light. No piston-engined fighters at all, just one or two Me262 fighter-bombers flying at about 5,000 feet. They were not after the airfield (Eindhoven) at this time; they were after our gun positions. The first morning they took us completely by surprise, coming over at 06.00 hours, and both dropped a canister full of anti-personnel bombs. When the canister hit the ground it exploded, throwing the smaller bombs over a large area. These kept going off all day long, injuring airmen that were near them. They were very hard to spot where they had landed in bush and hedge lines. Others that could be seen were thrown into pits where they could do little harm, but we would still jump out of skins when they went off. By the end of that first day, with our 'unwanted guests', everyone was a little jumpy.

"Each morning they attacked us we had no chance to open fire because, like modern jet aircraft at speed, you never heard them 'til they were going away. Some mornings we thought they were not coming, then 'whoosh - bang!', we had another lap full of bombs. Orders were to be as quiet as mice for the first hours of daylight, and this way we could hear the dull whine of the jets coming in at speed. As soon as we heard them coming we put up a barrage of fire with our Bofors. There was no point in using our gunsights because of their speed, but our fire did put them off their aim, making them break or climb away. They still dropped their bomb loads, but most of them went over the back of our position into open fields.

"One morning we did knock one down, but it was sheer luck on our part, as our gunsights were no good at their airspeed. We just pushed our sights right over 400 mph, as high as they went, and blazed away.

"I must state, the morning we hit one I was not our Bofors; it was the second gun crew's duty spell. Our guns had two crews, so they were always manned. I was awake in my trench a short distance behind the guns. Our Bofors put up the usual barrage as they heard the jets coming in. I saw the first Me262 flash through the *Flak* bursts. He dropped his bomb late and it went over our heads and exploded way outside our lines. Then the second jet came through. A *Flak* shell burst right in front of him and he must have sucked some shrapnel into his air intakes, because as he went over me his engines were making a noise like someone shaking coins in a tin. I spun around and watched him going away from us. Smoke was pouring out of his engines and the aircraft could be seen slowing down.

"What happened in the next few minutes I can only describe as a fantastic piece of flying skill. The German pilot's jet was at about 5,000 feet when it was hit; as he went away from us we could see him dropping, and going into a tight turn behind our positions. He must have dropped his bomb early, as I do not recall seeing it fall. The area was very flat and we could still see him although he was some distance away. He had now turned back towards our lines, but was very low, and a few seconds later had disappeared behind the hedge line into the next field to ours. Then we heard him hit and, a second or two later, the jet came skidding through the hedge sideways, jumped the ditch and stopped.

"We were not allowed to leave our positions, but some army lads were dug in behind us, very close to where the jet had stopped. I heard later that army personnel had got the pilot out of the cockpit and that he was alive, but I do not know if he was injured, and some officers whisked him off in a truck.

"A lot of smoke was coming from the jet but it was, on the whole, in one piece. We were not allowed to go near it and the army put guards around it until a group of Royal Engineers arrived with a tank transporter. Later in the day they had the wings off it, loaded the lot up, and that's the last we saw of it. I believe this was the first Me262 to be captured intact." [118]

Dennis Richardson has a particular reason for remembering one attack. He was serving with the East Riding Yeomanry in the Ardennes area, moving fuel and ammunition forward to tanks of the Royal Armoured Corps:

"We moved into a village one evening, that had just been cleared by Royal Engineers. It was very cold and we were glad to get a roof over our heads. It was only a small place, and five of us were billeted for the night in a butcher's shop in the centre of the village. One man, trooper Skinner, decided to have a shave in the sink in the shop before it got too dark. There was a group of civilians living in this house already; two nuns, who had five children in their care. They could speak a little English and some of us knew a few words of French, so we could communicate a little. We were all

May 1945. The Third Reich in ruins, an Me262 of JG 7 sits forlornly at Prague/Ruzyne airfield. Although its days of glory were over, it would not be forgotten. The life and death of the Me262 heralded the beginning of the jet age and ensured the Schwalbe's place in history.
(Z.Hurt)

talking loudly when Skinner, at the sink, shouted for everyone to be quiet. We all stopped talking. 'Listen', he said. 'Aircraft coming this way. Jet, by the sound of it.' He was one of those people who could hear things ages before anyone else. 'Jerrie!', someone shouted from the back. That did it. The nuns knew what that meant all right. They panicked and made a bolt for the door with the children, but we all dived on them, pulling them down onto the floor before they could leave. Just at that moment there was the whistle of a bomb. It hit the building on the other side of the street and the explosion blew in all the windows of our shop, covering all of us with glass, window-frame dust and bricks. If they had reached the door they would all have been killed, as the blast blew the door in too.

"As we all lay on the floor, they explained that they had been making for the shop cellar door, which was just outside. We all picked ourselves up, and got the nuns and children down into the cellar. Just as we made our way down the cellar steps, we heard the jet coming back. It passed over the village, machine-gunning as it went.

"It was not until the jet had finally gone that | I felt something running down the back of my head, and asked the corporal to have a look with his torch. I had to asked him several times, as he was cared to show a light, but when he finally did, he said, 'Christ! You'd better get down to the Medical Centre as soon as you can, with that!' I had a cut on the back of my head about three inches long and quite deep. It was funny really; I could not feel anything until later. I got down to the Medical Officer, who dressed the wound. I had been cut by flying glass, but it was not too bad, and I was put back on duty the following day.

"I had not seen the jet during that action, as I was inside for most of the time it was over the village, but I heard later that it was an Me262 fighter-bomber. We never saw or heard another one, but we were often bombed at night by conventional bombers." 119.

Perhaps the last thoughts should be left to an anonymous B-17 rear gunner, now deceased. Ronald Cole of the Sacramento police department, California, had a friend who flew with the 8th Air Force and he has never forgotten how his friend described the only time he saw Me262s at close quarters:

"He talked of his squadron's meeting with the Me262s many times, and his personal experience was one of sheer terror. Unlike the P-51s and P-47s, the B-17 could not turn inside the jets and he had to sit and watch it rip through the formation firing its rockets and cannon, while his shaking hands held machine-guns that were totally incapable of tracking it. His description of the jet attack will always remain with me. He described the cramped confines of his tail gunner's position, the small window through which he observed the enemy jets scream by in seconds that seemed an age, and the limited field of fire available to him. But most of all he remembered the complete breakdown of radio discipline as the crews observed the nightmare fighter, which they had all hoped was just a propaganda myth."120.

Notes

116. Correspondence Frank Belasco - S E Harvey.
117. Correspondence Leo Freedman - S E Harvey.
118. Hubert Hammett, a close friend of S E Harvey, who in 1972 first drew his interest - later obsession - with the combat history of the Me262.
119. Related to S E Harvey by marriage. It was a sheer coincidence that he too was attacked by Me262 fighter-bombers in 1944.
120. Correspondence Roland Cole S E Harvey.

Appendix I
Known Me262 Pilots.

Note: It is difficult to assess jet claims correctly, since the confused situation made it impossible for the normal claims procedure to be applied, and, due to Allied bombing and the speed of the advance, many documents have been lost. Thus it is impossible to ascertain which claims were not confirmed by Higher Command. The claims listed thus represent all known claims made whilst flying the Me262, followed by the pilot's total score on all types of fighter aircraft; '+' indicates 'at least'. Included in the jet claims are the 'Herausschusse', where known.

1) Day Fighter Units

Ofw Rudolf Alf	Kdo Now	?/12	KIFA
Lt Alfred Ambs	JG 7	7+/7+	
Ofw Helmut Anschütz	JG 7	?	
Uffz Fritz Anzer	JG 7	?	KIA
Ofw Heinz Arnold	JG 7	7/49	KIA
Ofhr Hans-Joachim Ast	JG 7	?	KIFA
Ofhr Willi Banzhaff	Kdo Now, JG 7	2/2+	KIA
Obstlt Heinz Bär	EJG 2, JV 44	16/220	+ 1957
Fw Ewald Barden	JG 7	0	
Maj Gerhard Barkhorn	JV 44	301/0	
Fw Kurt Baten	JG 7	?/24	
Ofw Helmut Baudach	Kdo Now, JG 7	5+/20+	KIA
Lt Max Beck	JG 7	?	
Ofw Otto Beckert	JG 7	0/1	
Lt Bell	EJG 2, JV 44	1+/1+	
Fw Bergmann	JG 7	?	
Uffz Hans-Joachim Berndt	JG 7	?	
Fw Aloys Biermeier	JG 7	?	
Hptm Günther Bischoff	JG 7	?/6	
Oblt Paul Bley	Ekdo 262 Kdo Now	1+/9+	KIFA
Oblt Blömert	JV 44	?	
Maj Hans-Ekkehard Bob	JV 44	0	
Ofw Böckel	JG 7	1+/12	
Ofw Bodes	JG 7	?	
Oblt Bohatsch	JG 7	4/17	

Oblt Josef Bohm	EJG 2	?	KIA
Uffz Peter Bongart	JG 7	?/11	
Lt Hans Bott	JG 7	?/1	
Uffz Erwin Böttge	JG 7	?/6	
Lt Hans Braun	JG 7	?	
Lt Karl Brill	JG 7	?/52	
Maj Brücker	JV 44	?/?	ex-KG(J)51
Uffz Wendelin Bruse	JG 7	?	
Ofw Hermann Buchner	Kdo Now, JG 7	12/58	
Uffz Burchardt	JG 7	?	
Hptm Lutz-Wilhelm Burckhardt	JG 7	?/61	
Ofw Burkschat	JG 7	?/3	
Lt Wilhelm Büschen	JG 7	?/9	
Ofw Erich Büttner	JG 7	8+/8+	KIA
Uffz Caatz	JG 7	?	
Uffz Herbert Chlond	JG 7	?/4	
Fhr Christer	JG 7	1+/1+	
Obst Walther Dahl	EJG 2	2/128	
Fw Karl Degener	JG 7	?/12	
Hptm Desdorffer	JG 7	?	
Uffz Detjens	JG 7	?/1	
Maj Dohler	JG 7	?	
Ofw Döring	JV 44	?	
Lt Hans Dorn	JG 7	?	
Fw Hubert Drfla	JG 7	?/18	
Maj Ernst Düllberg	JG 7	?/50	
Lt Hermann Eden	JG 7	?	
Maj Georg-Peter Eder	Kdo Now, JG 7	25/78	
Fhr Friedrich Ehrig	JG 7	5+/39	
Maj Heinrich Ehrler	JG 7	8/205	KIA
Maj Diethelm v.Eickel Streiber	JV 44	0/96	
Fw Erwin Eichhorn	JG 7	?	KIA
Fw Heinz Eichner	JG 7	?	KIA
Uffz Eischner	JG 7	?	
Lt Heinrich Engel	JG 7	?	
Uffz Wolfgang Engel	JG 7	?/1	
Hptm Rudolf Engleder	JG 7	1+/26	
Uffz Günther Engler	JG 7	3+/8+	
Hptm Esser	JV 44	?	
Hptm Franz Evers	JG 7	0/2	
Lt Gottfried Fährmann	JG 7, JV 44	4+/4+	
Lt Fall	JG 7	2+/2+	
Uffz Fick	JG 7	?	KIA
Uffz Kurt Flachs	JG 7	0	KIFA
Ofw Freutzer	Kdo Now	?	

Maj Siegfried Freytag	JG 7	?/102	
Obsting Franz Frodl	JG 7	?	
Lt Fröhlich	JV 44	?	ex-KG(J)51
Ofw Frohs	JG 7	?	
Lt Hein Führmann	JG 7	?/8	
Genlt Adolf Galland	JV 44	8/104	
Fw Benvenuto Gartmann	JG 7	?/54	
Ogfr Fritz Gehlker	JG 7	?	KIA
Uffz Ernst Giefing	JG 7	2+/2+	
Fw Heiner Geisthovel	JG 7	3+/3+	
Hptm Horst Geyer	Ekdo 262	?/35	
Lt Ernst-Rudolf Geldmacher	JG 7	?	KIA
Lt Rolf Glogner	JG 7	?/3	
Oblt Adolf Glunz	JG 7	0/72	
Lt Hubert Gobel	JG 7	9+/10+	
Fw Ernst Godde	JG 7	?/2	
Fw Heinz Gomann	JG 7	1+/13+	
Ofw Heinz Gossow	JG 7	?/9	
Hptm Hans Gottuck	JG 7	?/7	
Ofw Götz	JG 7	1+/1+	
Ofw Alfred Greiner	JG 7	1+/10+	
Oblt Kurt Grigo	JG 7	?/2	
Ofw Hans Gross	JG 7	?	
Maj Hans Grözinger	JG 7	?	+ 1945
Oblt Hans Grünberg	JG 7, JV 44	5/82	
Hptm Heinz Gutmann	JG 7	1+/1+	KIA
Fw Ebergard Gzik	JG 7	?	
Stfw Heinz Haack	JG 7	0	
Lt Reinhard Haas	JG 7	?	
Ofw Haase	JV 44	?	
Ofhr Eich Haffke	EJG 2	?	KIFA
Lt Walter Hagenah	JG 7	1+/17+	
Ofhr Karl-Heinz Hankammer	JG 7	?/2	
Oblt Norbert Hanning	JG 7	?/42	
Lt Rudolf Harbort	EJG 2, JG 7	5+/60+	
Uffz Karl Hartung	EJG 2	?	KIFA
Oblt Alfred Heckmann	JV 44	-/71	
Lt Günther Heckmann	JG 7	?/20	
Uffz Hubert Heckmann	JG 7	?/5	
Uffz Otto Heckmann	JG 7	?	KIA
Fw Hans Heidenreich	JG 7	?/11	
Gfr Heim	JG 7	5/5	KIA
Ofw Helmut Heiser	JG 7	1+/16+	
Uffz Helms	JG 7	?	KIA
Fw Rudolf Hener	JG 7	?/5	
Maj Wilhelm Herget	JV 44	1/72	
Fw Herlitzius	Ekdo 262	0/?	

Oblt Fritz-Erhard Herrmann	JG 7	?/2	
Fw Robert Heuer	JG 7	?/6	
Ofw Walter Hickethier	JG 7	?	
Fhr Helmut Hochleitner	JG 7	?	
Oblt Ernst-Otto Hocker	JG 7	?	
Lt Hofmann	JV 44	?	
Maj Erich Hohagen	JG 7	0/55	
Uffz August Holscher	JG 7	?/5	
Fw Franz Holzinger	JG 7	?/10	
Oblt Hondt	JV 44	?/16 approx	
Lt Hans Hoster	JG 7	?/2	
Lt Hans Hoyer	JG 7	?	
Ofw Hübl EJG2,	JG 7	2+/2+	
Ofw Heinz Humberg	JG 7	3/7	
Lt Heinz Jahner	JG 7	?/1	
Lt Walter Jahnke	JG 7	?/58	
Oblt Hans-Jochen Janke	JG 7	?/5	
FjFw Heinrich Jansen	JG 7	?	
Gfr Jan Janssen	JG 7	?	
Ofhr Günther Jelinski	JG 7	?/3	
Fhr Günter Jotten	JG 7	?	
Fhr Karl-Heinz Jurzitza	JG 7	?	
Ofw Erich Kaiser	EJG 2, JG 7	2+/2+	
Lt Herbert Kaiser	JV 44	0/68	
Lt Hans Kaiser-Dieckhoff	JG 7	?	
Fw Kammerdiener	JV 44	?	
Lt Karsten	JG 7	?	
Fhr Herbert Kaiser	JG 7	?	
Lt Fritz Kelb	JG 7	1+/3+	KIA
FjFw Heinrich Kempken	JG 7	?/2	
Lt Hans-Joachim Kindermann	JG 7	?	
Hptm Kirchays	JV 44	?	
Ofw Helmut Klante	EJG 2 JV 44	?	
Ofw Hans Klausen	JG 7	?	KIA
Hptm Knauth	JG 7	?	
Ofw Knier	JV 44	?	
Lt Gerhard Kobert	Kdo Now	?	KIA
Uffz Hans Kogler	JG 7	?	
Uffz Köhler	JG 7	?	KIA
Uffz Kurt Kolbe	JG 7	?	KIA
Uffz Harald König	JG 7	2+/2+	
Lt von Kortzfleisch	JG 7	?	
Uffz Peter Köster	EJG 2 JG 7 JV 44	7+/7+	
Hptm Gerhard Kostrzewa	JG 7	?	
Lt Karl Kraft	JG 7	?/5	
Ofhr Georg Kretzschmar	JG 7	?	

Appendix I

Ofw Kreutzberg	JG 7	?	
Hptm Kriegshammer	JG 7	?	
Hptm Walter Krupinski	JV 44	2/197	
Lt Elias Kuhlein	JG 7	?/36	
Uffz Heinz Kuhn	JG 7	?	KIFA
Oblt Franz Kulp	JG 7	3/10	
FjFw Landsenbacher	JG 7	?/10	
Fw Hans Langer	JG 7	?/10	
Hptm Kurt Lehmann	JG 7	0/0 ?	
Wolfgang Lehmann	JG 7	?	
Lt Alfred Lehner	JG 7	2+/37	KIA
Oblt Leikhoff	JG 7	?	
Ofhr Otto Leisner	JG 7	?/3	
Oblt Leitner	JG 7	?	
Fw Helmut Lennartz	Kdo Now JG 7	9/11	
Ogfr Leuthner	Kdo Now	?	
Fw Leverentz	JG 7	1+/1+	
Oblt Erwin Leykauf	JG 7	?/33	
Lt Heinrich Lonnecker	JG 7	? KIA	
Oblt Fritz Loose	JG 7	?/7	
FjFw Ferdinand Loschenkohl	JG 7	?/11	
Ofw Loschner	JG 7	?	
Ofw August Lübking	JG 7	3+/40+	KIA
Lt Hugo Luchs	JG 7	?	
Obst Günther Lützow	JG 7, JV 44	2/110	KIA
Ofw Heinz Mattuschka	JG 7	?	KIA
Uffz Karl Mayer	JG 7	?	
Uffz Hans Mehn	JG 7	?/1	KIA
Uffz Erich Meinhardt	JG 7	?	
Gfr Meinhold	JG 7	?	
Gfr Wille Mertz	JG 7	?	
Lt Harry Meyer	EJG 2, JG 7	1+/?	KIA
Hptm Meyer	JG 7	3/?	
Hptm Erich Mikat	JG 7	?	
Lt Bruno Mischkot	EJG 2 JG 7	5/7	KIA
Uffz Kurt Mühlbauer	JG 7	?	
Lt Erwin Müller	JG 7	2+/20+	
Lt Fritz Müller	JG 7	9/22	
Lt Herbert Müller	JG 7	?/6	
Lt Hermann Müller	JG 7	?/10	
Gfr Paul Müller	JG 7	1+/1+	
Lt Siegfried Müller	JG 7	?/17	KIA
Lt Wolfgang Müller	JG 7	?	
Uffz Herbert Müller-Welt	JG 7	?/1	
Uffz Müller	JV 44	?	
Lt Karl Munz	EJG 2	3/60	
Fhr Hans-Guido Mütke	EJG 2, JG 7	?	

The Me262 Combat Diary

Maj Johannes Naumann	JG 7	0/34	
Ofhr Neugebauer	JG 7	?	
Ofhr Josef Neuhaus	JG 7	2+/15+	
Lt Klaus Neumann	JG 7, JV 44	5/37	
Oblt Neumar	JG 7	?	
Ofw Nielinger	JV 44	?	
Flg Noher	JG 7	2+/2+	
Fw Germar Nolte	EJG 2	?	KIFA
Gfr Hermann Nötter	JG 7	2+/2+	
Oblt Karl Nordbruch	JG 7	?	
Maj Walter Nowotny	Kdo Now	3/258	KIA
Lt Walter Ohlerogge	JG 7	0/77	
Ogfr Fritz Pauleweit	JG 7	?	
Uffz Pelletier	JG 7	?	
Lt Viktor Petermann	JG 7	0/64	
Fhr Ernst Pfeiffer	JG 7	7+/7+	
Oblt Richard Philipp	JG 7	?/5	
Lt Hermann Pickrun	JG 7	?	
Uffz Rudolf Pings	JG 7	?	
Uffz Pöhling	JV 44	?	ex-KG(J)51
Lt Erik Prettner	JG 7	1+/1+	
Fhr Rolf Prigge	JG 7	3/16	
Fw Otto Pritzl	JG 7	8+/18+	
Uffz Hein Rach	JG 7	?	
Lt Rudolf Rademacher	JG 7	24/126	
Fw Rauchensteiner	EJG 2, JG 7	1+/1+	
Ofhr Richard Raupach	JG 7	?/23	
Ofw Reckers	Kdo Now JG 7 EJG 2, JV 44	1+/1+	KIA
Oblt Richter	JV44	?	
Uffz Gerhard Reiher	JG 7	4+/5+	
Hptm Ernst-Wilhelm Reinert	JG 7	0/174	
Ofw Gerhard Reinhold	JG 7	2+/43+	KIA
Ofw Fritz Reinke	JG 7	?/2	
Uffz Friedrich Renner	JG 7	?	KIFA
Lt Wolfgang Rentsch	JG 7	?/9	
Lt Günther von Rettberg	JG 7	?	KIA
Lt Roth	JV44	?	
Maj Erich Rudorffer	JG 7	14/222	
Ofw Heknut Ruffler	JG 7	?/63	
Ofhr Heinz Russel	Kdo Now JG 7	3+/4+	KIA
Fw Hans Rutt	JG 7 ?		
Lt Heinz Sachsenberg	JG 7, JV 44	?/104	
Gfr Ferdinand Sagemeister	EJG 2	?	KIFA
Oblt Franz Schall	Kdo Now JG 7	17/137	KIFA
Uffz Edward Schallmoser	JV 44	4+/4+	
Oblt Schätzle	JG 7	?	KIA

318

Fw Rudolf Scheibe	JG 7	?	
Fw Friedrich-Wilhelm Schenk	JG 7	3+/4+	
Uffz Kurt Schiebeler	JG 7	?/6	
Uffz Siegfried Schielicke	JG 7	?/?	
Fw Horst Schiesske	JG 7	?/2	
Lt Horst Schlick	JG 7	?/32	
Oblt Dietrich Schlüter	JG 7	?	
Lt Herbert Schlüter	JG 7	2+/17+	
Fhr Bruno Schmidt	JG 7	?	
Uffz Helmut Schmidt	EJG 2	?	
Uffz Dieter Schmitt	JG 7	?	
Lt Karl-Heinz Schmude	JG 7	?/31	
Uffz Werner Schneider	JG 7	?	
Maj Karl-Heinz Schnell	JV 44	2/72	
Uffz Wilhelm Schneller	JG 7	?	KIFA
Lt Karl Schnörrer	Ekdo 262, Kdo Now JG 7	11/46	
Ofhr Karl Schnurr	JG 7	?	KIFA
Ofw Helmut Scholz	JG 7	?/1	
Uffz Anton Schöppler	JG 7	7+/13+	
Oblt Hans Schrangl	JG 7	?/13	
Lt Alfred Schreiber	Kdo Now JG 7	7+/7+	KIA
Ofhr Günther Schrey	JG 7	?	KIA
Oblt Walter Schuck	JG 7	8/206	
Lt Leo Schuhmacher	JV 44	1/23	
Lt Erich Schulte	JG 7	?/1	KIA
Ofw Schwaneberg	JV 44	?	
Fw Christoph Schwarz	JG 7	?	
Oblt Karl-Heinz Seeler	JG 7	1+/9+	KIA
Oblt Alfred Seidl	JG 7	?/30	
? Georg Seip	JG 7	?	
Lt Seufert	JV 44	?	
Maj Rudolf Sinner	JG 7	3/39	
Lt Spangenberg	Kdo Now JG 7	?/37	
Maj Wolfgang Späte	JG 7	5/99	
Uffz Heinz Speck	EJG2	?	KIFA
Oblt Erwin Stahlberg	JG 7	?/9	KIA
Maj Hermann Staiger	JG 7	?/63	
Oblt Günter Stedtfeld	JG 7	?/25	
Lt Fritz Stehle	JG 7	11+/26+	
Fw Steiner	JV 44	?	
Obst Johannes Steinhoff	JG 7, JV 44	6/176	
Maj Wilhelm Steinmann	EJG 2, JV 44	4/44	
Oblt Stigler	JV 44 ?		
Lt Sträte	JV 44	?	ex-KG(J)51
Ofw Strathmann	Ekdo 262	0/?	
Uffz Stromm	JG 7	?	

Oblt Gustav Sturm	JG 7	4/21	
Hptm Gert Suwelack	JG 7	?/5	
Fw Adolf Tabbat	JG 7	1+/1+	
Fw Fritz Taube	JG 7	1+/7+	KIA
Lt Kurt Tangermann	JG 7	?/46	
Oblt Siegfried Tappe	JG 7	?	
Lt Fritz Tegtmeier	JG 7	?/146	
Oblt Alfred Teumer	Kdo Now	?	KIA
Fw Hans Theis	JG 7	?/10	
Ofw Arno Thimm	JG 7	?/4	
Hptm Werner Thierfelder	Ekdo 262	0	KIA
Lt Hans Timmermann	EJG 2 JG 7	2+/2+	
Ofw Hans Todt	JG 7	2+/13+	
Ofhr Harald Toennissen	JG 7	?	
Hptm Tollsdorf	JG 7	?	
Fw Trenke	JV 44	?	ex-KG(J)51
Oblt Wolf Trubsbach	JG 7	?	
Lt Willi Unger	JG 7	?/22	
Uffz Louis-Peter Vigg	JG 7	?	
Lt Walter Wagner	JG 7	? KIA	
Uffz Waldhofer	JG 7	?	
Oblt Hans Waldmann	JG 7	2/134	KIFA
Oblt Walter	JV 44	?	
Lt Joachim Weber	Kdo Now JG 7	9+/9+	KIA
Oblt Günther Wegmann	Ekdo 262, JG 7	8/21	
Lt Hans-Dieter Weihs	JG 7	9/9	
Ofhr Weindl	JV 44	?	ex-KG(J)51
Maj Theodor Weissenberger	JG 7	8/208	
Hptm Werner Wenzel	JG 7	?/18	
Uffz Hans Werner	JG 7	?	KIFA
Oblt Walther Wever	JG 7	?/44	KIA
Ofw Otto Wienberg	JG 7	?	
Fw Wilhelm Wilkenloh	JG 7	?	KIA
Ofhr Walter Windisch	JG 7	5+/7+	
Uffz Günther Wittbold	JG 7	2+/2+	
Lt Hermann Wolf	JG 7	1/57	
Oblt Ernst Worner	JG 7	1+/1+	
Hptm Hein Wübke	JV 44	0	
Fw Heinz Wurm	JG 7	?	KIA
Ofw Zander	Kdo Now	?	
FjFw Joachim Zeller	JG 7	1+/7+	
Fw Konstantin Zimmermann	JG 7	?	
Lt Rudolf Zingler	JG 7	1+/2+	
Uffz Aloys Zollner	Kdo Now	?	

2.) Night Fighter Units

Fw Karl-Heinz Becker	10/NJG11	6/6	
Oblt Behrens	E-Stelle Rechlin	?	

Appendix I

Lt Wilhelm Beier	Training	0/38	
Ofw Paul Brandl	10/NJG11	?	KIFA
Ofw Bockstiegel	10/NJG11	?	KIFA
Oblt Heinz Bruckmann	10/NJG11	?	KIFA
Oblt Walter Eppelsheim	10/NJG11	?	KIFA
Obst Hajo Hermann	LuftDiv 30	?	
Maj Gerhard Stamp	10/NJG11	?	
Ofw August Weibl	10/NJG11	?	KIFA
Maj Kurt Welter	10/NJG11	29/63	+ post-war

3.) Fighter-Bomber Units

Hptm Fritz Abel	KG(J)51	?	KIA
Hptm Rudolf Abrahamczik	KG(J)51	?	
Oblt Wolfgang Baetz	KG(J)51	?	
Ofw Baier	KG(J)51	?	
Maj Siegfried Barth	KG(J)51	?	
Hptm Hans-Georg Baetcher	KG(J)54	?	
Lt Wilhelm Batel	KG(J)51	1/?	
Fw Bernhard Bertelsbeck	KG(J)51	?	KIFA
Ogfr Jürgen Brink	KG(J)54	?	KIA
Hptm Hellmut Brocke	KG(J)51	?	KIFA
Maj Brücker	KG(J)51	?	to JV 44
Hptm Karl-Heinz Buhring	KG(J)51	?	KIFA
Hptm Hans-Christof Büttmann	KG(J)51	?	KIA
Uffz Friedrich Christoph	KG(J)51	?	KIA
Fw Heinz Clausner	KG(J)54	?	KIA
Uffz Edmund Delatowski	KG(J)51	?	
Lt Erwin Diekmann	KG(J)51	?	KIA
FjOfw Wilhelm Dikus	KG(J)54	?	KIFA
Oblt Walter Draht	KG(J)54	?	KIA
Uffz Adalbert Egri	KG(J)54	?	
Uffz Willi Ehrecke	KG(J)54	?	KIA
Fw Felix Einhardt	KG(J)54	?	KIA
Uffz Heinz Erben	KG(J)51	?	KIA
Uffz Wilhelm Erk	KG(J)51	?	KIFA
Uffz Alfred Farber	KG(J)51	?	KIA
Fw Joachim Fingerloos	KG(J)51	?	
Uffz Gerhard Franke	KG(J)51	?	KIFA
Lt Fröhlich	KG(J)51	?	to JV 44
Oblt Werner Gartner	KG(J)51	?	KIA
Ofw Gentzsch	KG(J)54	?	
Lt Gert Gietmann	KG(J)51	?	KIA
Fw Günther Gorlitz	KG(J)54	?	
Fw Heinrich Griems	KG(J)54	?	MIA
Maj Grundmann	KG(J)51	?	
Oblt Haeffner	KG(J)51	?	
Obstlt von Halensleben	KG(J)51	?	Killed.

Fw Willy Helber	KG(J)51	?	KIFA
Ofw Rudolf Hoffmann	KJ(J)51	?	KIA
Obstlt Hermann Hogeback	KG(J)6	?	
Ofhr Jürgen Höhne	KG(J)51	?	KIA
Oblt Hans Holzwarth	KG(J)51	?	KIA
Oblt Harald Hovestadt	KG(J)51	?	
FjFw Edgar Junghans	KG(J)51	?	DoW
Oblt Günther Kahler	KG(J)54	?	KIA
Ofw Erich Kaiser	KG(J)51	?	KIA
Oblt Hermann Kleinfeldt	KG(J)54	?	KIFA
Lt Hans-Georg Knobel	KG(J)54	?	KIA
Oblt Hermann Knodler	EKG 1	?	KIFA
Ofw Hans Köhler	KG(J)51	?	DoI
Ofhr Walter Kramer	KG(J)51	?	
Lt Josef Lackner	KG(J)54	?	KIA
Uffz Kurt Lange	KG(J)54	?	KIFA
Ofw Hieronymus Lauer	KG(J)51	?	
Oblt Hans-Georg Lamle	KG(J)51	?	KIA
Uffz Kurt Lange	KG(J)54	?	KIFA
Fw Herbert Lenk	KG(J)51	?	KIA
Lt Wolfgang Lübke	KG(J)51	?	KIA
Uffz Lothar Luttin	KG(J)51	?	
Lt Mai	KG(J)54	?	
Uffz Heinz Maurer	KG(J)54	?	KIFA
Uffz Günther Meckelburg	KG(J)51	?	KIA
Obst Wolf-Dietrich Meister	KG(J)51	?	
Ogfr Hajo Mentzel	KG(J)54	?	KIFA
Oblt Merlau	KG(J)51	?	KIA
Ofhr Horst Metzbrand	EKG 1	?	KIA
Fw Hans Meyer	KG(J)51	?	KIA
Lt Hans Moser	KG(J)51	?	
StFw Mosbacher	KG(J)51	?	KIA
Lt Wolfgang Oswald	KG(J)54	?	KIA
Ofw Karl-Heinz Petersen	KG(J)51	?	DoI
Lt Kurt Piehl	KG(J)51	?	KIA
Fw Pöhling	KG(J)51	?	to JV 44
Oblt Hans-Georg Richter	KG(J)51	?	KIA
Obstlt Volprecht Riedesel Frhr zu Eisenbach	KG(J)54	?	KIA
Lt Oswald von Ritter-Rittershain	KG(J)51	?	KIA
Ofhr Gerhard Röhde	KG(J)51	?	MIA
Hptm Rudolf Roesch	KG(J)51	?	KIA
Lt Walter Roth	KG(J)51	?	
Lt Eduard Rottmann	KG(J)51	?	KIFA
Ofw Georg Schabinski	KG(J)51	?	
Uffz Herbert Schauder	KG(J)51	?	KIA

Appendix I

Obstlt Wolfgang Schenk	KG(J)51	?	
Lt Schimmel	KG(J)51	?	KIA
Fw Erwin Schulz	KG(J)51	?	KIFA
Maj Josef Schloess	KG(J)51	?	
Ofhr Richard Schöpe	KG(J)54	?	KIFA
Ofw Adolf Schwachenwald	KG(G)51	?	
Hptm Matthias Schwegler	KG(J)51	? KIA	
Maj Ottfried Sehrt	KG(J)54	?	
Lt Sträte	KG(J)51	?	to JV 44
Lt Strothmann	KG(J)51	? KIA	
Oblt Franz Theeg	KG(J)54	?	KIA
Fw Trenke	KG(J)51	?	to JV 44
Maj Kurt Unrau	KG(J)51	?	
Oblt Joachim Valet	KG(J)51	?	KIA
Fw Walter Wehking	KG(J)51	?	
Lt Rolf Weidemann	KG(J)51	?	KIA
Obfhr Weindl	KG(J)51	?	to JV 44
Ofw Ernst Wiese	KG(J)51	?	KIFA
Oblt Benno Weiss	KG(J)54	?	KIFA
Hptm Eberhard Winkel	KG(J)51	?	KIA
Fw Werner Witzmann	KG(J)51	?	KIA
Oblt Christian Wunder	KG(J)54	?	Killed
StFw Hans Zander	KG(J)51	?	KIA
Uffz Axel von Zimmermann	KG(J)51	?	KIFA
Lt Wolf Zimmermann	KG(J)54	?	

4) Reconnaissance Units

Oblt Willi Knoll	NAG 6	0	KIFA
Lt Friedrich-Wilhelm Schlüter	NAG 6	0	+ post-war

Appendix II
Known Losses of Me262 Aircraft.

19.5.44	**EKdo 262 Me262V-7 130002 V1+AB** Crashed at Lechfeld on training flight. Uffz Kurt Flachs killed.
16.6.44	**EKdo 262 Me262V-12 130008 VI+AG** Crashed at Lechfeld on training flight. Ofw Becker badly injured.
14.7.44	**I/KG(J)51 Me262A-2a 130177** Crashed near Ammersee after bombing. Stfw Mosbacher killed.
18.7.44	**EKdo 262 Me262A-0 ——** Crashed near Landsberg. Hptm Werner Thierfelder (Kdr) killed.
19.7.44	**Leipheim Me262 130013** Destroyed by bombing.
19.7.44	**Leipheim Me262 170007** As above.
19.7.44	**Leipheim Me262 170009** As above.
19.7.44	**Leipheim Me262 170012** As above.
19.7.44	**Leipheim Me262 170062** As above.
19.7.44	**Leipheim Me262 170065** As above.
19.7.44	**Leipheim Me262 170066** As above.
19.7.44	**Leipheim Me262 170050** Badly damaged by bombing.
19.7.44	**Leipheim Me262 170057** As above.
19.7.44	**Leipheim Me262 170064** As above.
30.7.44	**Leipheim Me262A 170058** Crashed near Biberbach due to engine failure. Fhr Kaiser baled out unhurt.
3.8.44	**I/KG(J)51 Me262A-2a 130189 SQ+XB** Crashed force-landing at Lechfeld. Lt Eduard Rottmann died.
23.8.44	**I/KG(J)51 Me262A-2a ——** Crashed on take-off from Lechfeld.

23.8.44	I/KG(J)51 Me262A-2a —— Crashed on take-off from Lechfeld.	
23.8.44	I/KG(J)51 Me262A-2a —— Crashed on take-off from Schwabisch-Hall.	
23.8.44	I/KG(J)51 Me262A-2a —— Force-landed in France.	
28.8.44	I/KG(J)51 Me262A-2a —— Shot down near Termonde. Fw Hieronymus Lauer safe.	
8.9.44	I/KG(J)51 Me262A-2a 170040 9K+DL Shot down by *Flak* NE Diest. Lt Rolf Weidemann killed.	
10.9.44	I/KG(J)51 Me262A-2a 170013 9K+LL Shot down by *Flak* near Liege. Oblt Werner Gartner killed.	
12.9.44	I/KG(J)51 Me262A-2a 130126 9K+AL Shot down by own *Flak* near Arnhem. Uffz Herbert Schauder killed.	
17.9.44	I/KG(J)51 Me262A-2a 170298 Crashed at Leipheim. Fw Bernhard Bertelsbeck killed.	
27.9.44	I/KG(J)51 Me262A-2a 170046 KI+IZ Crashed near Sankt Ottilien. Uffz Wilhelm Urk killed.	
27.9.44	I/KG(J)51 Me262A-2a 170085 9K+UL Crashed near Lippstadt. Uffz Lothar Luttin killed.	
2.10.44	I/KG(J)51 Me262A-2a 170069 9K+NL Shot down by fighter near Rheine. Ofw Hieronymous Lauer wounded.	
4.10.44	2/Kdo Nowotny. Me262A-1a 170044 Crashed landing at Hesepe. Oblt Alfred Teumer killed.	
4.10.44	Kdo Nowotny Me262A-1a 170047 Crashed landing at Waggum. Oblt Franz Schall unhurt.	
5.10.44	2/Kdo Nowotny Me262A-1a 170292 Force-landed on autobahn near Braunschweig out of fuel. Ofw Helmut Baudach unhurt.	
5.10.44	I/KG(J)51 Me262A-2a 170082 9K+PL Crashed near Nordhorn. Uffz Gerhard Franke killed.	
5.10.44	I/KG(J)51 Me262A-2a 170093 9K+BL Shot down by Spitfires near Nijmegen. Hptm Hans-Christoph Büttmann killed.	
6.10.44	I/KG(J)51 Me262A-2a 170117 9K+XL Shot down by fighter near Rheine. Fw Joachim Fingerloos wounded.	
7.10.44	1/Kdo Nowotny Me262A-1a 110395 Shot down by P-51s over Achmer. Ofhr Heinz Russel wounded.	
7.10.44	1/Kdo Nowotny Me262A-1a 170307 Shot down by P-51s. Oblt Paul Bley baled out safely.	
7.10.44	2/Kdo Nowotny Me262A-1a 110405 Shot down by P-51s over Achmer. Lt Gerhard Kobert killed.	

Appendix II

7.10.44	2./Kdo Nowotny Me262A-1a —— Shot down by P-51 over Achmer. Hptm Arnold killed.
7.10.44	I./KG(J)51 Me262A-2a —— Shot down. Pilot baled out.
12.10.44	1./Kdo Nowotny Me262A-1a 110402 Force-landed near Bramsche; fuel. Fw Helmut Lennartz safe.
12.10.44	1./Kdo Nowotny Me262A-1a 110388 Force-landed near Steenwijk; fuel. Oblt Paul Bley safe.
13.10.44	1./Kdo Nowotny Me262A-1a 110401 Crashed landing at Hesepe. Ofhr Heinz Russel unhurt.
13.10.44	3./Kdo Nowotny Me262A-1a 110399 Crashed at Achmer. Ogfr Leuthner badly injured.
13.10.44	I./KG(J)51 Me262A-2a 170064 9K+FL Force-landed after combat with fighter near Volkel. Uffz Edmund Delatowski wounded.
14.10.44	10./EJG 2 Me262A-1a —— Crashed at Hochstadt/Donau. Ofhr Erich Haffke killed.
15.10.44	I./KG(J)51 Me262A-2a 170825 9K+UL Shot down by fighter near Rheine. FjFw Edgar Junghans wounded, died 21st.
15.10.44	I./KG(J)51 Me262A-2a —— Crash-landed on return from operations.
28.10.44	1./Kdo Nowotny Me262A-1a 110388 Crashed on take-off from Achmer. Oblt Paul Bley killed.
28.10.44	2./Kdo Nowotny Me262A-1a 110479 Nosewheel collapsed on landing at Hesepe. Oblt Franz Schall safe.
29.10.44	1./Kdo Nowotny Me262A-1a 110387 Rammed Spitfire over Nordhorn. Lt Alfred Schreiber slightly wounded.
1.11.44	3./Kdo Nowotny Me262A-1a 110386 Shot down by P-51s over Zwolle. Ofhr Willi Banzhaff slightly wounded.
2.11.44	1./Kdo Nowotny Me262A-1a 110368 Crashed on take-off from Achmer. Uffz Aloys Zollner badly injured.
2.11.44	2./Kdo Nowotny Me262A-1a 170278 Damaged at Achmer. Ofw Hubert Göbel safe.
2.11.44	5./KG(J)51 Me262A-2a 170010 9K+CL Hit by *Flak* near Graeve. Hptm Eberhard Winkel (StK) wounded.
3.11.44	3./Kdo Nowotny Me262A-1a 110483 Shot down by fighter near Hittfeld Ofhr Willi Banzhaff killed.
4.11.44	1./Kdo Nowotny Me262A-1a 110403 Force-landed near Bohmte out of fuel. Ofw Hubert Göbel safe.
4.11.44	2./Kdo Nowotny Me262A-1a 170310 Force-landed. Ofw Zander safe.

6.11.44	**1./Kdo Nowotny Me262A-1a 110389** Force-landed near Lehnwerder out of fuel. Lt Spangenberg safe.
6.11.44	**1./Kdo Nowotny Me262A-1a 110490** Damaged by fighters near Bremen and force-landed. Ofw Helmut Lennartz safe.
6.11.44	**2./Kdo Nowotny Me262A-1a 110402** Damaged by fighters near Ahlhorn and force-landed. Ofw Freutzer safe.
6.11.44	**2./Kdo Nowotny Me262A-1a 170045** Engine failure at Hesepe. Ofw Helmut Baudach safe.
8.11.44	**2./Kdo Nowotny Me262A-1a 110404** Shot down by fighters near Achmer. Oblt Franz Schall (StK) safe.
8.11.44	**2./Kdo Nowotny Me262A-1a ——** Shot down. Ofw Helmut Baudach baled out unhurt.
8.11.44	**Kdo Nowotny Me262A-1a 110400 'White 8'** Shot down near Achmer. Maj Walter Nowotny killed.
8.11.44	**Kdo Nowotny Me262A-1a 170293** Damaged on take-off from Achmer. Fw Büttner safe.
20.11.44	**2./KG(J)54 Me262A-2a 170107 B3+BK** Crashed on take-off from Giebelstadt. Ofhr Richard Schöpe killed.
25.11.44	**I./KG(J)51 Me262A-2a 170122 9K+KL** Shot down by Flak during low level airfield attack W Helmond. Hptm Rudolf Rosch killed.
26.11.44	**9./JG 7 Me262A-1a 110373** Crashed near Buchenau on test flight. Ofw Rudolf Alt killed.
26.11.44	**9./JG 7 Me262A-1a 110372** Crashed near Lechfeld. Lt Alfred Schreiber killed.
26.11.44	**I./KG(J)51 Me262A-2a 110372** Crashed 3km south of Kirchwistedt Oblt Heinz Lehmann killed.
26.11.44	**I./KG(J)54 Me262A** Damaged at Giebelstadt. Extent of damage not notified.
28.11.44	**2./KG(J)51 Me262A-2a 170120** Shot down by A.A. at Helmond. Uffz Horst Sanio killed.
2.12.44	**1./KG(J)54 Me262A-2a 110551 B3+DH** Crashed south of Gerolzhofen on training flight. Ogfr Hans-Joachim Mentzel killed.
3.12.44	**I./KG(J)51 Me262A-2a 150335 9K+BH** Shot down by fighter near Rheine. Oblt Joachim Valet killed.
3.12.44	**I./KG(J)51 Me262A-2a 170296 9K+EK** Crashed near Burgsteinfurt. Ofw Karl-Heinz Petersen died 5th.
6.12.44	**10./JG 7 Me262A-1a 110369** Crashed near Osnabrück. Uffz Friedrich Renner killed.

Appendix II

7.12.44	4./KG(J)51 Me262A-2a 500010 9K+KM
	Crashed near Schwabisch-Hall. Hptm Hellmut Brocke (StK) killed.
9.12.44	4./KG(J)51 Me262A-2a 500009 9K+IM
	Shot down by fighter N Schwabisch-Hall. Stfw Hans Zander killed.
9.12.44	I./KG(J)54 Me262A-1 ----
	Wings stressed due to overspeed on combat sortie. Hptm Kornagel safe. Aircraft 30% damaged.
10.12.44	I./KG(J)51 Me262A-2a 170281 9K+FL
	Shot down by fighter near Bevergen and force-landed. Lt Walter Roth wounded.
10.12.44	2./KG(J)54 Me262A-2a 110504 B3+FK
	Crashed near Fahrenbach/Baden during high altitude interception flight. Oblt Benno Weiss killed.
11.12.44	I./KG(J)51 Me262A-2a 170108 9K+WL
	Shot down by Flak S Wierden. Fw Herbert Lenke killed.
12.12.44	I./KG(J)51 Me262A-2a 170080 9K+RL
	Shot down by *Flak* near Aachen. Ofw Hans Kohler killed.
12.12.44	I./KG(J)54 Me262A ----
	Damaged by AA fire and force-landed near Obertraubling. Hptm Kornagel unhurt.
15.12.44	1./JG 7 Me262A-1a ----
	Crashed near Schwabstadt. Uffz Wilhelm Schneller killed.
17.12.44	II./KG(J)51 Me262A-2a 110501 9K+BP
	Shot down by fighter W Hesepe. Lt Wolfgang Lübke killed.
23.12.44	1./JG 7 Me262A-1a ----
	Shot down by fighters near Schwabstadt. Fw Wilhelm Wilkenloh killed.
24.12.44	II./KG(J)51 Me262A-2a 110591 9K+OP
	Crashed near Hessental. Uffz Axel von Zimmermann killed.
25.12.44	I./KG(J)51 Me262A-2a 170273 9K+MK
	Shot down by Spitfire mear Liege Fw Hans Meyer killed.
25.12.44	II./KG(J)51 Me262A-2a 110594 9K+MM
	Shot down by *Flak* near Liege. Oblt Hans-Georg Lamle killed.
25.12,44	I./KG(J)54 Me262A-1 ----
	Crashed and destroyed on combat sortie.
27.12.44	II./KG(J)51 Me262A-2a 110624 9K+AM
	Crashed near Bunde. Fw Walter Wehking badly injured.
29.12.44	I./KG(J)54 Me262A-2a ----
	Failed to return from conbat sortie. Lt Wolfgang Oswald missing.
1.1.45	9./JG 7 Me262A-1a 500021
	Shot down by fighters W Fassberg. Lt Heinrich Lonnecker killed
1.1.45	9./JG 7 Me262A-1a 500039
	Force-landed near Fassberg after combat. Uffz Detjens safe.

1.1.45	III./JG 7 Me262A-1a 110407 Crashed near Ulzen. Pilot safe
3.1.45	2./KG(J)51 Me262A-2a —— Lost in Lingen/Ems area. Ofw Erich Kaiser killed
7.1.45	10./EJG 2 Me262A-1a 170306 'White 4' Crashed at Lechfeld. Uffz Helmut Schmidt badly injured.
10.1.45	I/KG(J)51 Me262A-2a 170098 9K+HL Crash-landed W Giebelstadt. Ofw Ernst Wiese killed.
12.1.45	10./EJG 2 Me262A-1a 110494 'White 9' Crashed near Kleinaltingen. Gfr Ferdinand Sagmeister killed.
13.1.45	I/KG(J)51 Me262A-2a 110601 9K+FH Shot down by fighter near Giebelstadt. Uffz Alfred Farber killed.
13.1.45	I/KG(J)54 Me262A-1 —— Destroyed at Giebelstadt.
14.1.45	9./JG 7 Me262A-1a 110476 Shot down by fighter near Wittstock. Fw Heinz Wurm killed.
14.1.45	9./JG 7 Me262A-1a 500039 Shot down by fighter near Wittstock. Uffz Detjens baled out safely.
14.1.45	10./JG 7 Me262A-1a 110476 Crashed near Krivitz. Ofhr Hans-Joachim Ast killed.
14.1.45	III./JG 7 Me262A-1a 130180 'Red 14' Shot down near Logow, Neuruppin. Pilot believed safe.
14.1.45	I/KG(J)51 Me262A-2a 110578 9K+MK Shot down by *Flak* near Detweiler. Lt Oswald von Ritter-Rittershain killed.
14.1.45	6./KG(J)51 Me262A-2a 110543 9K+LP Shot down by Spitfire at Rheine. Uffz Friedrich Christoph killed.
14.1.45	I/KG(J)54 Me262A-1 —— Destroyed at Giebelstadt.
16.1.45	I/KG(J)54 Me262A-1 —— Destroyed in ground strafe at Giebelstadt. Unoccupied.
19.1.45	III./JG 7 Me262A-1a 111564 Crashed near Ingolstadt. Uffz Heinz Kuhn baled out, but parachute failed.
19.1.45	III./JG 7 Me262A-1a 110755 Undercarriage damaged landing.
19.1.45	I/KG(J)54 Me262A-1 —— Crashed at Giebelstadt due to engine fire. Aircraft 70% damaged.
19.1.45	I/KG(J)54 Me262A-1 —— Bellylanded at Giebelstadt due to undercarriage damage. Aircraft 20% damaged.
19.1.45	I/KG(J)54 Me262A-1 —— Damaged at Giebelstadt. Aircraft 10% damaged.

Appendix II

20.1.45	10./EJG2 Me262A-1a 110286 'White 9' Crashed 1km E Augsburg. Uffz Karl Hartung killed.
20.1.45	I/KG(J)54 Me262A-1 —— Destroyed at Giebelstadt.
21.1.45	I/KG(J)54 Me262A-1 500054 Crashed landing at Giebelstadt due to pilot error. Aircraft 40% damaged.
21.1.45	10./NJG 11 Me262A-1a 110610 Crashed on Wittstocker Heide. Oblt Heinz Brückmann killed.
22.1.45	9./JG 7 Me262A-1a Shot down on approach to Parchim. Hptm G-P Eder severely wounded.
23.1.45	9./JG 7 Me262A-1a 110564 Crashed near Lubz. Ofhr Karl Schnurr killed.
23.1.45	12./KG(J)51 Me262A-2a 170295 Shot down near Hopsten. Hptm Hans Holzwarth killed.
23.1.45	I/KG(J)54 Me262A-1 110788 Crashed on take-off from Giebelstadt due to pilot error. Aircraft 40% damaged.
29.1.45	1./KG(J)51 Me262A-2a 110361 Destroyed in strafe at Kitzingen.
29.1.45	I/KG(J)54 Me262A-1 500049 Force-landed at Giebelstadt due to technical failure. Aircraft 15% damaged.
30.1.45	III/EJG 2 Me262A-1a 110529 Force-landed at Lechfeld.
30.1.45	III/EKG 1 Me262A-1a 110779 Crashed on take-off from Alt Lonnewitz. Oblt Hermann Knodler killed.
30.1.45	I/KG(J)54 Me262A-1 500063 Force-landed at Giebelstadt due to technical failure. Aircraft 25% damaged.
31.1.45	10./EJG 2 Me262A-1a 110371 Force-landed near Schongau at 14.20. Ofw Helmut Klante injured.
2.2.45	III./JG 7 Me262A-1a 170112 Damaged landing at Neuburg.
2.2.45	I/KG(J)51 Me262A-2a 110615 9K+NL Crashed on take-off from Giebelstadt. Hptm Karl-Heinz Buhring killed.
2.2.45	III/KG(J)54 Me262A-2a 110651 Tyre burst on landing at Neuburg. Pilot unhurt. Aircraft 10% damaged.
2.2.45	ISS.1 Me262A-1a 111552 Damaged on take-off from Leipheim.

3.2.45	I./KG(J)54 Me262A-2a 110560 Crashed landing at Giebelstadt. Pilot safe. Aircraft 20% damaged.
4.2.45	III./JG 7 Me262A-1a 130163 Engine failure at Briest.
4.2.45	III./KG(J)55 Me262A-2a 500013 Crashed on take-off from Riem.
4.2.45	10./NJG 11 Me262A-1a/U1 110932 Crashed near Briest. Ofw Paul Brandl killed.
4.2.45	10./NJG 11 Me262A-1a 170051 Crashed N Belzig. Oblt Walter Eppelsheim killed.
6.2.45	III./EJG 2 Me262B-1a 111053 Crashed west of Landshut due to engine fire.
8.2.45	II./KG(J)51 Me262A-2a 110419 Damaged at Mulheim.
8.2.45	II./KG(J)51 Me262A-2a 110912 Damaged at Muhlheim.
8.2.45	II./KG(J)51 Me262A-2a 110377 Damaged down by German *Flak*.
8.2.45	9./KG(J)54 Me262A-2a 110663 B3+ET Crashed near Zuchering on training flight. Uffz Heinz Maurer killed.
9.2.45	Stab./KG(J)54 Me262A-2a 500042 B3+AA Shot down in combat east of Camberg. Obstlt Volprecht Riedesel Frhr zu Eisenach killed.
9.2.45	I./KG(J)54 Me262A-2a 110799 B3+AB Damaged in combat near Frankfurt/Main. Maj Ottfried Sehrt (GrKom) wounded. Aircraft 10% damaged.
9.2.45	I./KG(J)54 Me262A-2a 110791 B3+BB Shot down in combat near Meerholz. Oblt Walter Draht killed.
9.2.45	I./KG(J)54 Me262A-2a 110862 B3+GL Shot down in combat near Neuhof. Oblt Günther Kahler killed.
9.2.45	I./KG(J)54 Me262A-2a 110561 Belly-landed at Giebelstadt after combat. Aircraft 85% damaged.
9.2.45	I./KG(J)54 Me262A-2a 110609 Crashed landing at Giebelstadt after combat. Aircraft 50% damaged.
9.2.45	10./EJG 2 Me262A-1a 110415 'White 18' Crashed near Zusmalthausen at 17.00. Uffz Heinz Speck killed.
10.2.45	III./JG 7 Me262A-1a 501200 Force-landed.
10.2.45	II./KG(J)54 Me262A-2a 500018 Crashed landing at Kitzingen. Aircraft 20% damaged.
10.2.45	III./KG(J)54 Me262A-1 110651 Undercarriage damage at Neuburg.

Appendix II

11.2.45	11./JG 7 Me262A-1a —— Shot down by fighters. Maj Hans Grözinger (StK) killed.
11.2.45	III./EJG 2 Me262A-1a 110499 Crashed at Lechfeld.
13.2.45	I./KG(J)51 Me262A-2a 111920 Crashed near Köln. Ofhr Walter Kramer injured.
14.2.45	III./JG 7 Me262A-1a —— Shot down in combat. Pilot baled out.
14.2.45	I./KG(J)51 Me262A-2a 110498 Taxy accident at Muhlheim.
14.2.45	I./KG(J)51 Me262A-2a 110615 9K+NL Missing. Fw Rudolf Hoffmann lost.
14.2.45	I./KG(J)51 Me262A-2a 110811 Shot down in combat. Pilot baled out.
14.2.45	5./KG(J)51 Me262A-2a 170068 9K+BN Shot down by fighter near Coesfeld. Oblt Hans-Georg Richter killed.
14.2.45	5./KG(J)51 Me262A-2a 110571 9K+HN Shot down by fighter near Coesfeld. Fw Werner Witzmann killed.
14.2.45	II./KG(J)51 Me262A-2a 110538 Crashed landing at Muhlheim.
14.2.45	II./KG(J)51 Me262A-2a 500059 Crashed landing.
15.2.45	1./JG 7 Me262A-1a 130171 Crashed near Alveslohe. Uffz Hans Werner killed.
15.2.45	I./KG(J)54 Me262A-2a 110803 B3+GH Crashed near Bad Mergentheim on training flight. Uffz Kurt Lange killed.
15.2.45	I./KG(J)54 Me262A-1 110601 Force-landed at Mandelfeld. Aircraft 30% damaged.
15.2.45	I./KG(J)54 Me262A-1 110942 B3+LS Shot down at Obergrasheim. Uffz Litzinger baled out.
15.2.45	III./KG(J)54 Me262A-1 111621 Crashed landing at Neuburg. Aircraft 30% damaged.
15.2.45	10./NJG 11 Me262A-1a 500075 Damaged in combat and force-landed at Handorf. Fw Karl-Heinz Becker unhurt.
16.2.45	I./KG(J)54 Me262A-1 110665 Tyre burst on take-off from Giebelstadt. Aircraft 10% damaged.
16.2.45	III./KG(J)54 Me262A-1 110933 Strafed at Obertraubling. Aircraft destroyed.
16.2.45	III./KG(J)54 Me262A-1 —— Bombed at Neuburg.

16.2.45	III./KG(J)54 Me262A-1 ——	
	Bombed at Neuburg.	
16.2.45	III./KG(J)54 Me262A-1 ——	
	Bombed at Neuburg.	
17.2.45	I./JG 7 Me262A-2 111591	
	Force-landed north of Hamburg due to engine failure.	
17.2.45	I./JG 7 Me262A-1 110971	
	Damaged at Kaltenkirchen due to technical fault.	
17.2.45	III./JG 7 Me262A-1a 111008	
	Crashed at Briest. Ofw Hans Clausen killed.	
17.2.45	III./JG 7 Me262A-1a 501199	
	Force-landed at Briest.	
17.2.45	1./KG(J)54 Me262A-2a 110922 B3+LH	
	Shot down by fighter near Welkshausen. Oblt Franz Theeg killed.	
17.2.45	10./NJG 11 Me262A-1a/U1 110603 'Red 2'?	
	Crashed 5km E Burg. Ofw Walter Bocksteigel killed.	
19.2.45	Stab./JG 7 Me262A-1a 110608	
	Force-landed after attack on B-17s.	
	Maj Theodor Weissenberger slightly wounded.	
19.2.45	2./JG 7 Me262A-1a 111539	
	Crash-landed near Stubben, Bad Segeberg.	
	Fw Aloys Biermeier injured.	
19.2.45	I./KG(J)51 Me262A-2a 170091	
	Force-landed near Lingen.	
19.2.45	I./KG(J)51 Me262A-1 170312	
	Damaged taxiing at Rhein-Main.	
19.2.45	Stab./KG(J)54 Me262A-1 110581	
	Crash-landed near Wertheim due to fuel shortage.	
	Aircraft 20% damaged.	
19.2.45	I./KG(J)54 Me262A-1 110650	
	Crash-landed at Giebelstadt due to technical failure.	
	Aircraft 10% damaged.	
20.2.45	10./EJG 2 Me262A-1a 111616 'White 14'	
	Crashed S Lammerdingen at 16.37. Fw Germar Nolte killed.	
20.2.45	I./KG(J)54 Me262A-1 170081	
	Strafed at Giebelstadt. Aircraft 40% damaged.	
20.2.45	I./KG(J)54 Me262A-2 110519	
	Crashed at Oedheim due to engine fire. Pilot baled out and safe.	
20.2.45	1./NAufkgr6 Me262A-4 500095	
	Belly-landed at Lechfeld.	
21.2.45	II./JG 7 Me262A-1 110810	
	Tyre burst on take-off from Parchim.	
21.2.45	III./JG 7 Me262A-1a 110964	
	Crash-landed at Briest; technical failure.	

21.2.45	II./KG(J)51 Me262A-2a 170004	
	Damaged due to burst tyre.	
21.2.45	II./KG(J)51 Me262A-2a 500056	
	Damaged due to service failure.	
21.2.45	II./KG(J)51 Me262A-2a 170199	
	Possibly shot down in combat. Ofhr Gerhard Rohde missing.	
21.2.45	II./KG(J)51 Me262A-2a 170010	
	Crash-landed south Aschendorf due to fuel shortage.	
21.2.45	I./KG(J)54 Me262A-1 111600	
	Strafed at Giebelstadt. Aircraft 35% damaged.	
21.2.45	I./KG(J)54 Me262A-1 111600	
	Strafed at Giebelstadt. Aircraft 75% damaged.	
21.2.45	III./KG(J)54 Me262A-1 111612	
	Crashed at Giebelstadt; technical failure. Aircraft 15% damaged.	
21.2.45	10./NJG 11 Me262A-1a 110600	
	Damaged in combat, landed at Prenzlau.	
21.2.45	2./NAufkgr6 Me262A-1a/U3 110565 'Red 2'	
	Crashed SE Landsberg on training flight. Oblt Willi Knoll killed.	
22.2.45	Stab./JG 7 Me262A-1a 111544	
	Shot down in combat near Stade. Uffz Nötter injured.	
22.2.45	Stab./JG 7 Me262A-1a 110797	
	Shot down near Stade. Pilot safe.	
22.2.45	I./JG 7 Me262A-1a 110815	
	Force-landed at Kaltenkirchen after combat.	
22.2.45	III./JG 7 Me262A-1a 110967	
	Damaged in combat, crash-landed at Larz.	
22.2.45	III./JG 7 Me262A-1a 110466	
	Shot down near Larz. Pilot baled out.	
22.2.45	III./JG 7 Me262A-1a 110784	
	Crashed Doberitz; engine failure. Pilot killed.	
22.2.45	III./JG 7 Me262A-1a 110043	
	Combat damage Oranienburg.	
22.2.45	III./JG 7 Me262A-1a 170778	
	Shot down near Hagenow. Ofw Mattuschka baled out.	
22.2.45	10./JG 7 Me262A-1a 110781	
	Shot down by fighters near Schönwalde. Ofw Helmut Baudach baled out wounded and injured on landing. Died of injuries.	
22.2.45	2./KG(J)51 Me262A-2a 110918	
	Shot down by fighter near Aachen. Lt Kurt Piehl killed.	
22.2.45	II./KG(J)51 Me262A-2a 500026	
	Crashed due to pilot error.	
22.2.45	8./KG(J)54 Me262A-2a 111613 B3+GS	
	Shot down by fighter near Landsberg. Ogfr Jürgen Brink killed.	

23.2.45	I./KG(J)51 Me262A-2a 110590 Damaged in landing accident.
23.2.45	I./KG(J)54 Me262A-1 111633 Crashed at Giebelstadt due to technical failure. Aircraft 10% damaged.
23.2.45	III./KG(J)54 Me262A-1 120260 Bombed at Neuburg. Aircraft destroyed.
23.2.45	III./KG(J)54 Me262A-1 500016 As above. Aircraft 75% damaged.
23.2.45	III./KG(J)54 Me262A-1 110547 As above. Aircraft 50% damaged.
23.2.45	III./KG(J)54 Me262A-1 110920 As above. Aircraft 20% damaged.
23.2.45	III./KG(J)54 Me262A-1 110570 As above. Aircraft 20% damaged.
23.2.45	III./KG(J)54 Me262A-1 111571 As above. Aircraft 20% damaged.
24.2.45	I./KG(J)51 Me262A-2a 500061 Crashed near Essen-Kupferdreh. Fw Ernst Schulz killed.
24.2.45	II./KG(J)51 Me262A-2a 110817 Crashed on take-off
24.2.45	II./KG(J)51 Me262A-2a 110588 Strafed landing at Rheine.
24.2.45	II./KG(J)51 Me262A-2a 500050 Crash-landed at Rheine due to technical failure.
24.2.45	I./KG(J)54 Me262A-1 110737 Force-landed west of Giebelstadt. Fw Hans Brömel killed.
24.2.45	III./EKG1 Me262A-1 110827 Crashed at Neuburg due to technical failure. Lt Heinz Gratz injured.
25.2.45	Stab./KG(J)54 Me262A-1 500012 Bombed at Giebelstadt.
25.2.45	Stab./KG(J)54 Me262A-1 500012 B3+?A Strafed at Giebelstadt. Aircraft destroyed.
25.2.45	Stab./KG(J)54 Me262A-1 110799 B3+AB Strafed at Giebelstadt. Aircraft destroyed.
25.2.45	2./KG(J)54 Me262A-1 111887 B3+?L Crashed after combat near Giebelstadt. Lt Wolf Zimmermann wounded. Aircraft 40% damaged.
25.2.45	2./KG(J)54 Me262A-1 110928 B3+LL Crash-landed at Giebelstadt. Lt Becker safe. Aircraft 30% damaged.
25.2.45	I./KG(J)54 Me262A-1 111633 Strafed at Giebelstadt. Aircraft destroyed.

Appendix II

25.2.45	I/KG(J)54 Me262A-1 110569 Crashed after combat near Langenfeld. Fw Felix Einhardt killed.	
25.2.45	I/KG(J)54 Me262A-1 110799 Strafed at Giebelstadt.	
25.2.45	I/KG(J)54 Me262A-1 110787 Strafed at Giebelstadt.	
25.2.45	I/KG(J)54 Me262A-1 110787 Strafed at Giebelstadt. Aircraft 10% damaged.	
25.2.45	I/KG(J)54 Me262A-1 120539 Strafed at Giebelstadt. Aircraft destroyed.	
25.2.45	I/KG(J)54 Me262A-1 120549 Strafed at Giebelstadt. Aircraft destroyed.	
25.2.45	5/KG(J)54 Me262A-2a 110948 B3+AM Shot down by P-51 NE of Iphofen. Lt Hans-Georg Knobel killed.	
25.2.45	5/KG(J)54 Me262A-2a 111917 B3+BN Shot down by P-51 at Marktbreit. Lt Josef Lackner killed.	
25.2.45	5/KG(J)54 Me262A-2a 110947 B3+DP Shot down by P-51 over Giebelstadt. Fw Heinz Clausner killed.	
25.2.45	III/KG(J)54 Me262A-2a 110618 Crashed at Schwabisch-Hall. Technical failure. Aircraft 25% damaged.	
25.2.45	III/KG(J)54 Me262A-1 110937 Crash-landed at Neuburg.	
25.2.45	III/EJG 2 Me262A-1a 110491 Shot down by fighter near Deberndorf. Oblt Josef Bohm killed.	
25.2.45	St/NAG 6 Me262A-1 111570 Force-landed at Lechfeld.	
26.2.45	I/EKG 1 Me262A-1 170042 Crashed at Neuburg. Lt Gunther Elter killed.	
27.2.45	8/KG(J)54 Me262A-2a 111602 B3+DS Crashed near Ingolstadt on training flight. Oblt Hermann Kleinfeldt killed.	
27.2.45	III/KG(J)54 Me262A-1 111890 Crashed S Neuburg due to technical failure. Aircraft 30% damaged.	
27.2.45	III/KG(J)54 Me262A-1 110923 Damaged on take-off from Neuburg. Aircraft 20% damaged.	
28.2.45	III/JG 7 Me262A-1a 110784 Force-landed near Birkenwerder due to engine failure.	
28.2.45	III/JG 7 Me262A-1a 110807 Force-landed at Oranienburg due to engine failure.	
28.2.45	III/KG(J)54 Me262A-1 500209 Crash-landed at Leipheim due to pilot error. Aircraft 10% damaged.	

1.3.45	2./KG(J)54 Me262A-1 500218 B3+?K Shot down south of Giebelstadt. Lt Hans-Peter Haberle killed.
1.3.45	I./KG(J)54 Me262A-1 110562 Shot down east of Treuchtlingen. Fw Josef Herbeck killed.
2.3.45	5./KG(J)51 Me262A-2a 110553 9K+EN Shot down by fighter near Nijmegen. Hptm Fritz Abel (StK) killed.
2.3.45	II./KG(J)51 Me262A-2a 110941 Force-landed at Muhlheim due to technical failure.
2.3.45	II./KG(J)51 Me262A-2a 110516 Force-landed at Muhlheim due to technical failure.
2.3.45	I./KG(J)54 Me262A-1 110913 Shot down near Würzburg. Fw Gunther Gorlitz wounded.
2.3.45	I./KG(J)54 Me262A-1 111899 Shot down near Würzburg. Fw Heinrich Griems killed.
2.3.45	I.(E)./KG(J) Me262A-1 110655 Shot down south of Dillingen. Ofhr Horst Metzbrand killed.
3.3.45	9./JG 7 Me262A-1a 110558 Shot down during attack on B-17s SW Braunschweig. Hptm Heinz Gutmann killed.
3.3.45	III./JG 7 Me262A-1a 500058 Belly-landed at Oranienburg. Technical failure.
3.3.45	JG 7 Me262A-1a —— Shot down. Pilot safe.
3.3.45	JG 7 Me262A-1a —— Shot down. Pilot safe.
3.3.45	JG 7 Me262A-1a —— Shot down. Pilot safe.
3.3.45	JG 7 Me262A-1a —— Shot down. Pilot safe.
3.3.45	JG 7 Me262A-1a —— Shot down. Pilot safe.
3.3.45	10./NJG 11 Me262A-1a/U1 110610 Crashed north of Magdeburg. Ofw August Weibl killed.
4.3.45	III./EJG 2 Me262A-1 110472 Crashed at Lechfeld due to pilot error.
7.3.45	II./KG(J)54 Me262A-1 110500 Crashed landing at Kitzingen due to technical failure. Aircraft 30% damaged.
9.3.45	9./JG 7 Me262A-1a —— Missing near Laaland Island. Ofhr Heinz Russel killed.
9.3.45	II./KG(J)51 Me262A-2a 170124 Crashed at Erfurt-Bindersleben. Uffz Gunther Meckelburg killed.

Appendix II

9.3.45	II./KG(J)54 Me262A-1 111925 Force-landed at Bamberg out of fuel. Aircraft 30% damaged.
9.3.45	II./KG(J)54 Me262A-1 110943 B3+HL Crashed at Kitzingen. Lt Bernhard Becker.
10.3.45	I./KG(J)54 Me262A-1 110649 Tyre burst on take-off from Giebelstadt. Aircraft 10% damaged.
12.3.45	10./NJG 11 Me262A-1 111916 Severely damaged. No details notified.
13.3.45	I./KG(J)51 Me262A-2a 111966 9K+AB Combat with fighters near Xanten. Oblt Harald Hovestadt wounded.
13.3.45	I./KG(J)51 Me262A-2a 110915 9K+DL Shot down by fighter near Xanten. Ofhr Jurgen Hohne killed.
13.3.45	II./KG(J)51 Me262A-2a 170284 Fuel fire at Ludinghausen.
13.3.45	III./KG(J)51 Me262A-2a 111555 Crashed near Coesfeld. Ofw Georg Schabinski injured.
13.3.45	III./KG(J)51 Me262A-2a 110337 Crashed at Neunkirchen-Rheine.
14.3.45	III./KG(J)54 Me262A-1 110789 Abandoned at Ingolstadt due to engine fire.
17.3.45	8./KG(J)54 Me262A-2a 110938 B3+FS Crashed near Ingolstadt on training flight. FjOfw Wilhelm Dikus killed.
18.3.45	3./JG 7 Me262A-1b 170097 'Yellow 3' Collided with wingman near Schwarzenbeck. Oblt Hans Waldmann killed.
18.3.45	3./JG 7 Me262A-1b —— Collided with wingman near Schwarzenbeck. Lt Hans-Dieter Weihs baled out unhurt.
18.3.45	3./JG 7 Me262A-1b 500224 'Yellow 2' Shot down near Egenbüttel. Ofhr Gunther Schrey killed.
18.3.45	3./JG 7 Me262A-1b 110808 Shot down during attack on B-17s, Oblt Gunther Wegmann baled out wounded.
18.3.45	9./JG 7 Me262A-1b 110780 Shot down during attack on B-17s 5km SW Perleberg. Oblt Karl-Heinz Seeler killed.
18.3.45	III./JG 7 Me262A-1a —— Shot down. Pilot baled out.
19.3.45	10./JG 7 Me262A-1b 111005 Shot down by P-51s NE Eilenburg. Ofw Heinz Mattuschka killed.
19.3.45	11./JG 7 Me262A-1b 111545 Shot down by P-51s near Eilenburg. Lt Harry Meyer killed.

19.3.45	I./KG(J)54 Me262A-1 ---- Strafed at Giebelstadt. Aircraft destroyed.
19.3.45	I./KG(J)54 Me262A-1 ---- Strafed at Giebelstadt. Aircraft destroyed.
19.3.45	I./KG(J)54 Me262A-1 ---- Strafed at Giebelstadt. Aircraft 10% damaged.
19.3.45	III./KG(J)54 Me262A-1 ---- Strafed at Neuburg. Aircraft destroyed.
19.3.45	III./KG(J)54 Me262A-1 ---- Strafed at Neuburg. Aircraft 70% damaged.
19.3.45	III./KG(J)54 Me262A-1 ---- Strafed at Neuburg. Aircraft 40% damaged.
19.3.45	III./KG(J)54 Me262A-1 ---- Strafed at Neuburg. Aircraft 40% damaged.
19.3.45	III./KG(J)54 Me262A-1 ---- Strafed at Neuburg. Seven aircraft 5-20% damaged.
20.3.45	1./JG 7 Me262A-1b 111924 'White 7' Shot down by fighter over Kaltenkirchen. Uffz Hans Mehn killed.
20.3.45	10./JG 7 Me262A-1b 110598 Shot down by fighters near Bad Segeberg. Ogfr Fritz Gehlker killed.
20.3.45	10./JG 7 Me262A-1b 501196 Shot down by fighters near Kiel Ofw Erich Buttner wounded.
21.3.45	3./JG 7 Me262A-1a ---- Damaged in combat. Force-landed near Crimmitschau. Lt Hans-Dieter Weihs unhurt.
21.3.45	10./JG 7 Me262A-1b 500462 Shot down by fighters near Tharandt. Uffz Kurt Kolbe killed.
21.3.45	11./JG 7 Me262A-1a 110819 Shot down near Wenkwitz. Lt Joachim Weber killed.
21.3.45	JG 7 Me262A-1a ---- Shot down. Pilot wounded.
21.3.45	JG 7 Me262A-1a ---- Shot down. Pilot wounded.
21.3.45	3./KG(J)51 Me262A-2a 111973 9K+AL Shot down by fighter at Giebelstadt. Hptm Eberhard Winkel (StK) killed.
21.3.45	I./KG(J)51 Me262A-2a 170118 9K+CK Shot down by fighter at Giebelstadt. Lt Erwin Diekmann killed.
21.3.45	I./KG(J)51 Me262A-2a 111605 9K+DL Shot down by fighter at Giebelstadt. Uffz Heinz Erben killed.
21.3.45	I./KG(J)54 Me262A-2a 500069 B3+CH Shot down in combat near Giessen. Uffz Wille Ehrecke killed.

Appendix II

21.3.45	III./KG(J)54 Me262A-1 —— Bombed at Neuburg. Twelve Aircraft destroyed.
21.3.45	III./KG(J)54 Me262A-1 —— Bombed at Neuburg. Thirty-eight aircraft damaged.
22.3.45	11./JG 7 Me262A-1b 500436 Shot down by fighter near Alt-Dobern. Fw Heinz Eichmer killed.
22.3.45	JG 7 Me262A-1a —— Shot down. Pilot killed.
22.3.45	JG 7 Me262A-1a —— Shot down. Pilot killed.
22.3.45	JG 7 Me262A-1a —— Shot down. Pilot wounded.
22.3.45	Stab./KG(J)54 Me262A-1 —— Shot down near Würzburg. Oblt König killed.
22.3.45	Stab./KG(J)54 Me262A-1 —— Bombed at Giebelstadt. Aircraft 90% damaged.
22.3.45	I./KG(J)54 Me262A-2a 110602 B3+DK Shot down by P-51s near Giebelstadt. Uffz Adalbert Egri baled out wounded.
22.3.45	I./KG(J)54 Me262A-1 —— Bombed at Giebelstadt. Aircraft 80% damaged.
22.3.45	I./KG(J)54 Me262A-1 —— Bombed at Giebelstadt. Aircraft 60% damaged.
22.3.45	I./KG(J)54 Me262A-1 —— Bombed at Giebelstadt. Five aircraft 15% damaged.
22.3.45	I./KG(J)54 Me262A-1 —— Bombed at Giebelstadt. Three aircraft 5% damaged.
22.3.45	II./KG(J)54 Me262A-1 —— Bombed at Giebelstadt. Three aircraft 70% damaged.
22.3.45	II./KG(J)54 Me262A-1 —— Bombed at Giebelstadt. Aircraft 50% damaged.
22.3.45	II./KG(J)54 Me262A-1 —— Bombed at Giebelstadt. Four aircraft 7% damaged.
22.3.45	10./EJG 2 Me262A-1a 110485 NS+BM 'White 12' Shot down by P-51 on S perimeter of Lechfeld. FjOfw Helmut Reckers killed.
24.3.45	9./JG 7 Me262A-1b 111676 Shot down by fighter near Northeim. Oblt Ernst Worner baled out wounded.
24.3.45	11./JG 7 Me262A-1b 110999 Shot down by fighter near Wittenberg. Lt Alfred Ambs baled out wounded.
24.3.45	11./JG 7 Me262A-1b 110968 Damaged by fighters near Grossen. Uffz Ernst Giefing wounded.

24.3.45	JG 7 Me262A-1a —— Shot down. Oblt Kulp baled out wounded.
24.3.45	III./KG(J)54 Me262A-1 —— Bombed at Neuburg. Twenty-four aircraft destroyed.
24.3.45	III./KG(J)54 Me262A-1 —— Bombed at Neuburg. Thirty-six aircraft damaged.
25.3.45	9./JG 7 Me262A-1B —— Shot down by fighter near Rechlin. Oblt Schatzle killed.
25.3.45	9./JG 7 Me262A-1b 110796 Shot down by fighter 6km NW Parchim. Fhr Gunther Ulrich baled out but killed.
25.3.45	10./JG 7 Me262A-1b 110834 Shot down by fighter near Parchim. Lt Gunther von Rettberg killed.
25.3.45	10./JG 7 Me262A-1b 111738 Shot down by fighter near Rheinsehlen. Fw Fritz Taube killed.
27.3.45	3./JG 7 Me262A-1a —— Damaged in combat. Lt Hans-Dieter Weihs unhurt. (Bel 25th)
28.3.45	11./JG 7 Me262A-1b 111541 Damaged by exploding B-17 near Dresden. Ofw August Lübking killed.
30.3.45	2./JG 7 Me262A-1b 111593 Shot down by fighter near Hemdingen. Lt Erich Schulte believed killed on parachute.
30.3.45	11./JG 7 Me262A-1b —— Shot down by fighter near Hamburg. Lt Karl Schnörrer baled out wounded.
30.3.45	JG 7 Me262A-1a —— Shot down and crash-landed. Fw Geisthovel safe.
30.3.45	—— Me262A-1a 111711 Surrendered at Rhein-Main. Hans Fay, test pilot, captured.
31.3.45	JG 7 Me262A-1a —— Shot down. Pilot killed.
31.3.45	JG 7 Me262A-1a —— Shot down. Pilot missing.
31.3.45	JG 7 Me262A-1a —— Shot down. Pilot missing.
31.3.45	JG 7 Me262A-1a —— Shot down. Pilot safe.
31.3.45	I./KG(J)54 Me262A-1 —— Shot down by fighter near Zerbst. Pilot baled out safely.
31.3.45	2./KG(J)54 Me262A-1 —— Shot down by fighter near Halle. Oblt Dr Oberweg killed.

Appendix II

4.4.45	**Stab./JG 7 Me262A-1b** —— Shot down by P-51 NE Schaarlippe. Maj Heinrich Ehrler killed.
4.4.45	**Stab./JG 7 Me262A-1b** —— Shot down by P-51 near Neu-Chemnitz. Ofw Gerhard Reinhold killed.
4.4.45	**III./JG 7 Me262A-1b** —— Shot down by P-51 after take-off from Rechlin. Maj Rudolf Sinner (Kdr) baled out wounded.
4.4.45	**10./JG 7 Me262A-1a** —— Shot down near Parchim. Oblt Franz Schall baled ut unhurt.
4.4.45	**11./JG 7 Me262A-1b** —— Shot down by P-51 near Leipzig. Lt Alfred Lehner killed.
4.4.45	**11./JG 7 Me262A-1b** —— Shot down by P-51 near Leipzig. Uffz Heckmann killed.
4.4.45	**JG 7 Me262A-1a** —— Shot down. Pilot safe.
4.4.45	**JG 7 Me262A-1a** —— Shot down. Pilot safe.
4.4.45	**JG 7 Me262A-1a** —— Damaged in combat. Pilot safe.
4.4.45	**JG 7 Me262A-1a** —— Damaged in combat. Pilot safe.
4.4.45	**JG 7 Me262A-1a** —— Damaged in combat. Pilot safe.
4.4.45	**JG 7 Me262A-1a** —— Damaged in combat. Pilot safe.
4.4.45	**JG 7 Me262A-1a** —— Damaged in combat. Pilot safe.
5.4.45	**JG 7 Me262A-1A** —— Shot down, pilot missing.
5.4.45	**JG 7 Me262A-1A** —— Shot down, pilot missing.
7.4.45	**JG 7 Me262A-1a** —— Collided with B-24 over Luneburg. Pilot believed killed.
7.4.45	**JG 7 Me262A-1a** —— Shot down in combat, pilot missing.
7.4.45	**JG 7 Me262A-1a** —— Shot down in combat, pilot missing.
7.4.45	**I./KG(J)54 Me262A-1** —— **B3+White 8** Shot down by fighter near Hagenow. Hptm Tronicke killed.
8.4.45	**JV 44 Me262A-1a** —— Shot down by fighter over river Danube. Lt Fährmann baled out unhurt.

9.4.45	3./JG 7 Me262A-1a —— Damaged in combat. Force-landed at Dessau with damaged nosewheel. Lt Hans-Dieter Weihs unhurt.
10.4.45	2./JG 7 Me262A-1 —— Three aircraft destroyed in raid on Burg.
10.4.45	3./JG 7 Me262A-1b —— Shot down by fighter. Uffz Köhler killed.
10.4.45	3./JG 7 Me262A-1b —— Shot down by fighter near Berlin. Gfr Heim killed.
10.4.45	3./JG 7 Me262A-1a —— Shot down. Oblt Walter Schuck baled out unhurt
10.4.45	3./JG 7 Me262A-1b —— Shot down by fighter near Berlin. Lt Wagner killed.
10.4.45	7./JG 7 Me262A-1b —— Shot down by fighter near Neuruppin. Oblt Walther Wever (StK) killed.
10.4.45	10./JG 7 Me262A-1b —— Landed at Parchim after combat with fighters, rolled into bomb crater and exploded. Oblt Franz Schall (StK) killed.
10.4.45	JG 7 Me262A-1a —— Shot down. Fw Schwarz killed.
10.4.45	JG 7 Me262A-1a —— Shot down. Pilot missing.
10.4.45	JG 7 Me262A-1a —— Shot down. Pilot missing.
10.4.45	JG 7 Me262A-1a —— Shot down. Pilot missing.
10.4.45	JG 7 Me262A-1a —— Shot down. Pilot missing.
10.4.45	JG 7 Me262A-1a —— Shot down. Pilot missing.
10.4.45	JG 7 Me262A-1a —— Shot down. Pilot missing.
10.4.45	JG 7 Me262A-1a —— Shot down. Pilot missing.
10.4.45	JG 7 Me262A-1a —— Shot down. Pilot missing.
10.4.45	JG 7 Me262A-1a —— Shot down. Pilot missing.
10.4.45	JG 7 Me262A-1a —— Shot down. Pilot missing.
10.4.45	JG 7 Me262A-1a —— Shot down. Pilot missing.

10.4.45	JG 7 Me262A-1a ——	Shot down. Pilot missing.
10.4.45	JG 7 Me262A-1a ——	Shot down. Pilot missing.
10.4.45	JG 7 Me262A-1a ——	Shot down. Pilot missing.
10.4.45	JG 7 Me262A-1a ——	Shot down. Pilot wounded.
10.4.45	JG 7 Me262A-1a ——	Shot down. Pilot wounded.
10.4.45	JG 7 Me262A-1a ——	Shot down. Pilot wounded.
10.4.45	JG 7 Me262A-1a ——	Shot down. Pilot wounded.
10.4.45	JG 7 Me262A-1a ——	Shot down. Pilot wounded.

10.4.45   **10./NJG 11 Me262A-2 ——**
Three aircraft destroyed in raid on Burg.

10.4.45   **6./NAufkgr 6 Me262A-1 ——**
Three aircraft destroyed in raid on Burg.

10.4.45   **I./KG(J)54 Me262A-1 ——**
Crashed near Genthin on combat flight. Lt Paul Pallenda killed.

10.4.45   **1./KG(J)54 Me262A-1 ——**
Shot down by fighter at Bohmen. Oblt Beck killed.

10.4.45   **2./KG(J)54 Me262A-1 —— B3+Yellow 9**
Shot down by fighter near Barby. Lt Berhard Becker wounded.

10.4.45   **3./KG(J)54 Me262A-1 ——**
Shot down while on approach to Stendal.
Lt Jürgen Rossow wounded.

11.4.45   **I./JG 7 Me262A-1a ——**
Shot down on approach to Ruzyne,
Oblt Hans Grünburg baled out unhurt.

14.4.45   **II./JG 7 Me262A-1a ——**
Shot down. Lt Arno Thimm baled out wounded.

14.4.45   **9./JG 7 Me262A-1b ——**
Shot down by P-51 near Lonnewitz.
Oblt Erich Stahlberg killed.

14.4.45   **9./KG(J)54 Me262A ——**
Shot down near Neuburg. Uffz L.Ehrhardt baled out wounded.

16.4.45   **JG 7 Me262A-1a ——**
Shot down. Pilot killed

17.4.45   **3./JG 7 Me262A-1b ——**
Shot down by fighter near Prague. Uffz Fick killed

17.4.45	I./JG 7 Me262A-1a —— Shot down at Ruzyne. Pilot killed
17.4.45	I./JG 7 Me262A-1a —— Shot down at Ruzyne. Pilot killed.
17.4.45	I./JG 7 Me262A-1a —— Shot down at Ruzyne. Pilot killed.
17.4.45	I./JG 7 Me262A-1a —— Shot down at Ruzyne. Lt Grünberg safe.
17.4.45	11./JG 7 Me262A-1b —— Missing from ground attack in Thuringer Wald area. Ofw Heinz Arnold lost.
17.4.45	JV 44 Me262A-1a —— Collided with B-17. Uffz Eduard Schallmoser baled out unhurt.
18.4.45	JV 44 Me262A-1a —— Crashed on take-off from Riem. Obst Johannes Steinhoff severely burned.
19.4.45	III./JG 7 Me262A-1a —— Shot down. Fate of pilot not known.
19.4.45	III./JG 7 Me262A-1a —— Shot down. Fate of pilot not known.
19.4.45	III./JG 7 Me262A-1a —— Shot down. Fate of pilot not known.
19.4.45	III./JG 7 Me262A-1a —— Shot down. Fate of pilot not known.
19.4.45	I./KG(J)54 Me262A-1 —— Believed shot down by fighter at Slanem, Czechoslovakia. Uffz Bruno Reischke killed.
19.4.45	1./KG(J)54 Me262A —— Shot down near Dresden. Lt Mai killed.
20.4.45	12./JG 7 Me262A-1b —— Damaged in combat with B-26 near Rotenburg. Pilot baled out wounded.
20.4.45	JV 44 Me262A-1a —— Crash-landed due to engine failure. Maj Gerhard Barkhorn injured.
22.4.45	III./KG(J)54 Me262A —— Shot down near Erding. Unidentified Unteroffizier killed.
24.4.45	JV 44 Me262A-1a —— Shot down near Donauwörth. Obst Günther Lützow missing.
25.4.45	I./JG 7 Me262A-1a —— Crashed landing at Ruzyne. Pilot killed.
25.4.45	9./JG 7 Me262A-1a 500071 —— Force-landed at Dübendorf, Switzerland. Fhr Hans-Guido Mutke interned.

Appendix II

25.4.45	9./JG 7 Me262A-1a —— Strafed while landing at Rotenburg. Ofw Hermann Buchner safe.
26.4.45	JV 44 Me262A-1a —— Damaged in combat, strafed after landing at Reim. Genlt Adolf Galland wounded.
27.4..45	JG 7 Me262A-1a —— Shot down in combat with Russian aircraft. Pilot missing.
27.4.45	JG 7 Me262A-1a —— Shot down in combat with Russian aircraft. Pilot missing.
28.4.45	JG 7 Me262A-1a —— Shot down at Ruzyne. Lt Ernst-Rudolf Geldmacher killed.
29.4.45	III./KG(J)54 Me262A-1 —— **B3+Red 1** Engine fire on take-off from Ruzyne, Hptm Kornagel killed.
29.4.45	III./KG(J)54 Me262A-1 —— **B3+Red 3** Missing on sortie from Fürstenfeldbrück. Pulot lost.
29.4.45	III./KG(J)54 Me262A-1 —— **B3+Red 2** Shot down at Erding. Hptm Spadiut missing.
29.4.45	III./KG(J)54 Me262A-1 —— **B3+Red 4** Shot down at Erding. Lt Paukner missing.
30.4.45	1./JG 7 Me262A-1a —— Missing after combat. Lt Fritz Kelb lost.
30.4.45	I./KG(J)54 Me262A-2a —— Shot down by Russian A.A. fire. Pilot missing.
6.5.45	KG(J)51 Me262A-2a —— Shot down over Prague. Lt Schimmel killed.
7.5.45	KG(J)51 Me262A-2a —— Shot down over Prague. Lt Strothmann killed.
7.5.45	KG(J)51 Me262A-2a —— -Shot down over Prague. Lt Poling killed.
8.5.45	I./JG 7 Me262A-1a 500210 **Yellow 17** Surrendered to British Forces at Fassberg, Lt Hans Dorn interned.
8.5.45	I./JG 7 Me262A-1a 112372 **Yellow 7** Surrendered to British Forces at Fassberg. Uffz Günther Engler interned.
8.5.45	I./JG 7 Me262A-1a 111690 **White 5** Surrendered to British forces at Fassberg, believed by Lt Friedrich-Wilhelm Schlüter. Pilot interned.
8.5.45	I./JG 7 Me262A-1a 500443 **Yellow 5** Surrendered to British forces at Fassberg. Uffz Anton Schöppler interned.8.5.45 I./KG(J)54 Me262A-1 ----- Surrendered to American forces at Innsbrück.

8.5.45	**I./KG(J)51 Me262A-2a ——** Surrendered to Amewrican forces at Munich Riem. Hptm Rudolf Abrahamczik interned.
8.5.45	**I./KG(J)51 Me262A-2a ——** Surrendered to American forces at Riem. Lt Anton Haeffner interned.
8.5.45	**I./KG(J)51 Me262A-2a 500200 'X'** Surrendered to British forces at Fassberg. Lt Fröhlich interned.
8.5.45	**I./KG(J)51 Me262A-2a ——** Crash-landed on Lüneberg Heath. Lt Wilhelm Batel captured and interned.
8.5.45	**I./KG(J)54 Me262A-1 ——** Surrendered to American forces at Innsbrück. Crash-landed. Pilot interned.

Appendix III
Prisoner Interrogation Report: Generalleutnant Adolf Galland

SECRET APWIU (1st T.A.F.)
45/1945 AIR P/W INT UNIT
FIRST TACTICAL AIR FORCE
(PROV) APO 374

PREAMBLE

1. Towards the end of the struggle, and after he had been dismissed from his post as General der Jagdflieger (General of the Fighters), he received reluctant approval from GOERING to form a unit composed entirely of Me262 jet aircraft. The unit was variously known as Jadg Verband 44 (officially) or "Galland" Verband. The organisation was built up with some of the GAF's most experienced pilots and ground personnel, and when it became obvious that surrender was inevitable, GALLAND gave orders that contact be established with U.S.Air Forces in order to arrange for a mass surrender as a unit. Contact was established with XII TAC, and arrangements had been made, but for two days, weather closed in over SALZBURG and INNSBRUCK and thus delayed, the show never came off. Instead, land forces overran the area and General GALLAND, who had been wounded on 26 April, and the airfields used by his unit and his personnel stationed there, were taken by elements of the U.S. Seventh Army.

LAST BATTLE

2. On 26 April 1945, at about 1100 hours, GALLAND took off from MUNCHEN/RIEM with five other Me262s of his Jagdverband 44. One returned with engine trouble. Their mission was to attack a formation of B-26 Marauders flying in two tight vics of about 30 aircraft each. Coming in at 12 o'clock, the German fighters passed over the formation an wheeled around in a dive for an attack from about 8 o'clock from below. Galland, with his 'Katschmarek@ (his number two), who was an inexperienced

young non-com, had picked the outside rear-flying B-26 of the first vic as his target. As they closed in, the B-26 formation recognised them, and opened fire before the Germans did. GALLAND pulled up and fired his cannon. The Marauder exploded in mid-air. Meanwhile GALLAND, bypassing the exploded aircraft, lined up on the second, but since he failed to release the safety button for his rockets, they did not go off, and he obtained only a few cannon hits on his second target.

WE ALMOST GOT HIM

3. While banking away to observe the results of his attack on the second B-26, he sustained hits in the fuel tanks from that bombers gunners. At the same moment he was jumped by a U.S. fighter. GALLAND did not observe if it was a Thunderbolt (P-47) or a Mustang (P-51), who attacked from above and the rear. His aircraft was hit several times in the cockpit, and in the jet engines. GALLAND himself sustained splinters in his right leg. Thus incapacitated, and with his instrument board shot out, he dove straight down to get away from his attacker. Not pursued, GALLAND then followed the autobahn to MUNCHEN/ RIEM, to find upon his arrival there that Mustangs were attacking the flight strip. Because his aircraft was badly hit, and because he had lost control over the speed of his jet engines, he had to turn the fuel off and make a tree-top glide approach. He was able to land without being attacked once more.

4. The result of this encounter, according to GALLAND was four aircraft shot down: either four B-26s, or three B-26s and one Mustang. Losses were one Me262 shot down, but pilot safe. (These claims agree in general with the losses of the 42nd Bomb Wing of First Tactical Air Force: official records show that three B-26s were shot down, plus one B-26 crash-landed behind our lines due to enemy action.)

GAF PILOTS OPINION OF THE ME 262

5. Contrary to popular belief, GALLAND stated the the Me262 is not difficult to handle on landing and take-off. Rumors that jet pilots had orders not to land except with empty fuel tanks were false. He did state however, that many times his pilots had to land a few minutes after take-off, because of difficulties with the jet engines. After five flights of take-off and landing with a Me262, a fairly experienced pilot should be able to fly the

aircraft in combat. GALLAND was very enthusiastic about the capabilities of the Me262, whose efficiency in combat he rated very highly. According to statistics of his unit, the ratio was 5 to 1 of victories over aircraft shot down. He appeared to have uppermost in his mind the hope that his unit, with its experienced pilots and equipment, be used by U.S. Air Forces 'In the battle against Russia', which he was sure would come. He appeared less enthusiastic with the suggestion of combating the Japanese.

6. According to GALLAND, it was HITLER'S idea to use the Me262 as a bomber, which was cited as a typical instance of incompetence at the top. GALLAND considers the use of the Me262 as a bomber a ridiculous idea, and the efforts expended on training and modifications in design should have been spent on the development of this aircraft as a fighter. The Me262 flown by GALLAND, besides cannons in the nose, had twelve rockets mounted under the wings, outboards from the engine nacelles, which were fired in salvo. All fire was synchronised to converge at 600m. New Me262s as well as the current ones could be fitted with additional rockets mounted under the wings between the engine nacelles and the fuselage, making a total of fifty rockets carried.

THE DO 335

7. GALLAND had also flown the Do335, but although he found it a good aircraft, he believed it would require considerable improvements in design before it could be accepted as operational. As a two-engined fighter, it lacked the stability required and usually found in such aircraft. He attributed this lack of stability to the distance between the two engines. In comparison with a single engined fighter he stated that it handled 'too heavy'.

JAGDVERBAND 44

8. In forming his unit, General GALLAND was determined to gather around him the very best that the GAF could offer. It was known in GAF circles that if you wanted to belong to Jadgverband 44, you had to have at least the Ritterkreuz (Knight's Cross). This plan had been opposed by GOERING and General PELZ, and GALLAND had to fight them all along, but nevertheless succeeded in getting only the top-notch pilots.

9. General PELZ promoted the theory that former bomber pilots would make better pilots for the Me262 and other jet aircraft. Since PELZ had better connections at Air Ministry, his plan was adopted as the general scheme, although GALLAND managed to restrict his unit to fighter pilots.

GENERAL INFO

10. When it was known that the long-range Mustang had become operative in Europe, GALLAND expressed the opinion that U.S. Air Forces would soon commence escorted day attacks over the Ruhr area. This led to his having been called before GOERING, who told him in no uncertain terms that the spreading of such ideas would not be tolerated. As a result, GALLAND blamed the top GAF officials for wilfully ignoring facts, and failing to plan ahead to counter the Allied air offensive by waiting until the last moment before protecting vital industries. He was very bitter about the fact that hard-working and hard-fighting Air Units were blamed for these mistakes, and that the German public, realising that something went wrong, were told that the Luftwaffe was not doing it's share to hold back the stream of Allied bombers. GALLAND admitted that many mistakes were made by combat units, but the gravest and most telling were committed by the leaders and planners.
11. He severely criticised policies relating to the German Aircraft Industry. At the beginning of the war, when the GAF had its air superiority, Germany could well afford to build a considerable variety of experimental types. However when the GAF lost this superiority, he considered it a mistake to continue with it's vast experimental program. Experiments should have been continued on a reduced scale. To illustrate how inefficient the control over aircraft industry was, GALLAND cited that Do17s were still being manufactured in several plants only to be scrapped a few weeks later.
12. That GALLAND had not been popular with GOERING was evident for some time, and several attempts had been made to get rid of him. GALLAND stated that his telephone conversations were recorded, and that he was often called to explain some of the statements made in such conversations. GALLAND feels that GOERING was fully cognizant of the

Appendix III

conditions and the increasing threat of Allied air power. He accused GOERING of deliberately choosing the easiest way out, by just ignoring the signs and following an ostrich policy.

13. GALLAND discounted the tremendous importance generally attached to the V-weapons by the Germans. He considered it an advantage however, that during the V-attacks on England, a considerable number of Allied fighters were committed to combat this weapon. General GALLAND pointed out that the V-weapons did not prove effective enough to warrant the heavy burden on German industry they had become.

DETAILS OF PRISONER

14. This GAF ace flew every American fighter used in this theatre of war (including the P-39 Airacobra). He was invited to test captured Allied aircraft in his capacity as General of Fighters. He also flew the latest models and new aircraft developed for the GAF. From American aircraft he chose the Mustang as the best fighter. Of the U.S. bombers GALLAND considered the B-26 as the aircraft he would least enjoy to attack. He stated that B-26s, flying usually in very tight formations, were very difficult to approach. He had found through hard experience that they had devastating fire-power.

15. GALLAND had a rather spectacular career in the GAF. At the outbreak of war in 1939 he was an Oberleutnant (1st Lieutenant). After becoming a Hauptmann (Captain) he was promoted in 1940 first to Major and then Oberstleutnant (Lieutenant Colonel). The next year he became Oberst (Colonel) and exactly a year later he became a Generalmajor (Brigadier General). His final promotion to Generalleutnant (Major General) occurred in November 1944.

Appendix IV
USAAF Fighter Air Combat Claims Against Me262 Aircraft

Date	Unit	AF	Name	Claim
28.8.44	78 FG	8 AF	Maj J.Myers	} 1 dest
	78 FG	8 AF	Lt M.O.Croy	}
13.9.44	364 FG	8 AF	Lt J A Walker	1 dam
2.10.44	365 FG	9 AF	Capt V.J.Beaudrault	1 dest
6.10.44	353 FG	8 AF	Lt C.W.Mueller	1 dest
7.10.44	50 FG	9 AF	Capt S.Mamalis	1 dam
	78 FG	8 AF	Maj R.E.Connor	1 dest
	361 FG	8 AF	Lt U.L.Drew	2 dest
	479 FG	8 AF	Col H.Zemke	} 1 dest
	479 FG	8 AF	Lt N.Benoit	}
15.10.44	78 FG	8 AF	Lt H.H.Lamb	1 dest
	78 FG	8 AF	Lt H.O.Foster	1 dam
1.11.44	56 FG	8 AF	Lt W.L.Groce	} 1 dest
	352 FG	8 AF	Lt W.T.Gerbe	}
4.11.44	356 FG	8 AF	Capt R.A.Rann	1 dam
6.11.44	4 FG	8 AF	Lt W.J.Quinn	1 dest
	361 FG	8 AF	Lt J.R.Voss	1 dest
	357 FG	8 AF	Maj C. Yeager	1 dest, 2 dam
8.11.44	20 FG	8 AF	Lt E.C.Fiebelkorn	} 1 dest
	357 FG	8 AF	Lt E.R.Haydon	}
	361 FG	8 AF	Lt A.Maurice	1 dest
	362 FG	8 AF	Lt J.W.Kenney	1 dest
	364 FG	8 AF	Lt R.W.Stevens	1 dest
18.11.44	4 FG	8 AF	Lt J.M.Creamer	} 1 dest
	4 FG	8 AF	Capt J.C.Fitch	}
	353 FG	8 AF	Lt G.E.Markham	1 dam
26.11.44	50 FG	9 AF	Lt L.E.Willis	1 prob
2.12.44	325 FG	15 AF	Lt W.R.Hinton	1 dam
5.12.44	352 FG	8 AF	Lt B.Grabovski	1 dam
9.12.44	358 FG	8 AF	Lt H.L.Edwards	1 dest
15.12.44	82 FG	15 AF	Lt P.Kennedy	1 dam
	82 FG	15 AF	Lt W.Armstrong	1 dam
22.12.44	31 FG	15 AF	Capt E.P.McGlaufin	} 1 dest
	31 FG	15 AF	Lt R.L.Scales	}

Date	Unit	AF	Pilot	Claim
23.12.44	353 FG	8 AF	Capt H.D.Stump	1 dam
	353 FG	8 AF	Lt S.E.Stevenson	1 dam
31.12.44	339 FG	8 AF	Capt A.G.Hawkins	1 dam
1.1.45	4 FG	8 AF	Lt D.Pierine	1 dest (prob unconf)
	4 FG	8 AF	Lt F.W.Young	1 dest
	20 FG	8 AF	Capt W.M.Hurst	1 dam
13.1.45	55 FG	8 AF	Lt W.J.Konantz	1 dest
14.1.45	20 FG	8 AF	Lt K.D.McNeel	1 dam (poss Ar234)
	55 FG	8 AF	Maj D.S.Cramer	1 dam
	353 FG	8 AF	Lt B.J.Murray	1 dest
	353 FG	8 AF	Lt B.J.Murray	} 1 dest
	353 FG	8 AF	Lt J.W.Rohrs	}
	353 FG	8 AF	Lt G.J.Rosen	}
	353 FG	8 AF	Lt M.A.Arnold	} 1 dam
	353 FG	8 AF	Lt G.E.Markham	}
	10 PRG	9 AF	Lt C.G.Franklin	} 1 prob
	10 PRG	9 AF	Lt M.V.Logothetis	}
15.1.45	357 FG	8 AF	Lt R.P.Winks	1 dest
20.1.45	357 FG	8 AF	Lt D.E.Karger	1 dest
	357 FG	8 AF	Lt R.R.Wright	1 dest
3.2.45	364 FG	8 AF	Lt L.V.Andrew	1 dam
9.2.45	78 FG	8 AF	Lt W.E.Hydorn	1 prob
	78 FG	8 AF	Capt E.H.Miller	1 prob
	339 FG	8 AF	Lt J.J.Sainlar	1 dam
	339 FG	8 AF	Lt S.C.Ananian	1 dest
	357 FG	8 AF	Capt D.H.Bochkay	1 dest
	357 FG	8 AF	Lt J.L.Carter	1 dest
	357 FG	8 AF	Maj R.W.Foy	1 dam
14.2.45	20 FG	8 AF	Capt J.K.Brown	} 1 dam
	20 FG	8 AF	Lt K.D.McNeel	}
15.2.45	55 FG	8 AF	Lt D.M.Amoss	1 dest
17.2.45	365 FG	9 AF	Lt T.B.Westbrook	1 dam
	365 FG	9 AF	Lt C.E.Buchanan	1 dam u/c
21.2.45	356 FG	8 AF	Lt H.E.Whitmore	1 dest
22.2.45	20 FG	8 AF	Capt R.M.Howard	1 dam
	48 FG	9 AF	Capt M.F.Mason	1 dam
	352 FG	8 AF	Lt C.D.Price	1 dest
	352 FG	8 AF	Maj E.D.Duncan	1 dam
	352 FG	8 AF	Lt C.E.Goodman	1 dam
	353 FG	8 AF	Capt G.B.Compton	1 dest
	353 FG	8 AF	Maj W.K.Blickenstaff	1 dest
	363 FG	8 AF	Lt R.L.Hunt	1 dam
	363 FG	8 AF	Lt W.E.Randolph	1 dam
	363 FG	8 AF	Lt L.H.Phipps	1 dam

Appendix IV

	363 FG	8 AF	Lt L.L.Lefforge	1 dam
	363 FG	8 AF	Lt C.B.Kirby	1 dam
	353 FG	8 AF	Lt C.B.Kirby	} 1 prob
	353 FG	8 AF	Capt R.W.Stevens	}
	363 FG	8 AF	Lt G.O.Warner	2 dam
	364 FG	8 AF	Lt S.J.Price	1 dam
	364 FG	8 AF	Capt S.C.Phillips	1 dam
	365 FG	9 AF	Lt O.T.Cowan	1 dest
	366 FG	9 AF	Lt D.B.Fox	1 dest
	361 RS	9 AF	Lt W.A.Grusy	1 dam
25.2.45	4 FG	8 AF	Lt C.G.Payne	1 dest
	55 FG	8 AF	Capt D.E.Penn	1 dest
	55 FG	8 AF	Capt D.M.Cummings	2 dest
	55 FG	8 AF	Lt J.F.O'Neil	1 dest
	55 FG	8 AF	Lt M.O.Anderson	1 dest
	55 FG	8 AF	Lt D.T.Menegay	1 dest
	55 FG	8 AF	Lt B.Clemmons	1 dest
	365 FG	9 AF	Lt A.Longo	1 dam
	365 FG	9 AF	Lt J.L.McWhorter	2 dam
	365 FG	9 AF	Lt L.Freeman	1 dam (unconf)
	365 FG	9 AF	Capt C.Ready	1 dam (unconf)
	366 FG	9 AF	Lt M.R.Paisley	1 dam (unconf)
	366 FG	9 AF	Lt J.T.Picton	1 dam (unconf)
	373 FG	9 AF	Lt E.P.Gardner	1 dam
	373 FG	9 AF	Lt D.D.A.Duncan	2 dam
	405 FG	9 AF	Capt R.W.Yothers	1 dam (poss Ar234)
28.2.45	78 FG	8 AF	Lt W.F.Bechtelheimer	} 1 dam
	78 FG	8 AF	Lt J.E.Parker	}
1.3.45	355 FG	8 AF	Lt J.Wilkins	1 dest
	355 FG	8 AF	Lt W.W.Beaty	1 dest
	355 FG	8 AF	Maj H.H.Kirby	1 dam
	2 Sc Fce	8 AF	Maj F.B.Elliot	1 dam
	2 Sc Fce	8 AF	Capt C.W.Getz III	1 dam
2.3.45	354 FG	9 AF	Capt B.Peters	1 dest u/c
	354 FG	9 AF	Lt T.W.Sedvert	1 dest
	354 FG	9 AF	F/O R.Delgado	1 dest
	364 FG	8 AF	Lt F.T.O'Connor	1 dam
	107 RS	9 AF	Lt F.T.Dunmire	1 prob (unconf)
3.3.45	4 FG	8 AF	Col E.W.Stewart	1 dam
	339 FG	8 AF	Lt R.G.Johnson	1 dam
	353 FG	8 AF	Lt J.E.Frye	1 dam
	355 FG	8 AF	Lt W.S.Lyons	1 dam
	357 FG	8 AF	Capt J.L.Sublett	1 dam
	357 FG	8 AF	Capt I.L.Maguire	1 dam
9.3.45	55 FG	8 AF	Lt J.F.O'Neill	1 dam
13.3.45	365 FG	9 AF	Lt F.W.Marling	1 dest

Date	Unit	AF	Pilot	Result
14.3.45	56 FG	8 AF	Lt R S Keeler	1 dest (unconf)
	474 FG	9 AF	Lt G.G.Clark	} 1 dam
	474 FG	9 AF	Lt J.J.Kozlik	}
	474 FG	9 AF	Lt W.H.Barker	}
	474 FG	9 AF	Lt C.H.Darnell	} 1 dam
	474 FG	9 AF	Lt D.F.Lloyd	}
	474 FG	9 AF	Lt J.J.Kozlik	1 dam
	2 Sc Fce	8 AF	Lt C.R.Rodebaugh	1 dest
17.3.45	354 FG	9 AF	Lt Kuhn	1 dam
18.3.45	353 FG	8 AF	F/O W.V.Totten	1 dam
19.3.45	355 FG	8 AF	Capt C.H.Spencer	1 dest
	357 FG	8 AF	Maj R.W.Foy	1 dest
	357 FG	8 AF	Capt R.S.Fifield	1 dest
	357 FG	8 AF	Capt J.L.Carter	2 dam
	357 FG	8 AF	Lt J.W.Cannon	1 dam
	357 FG	8 AF	Capt A.G.Manthos	1 dam
	359 FG	8 AF	Maj N.K.Cranfill	1 dest, 1 dam
	15 RS	9 AF	Lt N.A.Thomas	1 dam
20.3.45	20 FG	8 AF	Lt J.C.Cowley	1 dam
	20 FG	8 AF	Lt C.Nicholson	1 dam
	339 FG	8 AF	Lt V.N.Barto	1 dest
	339 FG	8 AF	Lt R.E.Irion	1 dest
	339 FG	8 AF	Lt K.V.Berguson	1 dam
	339 FG	8 AF	Lt R.S.Hill	2 dam
	356 FG	8 AF	Lt E.G.Rudd	1 dam
21.3.45	78 FG	8 AF	Lt W.E.Bourque	1 dest
	78 FG	8 AF	Lt J.A.Kirk III	1 dest
	78 FG	8 AF	Lt A.A.Rosenblum	} 1 dest
	78 FG	8 AF	Lt W.H.Brown	}
	78 FG	8 AF	Lt R.D.Anderson	1 dest
	78 FG	8 AF	Capt E.H.Miller	1 dest
	78 FG	8 AF	Lt R.H.Anderson	1 dest
	339 FG	8 AF	Lt B.E.Langohr	} 1 dest
	339 FG	8 AF	Lt N.C.Greer	}
	354 FG	9 AF	Lt T.W.Sedvert	1 dest (unconf)
	361 FG	8 AF	Lt H.M.Chapman	1 dest
	12 RS	9 AF	Capt J.S.White	1 dam
22.3.45	31 FG	15 AF	Capt W.J.Dillard	1 dest
	31 FG	15 AF	Capt H.D.Naumann	1 dam
	31 FG	15 AF	Lt B.J.Bush	1 dam
	31 FG	15 AF	Lt R.R.Blank	1 dam
	31 FG	15 AF	Lt C.E.Greene	1 dam
	31 FG	15 AF	Lt N.R.Hodkinson	1 dam
	55 FG	8 AF	Lt J.W.Cunnick	1 dest
	55 FG	8 AF	Capt F.E.Birtciel	1 dam

Appendix IV

	78 FG	8 AF	Lt E.L.Peel	} 1 dest
	78 FG	8 AF	Lt M.B.Stutzman	}
	78 FG	8 AF	Capt H.T.Barnaby	1 dest
	27 FG	1 TAF	?	1 dam
24.3.45	31 FG	15 AF	Col W.A.Daniel	1 dest
	31 FG	15 AF	Lt W.M.Wilder	1 dest
	31 FG	15 AF	Capt K.T.Smith	1 dest
	31 FG	15 AF	Lt R.D.Leonard	1 dest
	31 FG	15 AF	Lt F.M.Keene	1 dest
	31 FG	15 AF	Lt J.C.Wilson	1 dam
	31 FG	15 AF	Lt W.H.Bunn	1 dam
	31 FG	15 AF	Lt G.E.Erichson	1 dam
	332 FG	15 AF	Lt R.C.Brown	1 dest
	332 FG	15 AF	F/O C.V.Brantley	1 dest
	332 FG	15 AF	Lt E.R.Lane	1 dest
	332 FG	15 AF	Lt R.Harder	2 dam
	332 FG	15 AF	Lt V.I.Mitchell	} 1 dam
	332 FG	15 AF	Capt Thomas	}
	332 FG	15 AF	?	1 prob
	332 FG	15 AF	?	1 prob
25.3.45	56 FG	8 AF	Capt G.E.Bostwick	1 dest, 1 dam
	56 FG	8 AF	Lt E.M.Crosthwait	1 dest
	339 FG	8 AF	Maj Schaffer	1 dam (unconf)
	352 FG	8 AF	Lt R.H.Littge	1 dest
	479 FG	8 AF	Lt E.H.Wendt	1 dest
	479 FG	8 AF	Lt F.W.Salze	1 dam
30.3.45	55 FG	8 AF	Lt P.L.Moore	1 dest
	55 FG	8 AF	Lt P.A.Erby	1 dam
	78 FG	8 AF	Col J.D.Landers	} 1 dest
	78 FG	8 AF	Lt T.V.Thain	}
	339 FG	8 AF	Lt R.F.Sargeant	1 dest
	339 FG	8 AF	Lt C.W.Bennett	1 dest, 1 dam
	339 FG	8 AF	Lt S.C.Ananian	1 dam
	339 FG	8 AF	Capt G.T.Rich	1 dam
	352 FG	8 AF	Lt J.C.Hurley	1 dest
	361 FG	8 AF	Lt K.J.Scott	1 dest, 1 dam
	364 FG	8 AF	Lt J.B.Guy	} 1 dest
	?		Unknown P-51	}
	364 FG	8 AF	Lt R.L.Hunt	1 dam
31.3.45	56 FG	8 AF	Lt F.H.Barrett	1 dam
	78 FG	8 AF	Lt W.L.Coleman	1 dest
	353 FG	8 AF	Lt H.B.Tordoff	1 dest
	357 FG	8 AF	Maj L.K.Carson	1 dam
	357 FG	8 AF	Lt M.A.Becraft	1 dam
	358 FG	9 AF	Lt P.M.Hughes	1 dam
	361 FG	8 AF	Lt G.R.Stockmeier	1 dam

	361 FG	8 AF	Lt E.E.Tinkham	1 dam
	371 FG	1 TAF	Capt W.T.Bales	1 dest
	479 FG	8 AF	Lt R.I.Bromschwig	1 dam
	2 Sc Fce	8 AF	Lt M.H.Castleberry	1 dest
	2 Sc Fce	8 AF	Capt R.W.Nyman	1 dam
1.4.45	162 RS	9 AF	Lt J.W.Waits	1 dam
	162 RS	9 AF	Lt W.R.Yarborough	1 dam
4.4.45	4 FG	8 AF	Capt R.H.Kanaga	1 prob
	4 FG	8 AF	Lt R.A.Dyer	1 dest
	4 FG	8 AF	Lt M.J.Kennedy	} 1 dest
	4 FG	8 AF	Lt H.H.Frederick	}
	4 FG	8 AF	Lt C.W.Harre	1 dam
	4 FG	8 AF	Lt H.H.Frederick	1 dam
	56 FG	8 AF	Capt W.D.Clark Jr	1 dam
	56 FG	8 AF	F/O J.W.Kassap	1 dam
	324 FG	1 TAF	Lt A.N.Kandis	1 dest
	324 FG	1 TAF	Lt R.T.Dewey	1 dam
	324 FG	1 TAF	Lt J.W.Haun	1 dest
	325 FG	1 TAF	Lt W.N.Clark	1 prob
	325 FG	15 AF	Lt W.K.Day	1 dam
	339 FG	8 AF	Lt N.C.Greer	1 dest
	339 FG	8 AF	Capt K.B.Everson	} 1 dest
	339 FG	8 AF	Capt R.C.Croker	}
	339 FG	8 AF	Capt H.R.Corey	1 dest
	355 FG	8 AF	Lt R.W.Cooper	1 dam
	361 FG	8 AF	Lt L.F.Gendron	4 dam
	361 FG	8 AF	Lt W.H.Street	2 dam
	361 FG	8 AF	Lt E.Jungling	1 dam
	361 FG	8 AF	Lt R.J.Farney	1 dam
	361 FG	8 AF	Lt H.A.Euler	1 dam
	361 FG	8 AF	Lt L.L.Jewell	1 dam
	361 FG	8 AF	Lt H.S.Dixon	1 dam
	364 FG	8 AF	Maj G.F.Ceuleers	1 dest
	364 FG	8 AF	Lt J.S.Rogers	1 dam
	474 FG	9 AF	Lt L.B.Alexander	1 dam
	479 FG	8 AF	Lt E.H.Sims	1 dam
	66 FW	8 AF	Lt Col W.C.Clark	1 dam
	2 Sc Fce	8 AF	Lt W.H.Bancroft	1 dam
5.4.45	56 FG	8 AF	Capt J.C.Fahringer	1 dest
	339 FG	8 AF	Lt S.C.Ananian	1 dam
	354 FG	8 AF	Lt R.C.Butler	1 dam
	364 FG	8 AF	Lt G.Z.Schroeder	1 dam
7.4.45	56 FG	8 AF	Capt G.E.Bostwick	1 dam
	339 FG	8 AF	Lt O.K.Biggs	1 dest
	339 FG	8 AF	Lt R.V.Blizzard	1 prob, 1 dam
	339 FG	8 AF	Lt P.E.Petitt	1 dam

	339 FG	8 AF	Lt L.M.Carter	1 dam
	339 FG	8 AF	Lt C.M.Mason	1 dam
	339 FG	8 AF	F/O J.J.Rice	1 dam
	355 FG	8 AF	Lt Reiff	} 1 dest (unconf)
	355 FG	8 AF	Lt Griswold	}
	355 FG	8 AF	Lt Hartzog	}
	355 FG	8 AF	Lt R.V.Finnessey	1 dam
	355 FG	8 AF	Lt Kouche	1 dam
	356 FG	8 AF	Lt P.C.O'Quinn	1 dam
	356 FG	8 AF	Capt S P M Kinsey	} 1 dam
	356 FG	8 AF	Lt T K Epley	}
	356 FG	8 AF	Lt E L Slanker	}
	356 FG	8 AF	Lt J S Thorough	}
	479 FG	8 AF	Lt R.G.Candelaria	1 prob
	479 FG	8 AF	Lt H.O.Thompson	1 dest
	479 FG	8 AF	Capt V.E.Hooker	1 dest
	479 FG	8 AF	Maj R.Olds	1 dam
8.4.45	50 FG	1 TAF	?	1 dest
	50 FG	1 TAF	?	1 dam
	358 FG	9 AF	Lt J.J.Usiatynski	1 dest
	111 RS	9 AF	Lt R.K.Wylie	1 dam
	162 RS	9 AF	Lt P.Reavis	1 dam
	162 RS	9 AF	Lt R.A.Rumbaugh	1 dam
9.4.45	55 FG	8 AF	Maj E.B.Giller	1 dest
	55 FG	8 AF	Lt G.Moore	1 dest
	86 FG	15 AF	?	1 dam
	324 FG	1 TAF	Lt J.Q.Peeples	1 dam
	339 FG	8 AF	Lt H.F.Hunt	1 dam
	339 FG	8 AF	Lt L.M.Orcutt Jr	1 dam
	359 FG	8 AF	Capt M.F.Boussu	1 dam
	359 FG	8 AF	F/O R.C.Muzzy	1 dam
	359 FG	8 AF	F/O R.C.Muzzy	} 1 dam
	359 FG	8 AF	Lt F.Rea Jr	}
	361 FG	8 AF	Lt J.T.Sloan	1 dest, 1 dam
	162 RS	9 AF	Lt M.W.Geiger	1 prob
10.4.45	4 FG	8 AF	Lt W.W.Collins	1 dest
	20 FG	8 AF	Lt W.D.Drozd	1 dest
	20 FG	8 AF	Lt A.B.North	1 dest
	20 FG	8 AF	F/O J.Rosenblum	} 1 dest
	20 FG	8 AF	Lt J.W.Cudd	}
	20 FG	8 AF	Capt J.K.Hollins	1 dest
	20 FG	8 AF	Capt J.K.Brown	1 dest
	20 FG	8 AF	Capt D.Michel	1 dam
	20 FG	8 AF	Lt R.W.Meinzen	1 dam
	20 FG	8 AF	Lt G.R.Hall	1 dam

	55 FG	8 AF	Lt K.R.McGinnis	1 dest
	55 FG	8 AF	Lt K.A.Lashbrook	1 dest
	55 FG	8 AF	Lt D.D.Bachman	} 1 dam
	55 FG	8 AF	Lt C.S.Chioles	}
	56 FG	8 AF	Capt W.Wilkerson	1 dam
	56 FG	8 AF	Lt W.J.Sharbo	1 dest
	56 FG	8 AF	Lt E.W.Andermatt	1 dam
	352 FG	8 AF	Lt.Col E.D.Duncan	} 1 dest
	352 FG	8 AF	Maj R.G.McAuliffe	}
	352 FG	8 AF	Lt J.W.Pritchard	} 1 dest
	352 FG	8 AF	Lt C.A.Ricci	}
	352 FG	8 AF	Lt C.C.Pattillo	1 dest
	352 FG	8 AF	Lt K.M.Waldron	1 dam
	353 FG	8 AF	Capt G.B.Compton	1 dest
	353 FG	8 AF	Capt R.W.Abernathy	1 dest
	353 FG	8 AF	Lt J.W.Clark	} 1 dest
	353 FG	8 AF	Lt B.D.McMahan	}
	354 FG	9 AF	Capt D.J.Pick	} 1 dest
	354 FG	9 AF	Lt H.C.Schwartz	}
	356 FG	8 AF	Lt W.C.Gatlin	1 dest
	356 FG	8 AF	Lt T.N.Mauldin	1 prob
	358 FG	9 AF	Lt R.B.Manwaring	1 dam
	359 FG	8 AF	Lt H Tenenbaum	1 dest
	359 FG	8 AF	Lt R.J.Guggemos	1 dest
	359 FG	8 AF	Lt J.T.Marron	1 dam
	359 FG	8 AF	Capt W.V.Gresham Jr	1 dam
	359 FG	8 AF	Lt R.R.Klaver	1 dam
11.4.45	31 FG	15 AF	Lt Col J.G.Thorsen	1 dam
	107 RS	9 AF	Lt C.W.Staats	1 dam (unconf)
14.4.45	353 FG	8 AF	Lt L.J.Overfield	1 dest
	354 FG	9 AF	Capt C.K.Gross	1 dest
	354 FG	9 AF	Lt A.J.Ritchey	1 dam
	162 RS	9 AF	Lt R.M.Kollar	} 1 dam
	162 RS	9 AF	Lt E.B.Scott	}
15.4.45	162 RS	9 AF	Lt W.P.Simpson	2 dam
	162 RS	9 AF	Lt G.B.Gremillion	2 dam
16.4.45	55 FG	8 AF	Maj E.E.Ryan	1 dest
	368 FG	9 AF	Lt H.A.Yandel	1 dest
	368 FG	9 AF	Lt V.O.Fein	1 dest
17.4.45	20 FG	8 AF	Lt R.M.Scott	1 dam
	20 FG	8 AF	F/O J.Rosenblum	1 dam
	324 FG	1 TAF	Lt D.L.Raymond	} 1 dam
	324 FG	1 TAF	Lt T.N.Theobald	}
	324 FG	1 TAF	Lt K.E.Dahlstrom	1 prob

Appendix IV

	324 FG	1 TAF	Lt R.Pearlman	1 dam
	324 FG	1 TAF	Lt J.V.Jones	1 prob
	339 FG	8 AF	Capt R.J.Frisch	1 dest
	339 FG	8 AF	Capt J.C.Campbell	1 dest
	354 FG	9 AF	Capt J.A.Warner	1 dest
	357 FG	8 AF	Lt J.A.Steiger	1 dest
	357 FG	8 AF	Lt Col J.W.Hayes	1 dam
	358 FG	9 AF	Lt E.E.Heald	1 dam
	358 FG	9 AF	Lt F.C.Bishop	1 prob
	358 FG	9 AF	Lt T.R.Atkins	1 prob
	364 FG	8 AF	Lt S.J.Price	1 dam
	364 FG	8 AF	Capt R.W.Orndorff	1 dest
	364 FG	8 AF	Lt W.F.Kissell	1 dest
	364 FG	8 AF	Capt W.L.Goff	1 dest
	371 FG	1 TAF	Lt J.A.Zweizig	1 dest
18.4.45	325 FG	15 AF	Maj R.F.Johnson	1 dest
	339 FG	8 AF	Lt Col J.S.Thury	1 dam
	356 FG	8 AF	Lt W.C.Gatlin	} 1 dam
	356 FG	8 AF	Lt G.W.Seanor	}
	356 FG	8 AF	Lt L.B.Proctor	}
	356 FG	8 AF	Lt O.L.Burwell	1 dam
	357 FG	8 AF	Maj L.K.Carson	2 dam
	357 FG	8 AF	Lt F.A.Dellorta	} 1 dam
	357 FG	8 AF	Lt R.H.Bradner	}
	357 FG	8 AF	Maj D.H.Bochkay	1 dest
	357 FG	8 AF	Capt C.E.Weaver	1 dest
19.4.45	55 FG	8 AF	Capt R.Deloach	1 dest
	357 FG	8 AF	Lt Col J.W.Hayes	1 dest
	357 FG	8 AF	Capt R.S.Fifield	1 dest
	357 FG	8 AF	Capt I.L.McGuire	} 1 dest
	357 FG	8 AF	Lt G.L.Weber	}
	357 FG	8 AF	Lt J.P.McMullen	1 dest
	357 FG	8 AF	Lt P.N.Bowles	1 dest
	357 FG	8 AF	Lt C.W.Ofthsun	1 dest
	357 FG	8 AF	Lt W.J.Currie	1 dam
	357 FG	8 AF	Lt G.A.Zarnke	1 dam
	357 FG	8 AF	Lt F.A.Kyle	1 dam
	357 FG	8 AF	Lt D.C.Kocher	1 dam
	404 FG	9 AF	Lt B.F.Baylies	1 dam
20.4.45	354 FG	9 AF	Lt L.R.Blumenthal	} 1 dam
	354 FG	9 AF	Lt J.E.Carl	}
	370 FG	9 AF	Capt M.P.Owens	1 prob, 1 dam
	370 FG	9 AF	Lt G.Caldwell	1 prob, 1 dam
23.4.45	27 FG	1 TAF	Lt B.V.Ackerman	1 dam
24.4.45	27 FG	1 TAF	Lt R.E.Prater	1 dam
	27 FG	1 TAF	Lt J.F.Lipiarz	1 dam

	358 FG	9 AF	Lt D.S.Renner	2 dam
	365 FG	9 AF	Lt O.T.Cowan	1 dam
	365 FG	9 AF	Capt J.G.Mast	} 1 dest
	365 FG	9 AF	Lt W.H.Myers	}
	365 FG	9 AF	Lt B.Smith Jr	1 dam
	365 FG	9 AF	Lt D.L.Seslar	1 dam
25.4.45	4 FG	8 AF	Lt W.B.Hoelscher	1 prob
	358 FG	9 AF	Lt M.M.Esser	} 1 dam
	358 FG	9 AF	Lt C.G.Dickerson	}
	358 FG	9 AF	Lt L.D.Volkmer	1 prob
	370 FG	9 AF	Lt R.D.Stevenson	} 1 dest
	370 FG	9 AF	Lt R.W.Hoyle	}
	370 FG	9 AF	Lt C.L.Harman	1 dam
	370 FG	9 AF	Lt I.B.McKenzie	} 1 dam
	370 FG	9 AF	Lt M.M.Deskin	}
	370 FG	9 AF	Lt S.H.Banks	1 dam
26.4.45	27 FG	1 TAF	Capt H.A.Philo	1 dest
	27 FG	1 TAF	?	1 dam
	50 FG	1 TAF	Lt J.Finnegan	1 dam
	50 FG	1 TAF	Capt R.W.Clark	1 dest
30.4.45	358 FG	9 AF	Capt J.H.Hall	} 1 dam
	358 FG	9 AF	Lt J.Richlitsky	}
4.5.45	365 FG	9 AF	Lt A.G.Sarrow	1 dam
	365 FG	9 AF	Lt A.T.Kalvastis	1 dam

Appendix V
RAF Fighter Air Combat Claims Against Me262 Aircraft

Date	Unit	Cmmd	Name	Claim
28.9.44	416 Sqn	2 TAF	F/L J.B.McColl	1 dam
30.9.44	132 Sqn	2 TAF	F/O F.Campbell	1 dam
30.9.44	441 Sqn	2 TAF	F/L R.G.Lake	1 dam
2.10.44	442 Sqn	2 TAF	F/O F.B.Young	1 dam
5.10.44	401 Sqn	2 TAF	F/L R.M.Davenport	} 1 dest
	401 Sqn	2 TAF	S/L R.I.A.Smith	}
	401 Sqn	2 TAF	F/L H.J.Everard	}
	401 Sqn	2 TAF	F/O A.L.Sinclair	}
	401 Sqn	2 TAF	F/O J.MacKay	}
13.10.44	3 Sqn	2 TAF	P/O R.W.Cole	1 dest
21.10.44	3 Sqn	2 TAF	F/L A.E.Umbers	1 dam
	3 Sqn	2 TAF	F/L G.R.Duff	} 1 dam
	3 Sqn	2 TAF	F/O R.Dryland	}
28.10.44	486 Sqn	2 TAF	F/S R.J.Danzey	1 dam
3.11.44	122 Wg	2 TAF	W/C J.B.Wray	1 prob
26.11.44	80 Sqn	2 TAF	F/L Price	} 1 dam
	80 Sqn	2 TAF	F/O Findlay	}
3.12.44	80 Sqn	2 TAF	F/L J.W.Garland	1 dest
5.12.44	274 Sqn	2 TAF	F/L R.B.Cole	} 1 dam
		2 TAF	F/O G.N.Mann	}
10.12.44	56 Sqn	2 TAF	F/S L.Jackson	1 dam
17.12.44	122 Wg	2 TAF	W/C J.B.Wray	1 dest
23.12.44	411 Sqn	2 TAF	F/L J.J.Boyle	1 dam
	486 Sqn	2 TAF	F/O R.D.Bremner	} 1 dest
	486 Sqn	2 TAF	F/O J.R.Stafford	}
25.12.44	403 Sqn	2 TAF	S/L J.E.Collier	1 dest
	411 Sqn	2 TAF	F/L J.J.Boyle	1 dest
26.12.44	411 Sqn	2 TAF	F/L E.G.Ireland	1 dam
	135 Wg	2 TAF	W/C R.H.Harries	1 dam
27.12.44	442 Sqn	2 TAF	F/O M.A.Perkins	1 dam
1.1.45	401 Sqn	2 TAF	F/L J.MacKay	} 1 dam
	401 Sqn	2 TAF	F/S A.K.Woodill	}
	442 Sqn	2 TAF	F/L J.P.Lumsden	1 dam

	442 Sqn	2 TAF	F/L R.K.Trumley	} 1 dam
	442 Sqn	2 TAF	F/L J.N.G.Dick	}
	442 Sqn	2 TAF	F/O W.H.Dunne	}
	442 Sqn	2 TAF	P/O E.C.Baker	}
14.1.45	332 Sqn	2 TAF	Capt K.Bolsted	1 dest
23.1.45	56 Sqn	2 TAF	F/L F.L.McLeod	} 1 dest
	56 Sqn	2 TAF	F/O R.V.Dennis	}
	118 Sqn	FC	F/L J.L.Evans	1 dam
	118 Sqn	FC	F/L K.M.Giddings	1 dam
	118 Sqn	FC	F/L W.Harbison	1 dam
	401 Sqn	2 TAF	F/O Church	1 dest
	401 Sqn	2 TAF	F/O G.A.Hardy	1 dest
	401 Sqn	2 TAF	F/L W.C.Connell	} 1 dest
	401 Sqn	2 TAF	F/O G.A.Hardy	}
	411 Sqn	2 TAF	F/L R.J.Audet	1 dest
24.1.445	411 Sqn	2 TAF	F/L R.J.Audet	1 dam
11.2.45	274 Sqn	2 TAF	S/L D.C.Fairbanks	1 dest
14.2.45	184 Sqn	2 TAF	Cpt A.F.Green DFC	1 dam
	274 Sqn	2 TAF	S/L D.C.Fairbanks	1 dam
	439 Sqn	2 TAF	F/L L.C.Shaver	1 dest
	439 Sqn	2 TAF	F/O A.H.Fraser	1 dest
	610 Sqn	2 TAF	F/L F.A.O.Gaze	1 dest
21.2.45	412 Sqn	2 TAF	F/L L.A.Stewart	1 dam
23.2.45	309 Sqn	FC	W/O A.Pietrzak	1 dam
24.2.45	274 Sqn	2 TAF	F/L R.C.Kennedy	1 dam
25.2.45	402 Sqn	2 TAF	F/L K.S.Sleep	} 1 dam
	402 Sqn	2 TAF	F/L B.E.Innes	}
	416 Sqn	2 TAF	P/O L.E.Spurr	1 dam
7.3.45	274 Sqn	2 TAF	F/L P.H.Clostermann	1 dam
12.3.45	401 Sqn	2 TAF	F/L L.H.Watt	1 dest
13.3.45	402 Sqn	2 TAF	F/O H.C.Nicholson	1 dest (Poss Ar234)
23.3.45	126 Sqn	FC	F/O A.D.Yeardley	1 dest
	129 Sqn	FC	F/L G.H.Davis	1 dam
	309 Sqn	FC	W/O A.Pietrzak	1 dam
31.3.45	126 Sqn	FC	F/O A.D.Yeardley	1 dam
9.4.45	309 Sqn	FC	F/L M.Gorzula	1 dest
	309 Sqn	FC	F/L J.Mancel	1 dest
	309 Sqn	FC	W/O A.Murkowski	1 dest, 1 dam
	306 Sqn	FC	S/L J.Zulikowski	1 dest
	64 Sqn	FC	F/O A.D.Woodcock	1 dest
15.4.45	56 Sqn	2 TAF	F/L J.A.McCairns	} 1 dest
	56 Sqn	FC	F/L N.D.Cox	}
				(Prob Ar234)

Appendix V

20.4.45	41 Sqn	2 TAF	W/O V J Rossow	1 dest
24.4.45	29 Sqn	2 TAF	F/L P.S.Compton	1 dest (Prob Me410)
25.4.45	41 Sqn	2 TAF	F/L P.Cowell	1 dest, 1 dam
	130 Sqn	2 TAF	F/L W.N.Stowe	} 1 Prob
	130 Sqn	2 TAF	W/O Ockenden	}
	350 Sqn	2 TAF	F/L Colwell	1 dest
	486 Sqn	2 TAF	F/O K.A.Smith	1 dest
26.4.45	263 Sqn	2 TAF	F/L W.J.Fowler	} 1 dest
	263 Sqn	2 TAF	P/O J.W.Shellard	}
	263 Sqn	2 TAF	W/O H.Barrie	}
2.5.45	402 Sqn	2 TAF	F/O G.N.Smith	1 dam

Appendix VI
Known Claims By Jet Pilots

Note: It is not possible to determine which claims were actually confirmed by the High Command, therefore this information should be regarded as claims and not necessarily actual victories. Herausschusse are noted as 'HSS'.

Date	Unit	Name	Type
26.7.44	Ekdo 262	Lt Schreiber	Mosquito
2.8.44	Ekdo 262	Lt Schreiber	Spitfire
8.8.44	Ekdo 262	Lt Weber	Mosquito
15.8.44	EKdo 262	Fw Lennartz	Fortress
24.8.44	Ekdo 262	Ofw Baudach	Spitfire
26.8.44	Ekdo 262	Lt Schreiber	Spitfire
	Ekdo 262	Ofw Reckers	Mosquito
5.9.44	Ekdo 262	Lt Schreiber	Spitfire
6.9.44	Ekdo 262	Ofw Göbel	Mosquito
11.9.44	Ekdo 262	Ofw Baudach	Mustang
12.9.44	Ekdo 262	Hptm Eder	Fortress
12.9.44	Ekdo 262	Hptm Eder	Fortress
12.9.44	Ekdo 262	Hptm Eder	Fortress prob
14.9.44	Ekdo 262	Lt Weber	Mosquito
18.9.44	Ekdo 262	Lt Weber	Mosquito
24.9.44	Ekdo 262	Hptm Eder	Fortress
	Ekdo 262	Hptm Eder	Fortress
	Ekdo 262	Hptm Eder	Fortress prob
28.9.44	Ekdo 262	Hptm Eder	Fortress prob
4.10.44	Ekdo 262	Hptm Eder	Fortress
	Ekdo 262	Hptm Eder	Fortress
6.10.44	Kdo Now	Hptm Eder	Lightning
7.10.44	Kdo Now	Oblt Schall	Liberator
	Kdo Now	Fw Lennartz	Liberator
	Kdo Now	Ofhr Russel	Liberator
10.10.44	Kdo Now	Oblt Bley	Mustang
12.10.44	Kdo Now	Ofw Lennartz	Mustang
13.10.44	Ekdo Lechfeld	Unknown pilot	Mosquito
28.10.44	Kdo Now	Oblt Schall	Mustang
	Kdo Now	Lt Schreiber	Lightning
29.10.44	Kdo Now	Lt Schreiber	Lightning
	Kdo Now	Lt Schreiber	Spitfire (collision)

	Kdo Now	Fw Büttner	Thunderbolt
	Kdo Now	Ofw Göbel	Thunderbolt
1.11.44	Kdo Now	Ofw Banzhaff	Mustang
2.11.44	Kdo Now	Fw Büttner	Mustang
	Kdo Now	Fw Büttner	Thunderbolt
	Kdo Now	Ofw Baudach	Thunderbolt
	Kdo Now	Hptm Eder	Fortress
4.11.44	Kdo Now	Ofw Göbel	Thunderbolt
	Kdo Now	Hptm Eder	Fortress
5.11.44	Kdo Now	Hptm Eder	Mustang prob
6.11.44	Kdo Now	Oblt Schall	Thunderbolt
8.11.44	Kdo Now	Oblt Schall	Thunderbolt
	Kdo Now	Oblt Wegmann	Thunderbolt
	Kdo Now	Oblt Schall	Mustang
	Kdo Now	Oblt Schall	Mustang
	Kdo Now	Maj Nowotny	Liberator
	Kdo Now	Maj Nowotny	Mustang
	Kdo Now	Hptm Eder	Mustang
	Kdo Now	Hptm Eder	Mustang
	Kdo Now	Hptm Eder	Mustang
	Kdo Now	Hptm Eder	Lightning prob
9.11.44	Kdo Now	Hptm Eder	Mustang
	Kdo Now	Hptm Eder	Mustang
21.11.44	III./JG 7	Hptm Eder	Fortress
23.11.44	III./JG 7	Lt Weber	Mustang
24.11.44	III./JG 7	Fw Büttner	Lightning
	III./JG 7	Lt Göbel	Mustang
	III./JG 7	Ofw Baudach	Lightning
25.11.44	III./JG 7	Hptm Eder	Mustang
	III./JG 7	Hptm Eder	Fortress prob
26.11.44	III./JG 7	Maj Sinner	Lightning
	III./JG 7	Ofw Buchner	Lightning
	III./JG 7	Lt Müller	Mosquito
27.11.44	III./JG 7	Ofw Lennartz	Spitfire
2.12.44	III./JG 7	Lt Weber	Lightning
2.12.44	III./JG 7	Ofw Lübking	Fortress
12.12.44	10./NJG 11	Oblt Welter	Lancaster (12/13th)
23.12.44	III./JG 7	Ofw Büttner	Lightning
	III./JG 7	Ofw Büttner	Mustang
	III./JG 7	Fw Böckel	Mustang
29.12.44	III./JG 7	Ofw Büttner	Mosquito
31.12.44	III./JG 7	Fw Baudach	Mosquito
	III./JG 7	Fw Baudach	Mustang
	III./JG 7	Unknown pilot	Fortress
??.12.44	III./JG 7	Hptm Eder	Fortress
2.1.45	10./NJG 11	Oblt Welter	Mosquito (2/3rd)
5.1.45	10./NJG 11	Oblt Welter	Mosquito (5/6th)

Appendix VI

10.1.45	10./NJG 11	Oblt Welter	Mosquito (10/11th)
1.2.45	III./JG 7	Lt Rademacher	Spitfire
3.2.45	III./JG 7	Lt Weber	Fortress
	III./JG 7	Lt Schnörrer	Fortress
	III./JG 7	Oblt Wegmann	Fortress
	III./JG 7	Uffz Schöppler	Mustang
	III./JG 7	Lt Rademacher	Liberator
	III./JG 7	Lt Rademacher	Liberator
5.2.45	III./EJG 2	Lt Harbort	Lightning
7.2.45	10./NJG 11	Unknown pilot	Lancaster (7/8th)
9.2.45	III./JG 7	Lt Rademacher	Fortress
	III./JG 7	Lt Rademacher	Fortress
	III./JG 7	Oblt Wegmann	Fortress
	III./JG 7	Lt Schnörrer	Mustang
	I./KG(J)54	Maj Sehrt	Fortress
	I./KG(J)54	Maj Sehrt	Fortress HSS
	I./KG(J)54	Unknown pilot	Fortress
	I./KG(J)54	Unknown pilot	Fortress HSS
14.2.45	III./JG 7	Lt Rademacher	Fortress
	III./JG 7	Uffz Schöppler	Fortress
	III./JG 7	Uffz Engler	Fortress
15.2.45	10./NJG 11	Fw Becker	Lightning
16.2.45	III./JG 7	Lt Rademacher	Mustang
20.2.45	10./NJG 11	Unknown pilot	Mosquito (20/21st)
	10./NJG 11	Unknown pilot	Mosquito (20/21st)
	10./NJG 11	Unknown pilot	Mosquito (20/21st)
22.2.45	III./JG 7	Ofw Buchner	Mustang
	III./JG 7	Oblt Wegmann	Mustang u/c
	III./JG 7	Uffz Nötter	Fortress
	III./JG 7	Uffz Nötter	Fortress
	III./JG 7	Lt Waldmann	Mustang
	III./JG 7	Lt Waldmann	Mustang
?.2.45	JV 44	Obstlt Steinhoff	Il-2
?.2.45	III./EJG 2	Uffz Köster	Spitfire
24.2.45	III./JG 7	Lt Rademacher	Fortress
	III./JG 7	Lt Weber	Mustang
27.2.45	III./JG 7	Lt Rademacher	Liberator
1.3.45	I./KG(J)54	Unknown pilot	Mustang
	I./KG(J)54	Fw Herbeck(?)	Fortress
3.3.45	III./JG 7	Hptm Gutmann	Fortress
	III./JG 7	Ofw Lennartz	Fortress
	III./JG 7	Ofhr Russel	Fortress
	III./JG 7	Lt Schnörrer	Fortress
	III./JG 7	Oblt Wegmann	Liberator
	III./JG 7	Oblt Wegmann	Mustang
	III./JG 7	Maj Sinner	Liberator
	III./JG 7	Maj Sinner	Liberator

	III./JG 7	Ofw Arnold	Fortress
	III./JG 7	Ofw Arnold	Thunderbolt
7.3.45	III./JG 7	Ofw Arnold	Mustang
	III./JG 7	Maj Sinner	Mustang
9.3.45	III./JG 7	Ofhr Russel	Recce aircraft
	III./EJG 2	Hptm Engleder	Marauder
12.3.45	III./EJG 2	Hptm Steinmann	Fortress
14.3.45	III./JG 7	Lt Ambs	Mustang
	III./JG 7	Lt Weber	Mustang
15.3.45	III./JG 7	Lt Weber	Liberator
	III./JG 7	Lt Weber	Liberator
	III./JG 7	Ofhr Pfeiffer	Fortress
	III./JG 7	Fhr Winisch	Fortress
	III./JG 7	Uffz Schöppler	Liberator
	III./EJG 2	Hptm Steinmann	Fortress
16.3.45	I./KG(J)51	Lt Batel	Thunderbolt
	Stab./JG 7	Maj Weissenberger	Mustang
17.3.45	III./JG 7	Oblt Wegmann	Fortress
	III./JG 7	Ofw Göbel	Fortress
	III./JG 7	Uffz Köster	Fortress
	III./JG 7	Uffz Köster	Fortress
18.3.45	Stab./JG 7	Maj Weissenberger	Fortress
	Stab./JG 7	Maj Weissenberger	Fortress
	Stab./JG 7	Maj Weissenberger	Fortress
	III./JG 7	Ofw Lübking	Fortress
	III./JG 7	Lt Rademacher	Fortress
	III./JG 7	Lt Sturm	Fortress
	III./JG 7	Oblt Schall	Mustang
	III./JG 7	Oblt Wegmann	Fortress
	III./JG 7	Oblt Wegmann	Fortress HSS
	III./JG 7	Lt Schnörrer	Fortress
	III./JG 7	Lt Schnörrer	Fortress HSS
	III./JG 7	Fhr Ehrig	Fortress
	III./JG 7	Fhr Ehrig	Fortress HSS
	III./JG 7	Ofhr Ullrich	Fortress
	III./JG 7	Ofhr Ullrich	Fortress HSS
	III./JG 7	Fhr Windisch	Fortress
	III./JG 7	Fhr Windisch	Fortress HSS
	III./JG 7	Oblt Seeler	Fortress
	III./EJG 2	Hptm Steinmann	Mustang
	III./EJG 2	Hptm Steinmann	Mustang
19.3.45	I./JG 7	Gfr Heim	Fortress
	I./JG 7	Uffz Koning	Fortress HSS
	III./JG 7	Ofw Lennartz	Fortress
	III./JG 7	Oblt Schall	Fortress
	III./JG 7	Ofw Arnold	Fortress
	III./JG 7	Lt Schnörrer	Fortress

Appendix VI

	III./JG 7	Ofw Reinhold	Fortress HSS
	III./JG 7	Lt Rademacher	Mustang
	III./JG 7	Unknown pilot	Fortress HSS
	III./JG 7	Unknown pilot	Fortress HSS
	III./EJG 2	Obstlt Bär	Mustang
	I./KG(J)54	Unknown pilot	Fortress
	I./KG(J)54	Unknown pilot	Fortress HSS
20.3.45	III./JG 7	Fw Pritzl	Fortress
	III./JG 7	Fw Pritzl	Fortress
	III./JG 7	Fhr Pfeiffer	Fortress
	III./JG 7	Ofw Heiser	Fortress
	III./JG 7	Fhr Christer	Fortress
	III./JG 7	Oblt Sturm	Fortress
	III./JG 7	Ofw Buchner	Fortress HSS
	III./JG 7	Fhr Ehrig	Fortress
	III./JG 7	Fhr Ehrig	Fortress
	III./JG 7	Fhr Ehrig	Fortress
21.3.45	Stab./JG 7	Maj Weissenberger	Fortress
	Stab./JG 7	Maj Ehrler	Fortress
	I./JG 7	Lt Weihs	Fortress
	I./JG 7	Gfr Heim	Fortress
	III./JG 7	Fhr Pfeiffer	Fortress
	III./JG 7	Lt Schnörrer	Fortress
	III./JG 7	Ofw Arnold	Fortress
	III./JG 7	Lt Weber	Fortress
	III./JG 7	Lt Ambs	Fortress
	III./JG 7	Lt Ambs	Fortress
	III./JG 7	Lt Ambs	Fortress
	III./JG 7	Uffz Giefing	Fortress
	III./JG 7	Uffz Giefing	Fortress
	III./JG 7	Lt Müller	Liberator
	III./JG 7	Oblt Schall	Mustang
	III./JG 7	Uffz König	Thunderbolt
	III./EJG 2	Obstlt Bär	Liberator
	III./EJG 2	Lt Bell	Lightning
	10./NJG 11	Fw Becker	Mosquito (21/22nd)
22.3.45	Stab./JG 7	Maj Weissenberger	Fortress
	Stab./JG 7	Maj Ehrler	Fortress
	III./JG7	Lt Schnörrer	Fortress
	III./JG7	Ofhr Petermann	Fortress
	III./JG7	Fhr Windisch	Fortress
	III./JG7	Fhr Pfeiffer	Fortress
	III./JG7	Ofw Lennartz	Fortress
	III./JG7	Ofw Buchner	Fortress
	III./JG7	Lt Ambs	Fortress
	III./JG7	Ofw Arnold	Fortress
	III./JG7	Uffz Köster	Fortress

	III./JG 7	Ofw Lübking	Fortress
	III./JG 7	Lt Schlüter	Fortress HSS
	III./JG 7	Oblt Schall	Mustang
	III./JG 7	Lt Lehner	Mustang HSS
23.3.45	Stab./JG 7	Maj Ehrler	Liberator
	Stab./JG 7	Maj Ehrler	Liberator
	Stab./JG 7	Ofw Reinhold	Fortress prob
	10./NJG 11	Fw Becker	Mosquito (23/24th)
24.3.45	Stab./JG 7	Maj Ehrler	Fortress
	I./JG 7	Maj Rudorffer	Tempest
	I./JG 7	Oblt Schuck	Mustang
	I./JG 7	Oblt Schuck	Mustang
	I./JG 7	Lt Weihs	Lightning
	III./JG 7	Ofw Arnold	Fortress
	III./JG 7	Lt Rademacher	Fortress
	III./JG 7	Lt Lehner	Fortress
	III./JG 7	Oblt Kulp	4-engined bomber
	III./JG 7	Lt Sturm	4-engined bomber
	III./JG 7	Oblt Schall	4-engined bomber
	III./JG 7	Ofw Pritzl	4-engined bomber
	III./JG 7	Ofw Buchner	4-engined bomber
	III./JG 7	Oblt Worner	4-engined bomber HSS
	III./EJG 2	Obstlt Bär	Liberator
	III./EJG 2	Obstlt Bär	Mustang
	10./NJG 11	Fw Becker	Mosquito (24/25th)
	10./NJG 11	Fw Becker	Mosquito (24/25th)
25.3.45	III./JG 7	Lt Rademacher	Liberator HSS
	III./JG 7	Lt Müller	Liberator
	III./JG 7	Fw Taube	Liberator
	III./JG 7	Ofw Buchner	Liberator
	III./JG 7	Ofhr Windisch	Liberator
	III./JG 7	Ofhr Ullrich	Liberator
	III./JG 7	Oblt Schall	Mustang
	III./JG 7	Lt Schnörrer	Mustang
27.3.45	I./JG 7	Lt Weihs	4-engined
	III./JG 7	Lt Heckmann	Lancaster (Bel 25th)
	III./EJG 2	Oberst Dahl	Thunderbolt
	III./EJG 2	Oberst Dahl	Thunderbolt
	III./EJG 2	Obstlt Bär	Thunderbolt
	III./EJG 2	Obstlt Bär	Thunderbolt
	III./EJG 2	Obstlt Bär	Thunderbolt
	III./EJG 2	Fw Rauchensteiner	Thunderbolt
	10./NJG 11	Fw Becker	Mosquito (27/28th)
	10./NJG 11	Oblt Lamm (?)	Mosquito (27/28th)
	10./NJG 11	Unknown pilot	Mosquito (27/28th)
	10./NJG 11	Unknown pilot	Mosquito (27/28th)
28.3.45	I./JG 7	Lt Stehle	Fortress

Appendix VI

	I./JG 7	Lt Stehle	Mustang
	I./JG 7	Oblt Schuck	Mustang
30.3.45	I./JG 7	Flg Reiher	Fortress
	I./JG 7	Maj Rudorffer	Fighter
	I./JG 7	Maj Rudorffer	Fighter
	I./JG 7	Fw Geisthovel	Mosquito
	I./JG 7	Gfr Heim	Mustang
	III./JG 7	Lt Schnörrer	Fortress
	III./JG 7	Lt Schnörrer	Fortress
	III./JG 7	Ofhr Petermann	Fortress
	10./NJG 11	Oblt Welter	Mosquito (30/31st)
	10./NJG 11	Oblt Welter	Mosquito (30/31st)
	10./NJG 11	Oblt Welter	Mosquito (30/31st)
	10./NJG 11	Oblt Welter	Mosquito (30/31st)
31.3.45	Stab./JG 7	Maj Weissenberger	Fortress
	Stab./JG 7	Maj Ehrler	Mustang HSS
	I./JG 7	Lt Weihs	Catalina on water
	I./JG 7	Oblt Stehle	Lancaster
	I./JG 7	Oblt Stehle	Lancaster
	I./JG 7	Oblt Stehle	Lancaster
	I./JG 7	Oblt Sturm	Lancaster
	I./JG 7	Oblt Sturm	Halifax
	I./JG 7	Oblt Grünberg	Lancaster
	I./JG 7	Oblt Grünberg	Lancaster
	I./JG 7	Lt Todt	Lancaster
	I./JG 7	Lt Todt	Lancaster
	I./JG 7	Flg Reiher	Lancaster
	I./JG 7	Lt Weihs	Lancaster
	III./JG 7	Lt Schenk	Lancaster
	III./JG 7	Lt Schenk	Lancaster
	III./JG 7	Oblt Schall	Lancaster
	III./JG 7	Oblt Schall	Lancaster
	III./JG 7	Ofw Buchner	Lancaster
	III./JG 7	Fhr Ehrig	Lancaster
	III./JG 7	Ofhr Windisch	Fortress
	III./JG 7	Ofw Pritzl	Fortress
	III./JG 7	Lt Rademacher	Mustang HSS
	I./KG(J)54	Unknown pilot	Liberator
	I./KG(J)54	Unknown pilot	Liberator HSS
	10./NJG 11	Fw Becker	Mosquito (31/1st)
1.4.45	I./JG 7	Oblt Stehle	Fortress
	III./JG 7	Uffz Köster	Spitfire
3.4.45	10./NJG 11	Unknown pilot	Mosquito (3/4th)
4.4.45	Stab./JG 7	Maj Ehrler	Fortress
	Stab./JG 7	Maj Ehrler	Fortress
	Stab./JG 7	Maj Weissenberger	Fortress
	I./JG 7	Lt Stehle	Fortress

	I./JG 7	Gfr Heim	Fortress
	I./JG 7	Lt Weihs	Thunderbolt
	I./JG 7	Lt Weihs	Mustang
	III./JG 7	Oblt Schall	Mustang
	III./JG 7	Lt Rademacher	Liberator
	III./JG 7	Lt Müller	Liberator
	III./JG 7	Lt Schenk	Fortress
	III./JG 7	Ofw Pritzl	Fortress
	III./JG 7	Fhr Pfeiffer	Fortress
	III./EJG 2	Obstlt Bär	Mustang
	I./KG(J)54	Lt Becker	Fortress
	I./KG(J)54	Unknown pilot	Fortress
5.4.45	JV 44	Unknown pilot	Fortress
	JV 44	Unknown pilot	Fortress
	JV 44	Unknown pilot	Liberator
	JV 44	Unknown pilot	Liberator
	JV 44	Unknown pilot	Liberator
7.4.45	I./JG 7	Oblt Schuck	Lightning
	III./JG 7	Ofw Göbel	Fortress
	III./JG 7	Uffz Schöppler	Liberator
	III./JG 7	Ofhr Neumann	Mustang
	III./JG 7	Fhr Pfeiffer	Mustang
	I./KG(J)54	Hptm Tronicke	Fortress
	I./KG(J)54	Hptm Tronicke	Fortress HSS
	I./KG(J)54	Unknown pilot	Fortress
	I./KG(J)54	Unknown pilot	Fortress
8.4.45	I./JG 7	Oblt Stehle	Lancaster
	I./JG 7	Lt Weihs	Lightning
	III./JG 7	Fw Geisthovel	Mustang
	III./JG 7	Fw Geisthovel	Mustang
	JV 44	Obstlt Steinhoff	Liberator
	JV 44	Lt Fährmann	Fortress
	JV 44	Lt Fährmann	Fortress
	I./KG(J)54	Unknown pilot	Bomber
	I./KG(J)54	Unknown pilot	Bomber
	I./KG(J)54	Unknown pilot	Bomber
	I./KG(J)54	Unknown pilot	Bomber
9.4.45	I./JG 7	Uffz Engler	Lancaster
	I./JG 7	Lt Zingler	Lancaster
	I./JG 7	Gfr Müller	Lancaster
	III./JG 7	Lt Müller	Thunderbolt
	III./JG 7	Oblt Schall	Lancaster
	III./EJG 2	Obstlt Bär	Marauder
	III./EJG 2	Obstlt Bär	Marauder
10.4.45	I./JG 7	Oblt Schuck	Fortress
	I./JG 7	Oblt Schuck	Fortress
	I./JG 7	Oblt Schuck	Fortress

Appendix VI

	I./JG 7	Oblt Schuck	Fortress
	I./JG 7	Oblt Grünberg	Fortress
	I./JG 7	Oblt Grünberg	Fortress
	I./JG 7	Oblt Stehle	Fortress
	I./JG 7	Oblt Bohatsch	Fortress
	I./JG 7	Ofhr Neuhaus	Fortress
	I./JG 7	Flg Reiher	Fortress
	III./JG 7	Lt Hagenah	Mustang
	III./JG 7	Fhr Pfeiffer	Fortress
	III./JG 7	Ofw Lennartz	Mustang
	III./JG 7	Lt Rademacher	Mustang
	III./JG 7	Ofw Greiner	Mustang
	III./JG 7	Fw Pritzl	Thunderbolt
	I./KG(J)54	Lt Palenda	Fortress
	I./KG(J)54	Lt Palenda	Fortress HSS
	I./KG(J)54	Lt Rossow	Fortress
	I./KG(J)54	Lt Rossow	Fortress
	I./KG(J)54	Lt Becker	Fortress
	I./KG(J)54	Unknown pilot	Fortress
	I./KG(J)54	Unknown pilot	Fortress
	I./KG(J)54	Unknown pilot	Fortress
	I./KG(J)54	Unknown pilot	Fortress
	I./KG(J)54	Unknown pilot	Fortress prob
	I./KG(J)54	Unknown pilot	Fortress prob
	I./KG(J)54	Unknown pilot	Fortress prob
12.4.45	JV 44	Obstlt Bär	Marauder
	I./JG 7	Flg Reiher	Thunderbolt
14.4.45	10./NJG 11	Unknown pilot	Mosquito (14/15th)
16.4.45	JV 44	Genlt Galland	Marauder
	JV 44	Genlt Galland	Marauder
17.4.45	JV 44	Uffz Schallmoser	Fortress (collided)
	I./JG 7	Hptm Späte	Fortress
	I./JG 7	Oblt Bohatsch	Fortress
	I./JG 7	Oblt Stehle	Fortress
	III./JG 7	Lt Müller	Fortress
	III./JG 7	Ofw Pritzl	Fortress
	III./JG 7	Ofw Göbel	Fortress
	III./JG 7	Uffz Schöppler	Fortress
	I./KG(J)54	Unknown pilot	Fortress
	I./KG(J)54	Unknown pilot	Fortress
	I./KG(J)54	Unknown pilot	Fortress
	I./KG(J)54	Unknown pilot	Fortress
	I./KG(J)54	Unknown pilot	Fortress
	I./KG(J)54	Unknown pilot	Fortress
	I./KG(J)54	Unknown pilot	Fortress HSS
	I./KG(J)54	Unknown pilot	Fortress HSS
	I./KG(J)54	Unknown pilot	Fortress HSS

Date	Unit	Pilot	Aircraft
18.4.45	JV 44	Obstlt Bär	Thunderbolt
	JV 44	Obstlt Bär	Thunderbolt
19.4.45	I./JG 7	Hptm Späte	Fortress
	I./JG 7	Uffz Schöppler	Fortress
	I./JG 7	Oblt Bohatsch	Fortress
	I./JG 7	Oblt Grünberg	Fortress
	III./JG 7	Ofw Göbel	Fortress
	JV 44	Obstlt Bär	Mustang
	JV 44	Obstlt Bär	Mustang
	I./KG(J)54	Lt Mai	Fortress
24.4.45	JV 44	Unknown pilot	Maurauder
	JV 44	Unknown pilot	Maurauder
	JV 44	Unknown pilot	Thunderbolt
25.4.45	I./JG 7	Maj Späte	Fortress
	I./JG 7	Maj Späte	Fortress
	I./JG 7	Maj Späte	Fortress
	I./JG 7	Uffz Schöppler	Fortress
	I./JG 7	Ofw Göbel	Fortress
	I./JG 7	Lt Kelb	Fortress
	I./JG 7	Uffz Engler	Fortress
	JV 44	Uffz Köster	Mustang
	JV 44	Uffz Köster	Mustang
26.4.45	JV 44	Genlt Galland	Marauder
	JV 44	Genlt Galland	Marauder
	JV 44	Unknown pilot	Marauder
	III./EJG 2	Oberst Dahl	P-51
27.4.45	JV 44	Obstlt Bär	Thunderbolt
	JV 44	Obstlt Bär	Thunderbolt
	JV 44	Maj Herget	Thunderbolt
	JV 44	Uffz Köster	Thunderbolt
	JV 44	Uffz Köster	Thunderbolt
28.4.45	JV 44	Obstlt Bär	Thunderbolt
30.4.45	I./KG(J)54	Unknown pilot	IL-2
?.4.45	III./JG 7	Oblt Schlüter	Yak-9
?.4.45	III./JG 7	Ofhr Wittbold	Il-2
	III./JG 7	Ofhr Wittbold	Il-2
8.5.45	I./JG 7	Oblt Stehle	Yak-9

Appendix VII

Royal Air Force Crash Report on Me262

SECRET
CRASHED ENEMY AIRCRAFT
Report Serial No.256 dated 14th October 1944
Me262

At 1500 hours on 5th October 1944, a Me262 jet-propelled aircraft was shot down by Spitfires 9 miles SW of Nijmegen, Map Ref. E/6454.

The pilot baled out at 2,000 ft. and the aircraft dived almost vertically into water-logged meadowland. The crater caused by the crash was 30 ft. by 12 ft. which filled up rapidly with water, a few pieces of the aircraft being thrown clear. A considerable fire occurred before water filled the crater, but some parts penetrated the soft ground to a sufficient depth to escape burning. Salvage operations are much hampered owing to the swampy nature of the ground, necessitating the use of two 3,000 gall/hour pumps.

Identification Markings:
(K + BK. Works No. 17093

Camouflage:
Pale blue undersurfaces, mottled green upper. The tips of some control surfaces, impossible to identify, are yellow.

Engines:
Jumo 004 (only one recovered)

Armament:
Two Mk.108 30mm guns in mountings were found and two further similar mountings, less guns. Two blast tubes plugged with wooden blocks confirm that only two 30mm guns were fitted

to this particular aircraft, which had apparently been carrying bombs.

Bomb Gear:

Parts of two bomb carriers suitable for 50 kg bombs, or supply containers, were found.

Armour Plate:

One very small piece of armour plate, 15mm thick, the location of which is unknown, was recovered. A bullet-proof screen, 100mm thick, with a built-in internal heating element, has been salvaged.

Internal Equipment:

The only definitely identifiable radio equipment was a FuG 25a, but it was considered that a FuG 16Z had been fitted, from the presence of certain small parts.

Crew:

One: Dead. Baled out, but parachute failed to open.

Remarks:

Particular search is being made for any parts of the pilot's seat to confirm the use of ejection apparatus.

One jet-unit has been recovered in fair condition and is being shipped to U.K. for further examination.

A.I.2.(g)   **(Sgd.) W.A.Lambert**

D.of I. (R)   **Squadron Leader**

14th October 1944   **for Wing Commander**

Index

Personnel - Luftwaffe

Abel, Hptm F.	164	Böttlander, Hptm.	64
Abrahamczik, Hptm R.	274	Brandl, Ofw P.	133
Alt, Ofw R.	100	Braunegg, Hptm H.	40, 103
Ambs, Lt A.	174, 190-191, 195, 199	Brink, Ogfr J.	154
		Brückmann, Oblt H.	133
Arnold, Hptm.	75	Buchner, Ofw H.	79, 90, 97-98, 99, 150-151, 167, 184, 195, 199, 200, 211, 218, 228, 229, 230, 266, 267, 286
Arnold, Ofw H.	168, 170, 182, 190, 195, 199, 250		
Ast, Ofhr H-J.	122		
Baetcher, Maj H-G.	160		
Baetz, Oblt W.	259	Büttmann, Hptm H-C.	71, 73, 308
Banzhaff, Ofw W.	84-85, 87	Büttner, Ofw F.	82, 86, 90, 97, 108, 114
Bär, Obstlt H.	82, 116, 182, 184, 191, 199, 202, 203, 224, 235, 244, 252, 255, 257, 258, 268, 277	Christer, Fhr.	184
		Christoph, Uffz F.	122
		Clausner, Fw H.	160
		Crump, Oblt P.	64
Barkhorn, Maj G.	217, 259	Dahl, Obst W.	45, 202, 268
Batel, Lt W.	175, 274, 275	Dahlmann, Uffz R.	192
Baudach, Ofw H.	52, 57, 59, 72, 86, 88, 90, 94, 97, 115, 152	Delatowski, Uffz E.	79
		Detjens, Uffz.	118, 122
		Denkhaus, Dr.	55,
Bauer, Uffz G.	192	Diekmann, Lt E.	192
Beck, Oblt.	240	Dorn, Lt H.	281, 284
Becker, Lt B.	170, 222, 240	Dortenmann, Oblt H.	64, 91
Becker, Fw K-H.	132, 134, 135, 136	Draht, Oblt W.	142
Behrens, Oblt.	131	Eder, Hptm G-P.	58, 62, 63, 68, 73, 76, 77, 84, 86, 88, 93, 94, 97, 115-116, 117, 119, 125-126, 203, 303
Bell, Lt.	191		
Biebel, Uffz J.	192		
Bley, Oblt P.	37, 74, 75-76, 77-78, 81		
Blömert, Lt.	154-155	Egri, Uffz A.	194
Böckel, Fw.	108	Ehrecke, Uffz W.	192
Bocksteigel, Ofw W.	134	Ehrhardt, Uffz L.	245
Bodenschanz, Gen.	38	Ehrig, Fhr.	179, 184, 211
Bohatsch, Oblt.	238, 252, 256	Ehrler, Maj H.	191, 194, 197, 199, 212-213, 224, 225
Bohm, Lt J.	158		
Borg, Fw B.	192	Eichmer, Fw F.	194

Einhardt, Fw F.	160	Heckmann, Lt.	202
Engleder, Hptm.	170	Heckmann, Uffz.	224
Engler, Uffz G.	147, 234, 265, 281	Heilmann, Oblt W.	64
Eppstein, Oblt W.	133	Heim, Gfr.	183, 187, 190, 204, 224, 243
Erben, Uffz H.	192		
Fährmann, Lt.	231-232, 252	Heiser, Ofw.	184
Farber, Uffz A.	120	Herbeck, Fw J.	163
Felden, Hptm H.	143	Herget, Maj W.	271, 273, 298
Fick, Uffz.	250	Herlitzius, Fw.	37
Fingerloos, Fw J.	72, 74	Herrmann, Obst H.	131
Flachs, Uffz K.	37, 38	Hoffmann, Fw R.	144
Franke, Uffz E.	194	Hoffmann, Ofw.	95
Franke, Uffz G.	72	Hogeback, Obstlt.	217
Freutzer, Ofw.	90	Hohagen, Maj E.	96, 119, 123, 217
Fröhlich, Lt.	274, 281, 286	Höhne, Ofhr J.	173
Galland, Genlt A.	28, 29, 30, 31, 32, 38, 90, 93, 119, 128, 128, 154, 217, 218, 235, 247, 248, 252, 260, 265, 267-268, 269, 270, 271. 273	Holzwarth, Hptm H.	127-128
		Hovestadt, Oblt H.	173
		Janssen, FjFw.	204
		Junghans, Fj-Fw E.	80
		Kahler, Oblt G.	142
		Kaiser, Lt E.	119
		Kaiser, Lt H.	217
Gärtner, Oblt W.	56	Kelb, Lt F.	265, 272, 273
Gehlker, Ogfr F.	185	Kippke, Hptgfr C.	192
Geisthovel, Fw. 204,	230	Klewin, Uffz H.	192
Geldmacher, Lt E-R.	271	Knobel, Lt H-G.	160
Geyer, Hptm H.,	29, 42, 47, 82	Kobert, Lt G.	75
Giefing, Uffz E.	174, 190	Köhler, Ofw H.	96, 106
Göbel, Ofw,	37, 56, 82, 88, 97, 175, 227, 252, 256, 265	Köhler, Uffz.	236
		Kolbe, Uffz K.	193
		König, Oblt H.	194
Goering, Reichsm H.	28, 30, 32, 34, 38, 119, 128, 171	König, Uffz	191
		Koning, Uffz.	184
Gollob, Obst G.	129	Kornagel, Hptm.	106, 272
Gorlitz, Fw G.	164	Korten, Gen.	38
Griem, Fw H.	164	Köster, Uffz.	175, 195, 218, 271
Greiner, Ofw.	243	Kowalewski, Obstlt R.	170
Grözinger, Maj H.	143	Kreutzberg, Ofw.	50
Grünberg, Oblt H.	209, 211, 238, 244, 250, 256	Krupinsky, Maj W.	217, 231
		Kruse, O.	283-284
Gutmann, Hptm.	167, 169	Kühn, Uffz H.	124
Haberle, Lt H-P.	163	Kulp, Oblt.	199
Haeffner, Lt.	274	Lackner, Lt J.	160
Hagenah, Lt W.	242	Lamle, Oblt H-G.	113
Halensleben, Obstlt.	192	Lange, Uffz K.	148
Harbort, Lt R.	140	Lauer, Ofw H.	53, 66-67
Hartung, Uffz K.	124	Lehmann, Oblt H.	100

Index

Lehner, Lt A.	195, 199, 224		243, 252, 270, 199, 200, 203, 213, 222, 243. 274
Lenke, Ofw H.	105		
Lennartz, Ofw H.	49, 50, 74, 77, 78, 90, 100, 167, 182, 195, 224, 242-243	Rauchensteiner, Fw.	202
		Reckers, FjOfw H.	37, 52-53
Leuthner, Ogfr.	80	Reiher, Flg.	204, 211, 238, 244
Litzinger, Uffz.	148	Reinhold, Ofw G.	182, 197, 224
Lonnecker, Lt H.	118	Reischke, Uffz B.	257
Lübke, Lt W.	108	Resch, Hptm R.	100
Lübking, Ofw A.	104, 178, 195, 203	v.Rettberg, Lt G.	202
Lützow, Obst G.	128, 129, 154, 261, 262	Richter, Lt H-G.	147
		Riedel, Hptm.	47
Mai, Lt.	257	Riedesel Frhr zu Eisenach, Obstlt V.	142, 143
Martius, Ogfr M.	192		
Mattuschka, Ofw H.	152, 183	v.Ritter-Rittershain, Lt O.	122
Mehn, Uffz H.	184		
Meister, Obst W-D.	38	Roesch, Hptm.	97
Merlau, Oblt.	95	Rohde, Ofhr G.	150
Metzbrand, Ofhr H.	164	Rossow, Lt.	240
Meyer, Lt H.	183	Roth, Lt W.	105
Meyer, Fw H.	113	Rudorffer, Maj E.	200, 202, 204, 205, 305
Milch, Genfeldm E.	27, 29, 30, 34		
Müller, Lt F.R.G.	97-98, 167, 187, 191, 200, 222, 223, 234, 252	Rupprecht, Uffz A.	274
		Russel, Ofhr H.	74, 80, 150, 167, 170
Müller, Oblt H.G.	37	Sachsenberg, Lt.	154
Müller, Gfr.	234	Sanio, Uffz H.	100
Mütke, Ofhr H-G.	265, 300	Schabinski, Ofw G.	172
Neuhaus, Ofhr.	238	Schall, Oblt F.	68, 74, 81, 82, 90-94, 119, 178, 182, 191, 195, 199, 201, 211, 220, 234, 242, 243
Neumann, Ofhr,	228		
Neumann, Lt.	231		
Nötter, Uffz H.	151, 152		
Nowotny, Maj W.	63, 74, 90-91, 93-95	Schallmoser, Uffz E.	249
Oswald, Lt W.	114	Schatzle, Oblt.	200
Overbeg, Ofw P.	194	Schauder, Uffz H.	58
Overweg, Oblt Dr. H.	214	Schenk, Lt.	211, 222
Palenda, Lt P.	240	Schenk, Hptm W.	44, 45, 49
Paukner, Lt.	272	Schimmel, Lt.	274
Petermann, Ofhr V.	194, 203	Schlüter, Lt F-W.	195, 272, 284
Petersen, Obst.	30, 38	Schnörrer, Lt K.	42, 50, 139, 142, 167, 179, 180, 182, 190, 194, 201, 203
Piehl, Lt K.	153		
Pfeiffer, Ofhr.	174, 190, 194-195, 222, 228, 242	Schöppler, Uffz A.	139, 147, 174, 227, 252, 256, 265, 281
Pöhling, Fw.	274		
Ponopp, Hptgfr G.	194	Schreiber, Lt A.	37, 44, 45, 47, 52, 81, 82, 100
Pritzl. Fw O.	184, 199, 213, 222,		

383

Schrey, Ofhr G.	180	Ullrich, Ofhr.	179, 180, 200, 202
Schuck, Oblt W.	199-200, 203, 205, 229, 238	Unrau, Maj K.	53
		Valet, Oblt J.	104, 105
Schulte, Lt E.	204-205	Vigg, Uffz.	243
Schuhmacher, Ofw L.	257	Vorwald, Genmaj.	31
Schwartz, Fw.	243	Wagner, Oblt W.	243
Seeler, Oblt.	179, 180	Waldmann, Oblt H.	151-152, 180, 181
Sehrt, Maj O.	141, 142	Weber, Lt J.,	37, 45, 58, 97, 104, 119, 139, 156, 174, 190, 193
Sinner, Maj R.	97-98, 99, 119, 123, 139, 167-168, 170, 217, 218-219, 220	Wegmann, Oblt G.	37, 90, 139, 142, 151, 167, 175, 179, 180, 182
Spadiut, Hptm.	272		
Spangenberg, Lt.	90	Wehking, Fw W.	114
Späte, Hptm W.	28, 219-220, 252, 256, 265	Weibling, Ofw A.	134
		Weihs, Lt H-D.	181, 187, 199-200, 202, 207, 209, 211, 224, 230, 236, 243, 272
Speck, Uffz H.	142		
Stahlberg, Oblt E.	245		
Staiger, Maj H.	175		
Stamp, Maj G.	131	Weiss, Lt B.	105
Stehle, Oblt F.	203, 209, 211, 218, 224, 230, 238, 252, 276, 281	Weiss, Hptm R.	64
		Weissenberger, Maj T.	119, 149, 175, 176, 178, 191, 194, 212, 224
Steinhoff, Oberst J.	119, 154-155, 231-232, 249, 252, 253, 254	Welter, Maj K.	131-132, 135, 136, 203, 275, 297
Steinmann, Hptm W.	172. 173, 174, 181	Wever, Obnlt W.	243
Strathmann, Ofw.	37	Wiedemann, Lt R.	56
Strothmann, Lt.	274	Wilkenloh, Fw W.	108
Sturm. Oblt G.	178, 184, 199, 211, 263	Windisch, Ofhr.	174, 179, 180, 194, 200, 212, 243
Suchert, Fw R.	192	Winkel, Hptm E.	86, 192
Tangermann, Lt.	187	Wittbold, Ofhr.	272
Taube, Fw.	200	Witzmann, Fw W.	147
Teumer, Hptm A.	68	Worner, Oblt E.	199
Theeg, Oblt F.	148	Wübke, Lt H.	252
Thierfelder, Hptm W.	34, 41, 42, 47	Wurm, Fw H.	122
Thimm, Fw A.	245	Zander, Ofw.	88
Todt, Lt.	211	Zander, Stfw H.	105
Traumüller, Uffz J.	192	Zimmermann, Lt W.	160
Trautloft, Obst J.	128	Zingler, Lt.	234
Tronicke, Hptm W.	229	Zollner, Uffz A.	86
Udet, Gen E.	27, 28		

Personnel - United States Army Air Forces

Name	Page(s)	Name	Page(s)
Abernathy, Capt R.W.	241	Benoit, Lt N.	74
Ackerman, Lt B.V.	260	Berguson, Lt K.V.	185
Adler, S/S W.E.	226, 228	Berry, Lt B.	95
Alison, Lt D.J.	84	Bigelow, Lt M.C.	168
Alexander, Lt L.B.	223	Bigg, Lt O.K.	228
Allen, Lt R.	125	Bird, S/Sgt L.B.	165-166
Almond, Lt.	245	Birtciel, Capt F.E.	194
Amoss, Lt D.M.	148	Birtle, Lt B.	184
Ananian, Lt S.C.	140, 206, 226	Bishop, Lt F.C.	251
Andermatt, Lt E.W.	241	Blank, Lt R.R.	194
Anderson, Lt R.D.	189	Blickenstaff, Maj W.K.	152
Anderson, Lt M.O.	159	Blizzard, Lt R.V.	228
Anderson, Lt R.H.	189	Bloomer, S/Sgt A.E.	287
Andrew, Lt L.V.	140	Blumenthal, Lt L.R.	259
Anspach, Lt R.J.	287, 290, 294	Bochkay, Maj D.H.	140, 253, 254
Arend, F/L P.	284	Bostwick, Capt G.E.	201-202, 228
Armstrong, Lt W.	107	Bourque, Lt W.E.	189
Arnold, Lt M.E.	122	Boussu, Capt M.F.	236
Atkins, Lt T.R.	251	Bowers, Lt A.A.	158, 159
Ayer, Lt W.H.	183, 220	Bowles, Lt P.N.	257
Bachmann, Capt C.M.	226	Box, S/Sgt E.T.	287
Bachmann, Lt D.D.	240	Bradner, Lt R.H.	254
Bales, Capt W.T.Jr.	214	Brantley, F/O C.V.	198
Bancroft, Lt W.H.	223	Brill, Lt M.	240
Banks, Lt S.H.	264	Bromschwig, Lt R.I.	214
Barker, Lt W.H.	173	Brown, Lt C.F.	123
Barnaby, Capt H.T.	193, 194	Brown, Lt J.F.	140
Barnhart, Lt H.	140	Brown, Capt J.K.	147, 238
Barr, S/Sgt C.A.	287	Brown, Lt R.C.	197
Barrett, Lt F.H.	214	Brown, Lt R.W.	287
Barto, Lt V.N.	184	Brown, Lt W.H.	189
Bast, Lt V.E.	84	Browning, Capt.	142
Baugh, Lt D.P.	220	Buchanan, Lt C.E.	149
Baylies, Lt B.F.	258	Buhrow, S/Sgt H.	178
Bazin, Lt R.	240	Bunn, Lt W.H.	199
Beaty, Lt W.W.	163	Burwell, Lt O.L.	254
Beaudreault, Lt V.J.	66-67	Bush, Lt B.J.	194
Bechtelheimer, Lt W.F.	160	Butler, Lt R.C.	226
Becraft, Lt M.A.	208	Bux, Lt A.J.	85
Beckmann, Capt J.H.	163	Caldwell, Lt.	259
Bedor, Lt K.L.	269	Campbell, Capt J.C.	250
Belasco, F.	304-305	Candelaria, Lt R.G.	223
Bell, Lt T.R.	159	Cannon, Lt J.W.	183
Bennett, Lt C.W.	204	Cantillon, Lt.	178

Carl, Lt J.E.	259	Dahlen, Lt H.	172
Carper, Lt W.	106	Dahlstrom, Lt K.E.	251, 287
Carroll, Lt J.A.	207, 209	Daniel, Col W.A,	198
Carson, Maj L.K.	207-208, 209, 254	Darnell, Lt C.H.	173
Carter, Lt J.L.	141, 142, 183	Dawson, Lt.	174
Carter, Lt L.M.	228	Day, Lt W.K.	223
Castanias, Lt.	178	Delgado, FO R.	164
Castleberry, Lt M.H.	214	Dellorta, Lt F.A.	254
Ceuleers, Maj G.	221	Deloach, Capt R.	256
Chance, Lt A.F.	97	Denson, Lt G.A.	159, 220, 263
Chapman, Lt H.M.	190, 191, 193	Deskin, Lt M.M.	264
Chestnutt, Sgt.	252	DeWeerdt, Lt P.	177
Chinn, Lt C.A.	104	Dewey, Lt R.T.	223
Chioles, Lt C.S.	240	Dickerson, Lt C.G.	264
Clark, Lt G.G.	173	Dickman, Col.	106
Clark, Lt J.W.	241	Dillard, Capt W.J.	193
Clark, Capt R.W.	268	Dixon, Lt H.S.	222
Clark, Col W.C.	221	Doody, Lt T.J.	118
Clark, Capt W.D.	222	Dorsett, Lt W.E.	165-166
Clark, Lt W.N.	223	Dotson, Lt J.	240
Clemmons, Lt B.	160	Drew, Lt U.L.	60-62, 74-76, 77, 303
Cohen, FO.	148		
Cole, S/Sgt W.H.	187	Drozd, Lt W.D.	238
Coleman, Lt W.L.	213	Duncan, Lt D.D.A.	158
Collins, Lt W.W.	241	Duncan, Lt.Col E.D.	151, 241
Compton, Capt G.B.	152, 241	Dunmire, Lt F.T.	164
Connor, Maj R.E.	76	Durkee, Maj M.L.	149
Cooper, Lt R.E.	223	Dyer, Lt R.A.	220
Corey, Capt H.R.	220	Edwards, Lt H.L.	105
Corwin, Lt W Jr.	91-93	Einhaus, Lt L.E.	125
Cowan, Lt O.T.	153, 260	Elliott, Maj F.B.	163
Cowley, Lt J.	185	Eneff, Sgt C.V.	166
Cox, Lt H.	198	England, Lt J.	92
Cranfill, Maj N.K.	183	Enoch, Lt C.	183
Crawford, Col T.W.,	221	Epley, Lt T.K.	229
Creamer, Maj D.S.	122	Erby, Lt P.A.	206
Creamer, Lt J.M.	95	Ergott, Lt.	97
Croker, Capt R.C.	219	Erichson, Lt G.	199
Crosby, Lt B.T.	148	Esser, Lt M.M.	264
Crosthwait, Lt E.M.	202	Euler, Lt H.A.	222
Croy, Lt M.D.	53	Everson, Capt K.B.	219
Cudd, Lt J.W.	238	Fahringer, Capt J.C.	226
Cummings, Capt D.M.	159-160	Farney, Lt R.J.	222
Cunnick, Lt J.W.	194	Fein, Lt V.O.	248
Cupp, T/S C.E.	221	Fiebelkorn, Lt E.C.	92, 93
Currie, Lt W.J.	257	Fifield, Capt R.S.	182-183, 257
Da Garcia, Lt.	228	Finnegan, Lt J.	268

Index

Finnessey, Lt R.V.	228	Hack, Lt.	262
Fitch, Capt J.C.	95	Hall, Lt G.R.	238
Florine, Lt R.N.	110, 111	Hall, Lt J.H	272
Flowers, Lt R.A.	84	Harder, Lt R.	198
Foster, Lt H.O.	80	Harmon, Lt C.L.	264
Fox, Lt D.B.	154	Harms, Lt F.	261
Foy, Maj R.W.	89, 142, 182-183	Harre, Lt C.W.	221
Francis, Capt R.	239	Harris, Lt B.H.	249
Franklin, Lt.	122	Hartzog, Lt.	228
Fredericks, Lt H.H.	220-221	Hauenstein, FO M.	240
Freedman, Maj L.	305	Haun, Lt J.W.	223
Freeman, Lt L.	157-158	Hawkins, Capt A.J.	115
Frisch, Capt R.J.	250	Haydon, Lt E.R.	93
Frye, Lt J.E.	168	Hayes, Lt.Col J.W.	250, 256
Gardner, Lt E.P.	158	Haynes, Lt W.V.	287
Gardner, Capt R.L.	163	Heald, Lt E.E.	251
Gatlin, Lt W.C.	241, 254	Heily, Capt W.T.	229-230
Geary, R.	125	Henderson, T/S J.V.	240
Geiger, Lt M.W.	236	Henry, Col J.B.	206
Gendron, Lt L.F.	222	Hewitt, Maj.	251
Gerbe, Lt W.T.	84	Higginbotham, Lt C.	184
Getz, Capt C.W.III.	163	Hill, Lt R.S.	185
Gilbert, R.	186	Hill, Maj.	260
Giller, Maj E.B.	234-235	Hillborn, Lt R.	56
Gilson, S/Sgt J.G.	287	Hillis, Lt F.I.	287, 292
Glazner, Lt R.	256	Hinton, Lt W.R.	104
Glynn, Lt E.	177	Hodkinson, Lt N.R.	194
Goff, Capt W.L.	250	Hoelscher, Lt W.B.	263
Goodman, Lt C.E.	151	Hoffert, Lt W.L.	91
Goth, Lt.	223	Hogan, Lt C.	151
Gould, Lt N.D.	104	Holbury, Capt R.	77
Grabovski, Lt B.	104	Hollins, Capt J.K.	238
Gray, Lt.	223	Holt, Lt J.K.	287, 290, 292, 295, 300
Greason, Lt C.	178		
Greenberg, Lt S.	74	Hooker, Lt F.F.	122
Greene, Lt C.E.	194	Hooker, Lt V.E.	228
Greer, Lt N.C.	193, 220	Horan, Sgt J.	113
Greigo, Sgt J.	177	Howard, Lt C.C.	191
Gremillion, Lt G.B.	247	Howard, Capt R.K.	150
Gresham, Capt W.V.	242	Hoyle, Lt R.W.	264
Griswold, Lt.	228	Hughes, Lt P.M.	214
Groce, Lt W.L.	84-85	Humphries, S/Sgt F.	178
Gross, Capt C.K.	245	Hunt, Maj H.F.	236
Gross, Brig.Gen W.	251	Hunt, Lt R.L.	151
Grusy, Lt W.A.	154	Hunt, Lt R.L.	206
Guggemos, Lt R.J.	241-242	Hurley, Lt J.C.	205
Guy, Lt J.B.	205	Hurst, Capt W.	118

Husband, H.P.	268	Kühn, Lt.	175
Hydorn, Lt W.E.	142	Kyle, Lt F.A.	257
Ilfrey, Capt J.	81, 84, 125	Kyler, Lt R.	222
Ingraham, S/Sgt R.	178	Lamb, Lt H.H.	80
Irion, Lt E.E.	184	Landers, Col J.D.	205
Jackson, FO D.E.	213	Lane, Lt E.R.	198
Jackson, Capt M.J.	104	Langohr, Lt B.E.	193
Jahnke, Lt J.E.	123	Lanham, Lt J.	198
Jahnke, Lt W.J.	163	Lapenas, Lt J.D.	206-207, 209
Jensen, Lt M.	177-178	Lashbrook, Lt K.A.	240
Jentz, Lt N.E.	178	Lefforge, Lt L.L.	151
Jewell, Lt L.L.	222	LeMay, Gen C.	293
Johnson, Maj R.F.	254-255	Leon, Lt E.E.	235
Johnson, Lt R.G.	168	Leonard, Capt R.D.	198
Jones, Lt J.V.	251	Lewis, Lt A.	140
Jones, Lt W.A.	57	Lipiarz, Lt J.F.	262
Jungling, Lt E.	222	List, T/S M.K.	249
Kalvastis, Lt A.T.	274	Littge, Lt R.H.	200
Kanaga, Capt R.H.	220	Lloyd, Lt D.F.	173
Kandis, Lt A.N.	223	Logothetis, Lt.	122
Karger, Lt D.E.	120-121, 123-124	Longo, Lt.	156-157
Kassap, FO J.W.	222	Love, Lt T.M.	156
Keeler, Lt R.S.	174	Lyons, Lt W.S.	168
Keene, Lt F.M.Jr.	199	Maguire, Capt I.L.	168
Kemp, Lt C.	177	Mains, Lt R.	221
Kennedy, Lt M.	220	Maltbie, Lt A.F.	163, 172
Kennedy, Lt P.	107	Mamalis, Capt S.	77
Kenney, Lt J.W.	91-92	Mankie, Lt J.A.	115
Kenny, R.	120	Manthos, Capt A.G.	183
Kiefer, 2/Lt R.A.	50	Manwaring, Lt R.B.	242
King, Lt R.	177	Markham, Lt G.E.	95, 122
King, Lt R.H.	125	Marling, Lt F.W.	172-173
Kinsey, Capt S.P.M.	229	Marron, Lt J.T.	242
Kirby, Lt C.B.	151, 152	Mason, Lt C.M.	228
Kirby, Maj H.H.	163	Mason, Col J L.	22
Kirk, Lt J.A.III.	189	Mason, Capt M.F.	153
Kirkland, Lt.	184	Mast, Capt J.G.	260, 261, 262
Kissel, Lt W.F.	250	Maurice, Lt A.	94
Klaver, Lt R.R.	242	Mauldin, Lt T,M,	241
Knupp, Lt D.F.	61	McAuliffe, Maj R.G.	241
Kocher, Lt D.C.	257	McCandliss, Lt R.	76
Kollar, Lt R.M.	245	McDaniel, Capt.	198
Konantz, Lt W.J.	120	McGinnes, Lt L.H.	240
Kortendick, Lt E.	151	McGinnis, Lt K.R.	240
Kouche, Lt.	228	McGlaufin, Lt E.P.	108
Kozlik, Lt J.J.	173	McGuire, Capt I.L.	256
Kuehl, Lt R.I.	189	McKelvey, Lt C.C.	91

Index

McKenzie, Lt I.B.	264		Overfield, Lt L.J.	245
McMahan, Lt B.D.	241		Owens, Capt M.P.	259
McMullen, Lt J.P.	256		Paisley, Lt M.R.	158
McNeel, Lt K.D.	122, 147		Panch, Lt H.P.	202
McWhorter, Lt J.L.	157		Parker, T/Sgt E.C.	286
Mead, F.M.Jr.	238		Parker, Lt J.E.	160
Meinzen, Lt R.W.	238		Pattillo, Lt C.C.	241
Menegy, Lt D.T.	159		Payne, Lt C.G.	158, 159
Meyer, Maj J C.	21, 38, 304		Pearlman, Lt R.	251
Meyer, Maj R.J.	150		Peel, Lt E.L.	193
Michel, Capt D.	238		Peeples, Lt J.O.	236
Miller, Capt E.H.	142, 189-190		Penn, Capt D.O.	159
Mitchell, Lt V.R.	198		Peters, Capt B.	164
Montague, FO W.W.	163		Peters, Lt.	67
Moon, T/Sgt N.D.	286		Peterson, Capt N.	124
Moore, Lt G.	235		Peterson, Lt.	184
Moore, Lt P.L.	205		Pettit, Lt P.E.	228
Moore, S/Sgt R.H.	287		Phillips, Capt S.C.	151
Mueller, Lt C.W.	72		Philo, Lt H.A.	264, 269
Murray, Lt B.J.	122		Phipps, Lt L.H.	151
Murray, Lt C.	73		Pick, Capt D.J.	242
Murray, Lt R.E.	238		Picton, Lt J.T.	158
Muzzy, FO R.C.	236		Pierine, Lt D.	118
Myers, Lt D.L.	206-207, 209		Pointer, Lt B.	184
Myers, Col J.	53		Powell, Lt H.G.	190
Myers, Lt W.H.	260, 261, 262		Prater, Lt R.E.	262
Nash, Lt R.J.	115		Price, Lt C.D.	152
Naumann, Capt H.D.	194		Price, Lt S.V.	151, 250
Needham, Lt C.S.	187-188		Pritchard, Lt J.W.	241
Newman, Lt.	255		Proctor, Lt L.B.	254
Nichols, Maj M.B.	150, 185		Purdey, Lt I.J.	110-111
Nicholson, Lt C.	185-186		Quinn, Lt W.J.	90
Nippert, Lt B.H.	184		Radley, Lt F.X.	151
Norley, Maj L.H.	247		Raidy, S/Sgt A.A.	276
Norsic, T/Sgt M.	178		Randle, Lt B.	224
North, Lt A.B.	238		Randolph, Lt W.E.	151
Nyman, Capt R.W.	214		Rann, Capt R.A.	88
O'Connor, Lt F.T.	164		Ray, Capt J.	221
O'Donnell, Capt W.	192		Raymond, Lt D.L.	251
Ofthsun, Lt C.W.	257		Rea, Lt F.	236
Olds, Maj R.	227, 228		Ready, Capt C.	157-158
Oliver, Lt L.	140		Reavis, Lt P.	230
O'Neil, Lt J.F.	159-160, 170		Reckland, Sgt W.L.	226
O'Quinn, Lt P.C.	229		Reeves, Lt D.	240
Orchard, Lt.	239		Reeves, Lt E.E.	269
Orcutt, Lt L.M.	236		Reeves, Lt R.W.	198
Orndorff, Capt R.W.	250		Reichel, Lt D.	177

Reiff, Lt.	228
Renner, Lt D.S.	262
Richey, Lt A.J.	245
Richlitsky, Lt J.	272
Renne, Lt.	98
Reynolds, Lt G.L.	125
Ricci, Lt C.A.	241
Rice, FO C.C.	228
Rich, Capt G.T.	206
Rickey, Lt I.J.	98
Roberts, Lt.	184
Robinson, Lt R.C.	198
Rodebaugh, Lt C.R.	174
Rodgers, Lt J.H.	156-157
Roebuck, Lt W.	201
Rogers, Lt J.S.	221
Rohrs, Lt J.W.	122
Rollo, Lt R.	164
Rosen, Lt G.J.	122
Rosenblum, Lt A.A.	189
Rosenblum, FO J.	238, 250
Ross, Lt F.	151
Rowlett, Capt B.	74
Royer, FO W.W.	88
Rudd, Lt E.G.	186
Rudd, Lt E.G.	91
Rudd, Lt F.G.	172
Rumbaugh, Lt R.A.	230
Rutledge, Lt H.C.	84, 86
Ryan, Maj E.E.	248
Sainlar, Lt J.J.	142
Salze, Lt F.W.	200
Sargent, Lt R.F.	204
Sarrow, Lt A.G.	274
Scales, Lt R.L.	108
Schaffer, Maj.	201
Schell, Lt.	198
Schroeder, Lt G.Z.	226
Schwikert, Lt J.	178
Scott, Lt E.B.	245
Scott, Lt K.J.	205
Scott, Lt R.M.	250
Seanor, Lt G.W.	254
Sears, Sgt D.A.	188
Sedvert, Capt T.W.	164, 192
Sells, Lt E.	239
Seslar, Lt D.L.	261
Shafter, Lt J.J.	221
Sharbo, Lt W.J.	241
Shatto, Lt A.P.	269
Shrull, Lt E.W.	241
Schwartz, Lt H.C.	242
Sime, Lt E.H.	222
Simpson, Lt W.P.	247, 255
Sink, T/Sgt P.F.	166
Skeetz, Lt K.	104
Slanker, Lt E.L.	229
Slates, Lt L.	261
Sloan, Lt J.T.	236
Smith, Lt B.	261
Smith, Lt G.	240
Smith, Capt K.T.	198
Spaatz, Gen C.	292-293
Spears, Lt L.W.	198
Spencer, Capt C.H.	182
Staats, Lt C.W.	244
Steiger, Lt J.A.	250
Stevens, Capt R.W.	93, 152
Stevenson, Lt R.D.	264
Stevenson, Lt S.E.	108
Stewart, Col E.W.	168
Stockmeier, Lt G.R.	214
Street, Lt W.H.	222
Strobell, Lt R.C.	286-295, 300, 305
Stroud, Lt J.D.	235
Stump, Capt H.D.	108
Stutzman, Lt M.B.	193
Sublett, Capt J.L.	92, 168
Swain, Capt R.	177
Taylor, S/Sgt T.L.	287
Tenenbaum, Lt H.	241
Thain, Lt T.V.	205
Theobald, Lt T.N.	251
Thomas, Lt J.	98
Thomas, Lt N.A.	183
Thomas, Capt.	198
Thompson, T/Sgt E.J.	286
Thompson, Lt H.O.	228
Thompson, Lt W.	177
Thompson, Lt.	239
Thorough, Lt J.S.	229
Thorson, Lt.Col J.G.	244
Thury, Lt.Col J.L.	254
Tinkham, Lt E.E.	214

Index

Tordoff, Lt H.B.	213	Wendt, Lt E.H.	201
Totten, FO W.V.	181	Westbrook, Lt T.B.	149
Truell, Lt.	223	White, Capt J.S.	192
Truver, S/S E.F.	261	Whitmore, Lt H.E.	150
Tyszkiewicz, Sgt E.S.	258-259	Wilder, Lt W.M.	198
Urban, Lt T.J.	178	Wilkerson, Capt W.	241
Usiatinski, Lt J.J.	230, 231	Wilkins, Lt J.K.	163
Valimont, Sgt J.A.	251-252	Willcoxen, S/Sgt D.J.	287
Volkmer, Lt L.D.	264	Williams, Lt J.	177
Voss, Lt J.R.	90	Willis, Lt L.E.	100
Wager, Lt E.L.	204	Wilson, Lt J.C.	199
Waits, Lt J.W.	218	Winks, Lt R.P.	123
Waldron, Lt K.M.	241	Wolfe, Lt C.W.	190
Walker, Lt E.L.	255	Wright, Lt R.R.	124
Walker, Lt J.A.	58	Wylie, Lt R.K.	230
Warner, Lt G.O.	151	Yandel, Lt H.A.	248
Warner, Capt J.A.	252	Yarbrough, Lt W.R.	218
Watson, Col H.E.	286, 287, 292, 293, 306	Yeager, Capt C.E.	89
		Yothers, Capt R.W.	158
Weaver, Capt C.E. 254		Young, Lt F.	118
Webb, Lt H.E.Jr. 166-167		Zarnke, Lt G.A.	257
Webb, Lt R.H. 150		Zemke, Col H.	74
Weber, Lt G.L.	256	Zweizig, Lt J.A.	252
Weihardt, Maj.	264		

Personnel - Royal Air Force and Commonwealth

Ackworth, S/L R.A.	66	Bradley, W/O.	115
Adams, F/O J.I.T.	274	Bremner, F/O R.D.	108
Andrews, F/O.	98	Brown, Capt E,	284
Ash, W/O E.J.	209	Bruce, F/L G.J.	139
Audet, F/L R.J.	111, 126, 127	Buckle, F/L.	108
Avis, F/O S.F.	211	Campbell, W/O F.	63
Baker, P/O E.C.	118	Camprey, F/S.	135
Baker, F/O.	266	Casey, F/S R.C.	210
Barrett, F/S J.	132	Church, F/O.	126
Barrie, W/O H.	269	Clostermann, F/L P.H.	169
Baxter, F/O J.	210	Cole, F/O R. 79,	80
Baxter, F/O R.	59	Cole, F/L R.B.	104
Benson, F/O.	212	Cole, F/S.	100
Berriman, F/O.	234	Collier, S/L J.E.	113
Bestwick, Sgt.	234	Connell, F/L W.C.	126
Blyth, F/O K.K.	212	Compton, F/L P.S.	260
Bolsted, Capt K.	122	Courtney, P/O L.	100
Bowes, F/O D.S.	212	Cowell, F/L P.	264, 267
Boyle, F/L J.J.	109, 110, 111-113, 309	Cowlin, F/O E.	210
		Cox, F/L N.D.	246

Craft, F/L H.C.	194	Hayton, Sgt J.	134
Crane, F/L F.N.	52	Heap, S/L J.	64
Danzey, F/O R.J.	81	Heaven, F/O E.G.	210
Davenport, F/L R.M.	70-71, 308	Henry, F/O.	132
Davis, F/L G.H.	196	Hill, F/S.	62
Dawson, F/O J.	210	Holland, P/O L.G.	206
Dennis, F/O R.V.	126-128	Holmes, S/L P.D.	209
Dick, F/L J.N.G.	118	Howard, F/L.	132
Dodd, F/L F.L.	50	Howes, F/S.	210
Donaldson, G/C E.M.	298	Huck, Sgt J.	234
Dow, S/L.	135	Humphries, F/O A.M.	210
Doyle, F/L E.O.	264	Hunter, F/O.	58
Dryland, F/O R.	80, 100	Hurley, F/L P.J.	212
Duff, F/L G.R.	80	Hyland, F/O G.A.	212
Dunne, F/O W.H.	118	Innes, F/L B.E.	160
Dykes, W/O T.	208	Ireland, F/L E.G.	114
Eagleston, P/O O.D.	97	Isenberg, F/O M.	210
Emmett, F/L.	266	Jackson, F/S L.	105
Evans, F/L J.	196	Jarvis, W/O J.G.	211
Everard, F/L H.	70-71	Johnson, W/C J.E.	64, 308
Fairbanks, S/L D.C.	143, 147	Jones, F/S R.	210
Findlay, F/O.	100	Jones, F/O R.R.	212
Fleming, S/L.	56	Keeley, V.	208
Foster, W/O.	78	Kennedy, F/L R.C.	156
Fowler, F/L W.J.	269	Krynauw, Lt D.	53
Fraser, F/O A.H.	119, 145-147, 169	Kuchma, F/S W.	210
Galliene, S/L	132	Lake, F/L R.G.	62
Garland, F/L J.W.	104, 105, 308	Lambert, F/S.	210
Gaze, F/L F.A.O.	143-144	Lambros, F/L A.	82
Giddings, F/L K.M.	196	Lelong, F/O R.E.	194
Gilbert, F/O.	196	Leprich, F/S J.O.	210
Gonsalvez, S/L.	284	Lesesne, F/L C.	212
Gosling, F/L C.	279-284	Lewandowski, P/O J.	234
Gorzula, F/L M.	233	Lewis, F/O.	212
Graham, F/S M.A.	210	Little, F/O.	195
Graham, F/L	135	Lyons, S/L E.B.	244
Green, Capt A.F.	147	Lobban, P/O A.S.	42-43, 202
Greenfield, F/O.	234	Lockhart, F/S D.	210
Haliburton, F/O G.P.	212	Lockhart-Ross, Lt A.	45-47
Hammett, H.J.	309	Lumsden, F/L J.P.	118
Harbison, F/L W.	196	Mackay, F/L J.	69-70, 117, 308
Hardy, F/O G.A.	126	Mancel, F/L J.	234
Harling, F/L D.W.A.	78	Mann, F/O G.N.	104
Harries, W/C R.	114	Martindale, S/L A.F.	284
Harris, P/O H.S.T.	135-136	Matthewman, F/L D.	45
Hawes, F/O F.	210	McCairns, F/L J.A.	246
Hawker, F/L H.C.V.	50-52	McColl, F/L J.B.	62, 78

Index

McKay, F/O R.	132	Shaver, F/O L.C.	144-145, 146
McKay, F/L S.S.	97, 202	Sheldon, Lt D.	80
McNeill, F/O D.L.	211	Shellard, F/O J.W.	269
McLeod, F/O E.F.	72, 126-128	Sinclair, F/O A.L.	70
McPhee, W/O.	134	Sleep, F/L K.S.	160
McRory, F/O.	134	Smith, F/O G.N.	274
Melhuish, F/L T.	284	Smith, F/O K.A.	264
Metiver, F/L H.A.	212	Smith, S/L R.I.A.	68-71, 308
Morgan, F/O D.E.	269	Snell, F/O P.	80
Morris, F/L R.	264	Spratt, F/S R.	210
Mouton, Lt C.	53	Spurdle, S/L R.L.	64
Moylan, F/S.	58	Spurr, F/O L.E.	160
Mozotwski, F/L J.	212, 234	Stafford, F/O J.R.	108
Murkowski, W/O A.	234	Stark, F/L J.B.	200
Nicholson, F/O H.C.	172	Stewart, F/L L.A.	150
Nunn, F/O G.	135-136	Stoffberg, Lt P.J.	98
Ockenden, W/O.	264, 266	Stokes, F/S C.H.	210
Ogilvie, G/C P.B.	105	Stopford, F/S W.	45
Olson, F/L.	115	Storms, F/L J.L.	210
Patterson, F/O.	195	Stowe, F/L. 264,	266
Payne, F/O D.M.	210	Sweetman, S/L.	100
Perkins, F/O M.A.	114	Taylor, F/S R.	210
Pienaar, Capt S.	45-47, 49	Taylor-Cannon, F/L K.B.	97
Pietrazak, Sgt A.	197	Trumley, F/L K.R.	118
Pietrzak, W/O H.A.	156	Umbers, F/L A.E.	80
Pike, F/O R.P.	210	Vardy, F/S A.E.	210
Pinney, F/L.	139	Voyce, W/C.	132
Platte, Sgt G.	208	Wall, F/L A.E.	42-43
Platts, F/L.	170	Wallace, F/O.	134
Pleiter, F/O D.	210	Watt, F/L L.N.	171
Pope, F/L.	212	Wilkins, F/L.	82
Price, F/L.	100	Wilson, F/L.	80
Purnell, F/O A.	132	Wolstenholme, F/O.	135
Robinson, F/S J.S.	210	Woodcock, F/O A.D.	234
Ross, F/O P.H.	88	Woodill, F/S A.K.	118
Rosser, F/L J.	57, 59	Wray, W/C J.B.	64, 87, 107-108, 109, 306-307
Rossow, W/O V.J.	259		
Russell, W/C D.	107	Yeardley, F/O A.D.	196, 212
Ruthig, W/O V.M.	209-210	Young, F/O F.B.	67
Schrader, S/L.	279-280, 283, 302	Zary, S/L H.P.M.	264
Scott-Malden, G/C F.D.	64	Zulikowski, S/L J.H.	234
Searles, F/L.	135		

Personnel - Miscellaneous

Baker, Sgt J. RE	244	Kozhedub, Col I.	148
Baur, K.	25, 26, 32, 288-289, 291, 292, 302	Lindner, G. 32, McConnell, Col J. Messerschmitt, Prof W.	40, 301, 302 203 22, 23, 29, 30, 31, 304
Beauvais, Dipl.Ing.	26		
Betts, Gnnr L.C.	60	Ostertag	28
Buchner, Käthe	90	Pericaud, L.	34
Caroli, G.	288-289	Richardson, D.	310
Cole, R.	312	Quill, J.	279
Fay, H.	206, 298, 300	Read, Spr F. RE	271
Heber, K.	175	Ring, H	76
Hitler, Reichsführer A.	30, 32, 34, 35, 38, 40, 119, 128, 309	Ritchie, Gen N. Saur, O.	245 40
Hoffmann, L.	288, 291, 293, 294	Skinner, Tpr.	310-311
Hughes, H.	300	Wendel, Flugkap F.	23, 24-25, 26, 27, 29, 32

Units - Luftwaffe

Eko Braunegg	40, 41, 103, 117	Jagdgeschwader 4	173
III./EJG 2	82, 95, 97, 124, 140, 142, 158, 159, 170, 171, 172, 173, 174, 181, 183, 184, 191, 194, 199, 202, 224, 235, 244, 269	Jagdgeschwader 5 Jagdgeschwader 7	119, 224 37, 108, 120, 155, 177, 186, 203, 205, 212, 214, 226, 227, 229, 236, 244, 248, 255, 270, 271, 286, 311
III./EKG 1	83		
E.Gr 210	45	Stab./JG 7	119, 149, 152, 167, 175, 176, 191, 194, 197, 212, 224
Ekdo 262	34, 37, 38, 40, 41, 44, 52, 56, 57, 58, 62, 63, 64, 152, 193	I./JG 7	147, 152, 183, 184, 195, 200, 204, 207, 209, 211, 217, 218, 224, 234, 238, 250, 252, 246. 265, 272, 273, 305
Ekdo Lechfeld	80		
E-Stelle Rechlin	131		
Gefechtsverband Hogeback	217, 245, 270-271, 276	1./JG 7	118, 243, 276
1 Jagddivision	167	2./JG 7	203, 230, 243
Jagdgeschwader 1	82, 217, 257, 275	3./JG 7	180, 199, 202, 203, 224, 229, 230, 236, 243, 244, 250
5./JG 1	183		
Jagdgeschwader 2	52		
Jagdgeschwader 3	82, 180, 261	II./JG 7	175, 245
I./JG 3	45		

Index

III./JG 7	96, 99, 100, 104, 108, 114, 115, 118, 119, 122, 123, 124, 139, 142, 147, 148, 149, 150, 152, 156, 160, 164, 168, 170, 174, 176, 181, 182, 184, 188, 190-191, 193, 195, 199, 200, 201, 211, 217, 218, 219, 222, 228, 230, 234, 242, 244, 249, 252, 256, 257, 258, 264	Jagdverbande 44	154, 155, 173, 202, 217, 225, 226, 227, 230, 231-232, 235, 241, 244, 247, 248, 249, 255, 257. 258, 259, 260, 261, 262, 265, 267, 269, 270, 271, 272, 273, 274
		Kampfgeschwader 51	
		I./KG 51	38
		II./KG 51	39
		III./KG 51	38, 192
		IV./KG 51	38
		Kampfgeschwader 76	169, 170
9./JG 7	63, 97, 100, 115, 117, 119, 122, 125, 152, 167, 182, 199, 243, 245, 266	I(E)./KG(J)	116, 164
		II(E)./KG(J)	116
		Kampfgeschwader (J) 6	116, 217
		Kampfgeschwader (J) 27	116
10./JG 7	119, 152, 167, 183, 185, 199, 202, 243	Kampfgeschwader (J) 30	116
		Kampfgeschwader (J) 51	39, 40, 45, 55, 61, 62, 64, 65, 67, 94, 119, 143, 153, 156, 163, 164, 173, 174, 217, 263, 274, 286, 309
11./JG 7	119, 143, 167. 183, 194, 199, 203, 224, 234, 250		
12./JG 7	259		
Jagdeschwader 11			
5./JG 11	49	I./KG(J)51	44, 53, 56, 58, 66, 71, 72, 73, 76, 79, 80, 83, 84, 96, 100, 104, 105, 106, 113, 117, 120, 122, 127, 144, 147, 169, 172, 175, 192, 258, 260
Jagdgeschwader 26	155		
8./JG 26	284		
Jagdgeschwader 27	173		
Jagdgeschwader 51	42		
I./JG 51	82		
Jagdgeschwader 52	155, 180		
Jagdgeschwader 53		1./KG(J)51	97
III./JG 53	98	2./KG(J)51	119
Jagdgeschwader 54	128, 139, 305	3./KG(J)51	44
I./JG 54	63	4./KG(J)51	105
III./JG 54	64, 91, 143	II./K(J)G51	100, 108, 114, 119, 122, 148, 150, 156, 259, 286
V./JG 54	154		
Jagdgeschwader 77	155		
I./JG 77	82	5./KG(J)51	86, 147, 164
Jagdgeschwader 101	63	III./KG(J)51	53, 172
Jagdgeschwader 300	131	IV./(E)KG(J)51	53, 217
II./JG 300	132	Kampfgeschwader 54	82
Jagdgeschwader 400	220, 272, 273	Kampfgeschwader (J) 54	65, 82, 116, 143, 229, 244, 249

Stab./KG(J)54	194		220
I./KG(J)54	82, 100, 105, 106,	2./Kdo Nowotny	68, 72, 88
	114, 115, 124, 140,	Kommando Schenk	44, 45, 53
	148, 150, 159-160,	Kommando Stamp	See 10./NJG 11
	163, 164, 171, 184,	Kommando Welter	See 10./NJG 11
	192, 194, 214, 217,	Nahaufklärungsgruppe 6	117, 243
	222, 232, 240, 244,	Nahaufklärungsgruppe 9	40
	248, 257, 272, 274,	Nachtjagdgeschwader 10	
	275	II./NJG 10	132
2./KG(J)54	170, 214	Nachtjagdgeschwader 11	
II./KG(J)54	82, 159-160, 200,	10./NJG 11	131, 132, 134, 135,
	217, 272		136, 137, 209, 212,
5./KG(J)54	160		214, 243, 275, 284,
III./KG(J)54	148, 156, 160, 182,		297
	192, 200, 259	Schnellkampfgeschwader	
7./KG(J)54	192	210	45
8./KG(J)54	154, 192	Zerstörergeschwader 1	45
9./KG(J)54	192, 245	Stab./ZG 26	37
Kampfgeschwader (J) 55	116	III./ZG 26	37, 63
Kommando Nowotny	63, 68, 73, 74, 77,	8./ZG 26	37
	78, 79, 81, 82,	9./ZG 26	37
	83-84, 85, 86, 87,	Zerstörergeschwader 76	257
	88-89, 90, 94-95,	1(F)./123	143
	96, 99, 123, 199,		

Units - United States Army Air Forces

Fighter Groups			205, 206, 234, 235,
1st FG, 15th AF	41, 98		240, 248, 256
4th FG, 8th AF	90, 96, 118, 123,	56th FG, 8th AF	84, 88, 104, 201,
	148, 159, 168, 183,		202, 214, 222, 226,
	192, 220, 228, 241,		228, 241, 243
	247, 250, 263	78th FG, 8th AF	53, 76, 80, 81, 142,
14th FG, 15th AF	97, 224		160, 168, 189, 193,
20th FG, 8th AF	81, 84, 92, 93, 118,		194, 205, 213, 251
	125, 147, 150, 185,	82nd FG, 15th AF	95, 106, 107, 114,
	237, 243, 250		140, 173, 186, 236
27th FG, 1 TAF	194, 245, 260, 262,	86th FG, 1 TAF	235, 236, 272
	264, 267, 268, 269	324th FG, 9th AF	223, 236, 250
31st FG, 15th AF	41, 108, 193, 194,	325th FG, 15th AF	104, 148, 174, 223,
	197, 244		254
48th FG, 9th AF	153	332nd FG, 15th AF	41, 197-198
50th FG, 9th AF	76, 100, 230, 267,	339th FG, 8th AF	57, 115, 140, 142,
	268		148, 184, 186, 193,
52nd FG, 15th AF	41, 184		201, 204, 206, 218,
55th FG, 8th AF	120, 122, 148, 156,		220, 226, 228, 236,
	159-160, 170, 194,		250, 254

Index

352nd FG, 8th AF	21, 22, 84, 85, 104, 150, 151, 152, 200, 201, 205, 241	79th FS, 8th AF	150
		95th FS, 15th AF	140
		334th FS, 8th AF	247
353rd FG, 8th AF	72, 96, 108, 121, 152, 181, 213, 241, 245, 286	353rd FS, 9th AF	192
		354th FS, 9th AF	222
		358th FS, 8th AF	184
354th FG, 9th AF	88, 164, 175, 192, 226, 245, 252, 259	363rd FS, 8th AF	182
		364th FS, 8th AF	142
355th FG, 8th AF	78, 80, 88, 124, 163, 168, 182, 184, 222, 228	375th FS, 8th AF	74
		386th FS, 9th AF	66, 156, 164
		387th FS, 9th AF	163
356th FG, 8th AF	79, 88, 150, 172, 186, 243, 254	388th FS, 9th AF	153, 163
		404th FS, 1 TAF	214
357th FG, 8th AF	88, 89, 91, 93, 120, 123, 123, 124, 140, 142, 168, 182, 183, 206, 207, 209, 227, 249, 250, 254, 256	487th FS, 8th AF	21
		523rd FS, 1 TAF	268
		Bomber Groups	
		2nd BG, 15th AF	68
		17th BG, 1 TAF	251, 260, 265, 267
358th FG, 9th AF	105, 214, 230, 242, 251, 262, 263, 272	25th BG, 8th AF	120, 125, 186
		34th BG, 8th AF	182
359th FG, 8th AF	91, 122, 140, 178, 183, 241	93rd BG, 8th AF	221
		94th BG, 8th AF	140, 156, 186
361st FG, 8th AF	60, 74-75, 88, 90, 94, 178, 190, 191, 205, 213, 222, 235	95th BG 8th AF	166
		96th BG, 8th AF	182, 305
		97th BG, 15th AF	68
363rd FG, 9th AF	150, 151	100th BG, 8th AF	57, 166, 176, 184, 227, 232, 238, 240
364th FG, 8th AF	58, 93, 140, 150, 151, 152, 164, 191, 205, 206, 221, 226, 242, 250	303rd BG, 8th AF	50, 97, 184, 203, 238
		305th BG, 8th AF	249
365th FG, 9th AF	66, 149, 152, 156, 163, 172, 260, 274	320th BG, 1 TAF	251
		322nd BG, 9th AF	247, 255, 258
366th FG, 9th AF	153, 158	323rd BG, 9th AF	225, 258
368th FG, 9th AF	183, 247	344th BG, 9th AF	170, 264
370th FG, 9th AF	259, 263	351st BG, 8th AF	238
371st FG, 1 TAF	214, 252	376th BG, 15th AF	304
373rd FG, 9th AF	158	379th BG, 8th AF	225, 226, 237
404th FG, 9th AF	258	381st BG, 8th AF	204
405th FG, 9th AF	158	384th BG, 8th AF	183, 237
474th FG, 8th AF	94, 171, 173, 223	385th BG, 8th AF	182
479th FG, 8th AF	74, 149, 200, 201, 214, 222, 227, 228	386th BG, 9th AF	149
		387th BG, 9th AF	235, 255
Fighter Squadrons		388th BG, 8th AF	226
55th FS, 8th AF	118, 150, 174, 185	389th BG, 9th AF	225, 227
63rd FS, 8th AF	201	390th BG, 8th AF	113-114, 115, 227
75th FS, 8th AF	84	392nd BG, 8th AF	85, 86
77th FS, 8th AF	84, 125, 185	394th BG, 9th AF	245, 258

397

398th BG, 8th AF	152	489th BS, 8th AF	74
401st BG, 8th AF	203, 226, 238	863rd BS, 8th AF	165
445th BG, 8th AF	167	**Reconnaissance Groups**	
446th BG, 8th AF	221	5th PRG, 15th AF	50, 104, 202
447th BG, 8th AF	256	7th PRG, 8th AF	56, 73, 82, 97, 98, 110, 150, 170
448th BG, 8th AF	167, 168, 189, 200, 221, 223	10th PRG, 9th AF	77, 122, 175
452nd BG, 8th AF	167, 182	**Reconnaissance Squadrons**	
453rd BG, 8th AF	226, 228	12th RS, 9th AF	192
457th BG, 8th AF	178, 238, 239	15th RS, 9th AF	183
466th BG, 8th AF	213	107th RS, 9th AF	164, 244
482nd BG, 8th AF	188	111th TRS, 9th AF	218, 230
483rd BG, 15th AF	247	162nd TRS, 9th AF	218, 230, 236, 245, 247, 255
486th BG, 8th AF	204		
487th BG, 8th AF	166, 238, 239	361st TRS, 9th AF	154
489th BG, 8th AF	85	**Other Units**	
490th BG, 8th AF	186, 256	2nd Scouting Force, 8th AF	163, 174, 214, 223
493rd BG, 8th AF	164-166, 204		
Bomber Squadrons		47th Troop Carrier Sqn, 9th AF	276
34th BS, 1 TAF	251, 261, 269		
95th BS, 1 TAF	268, 269	66th Fighter Wing, 8th AF	221
413th BS, 8th AF	305		

Units - Royal Air Force

Wings		132 Sqn	63
34 Wing	105	165 Sqn	230
122 Wing	87, 107, 109, 306	184 Sqn	147
125 Wing	64, 65, 107	222 Sqn	244
127 Wing	64, 65, 67	263 Sqn	269
135 Wing	114	274 Sqn	67, 104, 139, 143, 147, 156, 169, 200
Fighter Squadrons		309 (Polish) Sqn	156, 197, 212, 233, 234
3 Sqn	67, 79, 80, 100, 274		
41 Sqn	105, 143, 259, 264, 267	313 (Czech) Sqn	139
		332 (RNAF) Sqn	122
56 Sqn	72, 105, 126-127, 246	341 (Free French) Sqn	78
		401 (RCAF) Sqn	68-69, 117, 125, 171
64 Sqn	234		
66 Sqn	57, 59	402 (RCAF) Sqn	67, 160, 172, 274
80 Sqn	66, 67, 88, 100, 104, 105	403 (RCAF) Sqn	113, 259, 264, 266
		411 (RCAF) Sqn	109, 111, 114, 126, 127
85 Sqn	284		
118 Sqn	196	412 (RCAF) Sqn	150
126 Sqn	196, 212, 230	416 (RCAF) Sqn	62, 78, 160
129 Sqn	78, 196	418 (RCAF) Sqn	135
130 Sqn	67, 264, 266	438 (RCAF) Sqn	82

439 (RCAF) Sqn	119, 144, 147, 169	466 (RAAF) Sqn	196
441 (RCAF) Sqn	62	571 Sqn	132
442 (RCAF) Sqn	67, 114, 118	582 Sqn	133
486 (RNZAF) Sqn	81, 97, 108, 264	608 Sqn	135
515 Sqn	206	613 Sqn	136
602 Sqn	59	617 Sqn	224
610 Sqn	143	635 Sqn	212
616 Sqn	40, 279, 283, 298	692 Sqn	134, 135
Fighter Experimental Flt.	194, 260		

Bomber Squadrons

Reconnaissance Squadrons

		1 PRU	56
9 Sqn	135, 224	2 Sqn	108
50 Sqn	234	4 Sqn	82
61 Sqn	234	16 Sqn	105, 122
101 Sqn	134, 195	60 (SAAF) Sqn	45, 53, 80, 98
139 Sqn	132, 135	400 (RCAF) Sqn	80
156 Sqn	134, 212	414 (RCAF) Sqn	83
320 (Dutch) Sqn	120	430 (RCAF) Sqn	108
408 (RCAF) Sqn	212	540 Sqn	45, 56, 58, 62
415 (RCAF) Sqn	212	541 Sqn	170
419 (RCAF) Sqn	212	544 Sqn	42, 50, 58, 97, 115, 202, 204
424 (RCAF) Sqn	210		
425 (RCAF) Sqn	212	683 Sqn	50, 52, 100
427 (RCAF) Sqn	210-211		

Other Units

428 (RCAF) Sqn	134, 210	6 MU	285
429 (RCAF) Sqn	210, 211, 212	47 MU	284
431 (RCAF) Sqn	210, 212, 266	71 MU	284
433 (RCAF) Sqn	209-210	280 Sqn	208
434 (RCAF) Sqn	132, 210, 212	652 Sqn	224
464 (RAAF) Sqn	115	662 Sqn	74

Places

Aachen, Ger	105, 106, 152, 154	Ansbach, Ger	245
Achmer AD, Ger	61, 63, 64, 68, 72, 74, 75, 77, 79, 80, 86, 87, 90, 126, 191, 192, 306	Antwerp, Bel	53, 64
		Arnhem, NL	57, 58, 59, 63, 108, 147
		Aschaffenburg, Ger	56
Achym AD, Ger	266	Assen, Ger	89
Ahlhorn, Ger	90	Augsberg, Ger	25, 30, 34, 42, 97, 98, 114, 189, 236, 258, 272, 303
Airokopra, Cz	270		
Almelo, NL	119		
Altdobern, Ger	194	Aussig, Cz	250, 256
Altendorf, Ger	152	Bad Aibling, Ger	271
Alt Lonnewitz, Ger	83, 244, 245	Bad Bayerhausen, Ger	197
Amberg	148, 235	Bad Mergentheim, Ger	218
Ancona, Italy	48	Bad Segeberg, Ger	185

Bad Weissee, Ger	125	Chemnitz, Ger	134, 182, 183, 197
Bassum, Ger	90	Cherbourg, Fr	287, 293-294, 295
Bastogne, Bel	122	Chievres AD, Bel.	44
Baumenheim, Ger	186	Coesfeld, Ger	144, 145, 172
Beccles AD, UK	208	Constance, lake	245
Benson AD, UK	42	Cottbus, Ger	175, 230, 270
Berby, Cz?	240	Crailsheim, Ger	230, 242
Berlin, Ger	120, 131, 134, 136, 140, 142, 149, 154, 167, 174, 176, 178, 180, 203, 222, 224, 236, 238, 241, 242, 243, 249, 270, 304	Creil AD, Fr	44
		Czestochowa, Cz	270
		Danube (Donau) river	232, 258, 260
		Darmstadt, Ger	183
		Dayton, USA	300
		Debden AD, UK	159
Berlin-Schönefeld AD, Ger	22	Debendorf, Ger	158
		Derben, Ger	121
Betlinshausen, Ger	262	Dessau, Ger	158, 213, 221, 236, 241
Bevergen, NL?	105		
Birkenhead, UK	284	Dettelsau, Ger	251
Böblingen, Ger	226	Detweiler, Ger	122
Bodney AD, UK	22	Diest, Bel	56
Böhland, Ger	175	Dillingen, Ger	164, 258, 268
Böhmen, Ger	240	Döberitz, Ger	152
Böhmte, Ger	80, 88	Donauwörth, Ger	163, 255, 258
Bramsche, Ger	78	Dorsten, Ger	174
Brandenburg, Ger	152, 206, 212	Downham Market AD, UK	136
Brandenburg/Briest AD, Ger	119, 133, 154, 170, 174, 217, 238, 239, 241	Dreierwalde, Ger	100
		Dresden, Ger	133, 188, 190, 244, 250, 251, 252, 257
Brandis AD, Ger	244	Dübendorf AD, Switz	56, 265
Braunschweig, Ger	167, 214	Dummer Lake, Ger	88, 93, 97, 122, 227
Bremen, Ger	89, 90, 196, 203, 204, 222, 224, 227, 228, 229, 244, 266	Düren, Ger 100,	153, 156, 157
		Durlach, Ger	100
Brestau, Cz	See Wroclau	Düsseldorf, Ger	66
Brunswick, Ger	139, 140, 164, 203, 213, 214	Eberbach, Ger	58
		Eberswalde, Ger	175
Brussels, Bel	53	Eger, Cz	252
Buchen, Ger	200	Eggebeck AD, Den	218
Buena Park, USA	300	Eilenburg, Ger	183
Bunde, Ger	114	Eindhoven AD, NL	53, 109, 117, 309
Burg AD, Ger	131, 133, 217, 240, 243	Elbe river, Ger	186, 230, 240, 252, 271, 273
Canberra, Australia	286	Emmerich, Ger	144
Celle, Ger	228	Ems, Ger	119
Chartres, Fr	44	Enschede, Ger	88, 145
Chateaudun AD, Fr	44	Epe, Ger	93

Index

Erding, Ger	259, 264, 272	Haldern, Ger	169
Erkelen, Ger	158	Halle, Ger	160, 212, 214, 236, 244, 245, 251
Erlangen, Ger	217		
Erp, NL	113	Hamburg, Ger	115, 176, 184, 186, 195, 200, 203, 204, 206, 209-210, 211, 214, 221, 222, 228, 230, 234. 265, 273
Esch, Ger	100		
Etampes AD, Fr	44		
Euskirchen, Ger	100		
Fahrenbach/Baden, Ger	105		
Fährenhausen, Ger	97	Hamm, Ger	60, 97
Falkenst, Ger	250	Hannover, Ger	122, 127, 143, 148, 164, 165, 166, 222, 228, 238
Fano, Italy	98		
Farnborough, UK	275, 284		
Fassberg AD, Ger	118, 218, 221, 244, 274, 279, 280	Härz, mts, Ger	217
		Heesch AD, NL	111, 112, 113, 171
Feldkirchen	249	Helmond, NL	97, 100
Fermo AD, Italy	44	Hersfeld, Ger	160
Florennes/Juzaine		Hertogenbosch, NL	117
AD, Bel	163, 172	Hesepe AD, Ger	80, 90, 122
Ford AD, UK	284	Hildesheim, Ger	88, 164
Frankfurt, Ger	142, 164	Hittfeld, Ger	87
Frankfurt/Main, Ger	189, 225	Hoerstel AD. Ger	55, 100
Fulda, Ger	140, 160	Höhenlinden, Ger	224
Fürstenfeldbrück		Holzwickede, Ger	174
AD, Ger	264, 272	Hopsten AD, Ger	39, 55, 72, 100, 156, 172
Fürth, Ger	217		
Gablingen, Ger	247	Horgau, Ger	303
Gardelegen, Ger	140, 240, 241	Hörsching AD, Austria	248
Geisenhaim, Ger	182	Hoya AD, Ger	218
Gelsenkirchen, Ger	84	Ingolstadt, Ger	53, 124, 163, 184, 218, 254
Genthin, Ger	240		
Gerlingen, Ger	50	Innsbrück, Austria	275
Giebelstadt AD, Ger	50, 82, 100, 116, 120, 124, 140, 142, 148, 150, 159, 160, 163, 170, 172, 189, 192, 193, 194, 214	Insterburg, Ger	32
		Johannesburg, SA	285
		Jülich, Ger	100, 114, 154, 158
		Jüterbog, Ger	170
		Juvincourt AD, Fr	44
Giessen, Ger	192	Kaltenkirchen AD, Ger	152, 181, 185, 195, 204, 217, 246
Gilze-Rijn AD, NL	117		
Grave, NL	59, 64, 67, 78, 86, 308	Karlsruhe, Ger	76, 97, 225, 252
		Kassel, Ger	62, 80, 164
Graz, Austria	40	Kbely, Cz	298, 300
Grimbergen, NL	67	Kiel, Ger	218, 246
Guben, Ger	270	Kirchwistedt, Ger	100
Guernsey, Ch Is.	294	Kitzbühl, Austria	98
Gunzburg, Ger	230, 245	Kitzingen, Ger	170, 182, 189, 194
Hagenow, Ger	152, 229, 255, 259, 264	Klotsche, Ger	257
		Koblenz, Ger	174

Köln (Cologne), Ger	156, 164, 167, 172	Magdeburg/Rothensee, Ger	74
Kostian, Pol	178	Mahndorf, Ger	89
Kralupy, Cz	251	Main river, Ger	214
Krefeld, Ger	139	Mandelfeld, Ger	148
Krivitz	122	Manderfeld, Ger	120
Kummersbrück, Ger	235	Mannheim, Ger	97, 200
Laaland Island	170	Manston AD, UK	284
Landau, Ger	116, 244, 259	Marchtrenk, Austria	116
Landsberg, Ger	41, 154	Meerholz, Ger	142
Lärz AD, Ger	50, 56, 152, 222, 238	Melun AD, Fr	44, 287, 292, 293
Lechfeld AD, Ger	27, 28, 29, 31, 33, 34, 35, 37, 38, 39, 42, 43, 47, 50, 53, 56, 82, 83, 95, 97, 98, 100, 107, 116, 124, 171, 183, 194, 202, 267, 286, 287-292	Memmingen, Ger	41, 217, 258, 260
		Meppel, Ger	94
		Meppen, Ger	89
		Merseburg, Ger	62, 86, 90, 91, 125
		Metz, Fr	152, 163
		Meuthe-et-Moselle AD, Fr	164
		Milestin, Cz	263
Leck AD, Ger	136, 275, 279, 284	Minden, Ger	80, 85, 88
Leipheim AD, Ger	25, 26, 35, 40, 42, 45, 46, 96, 172, 192	Misburg, Ger	97
		Monchen-Gladbach, Ger	139
		Mount Farm AD, UK	56
Leipzig, Ger	57, 158, 160, 183, 224, 226, 236	Mühldorf, Ger	244, 270, 272
		Muiden, NL	73
Leiston AD, UK	253	Munich, Ger	42, 45, 47, 49, 50, 98, 104, 106, 107, 108, 123, 124, 140, 173, 186, 202, 218, 223, 234, 235, 236, 247, 248, 264, 265, 269, 300
Lichtenfels, Ger	217		
Liege, Bel	56		
Limburg, Ger	142, 175		
Lingen, Ger	88, 119, 126		
Linnich, Ger	148		
Linz, Aust	217		
Louvain, Bel	53	Munich/Riem AD, Ger	39, 53, 217, 231, 235, 241, 248, 249, 252, 253, 254, 260, 267, 268, 274
Lübeck, Ger	136, 176, 204, 205, 206, 240, 241, 242, 264, 279, 281, 282-283		
		Münster, Ger	126, 128, 172
Lübeck/Blankensee AD, Ger	264	Münster-Handorf AD, Ger	134
Ludwigshafen, Ger	192	Muritz Lake, Ger	174, 24
Ludwigslust, Ger	150, 220, 223	Neuburg/Donau AD, Ger	54, 82, 116, 123, 148, 156, 163, 181, 182, 192, 193, 194, 200, 206, 217, 245, 260
Lüneberg, Ger	200, 201, 206, 222, 227, 228, 275		
Maas, river	107		
Magdeburg, Ger	62, 108, 118, 133, 164, 167, 205, 206, 238, 240		
		Neuhof, Ger	142

Index

Neu Chemnitz, Ger	224		274, 298
Neumünster, Ger	199	Prague/Ruzyne AD, Cz	116, 217, 244, 250,
Neuruppin, Ger	122, 241, 243		252, 254, 256, 257,
Niebull, Ger	269-270		263, 274, 266, 270,
Niederaverbergen, Ger	258		271, 272, 311
Niederhausen, Ger	164	Prenzlau, Ger	134
Nijmegen, NL	59, 60, 62, 67, 68,	Quakenbrück, Ger	91, 104
	71, 73, 80, 164,	Rathenow, Ger	168, 179
	306, 308	Raumühle, Ger	50
Nordhausen, Ger	222, 226	Rechlin AD, Ger	201, 218
Nordhorn, Ger	72	Regensburg, Ger	226, 231, 252, 303
Nordlingen, Ger	230	Rehburg, Ger	90
Northeim, Ger	199	Reichenbach, Ger	188
Nürnberg, Ger	110, 218, 236, 247,	Reichswald Forest, Ger	197
	251, 255, 259	Riem AD, Ger	See Munich/Riem
Oberammergau, Ger	304	Reisa	245
Obergrasheim, Ger	148	Remagen, Ger	169, 170, 171, 172,
Oberoth, Ger	261		173
Oberstorf, Ger	41	Rendsburg, Ger	205
Obertraubling AD, Ger	106, 148, 303, 304	Rethem, Ger	245, 246
Odelzhausen, Ger	262	Rheine AD complex, Ger	44, 55, 72, 73, 80,
Oder river	154		88, 91, 96, 97, 100,
Oldenburg, Ger	156, 246		104, 105, 114, 118,
Oranienburg AD, Ger	119, 152, 174, 217,		122, 143, 147, 156,
	230, 236, 241, 243,		306
	259	Rhein-Main AD, Ger	206
Osnabrück, Ger	63, 74, 76, 88, 104,	Rheinsehlrn, Ger	200
	306	Rhine, river	108, 113, 171, 197,
Osthoven, Ger	192		200
Otersen, Ger	245	Rips AD, NL	68
Paderborn, Ger	143	Rohrensee, Ger	158
Parchim AD, Ger	119, 122, 125, 150,	Rosenheim, Ger	247
	201, 211, 218, 220,	Rotenburg AD, Ger	266
	221, 223, 227, 228,	Ruhland, Ger	175, 193, 197, 247
	230, 237, 238, 242,	Ruhr river, Ger	156
	243	Ruzyne AD, Cz	See Prague/
Paris, Fr	44		Ruzyne
Peenemünde, Ger	202	Saaz, Cz	252
Perleberg, Ger	122	Sacramento, USA	312
Pilsen, Cz	116, 250, 252	Salzberg, Austria	98, 270, 272
Pforzheim, Ger	98, 134	Salzwedel, Ger	150, 176, 222
Plattling, Ger	244	San Severo AD, Italy	45, 48
Plauen, Ger	184, 186, 188	Schaarlippe, Ger	224
Point Cook, Australia	286	Schiermonnikoog Is,	
Potsdam, Ger	136	Friesians	206
Prague, Cz	45, 175, 247, 250,	Schönewald/Niederbarin,	
	252, 254, 256, 263,	Ger	152

403

Schöngau AD	123		241
Schwabisch-Hall AD, Ger	53, 100, 105, 194, 206	Unterschönegg, Ger	261
		Valenciennes, Fr	110
Schwabmünchen, Ger	260, 265	Varrelbusch AD, Ger	78
Schwabstadt, Ger	108	Venlo, NL	57
Schwerin. Ger	220	Vienna, Austria	186
Sealand, UK	284	Volkel AD, NL	53, 308
Seesen, Ger	229	Waggum, Ger	68
Simbal	244	Wahrenholz, Ger	152
Slough, UK	284	Walchensee, Ger	52
Smirschitz, Cz	116	Washington DC, USA	296
Spesshardt, Ger	98	Wasserburg, Ger	58
St. Trond, Bel	93	Watton AD, UK	186
St. Vith, Bel	114	Weert, NL	107
Staaken AD, Ger	242	Wertheim, Ger	163
Stade, Ger	152	Wesel, Ger	167, 169, 171, 200
Stavanger, Nor	276	Wesendorf, Ger	218
Stavelot	114	Weser river, Ger	195, 244, 245
Steenwijk, NL	78	Wesermünde, Ger	172
Steinbrücken AD, Ger	192	Westen, Ger 244,	258
Steinhöring, Ger	104	Wildershausen, Ger	90
Steinhuder Lake, Ger	125, 214, 227, 228, 229, 266	Wilhelmshaven, Ger	203
		Willow Grove, USA	298, 300
Stendal, Ger	150, 200, 213, 218, 220, 222, 243	Wismar, Ger	125, 228
		Wittenberge	170, 179, 186, 189, 199
Stettin, Ger	124, 125, 150		
Stralsund, Ger	58	Wittstock, Ger	151, 152, 153
Strasbourg, Ger	255	Wittstocker Heide, Ger	133
Strasskirchen, Ger	259	Wright-Patterson AFB, USA	295, 300
Stuttgart, Ger	56, 98, 100, 147, 252		
		Wroclau, Cz	270
Tabor, Cz	254	Würzburg, Ger	149, 193, 194
Termonde, Bel	53	Zatec, Cz	274
Tharandt, Ger	193	Zeist AD, Bel	60
Treuchtlingen, Ger	163	Zeitz, Ger	133, 212
Trier, Fr	115	Zerbst, Ger	241
Tschenstochau, Cz	See Czestochowa	Zossen, Ger	174
Udine AD	48	Zuider Zee, NL	73, 150, 178
Ulm, Ger	58, 108, 193, 247, 258, 267	Zusmalthausen, Ger	142
		Miscellaneous	
Ulzen, Ger	118, 119, 200, 204,		

Miscellaneous

Ardennes offensive	100, 103, 113	Bendix Air Race	300
Avia S-92	297, 298, 300	Bodenplatte, Opn	117
Battle of the Bulge	See Ardennes offensive.	Clarion, Opn	150
		Cyclonite	176

Deutsches Museum	265	R4M rocket	175, 176, 179, 182, 227, 231-232, 239, 249, 270, 297, 298
Freya, radar	219		
Gisela, Opn	134		
Gloster Meteor	40, 279, 298		
He162 Volksjäger	275		
He280	24, 72, 123		
Hexogen	176	RAF Museum, UK	267
Hirschgeweih radar	131, 285, 297	Ramrod 1474	156
Industrie Schützstaffeln	129	Ramrod 1521	233
K-14 gunsight	129, 220, 238	Reaper, HMS	294
Lusty, opn	286 et seq	Rhenania oil refinery.	115
Market Garden, Opn	59	Robot 11	84
MBB	304	Royal Aircraft Establishment	275
McRae, SS	285		
Plunder, Opn	197	Sonderkommando Elbe	227-228
Projekt 1065	22	Spitfire Society	267